The "Conspiracy" of Free Trade

Following the Second World War, the United States would become the leading "neoliberal" proponent of international trade liberalization. Yet for nearly a century before, American foreign trade policy had been dominated by extreme economic nationalism. What brought about this pronounced ideological, political, and economic about-face? How did it affect Anglo-American imperialism? What were the repercussions for the global capitalist order? In answering these questions, *The "Conspiracy" of Free Trade* offers the first detailed account of the controversial Anglo-American struggle over empire and economic globalization in the mid to late nineteenth century. The book reinterprets Anglo-American imperialism through the global interplay between Victorian free-trade cosmopolitanism and economic nationalism, uncovering how imperial expansion and economic integration were mired in political and ideological conflict. Beginning in the 1840s, this conspiratorial struggle over political economy would rip apart the Republican party, reshape the Democratic, and redirect Anglo-American imperial expansion for decades to come.

MARC-WILLIAM PALEN is Lecturer in History at the University of Exeter, and a Research Associate at the US Studies Centre, University of Sydney.

The "Conspiracy" of Free Trade

The Anglo-American Struggle over Empire and Economic Globalization, 1846–1896

Marc-William Palen

University of Exeter

CAMBRIDGE
UNIVERSITY PRESS

CAMBRIDGE
UNIVERSITY PRESS

University Printing House, Cambridge CB2 8BS, United Kingdom

One Liberty Plaza, 20th Floor, New York, NY 10006, USA

477 Williamstown Road, Port Melbourne, VIC 3207, Australia

4843/24, 2nd Floor, Ansari Road, Daryaganj, Delhi - 110002, India

79 Anson Road, #06-04/06, Singapore 079906

Cambridge University Press is part of the University of Cambridge.

It furthers the University's mission by disseminating knowledge in the pursuit of education, learning and research at the highest international levels of excellence.

www.cambridge.org
Information on this title: www.cambridge.org/9781107109124

© Marc-William Palen 2016

First published 2016

A catalogue record for this publication is available from the British Library

Library of Congress Cataloging in Publication data
Palen, Marc-William, author.
The "conspiracy" of free trade : the Anglo-American struggle over empire and economic globalization, 1846–1896 / Marc-William Palen.
Cambridge, UK ; New York : Cambridge University Press, 2016. |
Includes bibliographical references and index.
LCCN 2015030769 | ISBN 9781107109124
LCSH: Free trade – United States – History – 19th century. | Free trade – Great Britain – History – 19th century. | United States – Foreign economic relations – Great Britain. | Great Britain – Foreign economic relations – United States. | United States – Commercial policy – History – 19th century. | Great Britain – Commercial policy – History – 19th century.
LCC HF1755 .P235 2016 | DDC 382/.71094109034–dc23
LC record available at http://lccn.loc.gov/2015030769

ISBN 978-1-107-10912-4 Hardback

Contents

Figures

Preface

Neoliberal policies of free trade and deregulation have become synonymous with economic globalization. As the close-knit global economy becomes ever more frayed, these same policies are also increasingly coming under fire.[1] Protectionism, the preferred political economic choice throughout the *longue durée* of world history, is now once again in fashion.[2] From this longer historical perspective, the international turn to trade liberalization since the Second World War – from GATT to the WTO – represents the rare exception to the protectionist rule. Aside from the notable case of Free Trade England, most nations in the latter half of the nineteenth century sought safety from the gales of modern global market competition behind ever higher tariff walls, buttressed with government subsidies to domestic industries and imperial expansion.

Few did so with more gusto than the United States, which from the 1860s adhered to stringent economic nationalist policies at home while increasing its imperial proclivities abroad. Not until the 1930s under the direction of FDR's State Department would free trade begin to displace protectionism as the preferred policy for American economic expansion. The inspiration for this book arose in seeking to explain this sizeable political, economic, and ideological about-face within the history of modern US domestic and foreign policy, a neoliberal turn that continues to perplex pundits, political scientists, historians, and economists alike. The origins awaited discovery within the nineteenth century, hidden amid the

---

[1] See, for instance, Gerard Dumenil, *The Crisis of Neoliberalism* (Cambridge, MA: Harvard University Press, 2011); Douglas A. Irwin, *Free Trade Under Fire* (Princeton: Princeton University Press, 2009 [3rd ed.]).

[2] Henryk Szlaijfer, *Economic Nationalism and Globalization*, trans. by Maria Chmielewska-Szlajfer (Leiden: Brill, 2012); Dani Rodrik, *The Globalization Paradox: Democracy and the Future of the World Economy* (New York: W. W. Norton, 2012); Anthony P. D'Costa, ed., *Globalization and Economic Nationalism in Asia* (Oxford: Oxford University Press, 2012); Ha-Joon Chang, *Bad Samaritans: The Myth of Free Trade and the Secret History of Capitalism* (New York: Bloomsbury Press, 2008).

conspiratorial conflict over free trade, imperialism, and global economic integration (economic globalization).[3]

Encompassing an era in which Great Britain effectively led the globe in capital investment, emigration, imperial expansion, and industrial productivity, *The "Conspiracy" of Free Trade* fast developed into a study of Anglo-American relations. Previous scholarship of Anglo-American imperialism, while prodigious, has focused primarily upon non-linear comparisons between the pre-1945 British Empire and the post-1945 American Empire.[4] This book offers instead a contemporaneous study that bridges the historiographical divide separating mid- to late-nineteenth-century American imperialism from histories of the British Empire and economic globalization. The book does so by focusing upon the ideological debates surrounding free trade and protectionism that came to dominate the era's international political economic landscape, a global contest over capitalism and imperialism that was fought with special ferocity within the United States and throughout the British Empire.

The "Conspiracy" of Free Trade argues that the late Victorian free trade-protectionist debate was not only a struggle over domestic prosperity, but also over the course of economic globalization. It was an ideological battle that would reshape the late-nineteenth-century US political economy and redirect Anglo-American imperial expansion for decades to come. This politico-ideological controversy correspondingly shines much-needed historical light upon today's ongoing debates over the future of economic globalization, alongside its complex relationship to global economic development.[5]

---

[3] This challenges recent scholarship that suggests neoliberal ideas originated in the twentieth century. See Daniel Stedman, *Masters of the Universe: Hayek, Friedman, and the Birth of Neoliberal Politics* (Princeton: Princeton University Press, 2012); Angus Burgin, *The Great Persuasion: Reinventing Free Markets Since the Depression* (Cambridge, MA: Harvard University Press, 2012); Jamie Peck, *Constructions of Neoliberal Reason* (Oxford: Oxford University Press, 2010); Philip Mirowski and Dieter Plehwe, eds., *The Road From Mont Pelerin: The Making of the Neoliberal Thought Collective* (Cambridge, MA: Harvard University Press, 2009).

[4] Phillip Darby, *Three Faces of Imperialism: British and American Approaches to Asia and Africa, 1870–1970* (New Haven: Yale University Press, 1987); Bernard Porter, *Empire and Superempire: Britain, America and the World* (New Haven: Yale University Press, 2006); Tony Smith, *The Pattern of Imperialism: The United States, Great Britain, and the Late-Industrializing World Since 1815* (Cambridge: Cambridge University Press, 1981); Patrick Karl O'Brien and Armand Cleese, eds., *Two Hegemonies: Britain 1846–1914 and the United States 1941–2001* (Aldershot: Ashgate, 2002); Julian Go, *Patterns of Empire: The British and American Empires, 1688 to the Present* (New York: Cambridge University Press, 2011).

[5] See, for example, Dani Rodrik, *One Economics, Many Recipes: Globalization, Institutions, and Economic Growth* (Princeton: Princeton University Press, 2007); Ray Kiely, *The New Political Economy of Development: Globalization, Imperialism, Hegemony* (New York:

The book is all the more timely considering that current critics of US-led neoliberalism commonly associate it with imperialism.[6] Imperial theorists of various stripes have similarly asserted that Anglo-American economic expansion in the nineteenth century was little more than free-trade imperialism in disguise. Such studies nevertheless overlook the fact that economic nationalism dominated the late-nineteenth-century American political economy and imperial expansion. They also gloss over how, in seeking greater domestic prosperity, the most avid Anglo-American free traders themselves subscribed to a cosmopolitan anti-imperial vision of peaceful economic expansion, non-interventionism, and global market integration.

Through an examination of the era's Anglo-American free-trade movement and its protectionist opposition, this book illuminates how so many ideological adherents to free trade during this period advocated *against* imperialism in its myriad manifestations. Rather, the principal Anglo-American proponents of empire were economic nationalists. In response to the diffusion of free-trade cosmopolitanism and the onset of the late-nineteenth-century Great Depression (*c.* 1873–1896), an expansionist doctrine of economic nationalism rose to prominence within protectionist circles. This imperial policy, the "imperialism of economic nationalism," coercively sought access to foreign markets while maintaining protectionism at home. The politico-ideological battle over economic globalization became particularly frenzied behind the high tariff walls of late-nineteenth-century America, where protectionist sentiment ran rampant. The US search for new markets would thus take on an imperial and protectionist cast – and American advocacy for free trade would become tantamount to a British conspiracy. This same controversial Victorian free-trade tradition would lay the ideological foundations for today's own neoliberal order.

Palgrave MacMillan, 2007); Ha-Joon Chang, *Globalization, Economic Development, and the Role of the State* (London: Zed Books, 2003); Chang, *Kicking Away the Ladder: Development Strategy in Historical Perspective* (London: Anthem, 2002).

[6] Et al., Ahmet H. Kose, Fikret Sense, and Eric Yeldan, eds., *Neoliberal Globalization as New Imperialism: Case Studies on Reconstruction of the Periphery* (New York: Nova Science Pub Inc., 2007); Francis Shor, *Dying Empire: US Imperialism and Global Resistance* (London and New York: Routledge, 2010); Richard A. Dello Buono and Jose Bell Lara, eds., *Imperialism, Neoliberalism and Social Struggles in Latin America* (Leiden: Brill, 2007); James Petras and Henry Veltmeyer, *Globalization Unmasked: Imperialism in the 21st Century* (New York: Zed Books, 2001); Robert E. Prasch, "Neoliberalism and Empire: How are They Related?" *Review of Radical Political Economics* 37 (Summer 2005): 281–287.

Acknowledgments

I am immeasurably grateful to Bill Brands, Tony Hopkins, and Mark Lawrence for their supervision, mentorship, and support throughout my career, as well as for their careful reading of the book itself. Many other scholars have also provided feedback and criticisms over the years, including Peter Cain, Duncan Campbell, Ed Crapol, Steve Davies, Dave Ekbladh, George Forgie, Jon Franklin, Frank Gavin, Tony Howe, Doug Irwin, Phil Magness, Steve Meardon, Mark Metzler, Phil Myers, Eddy Rodgers, Scott Shubitz, Jeremi Suri, and James Vaughn. Sections of the book were sharpened by the feedback I received at conferences, symposia, and workshops, including Society for Historians of American Foreign Relations conferences, the Massachusetts Historical Society, the Civil War-Global Conflict Conference at the University of Charleston, the University of Sydney's "History on Monday" series, the US Studies Symposium at Monash, the Porter Fortune Symposium on History at Ole Miss, Sydney's US Studies Centre postdoctoral series, International Security Studies at Yale, the British Scholar Conference at the University of Texas at Austin (UT), the British International History Group, and the Maple Leaf and Eagle Conference at the University of Helsinki. Thanks are also owed to the editors of the *Journal of Imperial and Commonwealth History*, *Diplomatic History*, the *Journal of the History of Economic Thought*, and the *Journal of the Civil War Era*, where some preliminary sections of the book have appeared as articles.

The generosity of the US Studies Centre at the University of Sydney since 2011 was invaluable, providing me with the opportunity to finish many of the book revisions as a postdoctoral fellow and then as a research associate. Bates Gill, Geoff Garrett, Margaret Levi, Brendon O'Connor, Tom Switzer, Craig Purcell, and Nina Fudala, among so many other amazing people at the Centre, were a constant source of support and inspiration, as were my fellow postdocs Niki Hemmer, Carrie Hyde, Rob Rakove, and Shawn Treier. Many thanks as well to Adam Tooze, Paul Kennedy, Amanda Behm, and Jeremy Friedman for welcoming me at Yale's International Security Studies at a particularly crucial point in the writing of the book. I am grateful to the History Department at UT, the Society for Historians of American Foreign Relations, the Canadian Embassy, UT's School of Liberal Arts, the Massachusetts Historical Society, and the New York Public Library for helping to fund the research that evolved into this book. And I have been very fortunate indeed to have had such supportive colleagues at the University of Exeter since my arrival in 2013, especially Martin Thomas, Andrew Thompson, Richard Toye, David Thackeray, and my head of department, Henry French.

Of course to Rachel Herrmann I owe an inestimable debt; she selflessly read my work with her constructive eye, and made sure that I never went hungry throughout the arduous journey. Last but by no means least, I would like to thank my parents, Andrea and Don, for their unwavering encouragement. Without them, this book would not exist; nor, for that matter, would I.

Abbreviations

ACLL	Anti-Corn Law League
AFTL	American Free Trade League
CC MSS	Cobden Club Manuscripts, Records Office, Chichester, West Sussex, England
CR	*Congressional Record*
FO	Foreign Office, National Archives, Kew, England
FRUS	*Foreign Relations of the United States*
IFL	Imperial Federation League
IFTA	International Free Trade Alliance
LAC	National Library and Archives, Ottawa, Canada
LOC	Library of Congress, Washington, DC
MHS	Massachusetts Historical Society, Boston, MA
NYPL	New York Public Library, New York City, NY
PRO	Public Records Office, National Archives, Kew, England
UETL	United Empire Trade League

Introduction

From the Civil War onward, the Republican party set out to place the United States on a pronounced protectionist path for domestic economic growth and imperial expansion abroad. American adherence to the Victorian English free-trade ideology known as "Cobdenism" – the belief that international free trade and non-interventionism would bring prosperity and peace to the world – duly became anathema within protectionist Republican circles. Despite intense Republican opposition, the influence of Cobdenism would reach its nineteenth-century apex during the non-consecutive Democratic administrations of Grover Cleveland (1885–1889, 1893–1897). As a result, in 1895 Republican Senator Henry Cabot Lodge would take Cleveland's second cabinet to task for having "been successfully Cobdenized, and that is the underlying reason for their policy of retreat" in the Pacific, Cleveland having opposed expanding US control in Hawaii and Samoa. President Cleveland's controversial 1887 annual message calling for freer trade during his first term had similarly shown him to be "an easy convert to Cobdenism."[1] For Republican economic nationalists, Cobdenism became tantamount to conspiracy: a secretive British-led attempt to stunt the growth of US "infant" industries and foil Republican imperial designs. Cobdenism's cosmopolitan ideology, in contestation with its economic nationalist counterpart, was interwoven within Anglo-American relations throughout the latter half of the nineteenth century, spindling alongside modern globalization's interconnecting threads of global trade, communications, ideas, people, and policies.

The overarching purpose of this book is to offer a much-needed reinterpretation of Anglo-American political economy, ideology, and empire. With the exception of Free Trade England, nations like the United States sought protection from global market uncertainty behind the aegis of economic nationalism throughout the late nineteenth century. Yet

---

[1] Henry Cabot Lodge, "Our Blundering Foreign Policy," *Forum* 19 (March 1895): 15; George B. Curtiss, *Protection and Prosperity: An Account of Tariff Legislation and its Effect in Europe and America* (New York: Pan-American Publishing, 1896), 626.

historians instead commonly portray this as an American era of laissez-faire and free trade, a misimpression that has seeped into the dominant American imperial narrative. The following chapters correct this political economic misconception by examining how ideological conflict between free traders and economic nationalists laid the imperial path for Anglo-American economic globalization.

The book argues that two ideological visions – "Cobdenite cosmopolitanism" and "Listian nationalism" – provided the central arguments for debates over the course of late-nineteenth-century industrial development and economic globalization. The fight was particularly fierce within the United States and the British Empire. The future of Anglo-American economic development, market integration, and imperial expansion rested upon the outcome.

Late-nineteenth-century America's free-trade cosmopolitans subscribed to the philosophy of Richard Cobden (1804–1865), who became Victorian England's free-trade apostle when he successfully led the overthrow of the British protectionist system in the 1840s. Cobden believed that international freedom of trade and a non-interventionist foreign policy would lead to domestic prosperity and world peace. He predicted that through universal free trade, nations would eventually become so interconnected and interdependent that war would become obsolete. Cobden's free-trade ideas found an avid audience among an influential group of Victorian America's liberal reformers.

The influence of American Cobdenism reached its anti-imperial height during the Democratic presidencies of Grover Cleveland. Cleveland's administrations opposed the era's imperial projects, be it forcibly prying open foreign markets, annexing Hawaii, or colonizing the Congo. Cleveland's cabinets advocated instead a Cobdenite policy of free trade, non-interventionism, and non-coercive market expansion. These Cobdenite policies provided a stark contrast both to the aggressive imperial designs of the antebellum Jeffersonian Democrats and to the postbellum Republican party, with the latter quickly discarding the remaining tattered vestiges of its more restrained antebellum Whig political tradition: that is, aside from its Whiggish dedication to protectionism.

This period's leading American protectionist intellectuals – most notably Henry C. Carey, James G. Blaine, and William McKinley – were Listian nationalists, who held an Anglophobic belief in infant industrial protectionism and internal improvements as enunciated by the German-American economic theorist Friedrich List (1789–1846). Listian nationalism was a progressive (i.e. forward-looking and reform-oriented) economic nationalist doctrine that viewed free trade as an ultimate ideal stage of economic development, and the coercive acquisition of foreign markets an eventual necessity for surplus goods and capital. Following the global onset of the era's Great Depression in 1873, disciples of this aggressive Listian ideology would begin to stand out from the Republican party's more orthodox home-market protectionists, who instead stuck to the belief that the US economy could forever supply its own demand.[2]

Friedrich List had lived in the American protectionist heartland of Pennsylvania from 1825 to 1832, during which he updated and elaborated upon eighteenth-century Hamiltonian protectionist theories. List expounded upon the burgeoning American System of governmental protectionism and internal improvements, and left his indelible progressive mark upon American economic nationalist ideology and imperialism for decades to come. His antebellum influence effectively represented the first wave of German-American economic nationalism, followed by the more widely studied second wave that struck American shores in the last decades of the nineteenth century, which would cement the List-inspired German Historical School's position within turn-of-the-century American economic thought, political economy, and imperial debates.

The complex relationship between economic globalization, imperialism, and economic development was hotly debated in the nineteenth century, a debate that continues today along surprisingly similar lines of argument. Throughout much of the nineteenth century, American protectionist policies had been advocated with little regard for acquiring foreign markets. This began to change in the final decades of the century as Listian nationalists took control of the Republican party. American Listians believed that both state intervention and coercive market expansion were crucial for US economic development and domestic prosperity, a belief that was closely linked to their progressive regionalized vision for American economic globalization. In contrast to many of their more orthodox protectionist political allies who disdained foreign markets, the Listian's economic nationalist ideology incorporated a sophisticated long-term understanding that, as America's infant industries matured and became internationally competitive, the United States would need more access to foreign markets – and Listians were willing to use imperial means to gain them. When informal protectionist reciprocity policies failed to coerce open new markets, Listians turned to more formal imperial methods.[3]

---

[2] I should note that whereas "Cobdenism," "Cobdenite," and "Manchester School" were terms used by nineteenth-century contemporaries, "Listian nationalist" is my own terminology to describe this imperial strand of protectionist thought. Nor were they isolated to the United States; they can be seen as national expressions of the wider Listian influence that took on a global cast by the late nineteenth century.

[3] Although there are invariably exceptions to these classifications, Listians also generally held a more sympathetic view toward the silver question than their Cobdenite

The Victorian American Empire was in many ways an inverse of that of the British Empire. In contrast to American continental expansion westward during much of the nineteenth century, the British Empire spread across the seas and across the globe; whereas the United States absorbed its continental territories within its federal political system, the global British Empire maintained a hierarchical imperial relationship with its overseas colonies, alongside a reliance upon foreign investment; and where economic nationalism dominated the late-nineteenth-century American political economy, free trade held sway in England.

Despite these differences, the similarity of the debate between Listians and Cobdenites within the British and American empires was remarkably similar. Drawing inspiration both from the writings of Friedrich List and the protectionist turn among Britain's competitors, the British Empire's new generation of economic nationalists would evolve into formidable late-nineteenth-century imperial opponents of Cobdenism, even within Free Trade England itself. This protectionist movement within the British Empire turned to the theories of Friedrich List. From the 1860s, onward Anglophobic American implementation of economic nationalist policies in turn greatly affected the British Empire, where List's theories began to vie with English Cobdenite orthodoxy.[4] Ever more imperial American protectionist policies strengthened internal calls throughout the British Empire to curb its Cobdenite proclivities and instead create a protectionist Greater Britain in order to politically and economically tie together its geographically disparate settler colonies in South Africa, Canada, Australia, and New Zealand. This idea of British imperial unity was made all the more viable owing to the development of more efficient tools of global transportation and communication such as railroads, canals, transoceanic telegraphic cables, and steamship lines. By century's end, Listians throughout the British Empire demanded imperial federation, protectionism, and intra-imperial trade preference, much as US Listians sought to expand American access to global markets through a mixture of high protective tariffs, restrictive reciprocity, and imperial expansion. Politico-ideological conflict thus paralleled Anglo-American imperial expansion and economic globalization.

In bringing this conflict to light, *The "Conspiracy" of Free Trade* therefore seeks to answer three broad questions: how Victorian free-trade

---

counterparts, as Listians tended to view US adherence to the gold standard as but a further fiscal shackle tying American markets to the City of London.

[4] On the influence of Cobdenism in the British Empire, see especially Anthony Howe, *Free Trade and Liberal England, 1846–1946* (Oxford: Clarendon Press, 1997); Frank Trentmann, *Free Trade Nation: Commerce, Consumption, and Civil Society in Modern Britain* (Oxford and New York: Oxford University Press, 2008).

cosmopolitanism reached and influenced American domestic and foreign relations; how economic nationalists opposed Cobdenism in the United States and the British Empire; and how these conflicting ideologies shaped Anglo-American relations, imperial expansion, and economic globalization. In doing so, the book describes how American Cobdenites fought fiercely for freer trade, anti-imperialism, and closer ties with the British Empire in an era dominated by protectionism, "new" imperialism, and Anglophobia. American economic nationalists in turn considered these transatlantic Cobdenite efforts to be part of a vast, British-inspired, free-trade conspiracy. The following chapters therefore incorporate an ideological approach to understanding nineteenth-century Anglo-American imperial expansion, politics, and economic globalization.

The ideological origins of American globalization

Tracing the ideological origins of a system or idea is always tricky, as one can easily get lost in the myriad intellectual tendrils trailing back through human history. Sleuthing the ideological origins of free trade is a case in point. The first systematic enunciation of free trade is of course commonly attributed to Adam Smith. Yet the universal principles of free trade originated at least two centuries before the 1776 publication of Adam Smith's *Wealth of Nations*.[5] As with the opposing principles of protectionism, the ideological origins of free trade can be traced back hundreds of years.

But these ideas were not static. Nineteenth-century free traders and protectionists would continue to update and adapt their theories for an increasingly global political economy. Late-eighteenth-century free-trade advocates like Adam Smith and economic nationalists like Alexander Hamilton had expounded their ideas from within a protean international economic system quite distinct from the global one that began to arise in the middle of the nineteenth century, when Richard Cobden and Friedrich List enunciated their conflicting creeds. It was the Victorian era that bore witness to the tumultuous booms and busts of modern globalization, whereupon the problems and promises of the foreign market began to rival those of the national, and wherein the disciples of Cobden and List fought to redirect the political economic course of an ever more integrated world. And it was during this later period that present-day ideological conceptions of trade liberalization originated.

[5] Douglas A. Irwin traces the idea back to Plato, Pliny, and Plutarch in *Against the Tide: An Intellectual History of Free Trade* (Princeton, NJ: Princeton University Press, 1996).

Cobden's and List's conflicting global visions would battle throughout the Victorian world, but most vociferously in the American political arena in the latter half of the nineteenth century. Economic nationalism came to dominate the US political economy and foreign policy, as protectionist policies, coupled with imperial expansionism, promised to help allay widely held economic nationalist fears that America's more nascent industries would prematurely be pulled into Britain's free-trade orbit.[6] American Cobdenites, in emulation of Britain's free-trade system, instead peaceably sought both an end to US protectionism and anti-imperial access to foreign markets through international trade liberalization. Their fight for freer trade was an uphill battle.

American economic nationalist fears of Free Trade England quickly turned into Anglophobic paranoia when American Cobdenites began to mobilize. This conspiratorial turn is not entirely surprising considering that British-oriented conspiracy theories had long been a rather ubiquitous American outgrowth of the widely held nineteenth-century fear of British encroachment in North America. So after England unilaterally turned to free trade at mid-century, American protectionists began seeing Adam Smith's invisible hand hidden behind any attempt to lower American high tariff walls. If the "paranoid style" were a Victorian American play, the alleged conspiracy of free trade would deserve top billing.[7]

The mid-century establishment of Britain's own free-trade policy – the leading source of American free-trade conspiracy theories – would also provide politico-ideological inspiration to an elite group of classical liberal abolitionist reformers in the American north like Edward Atkinson, William Cullen Bryant, and William Lloyd Garrison. The British policy

---

[6] Karl Polanyi described this as part of a "double movement" against the nineteenth-century British classical liberal system in *The Great Transformation* (New York: Rinehart & Co., 1944).

[7] On nineteenth-century US Anglophobic conspiracy theories, see, also, Richard Hofstadter, *The Paranoid Style in American Politics and Other Essays* (New York: Alfred A. Knopf, 1965); Lawrence A. Peskin, "Conspiratorial Anglophobia and the War of 1812," *Journal of American History* 98 (December 2011): 647–669; Kinley J. Brauer, "The United States and British Imperial Expansion, 1815–60," *Diplomatic History* 12 (January 1988): 19–37; Sam W. Haynes, *Unfinished Revolution: The Early American Republic in a British World* (Charlottesville: University of Virginia Press, 2010); Bradley J. Young, "Silver, Discontent, and Conspiracy: The Ideology of the Western Republican Revolt of 1890–1901," *Pacific Historical Review* 64 (May 1995): 243–265; Stephen Tuffnell, "'Uncle Sam is to be Sacrificed': Anglophobia in Late Nineteenth-Century Politics and Culture," *American Nineteenth Century History* 12 (March 2011): 77–99; William C. Reuter, "The Anatomy of Political Anglophobia in the United States, 1865–1900," *Mid-America* 61 (April–July 1979): 117–132; Edward P. Crapol, *America for Americans: Economic Nationalism and Anglophobia in the Late Nineteenth Century* (Westport, CT: Greenwood Press, 1973).

of free trade was adopted in 1846 with the overturning of England's Corn Laws, protective tariffs on foreign grain imports. Richard Cobden oversaw their overthrow as the leader of the Anti-Corn Law League (ACLL; 1838–1846), even as he tied the free-trade movement closely to that of transatlantic abolitionism. In marked contrast to the conspiratorial reception among American economic nationalists, the mid-century abolitionist leaders of the American free-trade movement took encouragement from Cobden's efforts. Their transatlantic free-trade cooperation, however, would spark even more conspiratorial conjecture when Cobden's friends and disciples created the Cobden Club (1866–1982) in London upon his death for the purpose of spreading free trade to the world, but especially to the United States.

US Listian nationalists, the nineteenth century's most progressive proponents of the "American System" of economic nationalism, became ever more outspoken and influential as the century came to a close. Even as American adherents to Cobdenism increased in number following the Civil War, Listian nationalist demands for protectionism coupled with coercive foreign market access were also reaching a fevered pitch. The politico-ideological battle over the future of American economic globalization – whether it would develop through a system of free trade and non-interventionism or protectionism and imperialism – became frenzied. How the United States would approach industrialization and the "Americanization of the world," as William T. Stead famously put it at the turn of the century, hinged upon the outcome.[8]

A matter of definitions

"Coleridge once said that abstract definitions had done more to curse the human race than war, famine, and pestilence," remarked Republican Congressman James Garfield to his friend Edward Atkinson in 1868. Garfield concluded that Coleridge "must have been reading financial literature just before he wrote that sentence."[9] The Ohio congressman's observation is as apt now as it was then. "Globalization" in particular is now thrown around so indiscriminately that it runs the risk of becoming meaningless. A. G. Hopkins describes modern globalization as occurring upon the arrival of the mid-nineteenth-century nation state and the expansion of industrialization, when "the sovereign state based on territorial boundaries was filled in by developing a wider and deeper sense of national consciousness and filled out, variously, by population growth,

---

[8] William T. Stead, *The Americanization of the World* (New York: Horace Markley, 1901).
[9] Garfield to Atkinson, August 11, 1868, Carton 1, Edward Atkinson Papers, MHS.

free trade, imperialism, and war."[10] The only addition to the latter list would be "protectionism." Broadly defined, globalization is the process of speeding up global integration via capital flows, markets, ideas, people, and technology. Nineteenth-century advances in technology not only aided in this process, but also provided new paths toward integrating the globe.[11] They allowed for the realistic projection of two conflicting economic systems – one of free trade and the other of protectionism – for modernization, for industrialization, and for tying international markets together. The book correspondingly expands from a transatlantic to a global study as the world became ever more interconnected through steamship lines, canals, transoceanic cables, transcontinental railroads, and imperial expansion in the latter half of the nineteenth century.[12] The following pages focus especially upon this Listian–Cobdenite conflict over *economic globalization*, the accelerating process of global economic integration and market interdependence.

The history of foreign relations and economic globalization includes the history of ideologies.[13] "Ideology" therefore also needs defining: a belief or doctrine that forms the basis of an ideal political, economic, social, or cultural system.[14] In the case of Listian nationalism and Cobdenite cosmopolitanism, these bases frequently overlapped.

Certain studies of the turn-of-the-century tariff in turn have taken a semantic stand regarding the label of "free trade." These works take an

---

[10] A. G. Hopkins, "Globalization – An Agenda for Historians," in *Globalization in World History*, ed. by A. G. Hopkins (New York: Norton, 2002), 7.

[11] For globalization in the long nineteenth century, see Jurgen Osterhammel, *The Transformation of the World: A Global History of the Nineteenth Century* (Princeton, NJ: Princeton University Press, 2014); Kevin H. O'Rourke and Jeffrey G. Williamson, *Globalization and History: The Evolution of a Nineteenth-Century Atlantic Economy* (Cambridge, MA: Harvard University Press, 1999); Dwayne R. Winseck and Robert M. Pike, *Communication and Empire: Media, Markets, and Globalization, 1860–1930* (Durham: Duke University Press, 2007); Roland Wenzlhuemer, *Connecting the Nineteenth-Century World: The Telegraph and Globalization* (Cambridge: Cambridge University Press, 2012); Emily S. Rosenberg, ed., *A World Connecting: 1870–1945* (Cambridge, MA: Belknap Press, 2012).

[12] On "global history" and the "history of globalization," see especially A. G. Hopkins, ed. *Global History: Interactions between the Universal and the Local* (New York: Palgrave Macmillan, 2006); Hopkins, ed., *Globalization in World History* (New York: Norton, 2002); Thomas Bender, *A Nation Among Nations: America's Place in World History* (New York: Hill and Wang, 2006); Bruce Mazlish and Akira Iriye, *Global History Reader* (New York: Routledge, 2005).

[13] Michael H. Hunt, *Ideology and U.S. Foreign Policy* (New Haven, CT: Yale University Press, 1987); John Gerring, "A Chapter in the History of American Party Ideology: The Nineteenth-Century Democratic Party (1828–1892)," *Polity* 26 (Summer 1994): 729–768.

[14] On political ideologies, see, also, Frank Ninkovich, "Ideology, the Open Door, and Foreign Policy," *Diplomatic History* 6 (September 1982): 185–208; Judith Goldstein, *Ideas, Interests, and American Trade Policy* (Ithaca, NY: Cornell University Press, 1993);

extreme view by suggesting that, in the nineteenth century, free trade entailed the complete and immediate elimination of tariffs, customs houses, and other trade barriers. As the liberal tariff reformers under examination here fought primarily for a "tariff for revenue only" and increases to the list of duty-free raw materials but rarely for a complete elimination of tariffs, historians like Tom Terrill and Paul Wolman prefer the label "tariff revisionist" rather than "free trader."[15]

However, this stark categorization of free trade is misleading. Throughout the nineteenth century, most governments, including those of the United States and England, obtained much of their revenue from tariffs.[16] Everett Wheeler, who helped establish the influential New York Free Trade Club, described what they meant by "free trade": "we did not advocate the repeal of the tariff. That was not our view of the meaning of free trade." Rather, free trade meant a "Tariff for Revenue only."[17] Nineteenth-century free traders, including Cobden himself, therefore predominantly sought a low tariff for revenue only, or what J. S. Mill and other political economists sometimes called a "free-trade tariff."[18]

American Cobdenites well understood that the country's political environment of the day would only allow for modest revisions and a gradual elimination of protective duties. The vast majority of them were therefore moderate – or gradualist – free traders, meaning they wanted a minimal tariff revenue system in imitation of the British free-trade system, but realized it might take decades to establish. Much fewer in number were absolute free traders, dogmatic doctrinaires who wanted immediate implementation of direct taxation and an elimination of all customs duties, although their numbers began to swell as the nineteenth century

---

Michael Freeden, *Ideologies and Political Theory: A Conceptual Approach* (Oxford: Clarendon Press, 1996).

[15] Tom E. Terrill, *The Tariff, Politics, and American Foreign Policy, 1874–1901* (Westport, CT: Greenwood Press, 1973), 10ff; Paul Wolman, *Most Favored Nation: The Republican Revisionists and U.S. Tariff Policy, 1897–1912* (Chapel Hill & London: University of North Carolina Press, 1992), xi.

[16] Even Adam Smith ceded the need for tariffs to provide revenue for national defense. See Adam Smith, *An Inquiry into the Nature and Causes of the Wealth of Nations*, ed. by Edwin Cannan (New York: The Modern Library, 1937 [1776]), 429–432; Jacob Viner, "Adam Smith and Laissez-Faire," *Journal of Political Economy* 35 (April 1927): 198–232; Irwin, *Against the Tide*, 78–83.

[17] William Graham Sumner, *Protectionism* (New York: Henry Holt and Company, 1888), 16; Everett P. Wheeler, *Sixty Years of American Life: Taylor to Roosevelt, 1850 to 1910* (New York: E. P. Dutton & Company, 1917), 152. See, also, David Ames Wells, "'A Tariff for Revenue': What It Really Means," *Forum* (September 1892): 51–66.

[18] Revenue tariffs are levied for gathering state revenue, not to discriminate against foreign imports. In contrast, protective tariffs are high import taxes designed to discourage or entirely prohibit foreign imports, thereby hindering foreign competition, normally for the purpose of artificially stimulating domestic industries.

drew to a close. It should therefore be kept in mind that free trade in practical application did not mean a complete absence of tariffs. Britain itself maintained a tariff revenue system at the height of its free-trade empire in the mid-nineteenth century.

Misunderstandings surrounding nineteenth-century free trade have also created confusion surrounding "reciprocity." The free-trade concept of trade reciprocity was epitomized in the 1860 Cobden–Chevalier Treaty, an Anglo-French agreement wherein Britain extended to the rest of the world without discrimination or conditions the same tariff concessions it offered to France through what has become known as the unconditional most-favored-nation clause. The postbellum Listian-Republican conception of trade reciprocity was very different; it was one of discrimination and retaliation, whereby imperial Republicans would seek to prize open new markets in Latin America and the Pacific through restrictive, conditional, bilateral reciprocity treaties, coupled with the coercive threat of massive tariff retaliation against foreign signatories. This restrictive reciprocity policy was enshrined within the Republican imperial playbook through the 1890 McKinley Tariff, which turned reciprocity into a protectionist tool for informal imperial expansion for many years to come.[19]

The majority Republican ideological adherence to economic nationalism became entrenched during the Civil War, which, as Richard Franklin Bensel has shown, brought about the rise of central state authority. Republicans thereafter instituted an economic system that involved a majority adherence to a national market and a protective tariff.[20] From its inception, a large proportion of the Republican party, controlling the executive for much of the time under consideration, subscribed to economic nationalism, an economic doctrine designed to protect the national market from international competition and crises through governmental control of trade, most commonly by way of protective tariffs, import restrictions, currency manipulation, and subsidization of domestic agriculture and industry. This economic nationalist doctrine

---

[19] A. A. Iliasu, "The Cobden-Chevalier Commercial Treaty of 1860," *Historical Journal* 14 (March 1971): 71; Jacob Viner, "The Most-Favored-Nation Clause in American Commercial Treaties," *Journal of Political Economy* 32 (February 1924): 117–118; James Laurence Laughlin and H. Parker Willis, *Reciprocity* (New York: The Baker & Taylor Co., 1903), chaps. 1, 6.

[20] Richard Franklin Bensel, *Yankee Leviathan: The Origins of Central State Authority in America, 1859–1877* (Cambridge: Cambridge University Press, 1990); Bensel, *The Political Economy of American Industrialization, 1877–1900* (Cambridge: Cambridge University Press, 2000). The most accessible treatment of nineteenth-century US tariff legislation to date remains F. W. Taussig, *The Tariff History of the United States* (New York & London: G. P. Putnam's Sons, 1931 [1892]).

historically has also been closely associated with political nationalism and a "realist" approach to international affairs.[21] For their part, American Cobdenites remained an independent cosmopolitan minority within the Republican party from the 1850s to the early 1880s, and became Mugwump party "traitors" after 1884 when they threw their support behind the Democratic presidential candidate, Grover Cleveland.

In correcting the era's common laissez-faire portrayal, *The "Conspiracy" of Free Trade* offers the first detailed transatlantic study of the free-trade movement in late-nineteenth-century America. The book also offers a reinterpretation of the Republican party's formation and ideological reorientation. In the United States, this new free-trade movement arose from among the leaders of the mid-century Liberal Republican movement. They were American subscribers to Cobdenism – sometimes referred to as the "Manchester School" – seeking a liberal world of free men, a reining in of protectionist-inspired monopolies and political corruption, and the establishment of world peace through global free trade. The book's online Appendix accordingly includes a detailed biographical list of American Cobdenites, many of whom were the politico-ideological leaders of free-trade, anti-imperial, abolitionist, and other liberal reform movements throughout the late nineteenth and early twentieth century.[22]

These American Cobdenites struggled but, in the short term, largely failed in their cosmopolitan goals. Their failure owed much to their independent spirit. They were too often unable to agree on a cohesive strategy to accomplish their shared goals, which helps to explain why the growing Cobdenite influence in the United States only rarely correlated with successful political reform. Their short-term failure owed even more, however, to the sizeable intellectual and political opposition of American economic nationalists.

Perhaps it is this lack of tangible success that helps explain why scholarship on the nineteenth-century free-trade movement in the United States has been minimal until now. Another reason certainly lies with the complexity of economic controversies that plagued the era. Just on the issues of protectionism and free trade alone – so often connected with nineteenth-century monetary issues surrounding the gold standard, international bimetallism, and the free coinage of silver (national bimetallism) – one

[21] Eric Helleiner, "Economic Nationalism as a Challenge to Economic Liberalism? Lessons from the 19th Century," *International Studies Quarterly* 46 (September 2002): 307–329; David Levi-Faur, "Friedrich List and the Political Economy of the Nation-State," *Review of International Political Economy* 4 (Spring 1997): 154–178; Robert Gilpin, *Global Political Economy* (Princeton, NJ: Princeton University Press, 2001).

[22] The Appendix, along with the full bibliography for the book, can be found online at www.cambridge.org/9781107109124.

can easily become lost in the vitriolic maze of contradictions, counter-arguments, bogeymen, and obfuscations used by all sides.

One desired end result is to clarify these subjects: to acknowledge their complexity without making them needlessly complicated. Protectionists promised high industrial employment and high wages for laborers, both of which would expand the market for farmers' and manufacturers' products. Free traders asserted instead that protectionism, unlike free trade, artificially increased costs for consumers, made American products internationally uncompetitive, and diminished agricultural exports for the sole benefit of a small segment of domestic industries, monopolies, and trusts.[23]

The tariff issue permeated nineteenth-century US politics like no other. Tariff disputes absorbed enormous quantities of congressional time and reflected the shifting balance of political power at any one time. As a result, it quite often divided the United States at a national, sectional, and local level. Free-trade outlets and organizations were promptly met with protectionist counterparts throughout the nation. Horace White's free-trade organ the *Chicago Tribune*, for instance, found a strong protectionist adversary in the *Chicago Inter Ocean*, as did William Cullen Bryant's *New York Evening Post* in Horace Greeley's *New York Tribune*. Nor was this a battle purely between intellectual elites. The ideological struggle over the road to domestic prosperity and global economic integration expanded from the east coast to the west, and both sides propagated propaganda campaigns, not on behalf of some mercurial hegemonic interest of the capitalist marketplace, but in the hopes of winning over the American people by making their respective economic ideologies an indelible part of American civil society and foreign policy.[24] Labor unions, manufacturers, and local farmers throughout the country aligned themselves with one side or the other. With less tangible success, both sides also sought the support of African Americans, women, the grassroots Granger movement, and its Populist successor.

As these different facets of the tariff issue demonstrate, internal divisions existed within both the free-trade and protectionist camps. Arguments for and against freer trade and protectionism were often amorphous, depending upon the time, place, and audience. Those seeking freer trade ran the gamut from a few of the most extreme, idealistic, absolute free-trade intellectuals; to more realistic pragmatists who sought

---

[23] Edward C. Kirkland, *Industry Comes of Age: Business, Labor, and Public Policy, 1860–1897* (Chicago, IL: Quadrangle Books, 1967), 187.

[24] Whereas economic nationalism reigned triumphant in the United States, Frank Trentmann has argued in *Free Trade Nation* that before the First World War, England could lay claim to a free-trade civil society.

moderate reductions as gradual steps toward ultimate free trade; to those who, bereft of ideological motivations, self-servingly desired reductions on particular duties that would favor their own business enterprises. The vast majority of the free traders within this study fall within the first two groups, since it focuses primarily upon the intellectual leadership of the free-trade and economic nationalist movements.

Protectionists similarly found themselves in internal disagreement over dutiable rates, dutiable goods, the efficacy of trade reciprocity and foreign markets, and the ultimate future of America's infant industries. More conservative protectionists believed the home market and insular freedom of trade among the states would forever guarantee high wages for the laborer and forever supply the demand for American goods, whereas progressive Listians argued that American products would eventually need foreign markets as outlets for American surplus goods and capital. Small businessmen looking for temporary tariff fortifications could easily find themselves at odds with other American businessmen in rival enterprises. The rise of trusts, monopolies, and combinations in turn led to powerful protectionist special interest groups and lobbyists that wielded great influence upon government policies and agencies. While it was generally understood that, theoretically, infant industries must one day reach adulthood, it thus became advantageous for some to stunt, or at least stubbornly deny, American industrial maturation. Nor was protectionism solely an issue in the more industrial Northeast. Kentuckians long sought protection for hemp, Louisianans for beet sugar, and Westerners for wool.[25]

Both Listians and Cobdenites were becoming ever more mindful of foreign markets during this time, covering as it does the interrelated rise of an integrated global cotton and food system, the "first age of globalization," and what some call America's second industrial revolution – the US development of widespread urbanization, consumption, innovation, and industrialization.[26] In the latter half of the nineteenth century, British investment in the United States skyrocketed; capital investment in manufacturing increased tenfold; the number of wage earners nearly fivefold; the amount of people living within cities increased by a third; and the total

[25] Entire books have been dedicated to these subjects. See, for example, Chester Whitney Wright, *Wool-Growing and the Tariff: A Study in the Economic History of the United States* (Cambridge, MA: Harvard University Press, 1910); Roy Gillespie Blakey, *The United States Beet Sugar Industry and the Tariff* (New York: Columbia University, 1912).

[26] Sven Beckert, "Emancipation and Empire: Reconstructing the Worldwide Web of Cotton Production in the Age of the American Civil War," *American Historical Review* 109 (December 2004): 1405–1438; Trentmann, *Free Trade Nation*, 15; O'Rourke and Williamson, *Globalization and History*. For the Second Industrial Revolution, see especially the work of Alfred Chandler.

population of the country more than doubled. Technological advances in turn drastically increased productivity. For instance, between 1865 and the end of the century, wheat production went up by 256 percent, sugar by 460 percent, corn 222 percent, coal 800 percent. During this same period, exports rose from $281 million to $1.231 billion, imports increased from $239 million to $616 million, and, as the turn of the century approached, American companies and missionaries spread throughout the globe.[27] The United States was fast closing in on Britain as the dominant industrial economy.

But with massive urbanization, innovation, immigration, trade, investment, and industrialization came as well a host of new problems, many of which entered debates over the tariff and global market expansion. Issues surrounding labor, wages, economic depressions, and trusts became particular areas of contention between American free traders and protectionists. Added to which, sectional demands of the Northeast, South, and West quite often conflicted, leading to further disagreements over what was truly in the national interest.[28]

Adding to the confusion, American historians have long mistaken Cobdenism for Jeffersonianism, despite their stark differences. For one thing, Cobdenism took root within the American manufacturing and financial centers of the Northeast – New York City and Boston – rather than the agrarian locales of the Jeffersonian South. For another, northern Cobdenism was tied closely to abolitionism, whereas the southern Jeffersonian free-trade ideology became associated with the defense of plantation slavery. Finally, American Cobdenites were Anglophiles, where Jeffersonians were Anglophobes. With the post-Civil War New South undergoing tremendous postwar social, political, and economic upheaval, it was left to the Cobdenite abolitionists to take charge of the postbellum free-trade movement.

In *Global Dawn*, Frank Ninkovich has drawn much-needed attention to the myriad cultural manifestations of late-nineteenth-century liberal

---

[27] Jay Sexton, *Debtor Diplomacy: Finance and American Foreign Relations in the Civil War Era, 1837–1873* (Oxford: Clarendon, 2005); P. L. Cottrell, *British Overseas Investment in the Nineteenth Century* (London: Macmillan, 1975), 11–15; Joseph A. Fry, "Phases of Empire: Late-Nineteenth-Century U.S. Foreign Relations," in *The Gilded Age: Essays on the Origins of Modern America*, ed. by Charles W. Calhoun (Wilmington, DE: SR Books, 1996), 262; David M. Pletcher, "1861–1898: Economic Growth and Diplomatic Adjustment," in *Economics and World Power: An Assessment of American Diplomacy since 1789*, ed. by William H. Becker and Samuel F. Wells, Jr. (New York: Columbia University Press, 1984), 120, 122; Emily Rosenberg, *Spreading the American Dream: American Economic and Cultural Expansion 1890–1945* (New York: Hill and Wang, 1982), 14–37.

[28] Peter Trubowitz, *Defining the National Interest: Conflict and Change in American Foreign Policy* (Chicago, IL: University of Chicago Press, 1998).

internationalism. Along these lines, Cobdenism's Anglo-American "free-trade culture" was indeed rich, and both men and women took part in it. The rhetoric of antislavery permeated the postbellum free-trade debate, acting as a linguistic bridge between the ante- and postbellum eras. Cobdenite cosmopolitans, many of whom were leading radical abolitionists, viewed the "unshackling" of the fetters of trade as but the next step in the universal emancipation of mankind and as a tool for "civilizing" less advanced societies.[29] Listian nationalists in turn believed that premature free trade kept society in a barbaric uncivilized state. They argued with similar antislavery language that free trade respectively enslaved American manufactures and laborers to the British market and European pauper labor. The free-trade debate even found outlets in the literature of Mark Twain, Walt Whitman, and Edward Bellamy. African Americans and women, although a small minority of the late-nineteenth-century free-trade and protectionist movements, also began to play a larger role as the century came to a close, as did the culture of manliness. These cultural aspects of the US controversy over free trade – its free-trade culture – would become ever more pronounced by the time of the late-1880s "Great Debate" over American tariff policy.[30]

American history as imperial history

Imperial historian Stephen Howe has observed how the "free-trade character" of late-nineteenth-century American imperialism has become the "dominant view."[31] The so-called Wisconsin School of diplomatic historians that rose to prominence in the 1960s and 1970s deserves due credit for this free-trade or open-door historiographical orthodoxy. Drawing inspiration in part from Marxist theories of economic imperialism, these revisionist foreign relations historians sought an overarching American imperial narrative: "empire as a way of life," as W. A. Williams, the founder of this radical school, put it. Revisionists provocatively

[29] Eric Williams controversially drew connections between the English free-trade and antislavery movements in *Capitalism and Slavery* (Chapel Hill: University of North Carolina Press, 1944).

[30] These aspects also complement the new socio-cultural histories of American capitalism and internationalism. See Frank Ninkovich, *Global Dawn: The Cultural Foundation of American Internationalism, 1865–1890* (Cambridge, MA: Harvard University Press, 2009), esp. 59–69; Michael Zakim and Gary J. Kornblith, eds., *Capitalism Takes Command: The Social Transformation of Nineteenth-Century America* (Chicago, IL: University of Chicago Press, 2012). On England's free-trade culture, see, also, Ayse Celikkol, *Romances of Free Trade: British Literature, Laissez-Faire, and the Global Nineteenth Century* (New York: Oxford University Press, 2011).

[31] Stephen Howe, "New Empires, New Dilemmas – and Some Old Arguments," *Global Dialogue* 5 (Winter/Spring 2003), worlddialogue.org/content.php?id=216.

suggest that late-nineteenth-century imperial presidents, with broad business and agrarian support, embarked upon a bipartisan quest for foreign markets that culminated in the acquisition of both a formal and informal American Empire. Williams termed this "Open Door imperialism," an American manifestation of John Gallagher and Ronald Robinson's "imperialism of free trade."[32]

In seeking an all-encompassing open-door imperial narrative, however, revisionist studies have tended to overlook the prevalence of economic nationalism in the United States. They have also tended to minimize the sizeable ideological and political conflicts over American imperial expansion between and within the Democratic and Republican parties.[33] They have thus recast postbellum American free traders – previously considered among the most vocal critics of American empire building – as advocates of informal imperialism.[34] Williams termed this seeming contradiction "imperial anticolonialism," and various other revisionists have similarly suggested that there was only a tactical difference between imperial and so-called anti-imperial commercial expansionists.[35]

---

[32] In their groundbreaking 1953 article Gallagher and Robinson revolutionized imperial studies by arguing that England's adoption of free trade from around 1850 onward had helped promote an informal British Empire that historians had previously overlooked. Robinson thereafter added that it entailed "coercion or diplomacy exerted for purposes of imposing free trading conditions on a weaker society against its will." John Gallagher and Ronald Robinson, "The Imperialism of Free Trade," *Economic History Review* 6 (August 1953): 1–15; Ronald Robinson, "Imperial Theory and the Question of Imperialism after Empire," in *Perspectives on Imperialism and Decolonization*, ed. by Robert F. Holland and Gowher Rizvi (London: Frank Cass, 1984), 48.

[33] Other influences included Charles Beard and an opposition to the Vietnam War. See, for instance, William Appleman Williams, *The Great Evasion: An Essay on the Contemporary Relevance of Karl Marx and on the Wisdom of Admitting the Heretic into the Dialogue about America's Future* (Chicago: Quadrangle Books, 1964); Emily S. Rosenberg, "Economic Interest and United States Foreign Policy," in *American Foreign Relations Reconsidered, 1890–1993*, ed. by Gordon Martel (London and New York, 1993); James G. Morgan, *Into New Territory: American Historians and the Concept of US Imperialism* (Madison: University of Wisconsin Press, 2014).

[34] For the anti-imperial interpretation, see E. Berkeley Tompkins, *Anti-Imperialism in the United States: The Great Debate, 1890–1920* (Philadelphia: University of Pennsylvania Press, 1970); David Patterson, *Toward a Warless World: The Travail of the American Peace Movement, 1887–1914* (Bloomington: Indiana University Press, 1976), 12–13, 32–33, 74–75, 80.

[35] William Appleman Williams, *The Tragedy of American Diplomacy* (Cleveland, OH: World Pub., 1959), 29, 46–47; Thomas McCormick, *China Market: America's Quest for Informal Empire, 1893-1901* (Chicago, IL: Ivan R. Dee, 1967), 45, 63; Walter LaFeber, *The New Empire: An Interpretation of American Expansion, 1860-1898* (Ithaca, NY and London: Cornell University Press, 1963), 412–417; Schoonover and Crapol, "Shift to Global Expansion," 140, 171–172; Thomas McCormick, "From Old Empire to New: The Changing Dynamics and Tactics of American Empire," in *Colonial Crucible: Empire in the Making of the Modern American State*, ed. by Alfred W. McCoy and Francisco A. Scarano (Madison: University of Wisconsin Press, 2009), 69–72. Such revisionist work

The continued salience of the free-trade imperial thesis also owes much to the cultural turn within US imperial historiography over the past few decades. This shift has borne witness to a variety of innovative gendered and racial studies of America's rise to empire. But owing to their cultural emphasis, they have effectively ceded the economic imperial impetus to the revisionists.[36] Subsequent work on American trade expansion within the broader history of modern globalization in turn has ably complemented – but has not supplanted – the "strongly influential" open-door imperial narrative.[37]

But more broadly, the dominant open-door imperial interpretation stems from the all too common historical depiction of the American late nineteenth century as a laissez-faire era, a shining example of what William Novak has described as "the myth of the 'weak' American state."[38] Aside from minimal governmental regulation of monopolies

has thereby indiscriminately equated "economic expansionism" with "imperialism." See J. A. Thompson, "William Appleman Williams and the 'American Empire,'" *Journal of American Studies* 7 (April 1973): 103–104. Similar criticisms were levelled against "The Imperialism of Free Trade." See, et al., D. C. M. Platt, "The Imperialism of Free Trade – Some Reservations," *Economic History Review* 21 (August 1968): 296–306.

[36] Matthew Frye Jacobson, *Barbarian Virtues: The United States Encounters Foreign Peoples at Home and Abroad, 1876–1917* (New York: Hill and Wang, 2000), xi; Kristin Hoganson, *Fighting for American Manhood: How Gender Politics Provoked the Spanish-American and Philippine-American Wars* (New Haven, CT: Yale University Press, 1998), 210, n. 14. Race now plays a larger role in the new edition of Walter Lafeber's *The New Cambridge History of American Foreign Relations Volume II: America's Search for Opportunity* (New York: Cambridge University Press, 2013). See, also, Ian Tyrrell, *Reforming the World: The Creation of America's Moral Empire* (Princeton, NJ: Princeton University Press, 2010); Paul Kramer, *The Blood of Government: Race, Empire, the United States, & the Philippines* (Chapel Hill: University of North Carolina Press, 2006); Eric T. Love, *Race over Empire: Racism and U.S. Imperialism, 1865–1900* (Chapel Hill: University of North Carolina Press, 2004); and Edward P. Crapol ed., *Women and American Foreign Policy: Lobbyists, Critics, and Insiders* (Wilmington, DE: Scholarly Resources, 1987).

[37] Mark Atwood Lawrence, "Open Door Policy," in *Encyclopedia of American Foreign Policy*, ed. by Alexander DeConde, Richard Burns, Fredrik Logevall, and Louise B. Ketz (New York: Scribners, 2002), 42. For the history of US globalization, see, for instance, Thomas W. Zeiler, "Just Do It! Globalization for Diplomatic Historians," *Diplomatic History* 25 (Fall 2001): 529–551; Rosenberg, *Spreading the American Dream*; Emily Rosenberg, *Financial Missionaries to the World: The Politics and Culture of Dollar Diplomacy, 1900–1930* (Durham: Duke University Press, 2003); Alfred E. Eckes, Jr. and Thomas W. Zeiler, *Globalization and the American Century* (Cambridge: Cambridge University Press, 2003); Thomas D. Schoonover, *Uncle Sam's War of 1898 and the Origins of Globalization* (Lexington: University of Kentucky Press, 2005); Paul A. Kramer, "Power and Connection: Imperial Histories of the United States in the World," *American Historical Review* 116 (December 2011): 1348–1391; Jay Sexton, "The Global View of the United States," *Historical Journal* 48 (March 2005): 261–276.

[38] William J. Novak, "The Myth of the 'Weak' American State," *American Historical Review* 113 (June 2008): 752–772. See, for instance, Rosenberg, *Spreading the American Dream*, 7; Vincent de Santis, "American Politics in the Gilded Age," *Review of Politics* 25 (October 1963), 554; Sidney Fine, *Laissez Faire and the General-Welfare State: A Study of Conflict in American Thought, 1865–1901* (Ann Arbor: University of Michigan Press,

and industrial practices, economic nationalist policies prevailed upon the American political economy, including massive governmental intervention to protect the home market through high protective tariffs, immigration restrictions, state and federal subsidization of industries and internal improvements, and governmental land redistribution.[39] It was thus economic nationalism that dominated the US political economic landscape in the late nineteenth century.

Debunking the myth of laissez-faire at home allows for a much-needed reconceptualization of late-nineteenth-century American imperialism abroad. *The "Conspiracy" of Free Trade* proffers the first in-depth analysis of the American influx of Victorian free-trade ideology and its global affect upon subsequent Anglo-American imperial debates. This has been made all the more feasible owing to the work of various intrepid scholars. British imperial historians in particular have led the way in connecting imperial history with that of the history of globalization.[40] Such approaches have encouraged a more dynamic understanding of British imperialism, one that has shifted away from the metropole–periphery model toward a more inclusive global study of British imperial networks, which increasingly include the United States within the interconnected British World of white settler colonies.[41] By bringing British

1956), 29; Louis Hartz, *The Liberal Tradition in America: An Interpretation of American Political Thought since the Revolution* (New York: Harcourt, Brace, Jovanovich, 1955); Harold U. Faulkner, *The Decline of Laissez Faire, 1897–1917* (New York: Rinehart, 1951); John G. Sproat, *"The Best Men": Liberal Reformers in the Gilded Age* (New York: Oxford University Press, 1968); Geoffrey Blodgett, *The Gentle Reformers: Massachusetts Democrats in the Cleveland Era* (Cambridge, MA: Harvard University Press, 1966); Eckes and Zeiler, *Globalization and the American Century*, 14.

[39] Novak, "Myth of the 'Weak' American State"; Marc-William Palen, "Foreign Relations in the Gilded Age: A British Free-Trade Conspiracy?," *Diplomatic History* 37 (April 2013): 217–247; Bensel, *Political Economy of American Industrialization*; Brian Balogh, *A Government Out of Sight: The Mystery of National Authority in Nineteenth-Century America* (New York: Cambridge University Press, 2009), chaps. 8–9; Mike O'Connor, *A Commercial Republic: America's Enduring Debate over Democratic Capitalism* (Lawrence: University Press of Kansas, 2014); Richard L. McCormick, *Party Period and Public Policy: American Politics from the Age of Jackson to the Progressive Era* (New York: Oxford University Press, 1986), 204–214; Richard Sylla, "The Progressive Era and the Political Economy of Big Government," *Critical Review* 5 (1992): 531–557.

[40] John Darwin, *Unfinished Empire: The Global Expansion of Britain* (London: Allen Lane, 2012); Gary B. Magee and Andrew S. Thompson, *Empire and Globalisation: Networks of People, Goods and Capital in the British World, c. 1850–1914* (Cambridge: Cambridge University Press, 2010); C. A. Bayly, *The Birth of the Modern World, 1780–1914: Global Connections and Comparisons* (Oxford: Oxford University Press, 2004); Hopkins, ed., *Globalization in World History*; Hopkins, ed., *Global History*; P. J. Cain and A. G. Hopkins, *British Imperialism, 1688-2000* (New York: Longman, 2002); Ronald Findlay and Kevin O'Rourke, *Power and Plenty: Trade, War and the World Economy in the Second Millenium* (Princeton, NJ: Princeton University Press, 2007), 387–395.

[41] See especially Magee and Thompson, *Empire and Globalisation*; James Belich, *Replenishing the Earth: The Settler Revolution and the Rise of the Angloworld, 1783–1939*

imperial history and historiography into intimate dialogue with the history of American imperialism and economic globalization, *The "Conspiracy" of Free Trade* proffers a corrective to the long-standing interpretation of the rise of an American Open Door Empire.

Like the open-door thesis, this book seeks to explain what spurred imperial demands for foreign markets. Also like revisionist scholarship, *The "Conspiracy" of Free Trade* integrates the domestic with the foreign. Trade policy, after all, contains a mixture of both. In this vein, Ed Crapol's *America for Americans* provides a rare exploration of Gilded Age American economic nationalism, foreign policy, and Anglophobia. But the era also had its fair share of cosmopolitan free traders and Anglophiles. As well as explicitly incorporating British viewpoints and reactions throughout the globe to American policies, and vice versa, the following study therefore examines those who preferred to "stroke the lion's mane" alongside those who enjoyed "twisting the lion's tail."

More generally, however, *The "Conspiracy" of Free Trade* challenges the revisionist argument that a bipartisan open-door or free-trade imperial consensus took hold in the latter half of the nineteenth century.[42] Although political historians have emphasized ideological differences between and within the Democratic and Republican parties, such differences largely disappear within revisionist studies of late-nineteenth-century imperialism.[43] Their tantalizing open-door imperial narratives thus quite often conceal or overlook the nuanced and very real ideological,

---

(New York: Oxford University Press, 2009); John Darwin, *The Rise and Fall of the British World-System, 1830–1970* (Cambridge: Cambridge University Press, 2009); Carl Bridge and Kent Fedorowich, *The British World: Culture, Diaspora and Identity* (London: Taylor and Francis, 2003); Alan Lester, *Imperial Networks: Creating Identities in Nineteenth Century South Africa and Britain* (London: Routledge, 2001).

[42] "Consensus" here refers to the revisionist approach of emphasizing continuity across political parties, interest groups, and classes regarding US support for imperial expansion. See, for instance, Williams, *Tragedy of American Diplomacy*; Terrill, *Tariff, Politics, and American Foreign Policy*, 4; Crapol, *America for Americans*, 46; Howard Schoonover and Edward P. Crapol, "The Shift to Global Expansion, 1865–1900," *From Colony to Empire: Essays in the History of American Foreign Relations*, ed. by William Appleman Williams (New York: John Wiley & Sons, 1972), 140, 171, 197; David A. Lake, *Power, Protection, and Free Trade: International Sources of U.S. Commercial Strategy, 1887–1939* (Ithaca, NY: Cornell University Press, 1988); Bender, *Nation Among Nations*, 183; Golub, *Power, Profit, and Prestige*.

[43] For the former, see H. Wayne Morgan, *From Hayes to McKinley: National Party Politics, 1877–1896* (Syracuse: Syracuse University Press, 1969); R. Hal Williams, *Years of Decision: American Politics in the 1890s* (New York: Wiley, 1978); McCormick, *The Party Period and Public Policy*, 200–204; Michael McGerr, *The Decline of Popular Politics: The American North, 1865–1928* (New York: Oxford University Press, 1978); Robert S. Salisbury, "The Republican Party and Positive Government: 1860–1890," *Mid-America* 48 (1986): 15–34; Charles W. Calhoun, "Major Party Conflict in the Gilded Age: A Hundred Years of Interpretation," *OAH Magazine of History* 13 (Summer 1999): 5–10; Lewis L. Gould, "Party Conflict: Republicans versus Democrats, 1877–1901," in *The Gilded Age: Essays on*

political, and economic conflict over global economic integration that was occurring between free traders and economic nationalists within the United States – and throughout the world.[44] As diplomatic historian David Pletcher once observed: "the continuity of the period was not that of a fully developed expansionism but of uncertainty, improvisation, and frequent arguments over foreign affairs – 'great debates' in the press and Congress."[45] This book strives to make sense of the pervasive uncertainty and politico-ideological conflict over American global economic integration.

Historians now generally agree that imperial history remains the most effective historical approach to late-nineteenth-century US foreign relations.[46] American imperialism – along with the era's other imperial

the Origins of Modern America, ed. by Charles W. Calhoun (Wilmington: SR Books, 1996); David Epstein and Sharyn O'Halloran, "The Partisan Paradox and the U.S. Tariff, 1877–1934," International Organization 50 (Spring 1996): 301–324; Worth Robert Miller, "The Lost World of Gilded Age Politics," Journal of the Gilded Age and Progressive Era 1 (January 2002): 49–67.

[44] Previous conflict-oriented studies include Ninkovich, "Ideology, the Open Door, and Foreign Policy"; Charles A. Beard, The Idea of National Interest: An Analytical Study in American Foreign Policy (New York: The Macmillan Company, 1934). The business community was also divided on the subject of imperialism and foreign market expansion, even amid the 1890s depression. See Julius W. Pratt, Expansionists of 1898: The Acquisition of Hawaii and the Spanish Islands (Chicago, IL: Quadrangle Books, 1964 [1936]); William H. Becker, The Dynamics of Business-Government Relations: Industry & Exports, 1893–1921 (Chicago, IL: University of Chicago Press, 1982). Critiques of consensus approaches to history include Robert L. Beisner, From the Old Diplomacy to the New, 1865–1900 (Wheeling, IL: Harlan Davidson, 1986 [1975]), 19, 69, 71; John Higham, "The Cult of the 'American Consensus': Homogenizing Our History," Commentary (February 1959): 93–100.

[45] David M. Pletcher, The Diplomacy of Trade and Investment: American Economic Expansion in the Hemisphere, 1865-1900 (Columbia: University of Missouri Press, 1998), 4. Similarly, see Lewis L. Gould, "Tariffs and Markets in the Gilded Age," Reviews in American History 2 (June 1974): 266–271.

[46] James A. Field, Jr., "American Imperialism: The Worst Chapter in Almost Any Book," American Historical Review 83 (June 1978): 644–668; Walter LaFeber and Robert L. Beisner, "Comments," American Historical Review 83 (June 1978): 669–678, 673; Robin W. Winks, "The American Struggle with 'Imperialism': How Words Frighten," in The American Identity Fusion and Fragmentation, ed. by Rob Kroes (Amsterdam: Amerika Instituut, 1980), 145, 170; Edward P. Crapol, "Coming to Terms with Empire: The Historiography of Late-Nineteenth-Century American Foreign Relations," in Paths to Power: The Historiography of American Foreign Relations to 1941, ed. by Michael J. Hogan (Cambridge: Cambridge University Press, 2000), 95, 106, 115; Hugh De Santis, "The Imperialist Impulse and American Innocence, 1865–1900," in American Foreign Relations: A Historiographical Review, ed. by Gerald K. Haines and J. Samuel Walker (Westport, CT: Greenwood Press, 1981); Fry, "Phases of Empire"; Philip S. Golub, Power, Profit, and Prestige: A History of American Imperial Expansion (London: Pluto Press, 2010). Notable exceptions include Jeremi Suri, Liberty's Surest Guardian: American Nation-Building from the Founders to Obama (New York: The Free Press, 2011); Elizabeth Cobbs Hoffman, American Umpire (Cambridge, MA: Harvard University Press, 2013).

projects – began to take on global proportions as the nineteenth century came to a close. However, *The "Conspiracy" of Free Trade* takes an imperial approach that highlights, where previous historians have often blurred or ignored, differences between informal imperialism, formal imperialism, and non-imperial commercial expansionism. Informal imperialism allowed exploited areas to maintain their sovereignty, and therefore involved more indirect economic, cultural, and political coercion to access and control foreign markets. Formal imperialism instead entailed direct control of foreign markets by means of annexation, territorial acquisition, or military occupation. Anglo-American Cobdenites instead primarily advocated anti-imperial, non-coercive commercial expansionism through international free trade, what British historian Oliver MacDonagh termed "the anti-imperialism of free trade." In contrast to the anti-imperialism of free trade, late-nineteenth-century American Listians utilized a mixture of informal and formal imperial approaches – "the imperialism of economic nationalism" – for seeking a more regionalized approach to economic globalization, particularly in Latin America and the Pacific. The imperialism of economic nationalism was implemented through informal high tariff walls and restrictive reciprocity if possible, by formal annexation and military power when necessary.[47] The progressive Listian program of an expansive closed door played a crucial role in American imperial expansion in the late nineteenth century, and thus in controlling the more regionalized course of US economic globalization for decades to come. Listian nationalism therefore was not an "anti-globalization" movement, but what Peter Evans terms "counter-hegemonic globalization," or what international business theorists call "regionalized integration."[48]

The book's ideological underpinnings bridge the ante- and postbellum eras and highlight the dueling approaches to nineteenth-century global economic integration. Although economic interests certainly played a role, the leading politico-intellectual advocates for foreign markets during

---

[47] Oliver MacDonagh, "The Anti-Imperialism of Free Trade," *Economic History Review* 14 (April 1962): 489–501.

[48] Peter Evans, "Counter-Hegemonic Globalization: Transnational Social Movements in the Contemporary Global Political Economy," in *The Handbook of Political Sociology: States, Civil Societies, and Globalization*, ed. by Thomas Janoski, Alexander Hicks, and Mildred Schwarts (Cambridge: Cambridge University Press, 2005), 655–670; Evans, "Is an Alternative Globalization Possible?," *Politics & Society* 36 (June 2008): 271–305; Peter J. Buckley and Pervez N. Ghauri, eds., *The Internationalisation of the Firm* (London: International Thomson Business Press, 1999); Barrie Axford, *The Global System: Economics, Politics and Culture* (Oxford: Polity, 1995). For the British World, Magee and Thompson refer to this as "the regionalized ... 'first wave' of modern globalisation that centred on the settler states of the empire," a "limited, culturally and regionally focused globalisation of the late nineteenth century" in *Empire and Globalisation*, 63, 235.

the latter half of the century were primarily driven by ideological rather than material motivation. Following the onset of multiple economic panics and the detrimental depression of the mid-1890s, a demonstrable number of farmers, manufacturers, and politicians also began to perceive the need for expanding foreign markets, albeit ultimately through a Listian rather than a Cobdenite worldview. Contrary to the common open-door portrayal, the late-nineteenth-century US imperial drive thus arose owing to the prevalence of the imperialism of economic nationalism – not the imperialism of free trade.[49]

Chapter outline

Chapters 1 and 2 explore the global reception of two new oppositional ideological movements that would thereafter vie over the proper course of economic globalization. Chapter 1 explores the mid-century rise of the "Cobdenite cosmopolitan" and "Listian nationalist" in the United States; the temporary unification of these two groups under the Republican party umbrella of antislavery; and the larger influence of Victorian free-trade ideology on antebellum Anglo-American relations. Chapter 2 examines the transatlantic repercussions – political, economic, and ideological – of American protectionism following the 1861 passage of the northern Morrill Tariff. Many in Free Trade England found northern protectionism reprehensible, whereas the Confederate promise of free trade garnered sympathy. The Morrill Tariff would therefore play an important part in transatlantic relations during the Civil War, and British and American Cobdenites would prove instrumental in undermining the Confederacy's "free-trade diplomacy."[50]

Chapters 3 and 4 trace the postbellum American free-trade-protectionist battle over US global economic integration, particularly where the debate intersected with party politics and foreign policy. Chapter 3 analyzes the Cobdenite free-trade movement in the postbellum United States. By way of this new perspective into American domestic and foreign policy, the chapter exhumes the myriad ways American tariff

---

[49] On the revisionist use of the "imperialism of free trade," see especially Marc-William Palen, "The Imperialism of Economic Nationalism, 1890–1913," *Diplomatic History* 39 (January 2015): 157–185; Morgan, *Into New Territory*, 20, 89, 105, 136; Richard H. Immerman, *Empire for Liberty: A History of American Imperialism from Benjamin Franklin to Paul Wolfowitz* (Princeton, NJ: Princeton University Press, 2010), 10–12; Ernest R. May, "Robinson and Gallagher and American Imperialism," in *Imperialism: The Robinson and Gallagher Controversy*, ed. by Wm. Roger Louis (New York: New Viewpoints, 1976), 228.

[50] Marc-William Palen, "The Civil War's Forgotten Transatlantic Tariff Debate and the Confederacy's Diplomacy of Free Trade," *Journal of the Civil War Era* 3 (March 2013): 35–61.

debates intersected with Cobdenism, Anglo-American relations, and protectionist charges of a free-trade conspiracy. Chapter 4 picks up with the Liberal Republican movement of the early 1870s. Led by America's Cobdenites, it ushered in the first concerted attempt at the national level to redirect the Republican party's economic nationalist path. The results of the Liberal Republican movement both upon the political party system and the free-trade movement reverberated throughout national politics and foreign relations for years to come, and laid the groundwork for the realignment of the US party system in 1884.

Entering office in 1885, Democratic President Grover Cleveland surrounded himself with American Cobdenites as they continued their attempt to replace the nascent imperialism of economic nationalism with the anti-imperialism of free trade. Chapter 5 examines Grover Cleveland's first presidential term, describing how America's economic nationalists spotted and attacked the alleged transatlantic free-trade enemies proliferating among Cleveland's Cobdenite supporters. His administration's advocacy for freer trade, anti-imperialism, the gold standard, and generally amicable Anglo-American relations would only add fuel to this conspiratorial fire.[51]

As the late-nineteenth-century American economy expanded ever outward, its economic relationship with the British Empire loomed ever larger in the formulation of US foreign relations, and vice versa. Chapter 6 correspondingly explores how postbellum Anglo-American conflicts led to a renewed Canadian-American movement toward North American commercial union in the late 1880s, accentuating North American disagreements over the future of Canadian economic globalization. One hundred years before NAFTA, US and Canadian Cobdenites advocated developing closer economic ties between the United States and Canada, while Canada's Listian nationalists sought with equal fervor to establish instead greater economic integration within the British Empire.

The imperialism of economic nationalism rapidly matured during the Republican presidency of Benjamin Harrison (1889–1893). American Listian nationalists correspondingly found themselves wielding tangible influence within Congress and Harrison's cabinet. Chapter 7 provides a politico-ideological reinterpretation of the Harrison administration's efforts to institute its progressive and expansionist protectionist policies. Republican Listians – under the leadership of Harrison, Secretary of State James G. Blaine, and Ohio Congressman William McKinley – sought to

---

[51] Thanks are owed to *Diplomatic History*, where some preliminary sections appeared in "Foreign Relations in the Gilded Age."

implement the imperialism of economic nationalism, and effectively used the innovative and coercive reciprocity provision of the 1890 McKinley Tariff to further this end. These Listian policies sent reverberations throughout the global economy, with a particularly shocking impact upon the British Empire. Chapter 8 therefore utilizes a global historical approach to the McKinley Tariff, examining how American protectionism helped call into question Britain's Cobdenite orthodoxy by drumming up Listian support for an imperial, protectionist, preferential Greater Britain. The shift in scale and scope from the study of the 1861 Morrill Tariff and the 1890 McKinley Tariff also exemplifies the broader integration taking place within the late-nineteenth-century global economy, particularly the extended economic reach of US protectionist policies.[52] Chapter 9 thereafter explores the second Cleveland administration's Cobdenite advocacy of the anti-imperialism of free trade, with American Cobdenites once again attempting to redirect the Listian nationalist course of American economic globalization, culminating in the controversial 1896 presidential election. As a result of this pivotal election, the Listians would steer the US political economy and the country's imperial course toward economic integration for years to come.

---

[52] See, also, Marc-William Palen, "Protection, Federation and Union: The Global Impact of the McKinley Tariff upon the British Empire, 1890–94," *Journal of Imperial and Commonwealth History* 38 (September 2010): 395–418.

1 Globalizing ideologies
Economic nationalism and free-trade cosmopolitanism, c. 1846–1860

> The opposite economical systems should be designated as those of the nationalistic and cosmopolitan schools. The nationalistic or protective-defensive school ... conceives of political economy as applicable only to the political bodies known as nations ... The cosmopolitan, or so-called free trade school, ignores the existence of nations ... Cobden would gladly see all boundary lines wiped from the map, and regards nations as necessary evils.
>
> John Hayes[1]

> The gospel of the modern "historical" and "scientific" school, put forward in Germany sixty years ago by Friedrich List, and preached by his disciples and successors ever since, has, they say, entirely superseded the ancient doctrine which they nickname "Smithsianismus," and "cosmopolitan Free Trade."... Friedrich List and his followers declare themselves to be the only worshippers at the shrine of true Free Trade, and that Richard Cobden's clumsy foot had desecrated her temple, his sacrilegious hand had torn down her veil, and his profane tongue had uttered her mysteries to nations who had for long ages to live and labour before they could be ready for initiation ... Round this dogma the Free Trade and Protectionist argument in all countries of the world ... has centered.
>
> Russell Rea[2]

On a January night in 1846, the triumphal stage was set within Manchester, England's Free Trade Hall. Never before had so many come to take part in the assemblages of the ACLL (1838–1846), nor had they such reason. After seven years of ravenous agitation, the ACLL could nearly taste its long-sought "cheap loaf." Sir Robert Peel's Parliament stood on the verge of overturning the Corn Laws, Britain's long-standing protective tariffs on foreign grain.

Public demand for the Manchester event was insatiable. Over 8,000 tickets had been purchased within the first hours of availability. More than 5,000 hopeful attendees would be turned away. The Free Trade Hall

---

[1] John L. Hayes, *Customs Duties on the Necessaries of Life, and their Relations to the National Industry* (Cambridge: John Wilson and Son, 1884), 36–37.

[2] Russell Rea, *Two Theories of Foreign Trade* (London: Henry Good & Son, 1905), 6–7.

was filled to capacity, the mad rush at the doors overwhelming. Ladies wore their finest dresses, gentlemen their sharpest suits. The hall gleamed with garish magnificence. Crimson draperies hung upon the platform wall. Crimson panels covered the end walls. The ceiling was white scattered with crimson ornaments and octagonal crimson shields bordered with gold. The gallery balconies were decorated with ornate trelliswork. Over the central iron columns hung a shield, behind which sprung the robed female statue of the Caryatides. A spectator could easily imagine, wrote a *Manchester Times* reporter at the scene, "that the great leaders of the League movement, fresh from new and yet more successful campaigns than any which they have heretofore achieved, had been met by their grateful fellow-citizens to be honoured with a 'TRIUMPH.'"[3]

At precisely half past seven, Richard Cobden, John Bright, and the other ACLL leaders entered the hall amid deafening cheers. Cobden, exuberant, was first to speak once the expectant crowd fell still. He observed that the free-trade feeling was spreading rapidly across the globe, especially to the United States: "There is one other quarter in which we have seen the progress of sound principles – I allude to America ... I augur ... that we are coming to the consummation of our labours." Loud applause greeted his prophetic vision for Anglo-American free trade.[4]

About six months after this cosmopolitan celebration, a German gentleman – dark-haired, bespectacled, with a receding hairline counterbalanced by a rather heavy beard – arrived in London. He coincidentally witnessed the expiration of the Corn Laws in the Upper House. A few hours later, this same man found himself in the House of Commons to watch Sir Robert Peel's ministry "receive its death-blow." A voice suddenly came from behind the German: "Mr. Cobden wishes to make your acquaintance." The man turned and Cobden, yet energetic at forty-two, with his unruly muttonchops, offered his hand. "Have you really come over to be converted?" asked Cobden. "Of course," Friedrich List, the German-American protectionist theorist, wryly answered: "And to seek absolution for my sins."[5]

Unbeknownst to either man, their chance meeting foreshadowed a worldwide ideological conflict over the future of economic globalization. Soon after meeting Cobden, List returned home. Suffering from severe depression, he had forebodingly mentioned to a friend in England just before returning to Germany: "I feel as if a mortal disease were in my frame

---

[3] *Manchester Times*, January 17, 1846.   [4] Ibid.
[5] Margaret E. Hirst, *Life of Friedrich List* (London: Smith, Elder, 1909), 100–102. See, also, W. O. Henderson, *Friedrich List: Economist and Visionary* (London: Frank Cass, 1985).

and I must soon die." On the morning of November 30, 1846, List went out for a walk. He did not return. His body was found that night, blanketed with freshly fallen snow. He had shot himself.[6] List's 1846 depression counterbalanced Cobden's euphoria. So too would Cobden's cosmopolitanism meet its match in List's legacy: the progressive advancement of economic nationalism that survived him in many parts of the globe.

Trade liberalization had certainly taken on an international cast at around this time. The major European powers began instituting freer trade throughout the mid-nineteenth century, picking up even more steam following the signing of the 1860 Cobden–Chevalier Treaty between Britain and France. In the United States, the modest 1846 Walker Tariff likewise appeared a promising start, as would further downward tariff revisions in 1857.[7] As the pro-free-trade *New York Evening Post* observed on New Year's Eve 1846, "a great movement of civilized mankind" on behalf of free trade had begun.[8] But US economic nationalists were skeptical, to put it mildly, of Cobdenism's promised panacea of free trade, prosperity, and peace. This looming ideological conflict between free-trade cosmopolitanism and economic nationalism was soon to play out on a global stage, but most controversially in the political arena of the United States.

Transatlantic radicals, subscribing to Richard Cobden's free-trade philosophy, were intimately involved not only with the fight to end the English Corn Laws and American protectionism, but also to abolish American slavery. For them, free men and free trade were far from disparate goals. Conversely, leading American economic nationalists viewed the free-trading plantation South and Free Trade England as respective enslavers of blacks and American manufacturers. These conflicting ideologies would play a critical role in reshaping the Republican party and Anglo-American relations for decades to come, as would rapid American westward expansion. The differences between Cobdenite cosmopolitans and Listian nationalists would, however, remain hidden beneath the Republican party's political surface until after the Civil War, as both ideological camps rallied to the party's antislavery banner.

---

[6] Ibid., 105, 106–107.

[7] The Walker Tariff included a fixed *ad valorem* duty of 30 percent, although a few exceptions were as low as 20 percent or as high as 40 percent. Duties on cotton goods and rail iron, for instance, were lowered from 70 percent (under the 1842 tariff) to 25 and 30 percent, respectively.

[8] Anthony C. Howe, "From Pax Britannica to Pax Americana: Free Trade, Empire, and Globalisation, 1846–1948," *Bulletin of Asia-Pacific Studies* 13 (2003), 141–142; F. W. Taussig, *Free Trade, The Tariff and Reciprocity* (New York: The MacMillan Company, 1924), 1–3; C. P. Kindleberger, "The Rise of Free Trade in Western Europe, 1820–1875," *Journal of Economic History* 35 (March 1975): 20–55; *New York Evening Post*, December 31, 1846.

Globalizing economic nationalism and free trade

Friedrich List had come to distrust the cosmopolitanism of orthodox economics after engrossing himself in Alexander Hamilton's economic philosophy contained in the *Report on the Subject of Manufactures* (1791) and Daniel Raymond's *Thoughts on Political Economy* (1820). List observed how free traders had developed the "cosmopolitical idea of the absolute freedom of the commerce of the whole world." List pointed out, however, that by focusing on the individual and the universal they had ignored the national.[9]

List believed that these prophets of economic cosmopolitanism were attempting to go about achieving their goals in the wrong order. "It assumes the existence of a universal union and a state of perpetual peace," confounding effects with causes. The world as it existed disproved their cosmopolitan theories. A precipitous global turn to free trade would be "a universal subjection of the less advanced nations to the supremacy of the predominant manufacturing, commercial, and naval power" of Britain. The rest of the world first needed to catch up. This leveling of the playing field, List argued, could only be accomplished through political union, imperial expansion, and economic nationalist policies of internal improvements and infant industrial protectionism.[10]

Building upon Alexander Hamilton's late-eighteenth-century theorizing, List argued that a country's economic policies were dependent upon its stage of development, and that imperial expansion could provide much-needed security for industrializing powers like Germany and the United States. England, with a strong home market and a heavily concentrated population, could focus more on manufacturing finer products and on dumping excess goods in foreign markets. The less advanced United States of the 1820s–1840s instead needed a mixed economy of manufacturers and agrarians working side by side, brought ever closer through the publicly and privately subsidized construction of canals and railroads. According to List, Latin American nations were at an even lower developmental stage, still "uninstructed, indolent and not accustomed to many enjoyments": a lack of "wants" that undercut the

---

[9] Keith Tribe, "Natural Liberty & *Laissez Faire:* How Adam Smith Became a Free Trade Ideologue," in *Adam Smith's Wealth of Nations: New Interdisciplinary Essays*, ed. by Stephen Copley and Kathryn Sutherland (Manchester: Manchester University Press, 1995), 28, 38–39; Tribe, "Friedrich List and the Critique of 'Cosmopolitical Economy,'" *Manchester School of Economic and Social Studies* 56 (March 1988): 17–36; Joseph Dorfman, *The Economic Mind in American Civilization, 1606–1865* (New York: A. M Kelley, 1946), II, 577; William Notz, "Frederick List in America," *American Economic Review* 16 (June 1926): 261–262; Friedrich List, *The National System of Political Economy*, trans. by Sampson S. Lloyd (London: Longmans, Green, and Co., 1904 [1885]), 97.

[10] List, *The National System*, 102–103.

Figure 1.1 Friedrich List (1789–1846)

cosmopolitan global free-trade vision. At their lower stage of development, these nations needed to focus on exchanging "precious metals and raw produce" for foreign manufactures, and would remain colonially dependent upon more developed manufacturing nations. As to the latter, List argued that America and a unified Germany needed imperial expansion. Aggressive American westward expansion was therefore becoming ever more necessary, with growing numbers of Americans passing "over the Mississippi, next the Rocky Mountains," to "at last turn their faces to China instead of to England." According to List, the German states had similarly progressed to the point that, upon unification, they would require the colonial acquisition of the Balkans, Central Europe, Denmark, and Holland (along with the latter's colonies) to more firmly establish his German Zollverein.[11]

---

[11] Friedrich List, "Letter IV," July 18, 1827, and "Letter V," July 19, 1827, in Hirst, *List*, 187–210; List, *The National System*, 28, 143, 327–328, 332, 342–344; Joseph Dorfman, *Economic Mind*, II, 575–584; Bernard Semmel, *The Liberal Ideal and the Demons of Empire: Theories of Imperialism from Adam Smith to Lenin* (Baltimore and London: Johns Hopkins University Press, 1993), 67–68; Jens-Uwe Guettel, *German Expansionism, Imperial Liberalism, and the United States, 1776–1945* (Cambridge: Cambridge University Press, 2012), 63–64; Henryk Szlaijfer, *Economic Nationalism and Globalization*, trans. by Maria Chmielewska-Szlajfer (Leiden: Brill, 2012), 56.

List thereby enunciated an international system of developmental stages coupled with "infant industrial" protectionism, coercive economic exploitation, and imperial expansion that Anglo-American imperialists in decades to come would work to implement at the local and global level. In 1897, Johns Hopkins political economist Sidney Sherwood would label it "young imperialism," when national political union was coupled with "a tariff wall of fortification around the imperial boundaries." And Sherwood laid much of the credit for America's own "youthful" imperialism at the feet of none other than "the successor of Hamilton," Friedrich List, whose protectionist doctrine "is rightly regarded as American in its origin."[12] This Listian imperialism of "young" industrializing nations – the imperialism of economic nationalism – would become manifest within late-nineteenth-century America.

In contrast to the imperialism of economic nationalism, List argued that England was practicing what historians have since termed the "imperialism of free trade." The leading industrially advanced island-nation sought to "manufacture for the whole world ... to keep the world and especially her colonies in a state of infancy and vassalage ... English national economy is *predominant*; American national economy aspires only to become *independent*." List believed that it was unfair to let the English reap the world's wealth. "In order to allow freedom of trade to operate naturally," underdeveloped nations needed to first be lifted up through artificial measures so as to match England's own artificially elevated state of cultivation.[13] List described one of the most "vulgar tricks of history" as "when one nation reaches the pinnacle of its development it should attempt to remove the ladder by which it had mounted in order to prevent others from following." He granted that universal free trade was the ultimate ideal, but first the world's infant industrial economies would need a combination of private and public investment, protectionism, and imperial expansion in order to catch up.[14]

List's protectionist prescription for the perceived pandemic of Victorian free-trade ideology found wide-ranging patients. Listian disciples spread and multiplied throughout the globe in subsequent decades.

[12] Sidney Sherwood, *Tendencies in American Economic Thought* (Baltimore: The Johns Hopkins Press, 1897), 12, 16.

[13] List, quoted in Tribe, "List and the Critique of 'Cosmopolitical Economy,'" 28; List, *The National System*, 106–107.

[14] List quoted in Leonard Gomes, *The Economics and Ideology of Free Trade: A Historical Review* (Cheltenham, UK, and Northampton, MA: Edward Elgar, 2003), 78; Friedrich List, *Professor List's Speech Delivered at the Philadelphia Manufacturers' Dinner* (s.I.: s. n., 1827), 5; Dorfman, *Economic Mind*, II, 581. See, also, Christin Margerum Harlen, "A Reappraisal of Classical Economic Nationalism and Economic Liberalism," *International Studies Quarterly* 43 (December 1999): 733–744.

List's desire for a German Zollverein, or customs union, would fall out of favor from the 1840s to the 1860s, but would be revived and fully implemented by the 1880s. List also became a source of inspiration for imperial protectionists in England, Australia, and Canada in the last decades of the nineteenth century.[15] Likewise, Japanese economists "imbibed" List's economic elixir following various Japanese tours of Europe in the 1870s and the translation into Japanese of List's work in the 1880s.[16] Russia's finance minister during the late-nineteenth century, S. Y. De Witte, would also look to List for inspiration when he reformed Russian finances and encouraged the construction of a trans-Siberian railway. Anglophobic French protectionists similarly leaned upon List's theories.[17] His work in turn received an avid audience among late-nineteenth-century South Asian anticolonial nationalists, to whom American and German industrial ascendency merely confirmed the value of List's work.[18] His writings thus found a welcome global audience, especially among modernizers beyond Western Europe.

List's economic philosophy would germinate first within the antebellum United States, where it would flourish by century's end. Exiled from Germany in 1825, he had fled to the United States, and was indebted to the earlier protectionist principles of Alexander Hamilton, Daniel Raymond, and Mathew Carey, the famous Philadelphia publisher, former president of the Pennsylvania Society for the Promotion of Manufactures and the Mechanic Arts, and father of Henry Charles

---

[15] See Chapters 6 and 8.

[16] Mark Metzler, "The Cosmopolitanism of National Economics: Friedrich List in a Japanese Mirror," in *Global History: Interactions between the Universal and the Local*, ed. by A. G. Hopkins (New York: Palgrave Macmillan, 2006); Tessa Morris-Suzuki, *A History of Japanese Economic Thought* (London: Routledge, 1989), 50–55; Tamotsu Nishizawa, "The Emergence of the Economic Science in Japan and the Evolution of Textbooks 1860s–1930s," in *The Economic Reader: Textbooks, Manuals, and the Dissemination of the Economic Sciences During the Nineteenth and Early Twentieth Centuries*, ed. by Massimo M. Augello and Marco E. L. Guidi (New York: Routledge, 2012).

[17] Szlaijfer, *Economic Nationalism and Globalization*, 62; *The Current Encyclopedia* (Chicago, IL: Modern Research Society, 1901), 447; W. O. Henderson, "Friedrich List and the French Protectionists," *Zeitschrift für die gesamte Staatswissenschaft* 138 (1982): 262–275; David Todd, *L'identité Economique de la France: Libre Échange et Protectionnisme, 1814–1851* (Paris: Grasset, 2008), chap. 13. On French protectionism, see Michael Stephen Smith, *Tariff Reform in France, 1860–1900: The Politics of Economic Interest* (Ithaca, NY: Cornell University Press, 1980).

[18] Bruce Tiebout McCully, *English Education and the Origins of Indian Nationalism* (New York: Columbia University Press, 1940), 270; Manu Goswami, *Producing India: From Colonial Economy to National Space* (Chicago, IL: University of Chicago Press, 2004), 215, 216, 337; Metzler, "Cosmopolitanism of National Economics," 104–105; P. K. Gopalakrisnan, *Development of Economic Ideas in India, 1880–1950* (New Delhi: People's Publishing House, 1959), chap. 3.

Carey (1793–1879). List would become a key player in the development of nineteenth-century Philadelphian protectionist thought.[19] By the end of the century, his influence would culminate in the creation of "the German-American school of economics."[20]

List became a leading defender of the American System of economic nationalism. It was fair to say, observed the editors of Boston's news organ the *Protectionist* in 1919, "that List the economist was 'made in America.'" In the fall of 1825, the Marquis de Lafayette introduced his friend List first to Mathew Carey and then to Henry Clay. After making a good first impression, List thereafter frequently gave protectionist speeches at conventions organized by Clay's friends. In the early decades of the century, Clay himself would become an arch-proponent of the "American System" of internal improvements and protectionism and would come to see free trade as but a new way for Great Britain to recolonize the United States through commercial domination.[21]

List exerted a great deal of influence not only on Clay's American System but also on Pennsylvania's progressive economic nationalist philosophy. In 1826, List became a newspaper editor in Pennsylvania, where he gained national recognition for his defense of the American System. He took part in the development of coal and railways in the area, and became a propagandist for the Pennsylvania Society of Manufactures. His letters to its vice president, Charles Ingersoll, were published in the United States as *Outlines of American Political Economy* (1827). List's published letters were then distributed to American congressmen later that year, influencing the 1828 tariff debate, and were at hand to be read by Mathew Carey's young and intellectually hungry son, Henry. Some scholars have even speculated that the timing of List's protectionist publications and the 1828 passage of the "Tariff of Abominations" was more than coincidental.[22]

---

[19] Hirst, *List*, 113–117; Kenneth V. Lundberg, "Daniel Raymond, Early American Economist" (PhD diss., University of Wisconsin Madison, 1953), 16; Tribe, "Natural Liberty & *Laissez Faire*," 37–38; H. Parker Willis, "Friedrich List: Grundlinien einer Politischen Okonomie und Andere Beitrage der Amerikanischen Zeit, 1825–1832," *American Economic Review* 22 (December 1932), 700.

[20] Robert Ellis Thompson, *Social Science and National Economy* (Philadelphia, PA: Porter and Coates, 1875), 132; Luigi Cossa, *An Introduction to the Study of Political Economy*, trans. by Louis Dyer (London: Macmillan, 1893), 477.

[21] Roland Ringwalt, "Friedrich List's American Years," *Protectionist* 31 (October 1919): 372; Henry Clay, *The Papers of Henry Clay*, ed. by James F. Hopkins, 4 vols. (Lexington: University of Kentucky Press, 1959–), IV, 629; Maurice Glen Baxter, *Henry Clay and the American System* (Lexington: University of Kentucky Press, 1995), 199, 200; James Barret Swain, ed., *The Life and Speeches of Henry Clay* (New York: Greeley & M'Elraith, Tribune Office, 1843), II, 24.

[22] Friedrich List, *Outlines of American Political Economy* (Philadelphia, PA: Samuel Parker, 1827); Gomes, *Economics and Ideology*, 73; Notz, "List in America," 248, 255–256.

After List's death in 1846, Henry Carey would take up List's forward-looking approach to the American System. Carey would become Pennsylvania's "Ajax of protectionism," a man well known for his imposing height, penetrating gaze, propensity for obscenities, and intellectual intimidation.[23] In his younger days, Carey had been a devout disciple of Adam Smith. Like List, Carey came to consider free trade an ultimate ideal for any country, but only after the proper implementation of economic nationalist policies – even England, he suggested, had jumped too far ahead when it abolished the Corn Laws.[24]

Carey began enunciating his progressive Listian nationalist creed by the late 1840s, noting that "war is an evil, and so are tariffs for protection," but "both *may* be necessary, and both *are* sometimes necessary." He had expressed similar sentiments to abolitionist senator Charles Sumner of Massachusetts in 1847: "Nobody *can* admire free trade more than I do ... I never in my life was more surprised than to find myself brought round to be a protectionist. It is all wrong – as much so as any other sort of war – but it is a necessary act of self defence." A temporary period of protectionism was needed, he suggested, and then the world might obtain free trade and peace.[25]

Carey's opposition to free-trade cosmopolitanism echoed List's. Carey thought that the country's vast expanse of available lands and a protective tariff were the twin panaceas to solve American economic ills. Protectionism was a cure-all that would increase morality and diversify labor productivity, invigorate the southern economy, and someday free the slaves. Like List, Carey also believed that the protective tariff remained essential only so long as American industries remained in

[23] William Elder, *The Memoir of Henry C. Carey* (Philadelphia, PA: Henry Carey Baird & Co., 1880), 32–35. Elder, while working for the Treasury Department, succinctly enunciated the Listian argument when he urged the imperial acquisition of new markets in the "tropical regions" for Western farm surpluses, in *How the Western States Can Become the Imperial Power in the Union* (Philadelphia, PA: Ringwalt & Brown, 1865), 18.

[24] On List's influence upon Carey, see, also, Thompson, *Social Science and National Economy*, 132; Sherwood, *American Economic Thought*, 14, 16, 22; Hirst, *List*, 118–122; Ernest Teilhac, *Pioneers of American Economic Thought in the Nineteenth Century*, trans. by E. A. J. Johnson (New York: The Macmillan Company, 1936), 79–80; Mark Thornton and Robert B. Ekelund, *Tariffs, Blockades, and Inflation* (Wilmington, DE: SR Books, 2004), 16–17; William J. Bernstein, *A Splendid Exchange: How Trade Shaped the World* (New York: Atlantic Monthly Press, 2008), 320–321; Szlaijfer, *Economic Nationalism and Globalization*, 55; Andrew Dawson, "Reassessing Henry Carey (1793–1879): The Problems of Writing Political Economy in Nineteenth-Century America," *Journal of American Studies* 34 (December 2000), 479; Frank A. Fetter, "The Early History of Political Economy in the United States," *Proceedings of the American Philosophical Society* 87 (July 14, 1943): 55–56.

[25] Henry C. Carey, *The Past, the Present, and the Future* (Philadelphia, PA: Carey & Hart, 1848), 302; Carey to Sumner, November 20, 1847, microfilm, reel 5, Charles Sumner Papers, Houghton Library, Harvard University, Cambridge, MA.

infancy. In proper Listian fashion, by the 1870s Carey would even tout restrictive trade reciprocity – a key US component of the imperialism of economic nationalism – alongside protective tariffs to aid in US regional economic integration.[26]

Carey saw the South's domestic slavery as but one manifestation of human bondage; the southern cotton growers themselves, with no home market to speak of, were slaves to the global cotton market. He expressed his dismay to Charles Sumner that antislavery men could simultaneously claim to be free traders. For Carey, free trade meant economic subservience to England. Britain wanted the people of the world to "have but one market in which to sell their produce, and one in which to buy their cloth linen – paying what she pleases for the one and charging what she pleases for the other. This is precisely what the planter desires his negro to do." Carey felt that free trade and southern slavery were therefore two sides of the same coin: "The one is just as much slavery as the other."[27] He believed that slavery and premature free trade were interconnected, an antislavery line of argument that postbellum American protectionists would continue to utilize. He thus came to view the British Empire's advocacy of free trade not only as an impediment to American maturation, but an evil – a threat to America's home industries and economic freedom.

Carey found a sympathetic national outlet for his Anglophobic brand of progressive economic nationalism. From around 1850 to 1857, he became the economic consultant of Horace Greeley, the editor of the widely disseminated *New York Tribune*.[28] Carey was now able to promote his Listian nationalist ideology as an editorial writer for Philadelphia's *North American* and the popular *Tribune*.[29] In recognition of his newfound

[26] Henry C. Carey, *Principles of Social Science*, 3 vols. (Philadelphia, PA: J. B. Lippincott, 1858), I, 28–31; III, 440–445, esp. 442; Sidney Fine, *Laissez Faire and the General-Welfare State: A Study in American Thought, 1865–1901* (Ann Arbor: University of Michigan Press, 1956), 16–17; A. D. H. Kaplan, *Henry Charles Carey: A Study in American Economic Thought* (Baltimore, MD: Johns Hopkins Press, 1931), 30; Arnold W. Green, *Henry Charles Carey: Nineteenth-Century Sociologist* (Philadelphia: University of Pennsylvania Press, 1951), 137, 140–141; Stephen Meardon, "Reciprocity and Henry C. Carey's Traverses on 'the Road to Perfect Freedom of Trade,'" *Journal of the History of Economic Thought* 33 (September 2011): 307–333.

[27] Carey to Sumner, November 20, 1847, microfilm, reel 5, Sumner Papers.

[28] On Greeley's mixture of radicalism and conservatism, see Adam-Max Tuchinsky, *Horace Greeley's* New-York Tribune: *Civil War-Era Socialism and the Crisis of Free Labor* (Ithaca, NY: Cornell University Press, 2009).

[29] Paul K. Conkin, *Prophets of Prosperity: America's First Political Economists* (Bloomington: Indiana University Press, 1980), xi; Elwyn B. Robinson, "The *North American*: Advocate of Protection," *Pennsylvania Magazine of History and Biography* 64 (July 1940): 346; Nathan A. Baily, "Henry Carey's 'American System'" (MA Thesis, Columbia University, 1941); Jeter A. Isley, *Horace Greeley and the Republican Party, 1853–1861: A Study of the New York Tribune* (Princeton, NJ: Princeton University Press, 1947), 59.

influence, the *Tribune*'s European correspondent Karl Marx described Carey at that time as "the only American economist of importance." He thereafter joined the Republican party and helped shape its protectionist platform, and was often consulted on economic matters by Lincoln, Lincoln's treasury secretary, Salmon P. Chase, and numerous other influential Republican politicians.[30] Carey's progressive Listian nationalism had thus found a sympathetic press and an attentive American readership. So too did List's *National System of Political Economy* (1841), especially once Carey's close friend Stephen Colwell solicited an American translation in the 1850s.[31]

Listian nationalism could not claim a monopoly upon American economic thought. Richard Cobden's cosmopolitan ideology was also finding American accommodation. Like List's doctrine, Cobdenism spread rapidly, making its way across the English Channel and spreading to France, Italy, Germany, Greece, and Spain during the 1840s. By the 1860s, Cobdenism would be propagated as far afield as Egypt, Siam, China, and Australia.[32] But Cobden's cosmopolitan ideology enlisted the most international recruits across the Atlantic, from within America's

---

[30] Michael Perelman, "Political Economy and the Press: Karl Marx and Henry Carey at the New York Tribune," *Economic Forum* 16 (Winter 1986): 111–128; Marx, quoted in Andrew Dawson, *Philadelphia Engineers: Capital, Class, and Revolution, 1830–1890* (Aldershot: Ashgate Publishing, 2004), 129; Green, *Carey*, 35; Conkin, *Prophets of Prosperity*, xi; Isley, *Greeley and the Republican Party*; Eric Foner, *Free Soil, Free Labor, Free Men: The Ideology of the Republican Party before the Civil War* (Oxford and New York: Oxford University Press, 1995), 19.

[31] See Frederick List, *National System of Political Economy*, trans. by G. A. Matile, preliminary essay by Stephen Colwell (Philadelphia, PA: J. B. Lippincott & Co., 1856), esp. vi, lx; Henry C. Carey, *A Memoir of Stephen Colwell* (Philadelphia, PA: Henry Carey Baird, 1872), 14.

[32] Anthony Howe, *Free Trade and Liberal England, 1846–1946* (Oxford: Clarendon Press, 1997), chap. 3; Alex Tyrrell, "'La Ligue Francaise': The Anti-Corn Law League and the Campaign for Economic Liberalism in France during the Last Days of the July Monarchy," in *Rethinking Nineteenth-Century Liberalism: Richard Cobden Bicentenary Essays*, ed. by Anthony Howe and Simon Morgan (Aldershot: Ashgate, 2006), 99–116; Robert Romani, "The Cobdenian Moment in the Italian Risorgimento," ibid., 117–140; Detlev Mares, "'Not Entirely a Manchester Man': Richard Cobden and the Construction of Manchesterism in Nineteenth-Century German Economic Thinking," ibid., 141–160; Pandeleimon Hionidis, "Greek Responses to Cobden," ibid., 161–176; *New York Evening Post*, November 18, December 31, 1846; Gabriel Tortella Casares, *Banking Railroads and Industry in Spain, 1829–1874* (New York: Arno Press, 1977), 506–550; Ernest Lluch, "La 'Gira Trionfal' de Cobden per Espanya (1846)," *Recerques* 21 (1988): 71–90; Christopher Schmidt-Nowara, "National Economy and Atlantic Slavery: Protectionism and Resistance to Abolitionism in Spain and the Antilles, 1854–1874," *Hispanic American Historical Review* 78 (November 1998): 607–608; David Todd, "John Bowring and the Global Dissemination of Free Trade," *Historical Journal* 51 (June 2008): 373–397; Craufurd D. W. Goodwin, *Economic Enquiry in Australia* (Durham, NC: Duke University Press, 1966), 11–12.

rapidly industrializing northeastern states – and from among the country's most radical abolitionist reformers.

Cobdenism's mid-century American arrival introduced a new free-trade tradition. Studies of nineteenth-century American economic thought have nevertheless tended to associate the US free-trade tradition solely with Jeffersonianism.[33] Yet Jeffersonianism represented a free-trade ideology based primarily upon agricultural production, Anglophobia, and a doctrine that had become tied to the defense of the southern slave system by mid-century.[34] Cobdenism instead took root within northeastern financial and manufacturing centers like New York and Boston, and its first American disciples were Anglophiles and abolitionists. Cobdenism was a very different free-trade ideology than that of Jeffersonianism.

Cobden's own classical liberal belief in the benign and universalizing principles of free trade, inspired by Adam Smith's *Wealth of Nations* (1776), contained a strong moral message that struck a familiar chord in transatlantic abolitionist ears.[35] Cobden believed that international commerce, when ultimately unfettered of the shackles of protectionism, would bring with it "the grand panacea, which, like a beneficent medical discovery, will serve to inoculate with the healthy and saving taste for civilization all the nations of the world." He had faith that the tools of globalization – among them free trade, cheap postage, and steamboats – would one day make the world so integrated and interdependent that war would become obsolete.[36]

---

[33] By mid-century, Jeffersonianism was in fact beginning to lose some ideological ground, even in the South. See John Majewski, *Modernizing a Slave Economy: The Economic Vision of the Confederate Nation* (Chapel Hill: University of North Carolina Press, 2009); Majewski, "Who Financed the Transportation Revolution? Regional Divergence and Internal Improvements in Antebellum Pennsylvania and Virginia," *Journal of Economic History* 56 (December 1996): 763–788; Brian Schoen, *The Fragile Fabric of Union: Cotton, Federal Politics, and the Global Origins of the Civil War* (Baltimore: Johns Hopkins University Press, 2009); Nicholas Onuf and Peter Onuf, *Nations, Markets, and War: Modern History and the American Civil War* (Charlottesville: University of Virginia Press, 2006), chap. 8, 324–333; Baxter, *Henry Clay and the American System*; Robert Royal Russel, *Economic Aspects of Southern Sectionalism* (Urbana: University of Illinois, 1924), 37, 40, 55–56, 151, 177; Jay Carlander and John Majewski, "Imagining 'a Great Manufacturing Empire': Virginia and the Possibilities of a Confederate Tariff," *Civil War History* 49 (December 2003): 334–352.

[34] See Schoen, *Fragile Fabric of Union*; Lacy K. Ford, "Republican Ideology in a Slave Society: The Political Economy of John C. Calhoun," *Journal of Southern History* 54 (August 1988): 405–424; Bruno Gujer, *Free Trade and Slavery: Calhoun's Defense of Southern Interests against British Interference, 1811–1848* (Zurich: aku-Fotodruck, 1971).

[35] On the influence of *The Wealth of Nations* upon subsequent British imperial debates, see Marc-William Palen, "Adam Smith as Advocate of Empire, c. 1870–1932," *Historical Journal* 57 (March 2014): 179–198.

[36] Richard Cobden, *Political Writings* (London: W. Ridgeway, 1867), I, 46; Frank Thistlethwaite, *America and the Atlantic Community: Anglo-American Aspects, 1790–1850*

Figure 1.2 Richard Cobden (1804–1865)

US Cobdenites, imbued with a similar moral underpinning, numbered among the mid-century leaders of the transatlantic free-trade and abolitionist movements. America's northeastern Cobdenites took inspiration from the seven-year struggle and ultimate success of England's ACLL, and quickly became cosmopolitan thorns in the side of not only the slave-ridden Jeffersonian, but also the northeastern Hamiltonian and

(Philadelphia: University of Pennsylvania, 1959), 155. On Cobden's foreign policy, see Peter Cain, "Capitalism, War, and Internationalism in the Thought of Richard Cobden," *British Journal of International Studies* 5 (October 1979): 229–247; William Harbutt Dawson, *Richard Cobden and Foreign Policy* (London: G. Allen & Unwin, Ltd., 1926); Nicholas C. Edsall, *Richard Cobden, Independent Radical* (Cambridge, MA: Harvard University Press, 1986); J. A. Hobson, *Richard Cobden: The International Man* (New York: Henry Holt and Company, 1918); Bernard Semmel, *The Rise of Free Trade Imperialism: Classical Political Economy and the Empire of Free Trade and Imperialism 1750-1850* (London and New York: Cambridge University Press, 1970), 158–175; David Nicholls, "Richard Cobden and the International Peace Congress Movement, 1848–1853," *Journal of British Studies* 30 (October 1991): 351–376; Richard Francis Spall, "Free Trade, Foreign Relations, and the Anti-Corn-Law League," *International History Review* 10 (August 1988): 405–432.

Madisonian, nationalist political traditions. For American Cobdenite radicals, free trade became entwined with free labor, free men, and free soil. Following the Civil War and the abolition of southern slavery, and ever aware of the burgeoning strength of American manufactures and the mounting need for foreign markets, much of their attention would turn to establishing free trade in the ACLL tradition and to righting the corruptive influences emanating from within the postbellum Republican party.

So how did Cobdenism take root in the Northeast, the heartland of mid-century American industrialism and protectionism? The Victorian free-trade tradition spread directly from Cobden, Bright, and other leaders of the ACLL to their radical counterparts in the United States. They did so by explicitly tying free trade and free labor together. Cobden asked his trans-atlantic disciples to "remember what has been done in the Anti-Slavery question. Where is the difference between stealing a man and making him labour, on the one hand, or robbing voluntary labourers, on the other, of the fruits of their labour?"[37] The ACLL would even begin replacing "repeal" with "abolition," as the latter contained more effective transatlantic resonance. The ACLL leadership also made sure to present their free-trade movement in universalist religious and humanitarian terms to transatlantic abolitionist correspondents. Cobden was quite clear on this point, urging the ACLL to appeal to "the religious and moral feelings ... the energies of the Christian World must be drawn forth by the remembrance of Anti-Slavery."[38] African American abolitionist Frederick Douglass's news organ noted as much, recalling how the "Anti-Corn Law movement" had "but one plank in its platform, and that was taken from the system of Christianity."[39] Personal friendships and a shared sense of moral economy directly led to the transatlantic germination of Cobdenism.

Added to this, the US and British economies had also become ever more interdependent throughout the nineteenth century. Through free trade, Anglo-American Cobdenites hoped to speed up this integrative process in order to cultivate greater prosperity and peace. Already, from

[37] Quoted in Stephen Meardon, "Richard Cobden's American Quandary: Negotiating Peace, Free Trade, and Anti-Slavery," in *Rethinking Nineteenth-Century Liberalism*, ed. by Howe and Morgan, 212.

[38] Morgan, "Anti-Corn Law League," 90–91; Howard Temperley, *British Antislavery, 1833–1870* (London: Longman, 1972), 195; Boyd Hilton, *The Age of Atonement: The Influence of Evangelicism on Social and Economic Thought, 1795–1865* (Oxford: Clarendon Press, 1988), chap. 2; Cobden to George Combe, August 1, 1846, Add. MS 43660, Vol. XIV, Richard Cobden Papers, British Library, London, England; Richard Cobden to Peter Alfred Taylor, May 4, 1840, in Richard Garnett, *The Life of W.J. Fox* (London: John Lane, The Bodley Head, 1910), 258. See, also, Stephen Meardon, "From Religious Revivalism to Tariff Rancor: Preaching Free Trade and Protection during the Second American Party System," *History of Political Economy* 40 (2008): 265–298.

[39] *Douglass' Monthly* (Rochester, NY), July 1859.

1820 to 1860 almost half of US exports went to Britain, and British goods made up around 40 percent of American imports. By 1860, Britain imported 80 percent of its raw cotton from the South, and nearly all US textile imports came from Britain. British and American commercial policies were thus indelibly linked when Cobdenism was exported to American shores.[40] US Cobdenites believed that free trade would link the two countries even further, to their mutual benefit. At a personal, moral, and material level, Cobdenites believed the United States required free trade.

For transatlantic Cobdenites, free trade and free labor were far from disparate goals.[41] Yet recent work has focused instead on the willingness of the ACLL to work with the slaveholding South for reciprocal tariffs: that by the mid-1840s the middle-class leaders of the ACLL had "subverted anti-slavery's moral authority." So, too, did leading Southerners encourage this perceived connection between transatlantic trade liberalization and the decline of antislavery sentiment.[42] But why, then, were the first Anglo-American Cobdenites a regular *who's who* of radical abolitionists? As Richard Huzzey illustrates, the British antislavery movement had not fallen away by the 1840s. It had splintered rather than declined, fractured rather than faltered. Though perhaps not "a nation of abolitionists," Free Trade England would remain an antislavery nation.[43] America's own first Cobdenites accordingly included some of the era's leading abolitionists, with close ties to British abolitionist free traders.

---

[40] Thistlethwaite, *America and the Atlantic Community*, 11; Scott C. James and David A. Lake, "The Second Face of Hegemony: Britain's Repeal of the Corn Laws and the American Walker Tariff of 1846," *International Organization* 43 (Winter 1989): 1–29; Patrick J. McDonald, *The Invisible Hand of Peace: Capitalism, The War Machine, and International Relations Theory* (Cambridge: Cambridge University Press, 2009), 141–155.

[41] Marc-William Palen, "Free-Trade Ideology and Transatlantic Abolitionism: A Historiography," *Journal of the History of Economic Thought* 37 (June 2015): 291–304.

[42] Simon Morgan, "The Anti-Corn Law League and British Anti-Slavery in Transatlantic Perspective, 1838–1846," *Historical Journal* 52 (February 2009), 89; Matt Karp, "King Cotton, Emperor Slavery," in *The Civil War as Global Conflict*, ed. by David T. Gleeson and Simon Lewis (Columbia: University of South Carolina Press, 2014), 36–52. See, also, Seymour Drescher, *The Mighty Experiment: Free Labor versus Slavery in British Emancipation* (Oxford: Oxford University Press, 2002); Catherine Hall, *Civilising Subject: Metropole and Colony in the English Imagination, 1830–1867* (Oxford: Oxford University Press, 2002), 338–339; Christine Bolt, *The Anti-Slavery Movement and Reconstruction: A Study in Anglo-American Co-Operation, 1833–1877* (London: Oxford University Press, 1969), 20.

[43] Richard Huzzey, *Freedom Burning: Anti-Slavery and Empire in Victorian Britain* (Ithaca, NY: Cornell University Press, 2012); Huzzey, "Free Trade, Free Labour, and Slave Sugar in Victorian Britain," *Historical Journal* 53 (2010): 359–379. Eric Williams famously connected the politico-ideological British turn to free trade and antislavery in *Capitalism and Slavery* (Chapel Hill: University of North Carolina Press, 1944). See, also, James L. Huston, "Abolitionists, Political Economists, and Capitalism," *Journal of the Early Republic* 20 (Autumn 2000): 487–521.

George Thompson, among a handful of other British abolitionists from the 1830s to the 1850s, was sent to the United States to link abolitionism and free trade together, and controversially so. Thompson was militant – some thought him mad – in his abolitionist quest. He even attempted to smuggle slaves out of Missouri in the 1830s, landing him a stint in prison. At his close friend William Lloyd Garrison's Boston home could be found a collection of handbills that had once been scattered about the city's streets, offering a $100 reward "for the notorious British Emissary, George Thompson, dead or alive."[44] Within this toxic antebellum environment, firebrand Thompson toured the United States, giving hundreds of speeches emphasizing the moral connection between free trade and abolitionism.[45] While feared and hated by many, he was held in high esteem among the more radical members of the American abolitionist movement, who often took their cue from the British and Foreign Anti-Slavery Society in England – so much so that Anglophobic southern congressmen opined that northern abolitionists were merely mouthpieces of their British counterparts. With the support of their American abolitionist contacts, by the early 1840s ACLL members saw the possibility of an internationalization of free trade, beginning with the abolition of the Corn Laws "as a key to advances" in America. Although not all-pervasive, the transatlantic abolitionist cause had become intimately associated with that of Victorian free trade.[46]

Massachusetts's Reverend Joshua Leavitt played a key role in tying American antislavery to Cobdenism. From the late 1830s onward, this onetime Whig, leader of the antislavery Liberty party, and editor of the

---

[44] Joseph Yannielli, "George Thompson among the Africans: Empathy, Authority, and Insanity in the Age of Abolition," *Journal of American History* 96 (March 2010): 979–1000; Giles B. Stebbins, *Upward Steps of Seventy Years. Autobiographic, Biographic, Historic* (New York: United States Company, 1890), 99; Samuel Finley Breese Morse, *The Present Attempt to Dissolve the American Union, A British Aristocratic Plot* (New York: John F. Trow, 1862), 34–38.

[45] Morgan, "Anti-Corn Law League," 90; Sam W. Haynes, *Unfinished Revolution: The Early American Republic in a British World* (Charlottesville: University of Virginia Press, 2010), 192–199; Hilton, *Age of Atonement*, chap. 2; C. Duncan Rice, "The Anti-Slavery Mission of George Thompson to the United States, 1834–35," *Journal of American Studies* 2 (April 1968): 13–31; Thistlethwaite, *America and the Atlantic Community*, 162; Wm. Lloyd Garrison, ed., *Lectures of George Thompson* (Boston, MA: Isaac Knapp, 1836), iii–xxxiii.

[46] Temperley, *British Antislavery*, 192–193; David Turley, *The Culture of English Antislavery, 1780–1860* (London and New York: Routledge, 1991), 126; Betty Fladeland, *Men and Brothers: Anglo-American Antislavery Cooperation* (Urbana: University of Illinois Press, 1972), chaps. 10–11; January 21, 1845, *Appendix to the Congressional Globe*, 28th Cong., 2nd Sess., 143; Sam W. Haynes, "Anglophobia and the Annexation of Texas: The Quest for National Security," in *Manifest Destiny and Empire: American Antebellum Expansionism*, ed by Sam W. Haynes and Christopher Morris (College Station: Texas A&M University Press, 1997), 123; Meardon, "Religious Revivalism to Tariff Rancor," 268.

abolitionist *Emancipator*, came to see that overturning the Corn Laws in England could shift British trade from the importation of southern slave-grown cotton to western free-grown wheat. "Our Corn Law project," Leavitt wrote to Liberty party presidential nominee James Birney in 1840, "looks larger to me since my return after seeing the very land where wheat grows .... We must go for free trade; the voting abolitionists can all be brought to that ... and the corn movement will give us the West."[47] English abolitionist and ACLL leader Joseph Sturge, upon his American arrival in 1841, made sure to contact Leavitt to inform him of the status of the Corn Law agitation in England.[48] With Sturge's added insight, Leavitt discovered that John Bright and a growing number of British manufacturers, weary of their dependence on southern slave-grown cotton, desired to turn instead to northern markets to sell their finished cotton cloth, but were sorely hampered in this endeavor owing to Corn Law restrictions and American protectionism.[49] According to his biographer, Leavitt hoped to move the antislavery movement into "independent political action" and "pounced on this antisouthern and antislavery dimension of the British league's message." Leavitt also denounced the English people (and by proxy the Corn Laws) for importing the products of slave labor while blocking staples produced by free labor from the American North and West throughout the early 1840s. Leavitt went so far as to propose that the people of the free states set up their own separate embassy in England in order to counteract the influence of southern slaveholders.[50]

[47] Leavitt to Birney, October 1, 1840, *Letters of James Gillespie Birney, 1831–1857*, ed. by Dwight L. Dumond, 2 vols. (New York: D. Appleton-Century Company, 1938), II, 604; Meardon, "Religious Revivalism to Tariff Rancor," 268, 273–275, 285–295; Edward P. Crapol, "The Foreign Policy of Antislavery, 1833–1846," in *Redefining the Past: Essays in Diplomatic History in Honor of William Appleman Williams*, ed. by Lloyd C. Gardner (Corvallis, OR: Oregon State University Press, 1986), 92–102.

[48] Joseph Sturge, *A Visit to the United States in 1841* (London: Hamilton, Adams, and Co., 1842); Martin, "Free Trade and the Oregon Question," 471–474. Sturge was a leading member of both the ACLL and the British and Foreign Anti-Slavery Society.

[49] See, for instance, Bright to Sturge, 1853, in Stephen Hobhouse, *Joseph Sturge: His Life and his Work* (London: J. M. Dent and Sons, 1919), 109; Sturge, *A Visit to the United States in 1841*, 156–158; Temperley, *British Antislavery*, 166; J. S. Buckingham, *The Eastern and Western States of America*, 3 vols. (London: Fisher, Son & Co., 1842), III, 242–243. See, also, Julian P. Bretz, "The Economic Background of the Liberty Party," *American Historical Review* 34 (January 1929): 250–264.

[50] Hugh Davis, *Joshua Leavitt: Evangelical Abolitionist* (Baton Rouge: Louisiana State University Press, 1990), 170; *Emancipator*, December 24, 1840; March 16, 1847. On the debate over free and slave-grown products, see, also, Thistlethwaite, *America and the Atlantic Community*, 161, 163–164; Carol Faulkner, "The Root of the Evil: Free Produce and Radical Antislavery, 1820–1860," *Journal of the Early Republic* 27 (Fall 2007): 377–405; Louis Billington, "British Humanitarians and American Cotton, 1840–1860," *Journal of American Studies* 11 (December 1977): 313–334; Merk, "The British Corn

Leavitt, with his newfound transatlantic inspiration, focused much of his attention upon overturning the Corn Laws. He did so by developing an American repeal strategy that would aid British manufacturers and northern farmers (suffering from scarce credit following the banking crisis of 1837), all while striking "one of the heaviest blows at slavery" by allowing the duty-free import of northern wheat to repay their foreign debts.[51] Leavitt then beseeched the Senate Committee on Agriculture to call for the repeal of the Corn Laws. He contended in 1840 that an antislavery American government might work toward such a repeal. "Next to the abolition of slavery," this was "the greatest question."[52] Leavitt's Liberty party also sent Ohio's John Curtis to Britain to support the ACLL in connecting Corn Law repeal with the abolition of American slavery. Leavitt thereafter presented to Congress another request for ending the Corn Law and for increasing northern trade with Britain by replacing the protectionist 1842 tariff with a tariff for revenue only.[53] He also began discussing the possibilities of Anglo-American free trade with English abolitionists while attending the 1843 antislavery convention in London. He then went on the ACLL tour circuit with Cobden and Bright, during which Leavitt claimed that a conspiracy existed between southern slaveholders and British aristocrats in opposing the Corn Law repeal.[54]

Leavitt reinforced his transatlantic ties through his correspondence with his English abolitionist friends and through the creation of American anti-Corn Law organizations. He encouraged his English

Crisis of 1845–46 and the Oregon Treaty"; C. Duncan Rice, "'Humanity Sold For Sugar!' The British Abolitionist Response to Free Trade in Slave-Grown Sugar," *Historical Journal* 13 (September 1970): 402–418; Harold Francis Williamson, *Edward Atkinson: The Biography of an American Liberal, 1827–1905* (Boston, MA: Old Corner Book Store, 1934), 4–10.

[51] *Emancipator*, May 1, 1840, 2; Davis, *Leavitt*, 171; Morgan, "Anti-Corn Law League," 95; Martin, "Mississippi Valley in Anglo-American Relations," 212–220; Thomas P. Martin, "Cotton and Wheat in Anglo-American Trade and Politics, 1846–1852," *Journal of Southern History* 1 (August 1935): 293–319; Martin, "Conflicting Cotton Interests at Home and Abroad, 1848–1857," *Journal of Southern History* 7 (May 1941): 173–194.

[52] *Memorial of Joshua Leavitt Praying the Adoption of Measures to Secure an Equitable Market for American Wheat*, Senate Documents, 26th Cong., 2nd Sess., No. 222, 1–8; *Ballot Box*, October 7, 1840, quoted in Davis, *Leavitt*, 171.

[53] Morgan, "Anti-Corn Law League," 96; John Curtis, *America and the Corn Laws* (Manchester: J. Gadsby, 1841); *Memorial of Joshua Leavitt, Praying That, in the Revision of the Tariff Laws, the Principle of Discrimination May be Inserted in Favor of Those Countries in Which American Grain, Flour, and Salted Meat, are Admitted Duty Free*, Senate Documents, 27th Cong., 2nd Sess., No. 339, pp. 117–124; *British and Foreign Anti-Slavery Reporter*, September 7, 1842, 142.

[54] *Leeds Mercury*, May 27, 1843; Crapol, "Foreign Policy of Antislavery," 98–99; Turley, *Culture of English Antislavery*, 126.

correspondents to think of American interests alongside their own, letters that were then published in the *Anti-Corn Law League Circular* in England. He also began establishing anti-Corn Law societies in the American Northwest and New York. Although in doing so he gained the disfavor of protectionists within the Whig party, his efforts provided further transatlantic moral support for the ACLL and strengthened Leavitt's connection to Cobdenism.[55]

Abolitionist firebrands Leavitt and Thompson were not alone in bringing the ACLL's free-trade fight to American shores. A variety of other American abolitionist free traders also took lessons from the ACLL. As W. Caleb McDaniel has recently noted, women of the ACLL staged Free Trade bazaars, giving direct and indirect encouragement to American abolitionists. Garrisonian pacifist Henry Clarke Wright similarly developed close ties with the ACLL, and the antislavery and free-trade work of Harriet Martineau fell within this transatlantic network, as well.[56]

William Cullen Bryant, former Barnburner Democrat, Free Soiler, poet, abolitionist, uncompromising free trader, and editor of the *New York Evening Post*, attended ACLL meetings in London during the 1840s. In admiration for Cobden, Bryant would afterward go on to edit the American edition of Cobden's *Political Writings* in 1865. He would also become an early leader of the subsequent Gilded Age American free-trade movement.[57]

Arch-abolitionist William Lloyd Garrison was heavily influenced by George Thompson and other British free traders. As one abolitionist (and protectionist) friend, Giles Stebbins, recollected, "Wm. Lloyd Garrison and others of the abolitionists whom I greatly respected, inclined to free trade; for their English anti-slavery friends were free-traders." In later years, Garrison became a member of, and corresponded frequently with, the Cobden Club upon its creation in 1866, avowing himself "a free-trader to an illimitable extent."[58] For him, free trade was but the next step to freeing mankind from bondage.

The humanitarian and religious antislavery rhetoric likewise entered the free-trade language of Reverend Henry Ward Beecher, himself a convert

---

[55] Davis, *Leavitt*, 180, 196, 202, 204; James M. McPherson, "The Fight Against the Gag Rule: Joshua Leavitt and Antislavery Insurgency in the Whig Party, 1839–1842," *Journal of Negro History* 48 (July 1963): 177–195.

[56] W. Caleb McDaniel, *The Problem of Democracy in the Age of Slavery: Garrisonian Abolitionists & Transatlantic Reform* (Baton Rouge: Lousiana State University Press, 2013), 122, 165–166; Clare Midgley, *Women Against Slavery: The British Campaigns, 1780–1870* (London and New York: Routledge, 1995), 130.

[57] Foner, *Free Soil*, 153; *Free-Trader* (March 1870), 170; John Bigelow, *William Cullen Bryant* (Boston and New York: Houghton, Mifflin, 1890), 182–183.

[58] Stebbins, *Upward Steps*, 194; *Morning Post*, September 7, 1875, 3.

from protectionism to Cobdenism, and famous in England for his transatlantic tours. In the years to come, he would beseech American free traders
to employ "the same energy and the same agitation" of the antislavery
struggle toward the burgeoning American free-trade movement. He hoped
that he would live long enough "to induce the American people to favor the
unshackling of intercourse between nation and nation."[59]

The "American Carlyle" Ralph Waldo Emerson was also involved in
the abolitionist and free-trade movements.[60] Emerson first met Cobden
in 1847 at a meeting of the Manchester Athenaeum, where he heard
Cobden give an "eloquent" address, spurring Emerson to comment
upon the shared traits "of that Anglo-Saxon race" that had "secured for
it the scepter of the globe." He would continue to meet with Cobden on
his English visits for years to come. During one such visit in 1848,
Emerson wrote to his friend Henry David Thoreau of the Free Trade
Banquet held the previous night, where he "heard the best man in
England make perhaps his best speech." Cobden, "the *cor cordis* ...
educated by his dogma of Free Trade ... as our abolitionists have been
by their principle .... It was quite beautiful, even sublime."[61] Emerson's
Cobdenite sentiments even found outlet in his literary musings. In his
1857 "Concord Ode," for example, he would beseech his country to "bid
the broad Atlantic roll, a ferry of the free."[62] Emerson, along with many of
these first-generation Cobdenites, would exude some of his own dogmatic energy when he helped create the American Free Trade League
(AFTL) in 1865.

Charles Sumner maintained perhaps the closest mid-century correspondence with Cobden and his man-at-arms, John Bright.
"Conscience" Whig Sumner left that party in 1848 for the antislavery
Free Soil party, before becoming an influential member of the Radical
Republicans in the late 1850s. Sumner first met Cobden in 1838 during a
trip to England, and they developed a friendship in the decades leading up
to and during the Civil War. Not coincidentally, Sumner's protectionist

---

[59] *New York Times*, May 27, 1882, 5; Lymon Abbott, *Henry Ward Beecher as His Friends Saw Him* (Boston and New York: The Pilgrim Press, 1904), 128.

[60] Len Gougeon, "The Anti-Slavery Background of Emerson's 'Ode Inscribed to W. H. Channing,'" *Studies in the American Renaissance* 9 (1985): 63–77; Gougeon, "Abolition, the Emersons, and 1837," *New England Quarterly* 54 (September 1981): 345–365; Gougeon, "Emerson and Abolition, the Silent Years: 1837–1844," *American Literature* 54 (December 1982): 560–575.

[61] *Liverpool Mercury*, November 23, 1847; Barbara L. Packer et al., ed., *Collected Works of Ralph Waldo Emerson: The Conduct of His Life* (Cambridge, MA: Harvard University Press, 1971), VI, 212; Emerson to Henry David Thoreau, January 28, 1848, in *Letters of Ralph Waldo Emerson*, ed. by Eleanor Marguerite Tilton (New York: Columbia University Press, 1939), 145.

[62] Excerpt reprinted in *Free Trade Broadside* 1 (April 1905), 1.

convictions began to soften during this period, even as he came around to Amasa Walker and Richard Cobden's condemnation of international war. Henry Carey would thereafter try without success to turn Sumner away from his Cobdenite convictions. Sumner's unwillingness to shift from his Cobdenite beliefs caused Carey to beseech him one final time in 1852 – if only Sumner could just satisfy himself "that protection is the real and the only road to freedom of trade and freedom in the fate of labour," and let go of "British free trade which leads everywhere to the subjugation of man."[63] Sumner instead became a strong advocate of Cobden's quest for "Universal Peace." In an inspirational 1849 speech before an audience of Free Soilers, for example, Sumner urged them to remember how the ACLL had successfully brought together Tories, Whigs, and Radicals to repeal the monopolistic Corn Laws. As economic historian Stephen Meardon notes, "The equation of tariff barriers with 'monopoly,' and their repeal with 'Freedom' . . . was the rhetoric of free trade. More to the point, in the broader context of peace and anti-slavery in which Sumner spoke, it was the rhetoric of Cobdenism."[64]

America's first Cobdenites were thus an imposing group of abolitionists with strong transatlantic ties.[65] Long after Cobden's death in 1865, many of these American radicals would maintain correspondence with the Cobden Club's leadership, and continue to work toward bringing about Cobden's universal vision of free trade, prosperity, and peace. These northern subscribers to Cobdenism were the vanguard of the Victorian American free-trade movement. William Freehling suggests that Jeffersonian free trade and slavery had become "intermeshed" in the South by the time of the Nullification Crisis (1832–1833). By the 1840s, so too were Cobdenism and abolitionism enmeshed within the American North.[66]

---

[63] Carey to Sumner, July 24, 1852, reel 9, Sumner Papers. His personal free-trade proclivities did not keep him from voting the Republican party line on the 1861 Morrill Tariff.

[64] Sumner to Cobden, February 12, 1849, reel 63, Sumner Papers; Sumner to Bancroft, March 15, 1846, Bancroft Papers; Charles Sumner, "Address to the People of Massachusetts, September 12, 1849," in *Orations and Speeches of Charles Sumner* (Boston, MA: Ticknor, Reed, and Fields, 1850), II, 294; Meardon, "Richard Cobden's American Quandary," 216. See, also, Thomas P. Martin, "The Upper Mississippi Valley in Anglo-American Anti-Slavery and Free Trade Relations: 1837–1842," *Mississippi Valley Historical Review* 15 (September 1928): 208–211.

[65] Other American abolitionists who would become leaders of the postbellum free-trade movement included Edward Atkinson, Amasa Walker, Gamaliel Bradford, William Earl Dodge, Parke Godwin, Benjamin Gue, Rowland Hazard, Edward Holton, James Redpath, F. B. Sanborn, Thomas Shearman, Joseph Thompson, Francis Stout, Francis Vincent, and Horace White (see Appendix).

[66] William W. Freehling, *Prelude to Civil War: The Nullification Controversy in South Carolina, 1816–1836* (New York: Harper & Row, 1966), 255.

Free trade, the Corn Laws, and westward expansion

The American arrival of Cobdenite ideology was closely linked not only to abolitionism, but also to connecting the ACLL with American westward expansion, a seemingly unexpected pairing. From the 1830s, the ACLL had sought to undo the British protectionist system. England's industrialization delivered with it a double punch of prosperity and poverty. The latter attribute, argued Richard Cobden, had only been compounded by the English aristocracy's militaristic atavism and the well-to-do land-owners' selfish adherence to protective tariffs. Such protectionism was exemplified by the Corn Laws, which for so long had artificially raised the price of bread stemming from the laws' protective tariffs on imported foreign grain. The ACLL therefore had clear cause for celebration in 1846 when the Corn Laws were repealed.[67] At long last, the promised "cheap loaf" proved politically palatable, as did Britain's ensuing free-trade policies. The era of the so-called *Pax Britannica* had arrived, yet with it came deteriorating Anglo-American relations arising from US westward expansion.

More than timing linked the rise of Free Trade England and American westward expansion. Just as Britain was turning to free trade, across the Atlantic, Jeffersonian Democratic President James K. Polk declared war against Mexico, marking the antebellum apogee of nationwide Manifest Destiny – the patriotic desire to expand the reach of the United States to every edge of North America. Antiwar Whigs tended to view the war with Mexico as an overt attempt to extend the territory of the southern "slave power." In response, as historian Sam Haynes paints the scene, western and southern expansionists tarred "the Whigs with a British brush." Antebellum Anglophobia had become a reliable "multipurpose bête noire."[68]

---

[67] In perhaps the first Listian response to Cobdenism in the UK, one Irish student of List wrote a defense of the Navigation Acts in 1847. "A Disciple of Friedrich List" [H. Forbes], *A Glance at the Proposed Abolition of the Navigation Laws, and the Principles of Free Trade* (Edinburgh: William Blackwood and Sons, 1847).

[68] Haynes, *Unfinished Revolution*, 139, 145. On Manifest Destiny and the war with Mexico, see especially Frederick Merk, *Manifest Destiny and Mission in American History* (New York: Vintage Books, 1966); Anders Stephanson, *Manifest Destiny: American Expansion and the Empire of Right* (New York: Hill and Wang, 1995); Thomas R. Hietala, *Manifest Design: Anxious Aggrandizement in Late Jacksonian America* (Ithaca, NY: Cornell University Press, 1985); Sam W. Haynes and Christopher Morris, *Manifest Destiny and Empire: American Antebellum Expansionism* (College Station: Texas A&M University Press, 1997); Charles G. Sellers, *James K. Polk: Continentalist, 1843–1846* (Princeton, NJ: Princeton University Press, 1966); Walter R. Borneman, *Polk: The Man Who Transformed the Presidency and America* (New York: Random House, 2008); John S. D. Eisenhower, *So Far from God: The U.S. War with Mexico, 1846–48* (New York: Random House, 1989); David M. Pletcher, *The Diplomacy of Annexation: Texas, Oregon, and the Mexican War* (Columbia: University of Missouri Press, 1973).

Anglophobia – defined as fear, distrust, or hatred of the British – was a multifaceted psychological condition that permeated American politics from the American Revolution onward, and remained prevalent even after Anglo-American rapprochement at the nineteenth century's *fin de siècle*. From the country's founding, southern Jeffersonians both feared British antislavery agitation and disliked their own continued reliance upon the British market for their agricultural exports. Many northern manufacturers instead feared Britain's pronounced advantages in the way of industrial production. And all sections generally remained wary of the British Empire's geopolitical presence in North America. More than a few Northerners and Southerners even set out to create a unique national identity in an effort to differentiate the fledgling American states from their English colonial heritage. While a strong vein of Anglophilia could be found among some northeastern elites, Anglophobia proved to be an effective and malleable tool for gaining electoral advantage; for creating a new sense of national identification that buttressed the American System of protectionism; and for further justifying American westward expansion.[69]

The decision for war against Mexico stemmed in no small part from an American geopolitical fear of British antislavery and annexationist agitation in Texas and California, followed closely by rumors that the British would support Mexico with men and money if a quarrel were to break out.[70] US Treasury Secretary Robert J. Walker warned that a pro-British Texas would lead to a slave exodus from the South and would give the British Empire a convenient base from which to invade the Mississippi

---

[69] On nineteenth-century American Anglophobia, see Kinley J. Brauer, "The United States and British Imperial Expansion, 1815–60," *Diplomatic History* 12 (January 1988): 19–37; Haynes, *Unfinished Revolution*; Schoen, *Fragile Fabric of Union*, chap. 1; Lawrence A. Peskin, "Conspiratorial Anglophobia and the War of 1812," *Journal of American History* 98 (December 2011): 647–669; Stephen Tuffnell, "'Uncle Sam is to be Sacrificed': Anglophobia in Late Nineteenth-Century Politics and Culture," *American Nineteenth Century History* 12 (March 2011): 77–99; William C. Reuter, "The Anatomy of Political Anglophobia in the United States, 1865–1900," *Mid-America* 61 (April–July 1979): 117–132; Edward P. Crapol, *America for Americans: Economic Nationalism and Anglophobia in the Late Nineteenth Century* (Westport, CT: Greenwood Press, 1973).

[70] Haynes, *Unfinished Revolution*, 230–250; Temperley, *British Antislavery*, 197–202; Harriet Smither, "English Abolitionism and the Annexation of Texas," *Southwestern Historical Quarterly* 32 (January 1929): 193–205; Ephraim Douglas Adams, *British Interest and Activities in Texas, 1838–1846* (Baltimore: Johns Hopkins Press, 1910); Adams, "English Interest in the Annexation of California," *American Historical Review* 14 (July 1909): 744–763; Lelia Roeckell, "Bonds over Bondage: British Opposition to the Annexation of Texas," *Journal of the Early Republic* 19 (Summer 1999): 257–278; Sheldon G. Jackson, "The British and the California Dream: Rumors, Myths, and Legends," *Southern California Quarterly* 57 (Summer 1975): 251–268; Jackson, "Two Pro-British Plots in Alta California," *Southern California Quarterly* 55 (Summer 1973): 105–140.

delta. Perhaps in the hope of striking a sympathetic chord with Whig protectionists, others suggested that the British might even use the recently minted Texas Republic to bypass US tariff schedules. As a complement to this British antislavery and free-trade fearmongering, still other expansionists would dangle the tantalizing possibility of accessing Pacific-rim markets – that the new territories would open up the western coastline of North and South America, as well as the markets of Russia, India, and China, for American exports.[71]

The war with Mexico also contained the problematic promise of acquiring massive tracts of new American territory. Would these new lands ultimately become free or slave states? This difficult question surrounding slavery's expansion fertilized the dormant seeds of sectionalism and secession: seeds that would sprout into Civil War in 1861. Yet even though slavery monopolized the era's political scene like no other issue in American history, the influence of Victorian free trade also reverberated throughout antebellum US foreign relations and domestic politics, from the Oregon boundary dispute to the formation of the Republican party.[72]

During this era of massive economic growth and transatlantic interconnectivity, some paternalistic Listian nationalist intellectuals in the United States also were slowly coming to accept that American infant industries would one day reach adolescence and adulthood – and that reciprocal trade and expanding foreign markets would in the near future not only become desirable, but necessary. They also viewed Britain's newly christened free-trade imperialism as a formidable stumbling block to proper American industrial maturation.[73]

Such Anglophobic sentiments had already begun to spill over into international politics stemming from an Anglo-American boundary dispute surrounding the Oregon territory in the early 1840s, a conflict commonly remembered by Polk's 1844 expansionist presidential campaign slogan "Fifty-Four Forty or Fight!" The pro-free-trade *New York Evening Post* even reported that some conspiratorial protectionists in Congress and the Whig press were considering "making the apprehension of war a pretext for spending large amounts of money in military and naval preparations," thereby creating enough new expenditures to justify the high tariff of 1842. The paper also speculated with less cynicism that there was now the possibility of combining the Oregon boundary question with Anglo-American free trade. A "free trade tariff on both sides will settle the

---

[71] Robert J. Walker, *Letter of Mr. Walker Relative to the Annexation of Texas* (Washington, DC: The Globe Office, 1844); Haynes, "Anglophobia, Annexation," 133; Ximenes, *Mr. Calhoun – Mr. Van Buren – Texas* (July 1, 1843).

[72] David M. Potter, *The Impending Crisis, 1848–1861* (New York: Harper & Row, 1976), 49.

[73] Brauer, "United States and British Imperial Expansion."

matter quickly," the *Post* predicted in late January, "and give us something better to do than fighting." Such speculation received encouragement from the ACLL, with one of its member's expressing the hope that, now that England was embracing free trade, "if your President can only carry out his sensible trade views, the extended intercourse between the two countries will be the surest guarantee for peace." Treasury Secretary Walker, temporarily putting aside his own expansionist impulse for the sake of tariff reform, had noted in his 1845 annual Treasury report that if the US tariff were reduced, "the party opposed to the Corn Laws of England would soon prevail," leading to Anglo-American free trade. Even as Whig antiwar politicians were being labeled pro-British, protectionist Whig opponents of Polk were quick to portray him as a paid British agent, drawing conspiratorial connections between British industrialists, free-trade propaganda, and Polk's liberal stance on the tariff.[74]

At the same time, the British were also beginning to take notice of the bountiful wheat crop and the expansive agricultural development of the American West. Discussion arose on both sides of the Atlantic as to whether these vast western territories might become Britain's next breadbasket, especially after the onset of a severe harvest shortage throughout the United Kingdom in 1845, culminating in the horrific Great Famine of Ireland (1845–1852).[75] Alongside potentially solving the food shortage through increased importation of American wheat, British free traders believed that repeal of the Corn Laws would create such strong commercial connections between the British Empire and the United States that future Anglo-American hostilities like the boundary issue would disappear. British free traders' desire for western wheat as part of the promised "cheap loaf," alongside a general British turn toward internationalism, strengthened repeal and laid the groundwork for a peaceable solution to the Oregon boundary dispute.[76]

[74] *New York Evening Post*, January 12, Janaury 19, January 26, Janaury 28, 1846; Robert J. Walker, "Report from the Secretary of the Treasury," in *State Papers and Speeches on the Tariff*, ed. by Frank W. Taussig (Cambridge, MA: Harvard University Press, 1893 [1845]), 11; Haynes, *Unfinished Revolution*, 129–131, 149–151; McDonald, *Invisible Hand of Peace*, 141–145.

[75] David Sim, *A Union Forever: The Irish Question and U.S. Foreign Relations in the Victorian Age* (Ithaca, NY: Cornell University Press, 2014) 40–43; Harry J. Carman, "English Views of Middle Western Agriculture, 1850–1870," *Agricultural History* 8 (January 1934): 3–19; Thomas Stirton, "Free Trade and the Wheat Surplus of the Old Northwest, 1839–1846" (MA Thesis, University of Chicago, 1952), 67–139. Wheat continued to play an important diplomatic role in subsequent years. See Morton Rothstein, "America in the International Rivalry for the British Wheat Market, 1860–1914," *Mississippi Valley Historical Review* 47 (December 1960): 401–418.

[76] *London Times*, November 11, 1845, 4; November 18, 1846, 4; Blanche Cecil Woodham-Smith, *The Great Hunger: Ireland, 1845–49* (New York: Harper & Row, 1962), 40; Frederick Merk, *The Oregon Question: Essays in Anglo-American Diplomacy and Politics*

Figure 1.3 "Peel and Polk." London's humor magazine *Punch* offers a cartoon depicting Peel [left] pelting a militant Polk [right] with "Free Corn," so as to bring a peaceful settlement to the Oregon dispute. *Punch* (1846), X, 155

Yet support for repeal was far from universal. American protectionists preferred fearmongering to tariff reductions. Baltimore's protectionist news organ *Niles' Weekly Register* speculated that the Peel government

(Cambridge, MA: Belknap Press, 1967), 309–336, 391; Merk, "The British Corn Crisis of 1845–46 and the Oregon Treaty," *Agricultural History* (July 1934): 95–123; Thomas P. Martin, "Free Trade and the Oregon Question, 1842–1846," in *Facts and Factors in Economic History: Articles by Former Students of Edwin Francis Gay* (Cambridge, MA: Harvard University Press, 1932), 485–490; R. C. Clark, "British and American Tariff Policies and their Influence on the Oregon Boundary Treaty," *Pacific Coast Branch of them American Historical Association Proceedings* 1 (1926): 32–49; Henry Commager, "England and Oregon Treaty of 1846," *Oregon Historical Quarterly* 28 (March 1927), 34–38; Howard Jones and Donald A. Rakestraw, *Prologue to Manifest Destiny: Anglo-American Relations in the 1840s* (Wilmington, DE: SR Books, 1997), 228, 236; Pletcher, *Diplomacy of Annexation*, 417–420. For further speculation about free trade bringing a peaceful settlement, see *European Times*, November 20, December 4, 1845, in *Littell's Living Age* (Boston, MA: Waite, Peirce & Company, January–March 1846), VIII, 54; Russell, quoted in Merk, "The British Corn Crisis of 1845–46 and the Oregon Treaty," 104; Everett to Bancroft, February 2, 1846, carton 14, George Bancroft Papers, MHS.

would use the Oregon dispute to sway recalcitrant ministers toward repeal, and that American trade liberalization would mean that the United States "may again be courted into colonial reliance ... the glorious old colonies are coming back to a proper dependence upon British manufactures."[77] For some, free trade appeared to be bringing its promised panacea of peace through more amicable Anglo-American relations, but for others it also carried with it the possibility of British free-trade imperialism in the United States.

Cobdenite free-trade agitation in favor of Anglo-American rapprochement also met staunch opposition from some Anglophobic Jeffersonians hoping to undermine the growing transatlantic abolitionist–Cobdenite alliance. In 1842, Duff Green, a southern agent, was sent to Europe with the mission of cutting the ties between northern abolitionists and the ACLL so as to maintain the current southern–western free-trade alliance in American politics. He even claimed to have discovered a vast British conspiracy involving the repeal of the Corn Laws, British emancipation agitation in Texas, and the destruction of US commerce. Green's allegations caused alarm back home.[78]

Nor did North American prosperity immediately follow transatlantic trade liberalization. In the short term, at least, the reality of Corn Law repeal meant that Canada and the United States now had to compete directly with the agricultural exports of the so-called pauper labor of Europe.[79] This newfound economic competition was compounded by the realization that the United States had lost its backdoor trade route through Canada, a British colony that, until repeal in 1846, had been receiving preferential commercial treatment from England. Owing to the sudden increase in European competition, agricultural prices in North America fell. By 1849, this sharp agricultural price decline produced an economic depression in Canada, and a corresponding demand from Montreal's merchant community for American annexation of Canada. Alongside placating this annexationist sentiment, avoiding the era's

---

[77] McDonald, *Invisible Hand of Peace*, 146–148; *Niles National Register* (Baltimore), LXIX, January 24, 1846, 322; January 31, 1846, 340; February 21, 1846, 386. On Peel's "realist" repeal of the Corn Laws, see Anthony Howe, "Radicalism, Free Trade, and Foreign Policy in Mid-Nineteenth-Century Britain," in *The Primacy of Foreign Policy in British History, 1660–2000*, ed. by William Mulligan and Brendan Simms (Basingstoke: Palgrave Macmillan, 2010), 170–171.

[78] Pletcher, *Diplomacy of Annexation*, 22–23; Malcolm Rogers Eiselen, "Rise of Pennsylvania Protectionism" (PhD diss., University of Pennsylvania, 1932), chaps. 9–10; Martin, "Free Trade and the Oregon Question," 475–480; Karp, "King Cotton, Emperor Slavery."

[79] *Cleveland Herald*, February 27, 1846; *American Review: A Whig Journal of Politics, Literature, Art and Science* (New York: George H. Colton, 1846), III, 218; *Congressional Globe* (Washington, 1846), 29th Cong. 1st Sess., 339–340, 460.

seemingly endless Canadian–American fisheries disputes, and the loss of Canada's preferential treatment with England, the closing of this American backdoor trade route thereafter played a sizeable role in the development of US–Canadian reciprocity in 1854. Protectionist Whigs like Daniel Webster and some western farmers – the latter still seething over the Oregon issue – instead believed that the weak increase in US wheat exports and declining agricultural prices following repeal only strengthened the protectionist home-market argument.[80]

The 1846 repeal of the Corn Laws, the passage of the low US Walker Tariff, and the peaceful settlement of the Oregon boundary dispute also did little to diminish American Anglophobia. All of these events held out the possibility for a new era of transatlantic trade liberalization and closer Anglo-American relations.[81] But these events and their aftermath also demonstrated that Anglophobia and tense Anglo-American relations were anything but dissipating. The ideological dividing wall between free traders and economic nationalists was already proving to be formidable.

So how did America's estranged free traders and protectionists come to lie together within the Republican party? Put simply, a radical minority of northeastern Cobdenites initially gave their support to the Republican party – a party made up predominantly of former Whig protectionists – owing to the fledgling party's ideology of free labor, free soil, and antislavery. The Republican party's minority of Cobdenite free-trade radicals, drawing upon the ACLL's leadership and success, hoped to bring the same promised panacea of free trade and peace to American shores. As *Frederick Douglass' Paper* described it, the American Cobdenites' proposed Republican doctrine was "Free Men, Free Soil, Free Labor, and Free Trade."[82] The Whig-Republican

---

[80] Edwin Williams, *The Wheat Trade of the United States and Europe* (New York: New York Farmers' Club, 1846), 17–19; Merk, "The British Corn Crisis of 1845–46 and the Oregon Treaty," 108–117; D. L. Burn, "Canada and the Repeal of the Corn Laws," *Cambridge Historical Journal* 2 (1928): 252–272; Frederick E. Haynes, "The Reciprocity Treaty with Canada of 1854," *Publications of the American Economic Association* 7 (November 1892): 9–12; Thomas P. Martin, "The Staff of Life in Diplomacy and Politics during the Early Eighteen Fifties," *Agricultural History* 18 (January 1944): 1–15; Peter J. Parish, "Daniel Webster, New England, and the West," *Journal of American History* 54 (December 1967), 535. On the Reciprocity Treaty of 1854, see Robert E. Ankli, "The Reciprocity Treaty of 1854," *Canadian Journal of Economics* 4 (February 1971): 1–20; Lawrence H. Officer and Lawrence B. Smith, "The Canadian-American Reciprocity Treaty of 1855 to 1866," *Journal of Economic History* 28 (1968): 598–623.

[81] A point that Polk himself noted to Congress later that year. James K. Polk, "Second Annual Message," December 8, 1846, *Tariff Proceedings and Documents 1839–1857 Accompanied by Messages of the President, Treasury Reports, and Bills*, 3 vols. (Washington: Government Printing Office, 1911), III, 1653.

[82] "Free Labor and Protection," *Frederick Douglass' Paper*, March 24, 1854. The motto is similar to that adopted at the Free Soiler Herkimer Convention of October 26, 1847, led

supporters of the "American System" – revamped by Friedrich List, Henry Clay, and Henry Carey – would instead seek to move the Republican party away from antislavery and toward a platform of protective tariffs and government-subsidized internal improvements. With a tenuous thread and needle, antebellum antislavery stitched the Republican party together. Free traders and protectionists in the North and West had thus found a common cause and tenuous party loyalty under the broad Republican banner of antislavery, a northern–western alliance that was buttressed by the construction of Great Lakes canals and railroad lines.[83] When American Cobdenite desires for freer trade increasingly became a postbellum Republican pipedream, however, the party's precarious free-trade–protectionist alliance would begin to wear. As examined in subsequent chapters, upon the Civil War's conclusion and the manumission of southern slaves, the tempestuous tariff issue would tear this fair-weather friendship apart.

Moreover, the Panic of 1857 would have lasting reverberations, in both the ante- and postbellum Republican party. The moderate Democratic revenue tariffs of 1846 and 1857 appeared to have indicated a national move toward a policy of trade liberalization: a move that had partially placated both southern Jeffersonians and northeastern Cobdenites. But the low tariffs also earned the ire of Henry Carey and protectionist politicians from the infant industrial Midwest and Northeast. Economic nationalist ire was heightened following the onset of the 1857 economic panic, which coincided closely with the passage of the low 1857 tariff. The timing may have been coincidental, but it revitalized the Whig-Republican argument that only protectionism could return prosperity, stability, and high wages to the American laborer. This line of argument garnered further protectionist support in

by Cobdenite David Dudley Field: "Free Trade, Free Labor, Free Soil, Free Speech and Free Men." See Jonathan Halperin Earle, *Antislavery and the Politics of Free Soil, 1824–1854* (Chapel Hill: University of North Carolina Press, 2004), 71–72.

[83] Foner, *Free Soil*, xiv, xxiv, 9, 19, 59, 61, 105, 153; William A. Williams, *The Contours of American History* (Cleveland, OH: World Pub. Co., 1961), 248; William D. Carleton, "Tariffs and the Rise of Sectionalism," *Current History* 42 (June 1962): 333–338; Edward Stanwood, *American Tariff Controversies in the Nineteenth Century*, 2 vols. (Boston and New York: Houghton, Mifflin, 1903), II, 71–81; Charles A. Beard, *The Idea of National Interest: An Analytical Study in American Foreign Policy* (New York: The Macmillan Company, 1934), 58; Douglas Irwin, "Antebellum Tariff Politics: Coalition Formation and Shifting Regional Interests," *National Bureau of Economic Research Working Paper Series*, No. 12161 (April 2006): 1–43; Marc Egnal, *Clash of Extremes: The Economic Origins of the Civil War* (New York: Hill and Wang, 2009); Carleton, "Tariffs and the Rise of Sectionalism"; Thomas M. Pitkin, "Western Republicans and the Tariff in 1860," *Mississippi Valley Historical Review* 27 (December 1940): 401–420.

the West and generally intensified prevailing sectional views.[84] Carey and his Listian acolytes would continue to use subsequent economic panics in seeking to make the Republican party "a protective party *en bloc*."[85]

The Republican party's Cobdenite minority unsuccessfully sought to counter this Whig-Republican protectionist insurgency. They even tried to include a "tariff for revenue only" plank into the new Republican party platform. In 1857, John Bigelow wrote to William Cullen Bryant that Horace Greeley was instead "trying very hard to get up a clamor for *protection*" by "hammering at the Tariff of '46 and the bill of last winter as the cause of all our troubles constantly." Bryant's *Evening Post* thereafter charged that there was a conspiracy underway "to pervert the Republican party to the purposes of the owners of coal and iron mines" through high tariff legislation. Charles Francis Adams, Sr. similarly warned that "the old Whig side" was attempting "to stuff in the protective tariff as a substitute for the slave question."[86] As the outbreak of the Civil War neared, the Republican party's free-trade–protectionist political alliance was already showing strain.

Conclusion

The burgeoning struggle between Listian nationalism and Cobdenite cosmopolitanism over the political economic course of American economic expansion thus coincided with Manifest Destiny's mid-century westward push and England's own turn to free trade. Contrary to the common narrative that antebellum free trade only went hand in hand with southern Jeffersonianism and slavery, a study of the arrival of Cobdenism illuminates how Anglo-American free trade and abolitionism had also become entwined in the Northeast. American abolitionist free traders, the

---

[84] Egnal, *Clash of Extremes*, 242–244; Eiselen, "Rise of Pennsylvania Protectionism," chap. 12; James L. Huston, *The Panic of 1857 and the Coming of the Civil War* (Baton Rouge: Louisiana State University Press, 1987), 1; Huston, "A Political Response to Industrialism: The Republican Embrace of Protectionist Labor Doctrines," *Journal of American History* 70 (June 1983): 35–57; Pitkin, "Western Republicans and the Tariff."

[85] E. Pershine Smith to Carey, February 6, January 16, 1859, Edward Carey Gardiner Collection, Historical Society of Pennsylvania, Philadelphia, PA. See, also, Henry C. Carey, *Letters to the President on the Foreign and Domestic Policy of the Union, and Its Effects, as Exhibited in the Condition of the People and the State* (Philadelphia, PA: J. B. Lippincott & Co., 1858); Foner, *Free Soil*, 173; Arthur Lee, "Henry Carey and the Republican Tariff," *Pennsylvania Magazine of History and Biography* 81 (July 1957), 285–290.

[86] Bigelow to Bryant, October 12, 1857, box 1, John Bigelow Papers, NYPL; *New York Evening Post*, January 14, 1860; Adams to Sumner, August 1, 1858, microfilm reel 162, Charles Francis Adams Letterbook, Adams Family Papers, MHS; Foner, *Free Soil*, 175–176, 203.

country's first Cobdenites, worked closely with their British counterparts in the overthrow of both the English Corn Laws and American slavery. At the same time, forward-looking economic nationalists within the Republican party sought instead an aggressive protectionist path for American expansion. The newly formed Republican party's rally around antislavery may have temporarily overshadowed the Republican coalition's conflicting free-trade and protectionist ideologies, but a culmination of events would soon usher in an ideological, territorial, and racial conflagration that would reshape the transatlantic political economic landscape for decades to come: especially once the postbellum Republican party began turning its main focus from antislavery to protectionism.

The Republican reorientation toward infant industrial protectionism began in 1860 with the proposal of a protective tariff bill by Vermont's Republican congressman, Justin Morrill, with the aid and encouragement of Henry Carey as well as more orthodox home-market protectionists. Georgia politician Robert Toombs certainly misread the situation in November 1860 at the Georgia secession convention, however, when he stated: "The free-trade abolitionists became protectionists; the non-abolition protectionists became abolitionists. The result of this coalition was the infamous Morrill bill." Rather, the proposed bill had backing from Midwesterners and Pennsylvanians, as it offered protection to wool, iron, and coal, among other industries. But opposition arose to the tariff not only in the South, but also in the Northeast, particularly among Republican Cobdenites.[87]

However unintentionally, the Morrill Tariff further alienated Republican Cobdenites from the party's protectionist majority. The demands and the lobbying tactics of the protectionists would prove more than a match for the country's cross-sectional free-trade opposition, especially following the secession of various southern states, whose Jeffersonian congressmen might otherwise have voted against the bill. Hoping to woo voters in protectionist Pennsylvania, the Republican

---

[87] William W. Freehling and Craig M. Simpson, eds., *Secession Debated: Georgia's Showdown in 1860* (New York: Oxford University Press, 1992), 38; *New York Times*, February 6, 1861, 1; Egnal, *Clash of Extremes*, 249. Some manufacturers did warn Morrill against raising dutiable rates. See J. M. Forbes to Morrill, February 18, 1859; Henry S. Pierce to Morrill, April 26, 1860; J. Sting Fray Bigs[?] to Morrill, May 7, 1860, reel 4; Jed Jewitt to Morrill, February 2, 1861; copy, Portuguese legate De Figaniere e Mordo to J. S. Black, February 12, 1861; J. M. Forbes to Sumner, February 21, 1861; Lombard, Whitney & Co. to A. H. Rice, February 21, 1861, reel 5, microfilm, Justin Morrill Papers, LOC. See, also, Richard Hofstadter, "The Tariff Issue on the Eve of the Civil War," *American Historical Review* 44 (October 1938): 50–55; *Cong. Globe*, 36th Cong., 1st Sess., 2053; J. L. Bishop, *A History of American Manufactures*, 2 vols. (Philadelphia, PA: F. Young & Co., 1864), II, 427.

party majority ignored the northeastern free-trade rumblings of dissent and fell in behind the high tariff bill. Morrill wrote in April 1861, two months after the tariff's passage: "Our Tariff Bill is unfortunate in being launched at this time as it will be made the scape-goat of all difficulties."[88] Morrill's prescience was remarkable.

[88] Phillip W. Magness, "Morrill and the Missing Industries: Strategic Lobbying Behavior and the Tariff, 1858–1861," *Journal of the Early Republic* 29 (Summer 2009): 287–329; Justin Smith Morrill to John Sherman, April 1, 1861, GLC02762, Gilder Lehrman Institute Archives, New York City.

2   "The most successful lie in history"

The Morrill Tariff and the Confederacy's
free-trade diplomacy

> The Confederate constitution made slavery and free trade its chief
> corner stones. This was not an attempt to mix oil and water. Free
> trade was not adopted because of any love of freedom. The
> Confederates knew very well that it would help them to perpetuate
> slavery and it did secure for them a large measure of British sympathy
> and aid.
>
> Albert Clarke.[1]

> Into your confounded quarrel
> Let myself be dragged I'll not
> By you, fighting for a Morrill Tariff; or your slavery lot.
>
> "Mr. Bull to His American Bullies," *Punch*, reprinted in
> *Leeds Mercury*, October 1, 1863.

> If it be not in slavery, where lies the partition of the interests that has led
> at last to actual separation of the Southern from the Northern States? . . . .
> The last grievance of the South was the Morrill tariff . . . it has severed the
> last threads which bound the North and South together.
>
> Charles Dickens, 1861.[2]

The Morrill Tariff, passed in early March 1861, was a key domestic
component of the new Republican platform, which also called for internal
improvements, a Pacific railroad, and a homestead law.[3] Listian

---

[1] Albert Clarke, "Free Trade Is Not Free," in *A Tariff Symposium* (Boston, MA Home Market Club, 1896), 9.

[2] "The Morrill Tariff," *All the Year Round*, December 28, 1861, 328–330.

[3] Frank W. Taussig, *The Tariff History of the United States* (New York and London, 1931 [1892]), 158–160. On Justin Morrill and the Morrill Tariff, see especially Phillip W. Magness, "Morrill and the Missing Industries: Strategic Lobbying Behavior and the Tariff, 1858–1861," *Journal of the Early Republic* 29 (Summer 2009): 287–329; Jane Flaherty, "Incidental Protection: An Examination of the Morrill Tariff," *Essays in Economic and Business History* 19 (2001): 103–118; Thomas M. Pitkin, "Western Republicans and the Tariff in 1860," *Mississippi Valley Historical Review* 27 (December 1940): 401–420; Edward Stanwood, *American Tariff Controversies in the Nineteenth Century*, 2 vols. (New York: Houghton Mifflin, 1903); Heather Cox Richardson, *The Greatest Nation of the Earth: Republican Economic Policies During the Civil War* (Cambridge, MA: Harvard University Press, 1997), 104–110, 113–114, 116; and William Belmont Parker, *The Life and Public Services of Justin Smith Morrill* (Boston, MA: Houghton Mifflin, 1924).

nationalist Henry C. Carey had lobbied especially hard for the protectionist legislation, which contrasted sharply with the South's Jeffersonian free-trade advocacy. The 1861 tariff would usher in nearly a century of American protectionism. Anglo-American Cobdenites would correspondingly condemn the country's economic nationalist turn, heralding a decades-long Listian–Cobdenite battle over American economic development and foreign market integration.

But passage of the Morrill Tariff also created a more immediate problem for Anglo-American relations during the first years of the Civil War. Southern congressmen had opposed the protectionist legislation, which explains why it passed so easily after several southern states seceded in December 1860 and the first months of 1861. However, this coincidence of timing fed a mistaken inversion of causation among the British public, with many initially speculating that it was an underlying cause of secession, or at least that it impeded any chance of reunion. As Richard Cobden pointed out in December 1861, the new tariff also proved antithetical to a subject about which the British "are unanimous and fanatical." That subject was free trade. The Morrill Tariff significantly raised rates on imports, with duties on specific items such as pig iron and wool raised to nearly 50 percent: levels of protection that severely hit at Britain's exports to its largest single market, the United States.[4] The seceding southern states, providing Free Trade England with nearly 80 percent of its raw cotton imports, instead offered the promise of free trade. The tariff thus played an integral role in confounding British opinion about the causes of southern secession, and in enhancing the possibility of British recognition of the Confederacy.[5]

---

[4] Cobden to Charles Sumner, December 5, 1861, microfilm reel 23, Charles Sumner Papers, Houghton Library, Harvard University, Cambridge, MA; Taussig, *Tariff History of the United States*, 158–159; Magness, "Morrill and Missing Industries," 327–328; Flaherty, "Incidental Protection"; Duncan A. Campbell, *English Public Opinion and the American Civil War* (Campbell, CA: Boydell & Brewer, 2003), 41. Between 1830 and 1860, a quarter of British exports went to the United States. David P. Crook, *The North, the South, and the Powers, 1861–1865* (New York: Wiley, 1974), 4–9.

[5] Bernard Schmidt, "The Influence of Wheat and Cotton in Anglo-American Relations during the Civil War," *Iowa Journal of History and Politics* 16 (1918): 401–439; Eli Ginzberg, "The Economics of British Neutrality during the American Civil War," *Agricultural History* 10 (October 1936): 147–156; Robert H. Jones, "Long Live the King?" *Agricultural History* 37 (July 1963): 166–169; William G. Carleton, "Tariffs and the Rise of Sectionalism," *Current History* 42 (June 1962): 333–338; Richard H. Luthin, "Abraham Lincoln and the Tariff," *American Historical Review* 49 (July 1944): 614; John Majewski, *Modernizing a Slave Economy: The Economic Vision of the Confederate Nation* (Chapel Hill: University of North Carolina Press, 2009), 108–139; Robert A. McGuire and T. Norman van Cott, "The Confederate Constitution, Tariffs, and the Laffer Relationship," *Economic Inquiry* 40 (July 2002): 428–438.

When the Union did not immediately declare itself on a crusade for abolition, there were some in Great Britain who initially thought that it was the Morrill Tariff that had sparked secession and war. They either sympathized outright with the South, or at the very least took a neutral stance.[6] Transatlantic abolitionists would afterward maintain that slavery had been the war's primary issue all along, while the Confederacy's transatlantic supporters and various members of the British press at first commonly portrayed the war as one fought between northern proponents of protectionism and southern advocates of free trade. This was a view that contemporary Southerners and their British sympathizers made sure to encourage, and one that historians have since neglected.[7]

Some of the most persuasive studies of Civil War foreign relations have offered strong arguments for why Britain maintained its neutral stance throughout the conflict. They emphasize the sizeable diplomatic and financial ties that had developed between England and the North by mid-century, but, in doing so, they have overlooked the transatlantic tariff debate.[8] The tariff may not have endangered British investment in the United States, but it certainly ruffled Britain's commercial feathers and editorial pages. As Martin Crawford has observed, the Morrill Tariff's impact upon British opinion was "greater than most modern historians have been willing to admit."[9] Granted, the tariff would only play a marginal role in affecting the major decisions of Britain's top

---

[6] Douglas A. Lorimer, "The Role of Anti-Slavery Sentiment in English Reactions to the American Civil War," *Historical Journal* 19 (June 1976): 405–420.

[7] Regarding the latter, see Donaldson Jordan and Edwin J. Pratt, *Europe and the American Civil War* (Boston, MA: Houghton Mifflin, 1931); Richard J. M. Blackett, *Divided Hearts: Britain and the American Civil War* (Baton Rouge: Louisiana State University Press, 2001); Joseph M. Hernon, Jr., "British Sympathies in the American Civil War: A Reconsideration," *Journal of Southern History* 33 (August 1967): 356–367; James Morton Callahan, *The Diplomatic History of the Southern Confederacy* (Baltimore: The Johns Hopkins Press, 1901), 277; Brian Jenkins, *Britain & the War for the Union*, 2 vols. (Montreal: McGill-Queen's University Press, 1974–1989), I, 81; Howard Jones, *Blue and Gray Diplomacy: A History of Union and Confederate Foreign Relations* (Chapel Hill: University of North Carolina Press, 2010), 18; Crook, *The North, the South, and the Powers, 1861–1865*, 21–22. For a notable exception, see Campbell, *English Public Opinion*, 41–48.

[8] Phillip E. Myers, *Caution & Cooperation: The American Civil War in British-American Relations* (Kent, OH: Kent University Press, 2008); Jay Sexton, *Debtor Diplomacy: Finance and American Foreign Relations in the Civil War Era, 1837–1873* (Oxford: Oxford University Press, 2005).

[9] Martin Crawford, *The Anglo-American Crisis of the Mid-Nineteenth Century: The Times and America, 1850–1862* (Athens: University of Georgia Press), 93. Previous studies have precipitously concluded that the Morrill Tariff had no effect on forming editorial opinion, or that few British journals "actually laid part of the blame for secession on the tariff." See, respectively, Thomas J. Keiser, "The English Press and the American Civil War" (PhD diss., University of Reading, 1971), 101; Campbell, *English Public Opinion*, 44–45.

policymakers. If, however, the Confederacy's "free-trade diplomacy" is expanded to include not only official state-to-state interactions, but also the efforts of non-state southern sympathizers and pro-Confederate propagandists to influence English public opinion, then the tariff debate takes on new significance.[10]

Following the Morrill Tariff's passage, the Confederacy and its transatlantic supporters would dangle the carrot of free trade before Europe while simultaneously brandishing King Cotton's stick. While southern free-trade diplomacy did not ultimately help gain British recognition any more than did that of King Cotton, the South's *ex post facto* free-trade justification for secession would be picked up by numerous British news outlets and draw an impressive amount of initial sympathy in England, which was riding high on its newfound free-trade ideology, Cobdenism.[11] This chapter therefore examines the British reaction to the northern tariff by incorporating English, Scottish, and Irish responses.[12] In doing so, it illuminates how British support for the South went beyond an opposition to fratricide, blockades, or democracy; it was also an opposition to northern protectionism.[13] The secession of southern states made the Morrill

---

[10] What attention the tariff issue has received primarily has revolved around Charles and Mary Beard's emphasis on domestic economic motivations for the Civil War's onset. As William Freehling has persuasively argued, however, the tariff question and slavery agitation had largely become "intermeshed" by the earlier crisis of nullification. William W. Freehling, *Prelude to Civil War: The Nullification Controversy in South Carolina, 1816–1836* (New York: Harper & Row, 1966), 255. See, also, Charles A. Beard and Mary Beard, *The Rise of American Civilization*, 2 vols. (New York: Macmillan, 1927), II, 35–38; Richard Hofstadter, "The Tariff Issue on the Eve of the Civil War," *American Historical Review* 44 (October 1938): 50–55; Marc Egnal, "The Beards Were Right: Parties in the North, 1840–1860," *Civil War History* 47 (March 2001): 30–56; Jane Flaherty, "'The Exhausted Condition of the Treasury,' on the Eve of the Civil War," *Civil War History* 55 (June 2009): 248–252; Mark Thornton and Robert B. Ekelund, *Tariffs, Blockades, and Inflation: The Economics of the Civil War* (Wilmington, DE: SR Books, 2004), 2, 22–26.

[11] Foner, *British Labor*, 3–4; Campbell, *English Public Opinion*, 41. See, also, Mary Ellison, *Support for Secession: Lancashire and the American Civil War* (Chicago, IL: University of Chicago Press, 1972); and Wright and Wright, "English Opinion on Secession," 151–153. The tariff issue was occasionally raised in the secessionist conventions of South Carolina, Georgia, and Virginia, but was utterly overwhelmed by speeches concerning slavery.

[12] A wide sampling of British news outlets has been drawn upon to avoid potential pitfalls when discussing British "opinion." See, also, D. G. Wright and D. E. Wright, "English Opinion on Secession: A Note," *Journal of American Studies* 5 (August 1971): 151–154; Lorraine Peters, "The Impact of the American Civil War on the Local Communities of Southern Scotland," *Civil War History* 49 (June 2003): 133–152.

[13] Philip S. Foner, *British Labor and the American Civil War* (New York: Holmes & Meier, 1981), 3; Ephraim D. Adams, *Great Britain and the American Civil War*, 2 vols. (New York: Longmans, Green, and Co., 1925); Jordan and Pratt, *Europe and the American Civil War*; Donald Bellows, "A Study of British Conservative Reaction to the American Civil War," *Journal of Southern History* 51 (November 1985): 505–526.

Tariff's passage possible, an order of events that few in free-trading Great Britain were certain of at the time. For British abolitionists, such uncertainty was compounded by the Union's refusal to tackle southern slavery head-on at the war's outset.[14] Along with the northern blockade of the South, British recognition of southern belligerency in May 1861, the *Trent* Affair in November 1861, and the September 1862 preliminary Emancipation Proclamation, the South's free-trade diplomacy created ambiguity, division, confusion, and even Confederate support across the Atlantic. Not until Anglo-American Cobdenites effectively countered the tariff argument with one of antislavery did British public sentiment demonstrably begin to shift toward the North. Responding with proclamations, editorials, and speeches of their own, transatlantic Cobdenites were able to turn British attention away from the North's antagonistic policies of blockades and protectionism, and toward the Union's fight to destroy the southern system of slavery.

The Morrill Tariff's transatlantic reception

The Morrill Tariff became a campaign issue in 1860. It passed through the House of Representatives on May 10, 1860, on a sectional vote, with nearly all northern representatives in support and nearly all southern representatives in opposition. The bill was then tabled in the Senate until after the 1860 elections by Virginia's Robert Hunter, future Confederate secretary of state and author of the low 1857 tariff. While the bill hung in political limbo, its advocates and adversaries alike sprung into action. Democratic senators sought to postpone a vote on the bill, whereas Republican president-elect Abraham Lincoln – a Whig disciple of the American System who favored "the internal improvement system, and a high protective tariff" – promised a sympathetic Pittsburgh audience that he would make sure that "no subject should engage your representatives more closely than the tariff," so as to nurse the country's infant industries.[15]

---

[14] Richard Huzzey, *Freedom Burning: Anti-Slavery and Empire in Victorian Britain* (Ithaca, NY: Cornell University Press, 2012), chap. 2.

[15] Pitkin, "Western Republicans"; Magness, "Morrill and Missing Industries"; Henry Harrison Simms, *Life of Robert M. T. Hunter: A Study in Sectionalism and Secession* (Richmond, VA: The William Byrd Press, 1935), 108–109; Osborn H. Oldroyd, *The Lincoln Memorial* (New York: G. W. Carleton, 1882), 76; Jesse W. Weik, *Herndon's Lincoln*, 2 vols. (Chicago, IL: Belford-Clarke Co., 1889), I, 102; Luthin, "Lincoln and the Tariff"; Speech of February 15, 1861, *The Collected Works of Abraham Lincoln*, 4 vols. (New Brunswick, NJ: Rutgers University Press, 1953–1955), IV, 213; F. W. Taussig, *Free Trade, the Tariff and Reciprocity* (New York: The MacMillan Company, 1924), 35.

The tariff generated a predictable outcry in much of the South. Its loudest critics, however, conveniently overlooked the fact that, following secession, a number of southern senators had resigned that might otherwise have voted against the bill and thereby stopped its congressional passage. The Morrill Tariff of March 2, 1861, therefore became law in part *as a result* of southern secession.

Democratic President James Buchanan, hailing from the protectionist heartland of Pennsylvania, signed the bill into law with characteristic loyalty to his state. Ad valorem rates were raised from a low 17 percent to an average of 26 percent. The tariff also contained specific protective duties approaching the high level of 50 percent or more on items such as pig iron and cutlery for the express purpose of protecting American infant industries. To southern agrarians and British manufacturers whose livelihoods depended upon foreign trade, as well as Cobdenite idealists, the bill appeared punitive, incendiary, and economically backward.

Even as this Union–British trade crisis unfolded, some northerners began turning an expansive eye toward Canada. The Morrill Tariff only exacerbated Canadian–American tensions. The *New York Herald* loudly called for Canadian annexation, an expansionist refrain that fostered anti-northern sentiment in Britain's North American colony. Southern sympathizers in England and Canada then used the *Herald*'s annexationist calls and northern protectionism to generalize the hostility of northern attitudes toward the British Empire. The *Ottawa Citizen*, for example, thereafter made sure to differentiate between the South's advocacy of "a free trade policy" from the North's "hollow contemptuous sympathy" for "the negro" and an "unbearably arrogant and menacing" conduct of foreign relations.[16]

Northern congressmen only grew more upset at such apparent anti-Union sentiment proliferating in Canada, as well as the growth of Canadian protectionism. Republican protectionists had previously expressed outrage over Canada's breach of the 1854 Canadian–American reciprocity treaty, when Canadian finance ministers heightened tariff rates from 1858 to 1860. While some in the Great Lakes area had benefited from the 1854 reciprocity treaty, and others in the North viewed reciprocity's continuance as a logical step toward the eventual annexation of Canada, the increasingly Anglophobic *New York Herald* again took the lead, demanding an end to Canadian–American reciprocity.[17] Canadian–American protectionism thus compounded Anglo-American tensions.

---

[16] Goldwin Smith, *A Letter to A Whig Member of the Southern Independence Association* (Boston, MA: Ticknor and Fields, 1864), 12; *Ottawa Citizen*, February 15, 1861; February 19, 1861.

[17] This Anglophobic Republican movement against Canadian reciprocity would reach fruition in 1866 with the treaty's official abrogation, which, along with the threat of

Alongside this added anti-northern agitation in a contiguous British North American colony, the Morrill Tariff fast garnered support for southern free trade across the Atlantic. The diplomatic consequences of the bill's passage promptly became clear to the *London Times*, noting in late March 1861 that the South's goal was to gain the goodwill of England "by placing Southern liberality in contrast with the grasping and narrow-minded legislation of the Free States . . . . So far the game is still in favour of the new Confederacy."[18] John Lothrop Motley, an American in England, observed in a letter to his mother that the Morrill Tariff's passage had "done more than any commissioners from the Southern Republic could do to alienate the feelings of the English public toward the United States."[19] As a result, the *New York Times* reported in mid-March 1861 that the British had "entirely misapprehended the controversy," believing instead that slavery did "not constitute the essence of the quarrel; that it has been merely introduced as a blind, or as an instrument of provocation, and that the real point of contention lies in the national Tariff."[20] The tariff argument had found an accepting English audience.

Some northerners warned of the Morrill Tariff's potential transatlantic fallout. As early as February 1861, with the successive secession of six southern states and with the possibility of reunion yet tossed around, Democratic Congressman Daniel Sickles of New York had decried the tariff's approaching passage because it offered "the strongest provocation to England to precipitate recognition of the southern confederacy." The pro-free-trade *New York World* acknowledged as well that the tariff

Northern invasion during the Civil War, acted as a strong, albeit unintended, impetus for Canadian confederation in 1867. Robin W. Winks, *Canada and the United States: The Civil War Years* (Montreal: Harvest House, 1971), 28–29, 343–346, 379.

[18] *London Times*, March 26, 1861. On Canadian opinion, see, also, Fred Landon, "Canadian Opinion of Southern Secession, 1860–61," *Canadian Historical Review* 1 (September 1920): 255–266; Jenkins, *Britain & the War*, I, 60, 61, 65; Winks, *Canada and the United States*; Marc-William Palen, "A Canadian Yankee in King Cotton's Court," *Civil War History* 18 (June 2012): 224–261.

[19] Motley, quoted in Crawford, *Anglo-American Crisis*, 93. On the initial lack of northern support in England, see Edwin de Leon, *Secret History of Confederate Diplomacy Abroad*, ed. by William C. Davis (Lawrence: University Press of Kansas, 2005), 145–146; Lorimer, "Role of Anti-Slavery Sentiment," 405; Peter d'A. Jones, "The History of a Myth: British Workers and the American Civil War," in Ellison, *Support for Secession*, 199–219; Royden Harrison, "British Labour and the Confederacy: A Note on the Southern Sympathies of Some British Working Class Journals and Leaders during the American Civil War," *International Review of Social History* 2 (April 1957): 78–105; Campbell, *Unlikely Allies: Britain, American and the Victorian Origins of the Special Relationship* (London: Hambledon Continuum, 2007), 165, 167–169.

[20] See, also, *New York Times*, March 23, 1861, 2; Bigelow to Hargreaves, September 14, 1861, John Bigelow Papers, NYPL; Charles Francis Adams, Jr., *The Richard Cobden Centennial. Speech of Charles Francis Adams at the Dinner of the Free Trade League at the Hotel Vendome, Boston, on the Evening of June 2, 1904*, 2.

"greatly disaffects England and France ... and presents them a direct inducement to recognize, at the earliest day, the independence of the states which reject both it and the policy on which it rests."[21]

Southerners also speculated about the tariff issue's usefulness in Europe. The editor of the *Charleston Mercury* observed a month before the tariff's passage that offering free trade to Europe trumped King Cotton in providing "the strongest possible inducement for our immediate recognition."[22] Further confounding the British, Confederate President Jefferson Davis waded into the transatlantic tariff debate early on with his mid-February inaugural address, less than a month before the Morrill Tariff was signed into law. He cannily played the South's free-trade trump card that "our true policy is peace and the freest trade which our necessities permit." His speech also notably excluded any direct reference to slavery.[23] Early on, the Confederacy showed awareness of the European ramifications of its free-trade diplomacy.

Davis's address was disseminated in the British press at about the same time as news arrived of the Morrill Tariff's passage, both of which added to the confusion. If Britons were unclear as to why the North was seemingly making any chance of reunion impossible through its protectionist legislation, they also found Davis's inaugural address inscrutable, as was the South's "object" of secession. One contemporary study of English public opinion emphasized editorial consternation regarding the address: "Is it the question of slavery or that of free trade? We have never read a public document so difficult to interpret." The *London Times* similarly asked: "Is the question of Slavery subordinate to that of Free Trade, or is Free Trade the bribe offered to foreign nations to consideration of their pocketing their scruples about Slavery?"[24] The British free-trade apostle Richard Cobden himself, though eventually a strong supporter of the Union, explained England's confusion to his long-time friend, Republican Senator Charles Sumner: "We [the English] observe a mighty quarrel: on one side protectionists, on the other slave-owners. The protectionists say they do not seek to put down slavery. The slave-owners say they want Free Trade. Need you wonder at the confusion in John Bull's poor head?"[25]

---

[21] *Congressional Globe*, 36th Cong. 2nd Sess., Appendix, 1153, 1190; *New York World*, quoted in S. D. Carpenter, *Logic of History* (Madison: S. D. Carpenter, 1864), 147; *New York Times*, February 14, 1861, 4. See, also, *New York Times*, March 26, 1861, 4.

[22] *Charleston Mercury*, February 5, 1861.

[23] *Sheffield & Rotherham Independent*, March 9, 1861, 3.

[24] John William Draper, *History of the American Civil War*, 3 vols. (New York: Harper & Brothers, 1868), II, 510; *London Times*, March 8, 1861, reprinted in *New York Times*, March 26, 1861, 5; Crawford, *Anglo-American Crisis*, 95. See, also, *Once a Week*, March 16, 1861.

[25] Cobden to Sumner, December 5, 1861, reel 23, Sumner Papers; Stephen Meardon, "Richard Cobden's American Quandary: Negotiating Peace, Free Trade, and Anti-

Transatlantic speculation over the connection between southern secession and the passage of the Morrill Tariff had only just begun. London's
Morning Chronicle recognized that the bill was crafted to appeal to
Pennsylvania voters, but that the tariff also "has laid the first foundation
of disunion and secession." This was therefore an inopportune time for
the tariff, as it would only "confirm the alienation of the South from the
Union," and "strengthen" the motivation of the European powers "to
recognize the free-trade Southern Confederacy." Scotland's *Caledonian
Mercury* concurred, noting that the English, French, and Germans "will
have to fraternize with the South," owing to the Morrill Tariff.[26] Within
Great Britain's editorial pages, recognition of the South appeared promising owing to its free-trade diplomacy. The British press was particularly quick to note that the irreconcilable nature of the conflict was not
relegated to ideological debates about slavery; transatlantic commercial
considerations had at first figured heavily.

While civil war itself yet remained uncertain in early 1861, to spectators
across the Atlantic the tariff issue appeared to have made any chance for
peaceful reunion impossible. British newspapers continued to voice their
discontent with the Morrill Tariff, even as they highlighted growing sectional divisions in the United States. "Protection was quite as much a cause
of the disruption of the Union as Slavery," the *London Times* pronounced
on March 12, 1861, ten days after the Morrill Tariff had become law.[27] The
Times also remarked upon how the tariff "has much changed the tone
of public feeling with reference to the Secessionists." London's *Morning
Post* aptly summed up the dilemma: "Slavery, no doubt, is the blight and
plague-spot of the South; but the North has its plague-spot in this prohibitive tariff ... It were well if North and South would say to each other ...
'Brother, brother, we are both wrong.'"[28] Ever the stubborn siblings,
neither would.

Owing in part to the passage of the Morrill Tariff, the idea of English
recognition of the Confederacy had become a source of serious speculation.
The *Sheffield & Rotherham Independent* warned that, as things stood, "our

Slavery," in *Rethinking Nineteenth-Century Liberalism: Richard Cobden Bicentenary Essays*,
ed. by Anthony Howe and Simon Morgan (Aldershot: Ashgate, 2006), 213–216. For
Cobden's criticism of Northern protectionism, see Cobden to Sumner, December 5,
1861, reel 23; December 12, 1861; December 19, 1861; January 23, 1862, reel 24,
Sumner Papers.

[26] *Morning Chronicle* (London), February 12, 1861; February 26, 1861; *Caledonian
Mercury*, February 28, 1861. See, also, Campbell, *English Public Opinion*, 44.

[27] That day's editorial may "legitimately be viewed as the *Times*'s editorial manifesto on the
disunion crisis." Crawford, *Anglo-American Crisis*, 95–96.

[28] *London Times*, March 12, 1861; *Morning Post*, March 13, 1864, 4. See, also, *Bradford
Observer*, March 7, 1861, 4; *London Star*, March 12, 1861; *New York Times*, March 29,
1869, 2.

Figure 2.1 "Before and After the Morrill Tariff." *Harper's*, a pro-Union magazine, portrays the North's outrage over Britain's apparent shift from moral outrage to support for southern slavery owing to the Morrill Tariff's passage. [Left panel] "Before the Morrill Tariff: Mr. Bull (*very indignant*), 'Back, Sir! – stand back, Sir! I shall protect the poor Negro from your bloodthirsty prosecutions!'" [Right panel] "After the Morrill Tariff: Mr. Bull (*very indignant once more*), 'Take that, you Black Rascal! can't you attend to your task, and keep the flies off my Friend from the South? My Dear Sir! the only way to manage with those lazy Niggers is to drive 'em, drive 'em, Sir! with the lash, Sir!'" *Harper's Weekly*, April 20, 1861, 256

government cannot do less than recognize the *de facto* government of the South." The South's constitution, the newspaper further noted, prohibited industrial protectionism and instead reduced duties enough to compensate Europe "for the loss sustained by the Morrill tariff bill," whereas all the North had offered in return were prohibitive trade restrictions.[29] British conservatives and the *Lancaster Gazette* even began speculating that the North was in reality going to war for the sake of protectionism and empire.[30] It appeared to critics on both sides of the Atlantic that the North

[29] *Sheffield & Rotherham Independent*, March 30, 1861, 6; *Morning Chronicle*, April 6, 1861; *Morning Post*, April 9, 1861. See, also, *Glasgow Herald* (Scotland), April 6, 1861; *Daily News*, March 18, 1861. The *New York Herald* frequently castigated the Morrill Tariff. See *New York Herald*, March16; March19; April 3, 1861. See, also, "Constitution for the Provisional Government," Article I, in James D. Richardson, ed., *A Compilation of the Messages and Papers of the Confederacy Including the Diplomatic Correspondence 1861–1865*, 2 vols. (Nashville, TN: United States Publishing Company, 1905), II, 3–8.
[30] Bellows, "British Conservative Reaction," 525; Ellison, *Support for Secession*, 53.

had to change tactics if it were to undercut possible European recognition of the Confederacy. The South, hoisting the banner of "Free Trade" for its foreign observers, appeared to be starting strong at the war's outset in garnering British sympathy – and perhaps even recognition.

The Confederacy's free-trade diplomacy

The Confederacy's free-trade diplomacy took shape not only within British editorial pages, but also within more formal diplomatic circles. In the first week of May 1861, the Confederate commissioners to England – Mann, Rost, and Yancey – gained an interview with Lord John Russell, the British foreign secretary, through the efforts of William Gregory, a sympathetic member of the House of Commons. They stated to Russell that the Morrill Tariff was the principal cause of secession, and that the South only desired free trade with the world. They repeated this sentiment to Russell in writing. The commissioners were acting under the direct orders of Robert Toombs, then Confederate secretary of state. Toombs had instructed the commissioners in March to meet with Russell as quickly as possible, and urged them to emphasize that secession was necessary owing to the North having forced the South to "pay bounties to northern manu-facturers in the shape of high protective duties on foreign imports" since 1828. The Morrill Tariff of 1861 "strikingly illustrated" this unjust policy, Toombs continued. He believed that this line of argument would show the wisdom of the Confederacy, "especially in the estimation of those countries whose commercial interests, like those of Great Britain, are diametrically opposed to protective tariffs." He even quoted the maxim of Richard Cobden: The Confederate states would "buy where you can buy cheapest, and sell where you can sell dearest." As a result, Toombs expected Britain "will speedily acknowledge our independence."[31] Thus, by March 1861 the Confederate State Department had enunciated through official chan-nels its free-trade diplomacy toward Europe. Toombs and his successors would soon extend this policy to Spain, Cuba, and Russia, as well as to the British, Danish, and Spanish West Indies.[32]

[31] Callahan, *Diplomatic History of the Southern Confederacy*, 111; Robert Toombs to William L. Yancey, Pierre A. Rost, and A. Dudley Mann, March 16, 1861, in Richardson, ed., *Messages and Papers of the Confederacy*, II, 4–5, 7; Yancey, Rost, and Mann to Russell, August 14, 1861, ibid., 67. See, also, Toombs to Yancey, Rost, and Mann, April 24, 1861, ibid., 17.
[32] See Toombs to Charles J. Helm, July 22, 1861, Richardson, ed. *Compilation of Messages*, 46–48; Hunter to Yancey, Rost, and Mann, August 24, 1861, ibid., 76. Confederate Secretary of State Judah P. Benjamin also requested Lucius Q. C. Lamar, commissioner to Russia, to promise unrestricted commercial relations. See Benjamin to Lamar, November 19, 1862, ibid., 365–366.

The South's governmental and nongovernmental free-trade diplomacy was paying propagandistic dividends, compounded by the Union government's initial unwillingness to declare slavery the primary issue of secession and reunion. Confederate diplomat Edwin de Leon wrote a letter to the editors of the *London Times* in late May that slavery was "a mere pretext" for secession, as shown by continued northern defenses of the institution through its guarantee of slavery where it existed and through its enforcement of the fugitive slave law. The *Preston Guardian* even asserted that when northerners cried "no slavery," they really meant "protection."[33] William H. Gregory called for British recognition in the House of Commons. He argued that it would bring an end to the slave trade; keep the states from fighting a "fratricidal, needless war"; and provide retaliation against the North's "selfish, short-sighted, retrograde" protectionist policy. The Union minister to England, Charles Francis Adams, Sr., after meeting with Britain's foreign secretary, Lord John Russell, noted that the Morrill Tariff and the conflict's seeming nonissue of slavery yet left southern recognition on the table.[34]

All the while, Britain's maintenance of neutrality appeared to benefit the South and antagonize the North. The 1862 construction in British ports of Confederate war vessels like the *Alabama* further outraged the Union, many of whom viewed their construction as a covert act of war by the British against the North. The issue would remain a source of Anglophobic ire for years to come. Alongside northern protectionism, British neutrality heightened Anglo-Union animosity.

British pro-South sympathizers made sure that the tariff argument remained prominent for many months to come. James Spence, Liverpool's pro-Confederate merchant and *London Times* writer, spent but one chapter on slavery in his influential publication *The American Union* (1861). He spent the other seven on the Morrill Tariff, the right to secession, and why he thought a future reunion was culturally and philosophically impossible. After a close reading of Spence in late 1861, Charles Dickens himself became decidedly pro-South, and argued in the pages of *All the Year Round* that the Morrill Tariff had "severed the last threads which bound the North and South together." John Bright wrote to Charles Sumner that the subject of the tariff was of such "great importance" that little "would more restore sympathy between England

---

[33] *London Times*, May 25, 1861, 12; *Preston Guardian*, May 29, 1861. See, also, *Belfast News-Letter*, June 14, 1861; *Sheffield & Rotherham Independent*, June 8, 1861, 8.

[34] *London Times*, June 12, 1861, 12; *New York Times*, June 24, 1861, 5; Howard Jones, *Union in Peril: The Crisis over British Intervention in the Civil War* (Chapel Hill: University of North Carolina Press), 1993, 34; Callahan, *Diplomatic History of the Southern Confederacy*, 116.

and the States than the repeal of the present monstrous and absurd Tariff," as it gave "all the speakers and writers for the South an extraordinary advantage in this country."[35]

Northern attempts to acquire loans from England further illustrated the tariff's unfavorable transatlantic traction. Following the southern rout of northern troops at Bull Run in July 1861, New York banker August Belmont sought a Union loan from the British. As leverage, he reminded Prime Minister Palmerston of the South's continued maintenance of slavery, to which Palmerston retorted: "We do not like slavery, but we want cotton and we dislike very much your Morrill tariff."[36]

Such continued British support for the Confederacy's free-trade diplomacy is all the more remarkable considering that the North controlled much of the outgoing information to Europe regarding the war, and that the Confederacy's official European propagandistic and diplomatic activities were negligible until the end of 1861. Whatever favorable coverage they had received thus far was owed predominantly to Britain's non-governmental southern sympathizers.

Nevertheless, northern control of transatlantic information flows began taking its toll on pro-Confederate sympathies in Europe. Such imbalanced war coverage first inspired Toombs's Confederate State Department successor, R. M. T. Hunter and, afterward, Hunter's 1862 replacement, Judah P. Benjamin, to send Henry Hotze to England in order to ghost-write editorials in leading London newspapers, emphasizing northern tyranny, scientific racialism, and the benefits offered to Great Britain by the Confederacy's free-trade policies.

Upon his arrival, Hotze was shocked to find a near lack of any professional Confederate propaganda machine within the British press. Hotze's own first successes did not come about until February 1862, with the *Morning Post* editorial page opening itself as a promising outlet for encouraging British recognition of the Confederacy. Playing on British anti-Chinese sentiment brought on by the Opium Wars (1839–1842, 1856–1860), he asked if Britain could sit back and watch the world's cotton and tobacco fields walled in by "legislation like the Morrill tariff," which resembled "the favorite legislation of the Chinese empire." A united America and a

---

[35] James Spence, *The American Union* (London: Richard Bentley, 1862); De Leon, *Secret History*, 149; "The Morrill Tariff," *All the Year Round*, December 28, 1861, 330; John O. Waller, "Charles Dickens and the American Civil War," *Studies in Philology* 57 (July 1960): 535–548; Bright to Sumner, November 29, 1861, reel 23, Sumner Papers. See, also, *Dundee Courier*, July 3, 1861.

[36] Belmont to Seward, July 30, 1861, reel 64, William H. Seward Papers, LOC; Irving Katz, *August Belmont: A Political Biography* (New York: Columbia University Press, 1968), 101–103; Jones, *Blue and Gray Diplomacy*, 62; Sexton, *Debtor Diplomacy*, 92; Campbell, *English Public Opinion*, 41–43.

dependent South, he warned, would offer a similarly autarkic empire. In subsequent weeks, he also began contributing to the *London Times*, the *Standard*, the *Herald*, and the *Money Market Review*. He next created his own paper, the *Index*, to better disseminate Confederate propaganda in Britain and France, and its printing would continue until August 1865.[37]

The South's free-trade diplomacy received more bolstering following the Union seizure of the Confederacy's special commissioners bound for Europe upon the *Trent* in early November 1861. It provoked British outrage, and the South took advantage. Amidst the affair, Lord Lyons, British minister in Washington, expressed to Lord John Russell his hope that the Morrill Tariff might be replaced by a tariff for revenue only.[38] Furthermore, Confederate Secretary of State Hunter's order to the recently released commissioner to Britain, James Mason, was to continue on to London and express the South's dedication to low import duties and its "great interest" in producing and exporting staples, thereby binding "them to the policy of free trade." Playing upon Britain's Cobdenite heartstrings, he was also to stress that the Confederacy's "free trade" was essential to the progress of humankind and "to preserve peace."[39] John Slidell, Confederate special commissioner to France, similarly reported to the French foreign minister on February 7, 1862, that upon recognition the Confederate States would commit to a policy of free trade and peace.[40]

Slidell's report illustrated how the advance of southern free-trade diplomacy in Britain had now made its way across the English Channel to France. Thurlow Weed, the Union's unofficial emissary to France, reported to Secretary of State William Seward that the French emperor

---

[37] Lonnie A. Burnett, ed., *Henry Hotze, Confederate Propagandist: Selected Writings on Revolution, Recognition, and Race* (Tuscaloosa: University of Alabama Press, 2008), 15–21; Charles C. Cullop, *Confederate Propaganda in Europe 1861–1865* (Coral Gables, FL: University of Miami Press, 1969), 28–29, 32–35, 36, 40, 63–64; *Morning Post*, March 24, 1862, in Burnett, *Hotze*, 127.

[38] Lyons to Russell, July 8, 1861, F.O. 5/767–327, ff. 106–107, in James J. Barnes and Patience P. Barnes, *The American Civil War through British Eyes, Dispatches from British Diplomats, Volume 1: November 1860–April 1862* (Kent, OH: The Kent State University Press, 2003), 138–141; Lyons to Russell, November 22, 1861, PRO 30/22/35, ff. 321–323, in James J. Barnes and Patience P. Barnes, *Private and Confidential: Letters from British Ministers in Washington to the Foreign Secretaries in London, 1844–1867* (Selinsgrove, PA: Sushquehanna University Press, 1993), 267–268; Gordon H. Warren, *Fountain of Discontent: The Trent Affair and Freedom of the Seas* (Boston, MA: Northeastern University Press, 1981).

[39] Richardson, ed., *Compilation of the Messages and Papers of the Confederacy*, II, 89–90.

[40] "Inclosure," Slidell to Benjamin, July 21, 1862, in Richardson, ed., *Compilation of the Messages and Papers of the Confederacy*, II, 279, 282. On negative French reaction to the tariff, see *New York Times*, March 18, 1861, 1; George M. Blackburn, *French Newspaper Opinion on the American Civil War* (Westport, CT: Greenwood Press, 1997), 64, 74; Serge Gavronsky, *The French Liberal Opposition and the American Civil War* (New York: Humanities Press, 1968), 81.

was hinting at breaking the Union blockade or even recognizing the
Confederacy owing to the detrimental economic problems striking
France, continued northern military failures, and the unpopularity
of the Morrill Tariff. Just weeks after Weed's message, William
S. Lindsay, a radical member of English Parliament and a wealthy
British ship-owner, hurt by the North's tariff and its southern blockade,
traveled to Paris in order to urge Napoleon III to spur action on the
matter. Lindsay emphasized Confederate propagandistic talking points
to the French emperor: The North had gone to war, not for emancipation,
but for the Morrill Tariff and southern subjugation. And the emperor
expressed agreement with Lindsay's assessment.[41]

The transatlantic antislavery counterattack

Cobdenites began to counter the pernicious tariff argument with one of
antislavery. In December 1861, John Bright turned the conversation to
the Morrill Tariff when asked to give his views of the *Trent* Affair in
Rochdale, England. In emphasizing that the Civil War was at heart over
the issue of slavery, he noted how "there is another cause which is sometimes in England assigned for this great misfortune ... the protective
theories in operation in the Union, and the maintenance of a high tariff."
Yet this tariff argument used "by ignorant Englishmen" did not exist in
America itself, he retorted. Nor had the tariff question arisen during the
attempts at compromise in December of the previous year. "It is a question of slavery" and nothing else, he reiterated to his English audience.[42]

Bright's counterattack alongside continued Union control of transatlantic information flows spurred Judah P. Benjamin to action when he
took over the Confederate State Department in the spring of 1862. He
wrote to Mason that, owing to the North's "system of deception so
thoroughly organized as that now established by them abroad," it was
not wise to ignore public opinion. Benjamin supplied Mason, Hotze, and
the Confederate minister to France, John Slidell, with the services of
Edwin de Leon along with $25,000 to be used to enlighten public opinion
"through the press" in Great Britain and France.[43] Mason thereafter put

---

[41] Weed to Seward, Paris, January 20, 1862, reel 68, Seward Papers; Case and Spencer,
United States and France, 252; Slidell to Benjamin, Memorandum of dispatch No. 5,
April 14, 1862, box 18, Bigelow Papers; Charles M. Hubbard, *The Burden of Confederate
Diplomacy* (Knoxville: University of Tennessee Press, 1998), 80–85.

[42] John Bright, *Speeches on Questions of Public Policy*, 2 vols. (London: Macmillan and Co.,
1868), I, 174–176. See, also, John W. Hinton, *Free Trade and Southern Rebellion*
(Milwaukee, WI: Self-published, 1883), 3.

[43] Benjamin to Mason, April 12, 1862, *Public Life of Mason*, 292–293. See, also, Paul
Pecquet du Bellet, *The Diplomacy of the Confederate Cabinet of Richmond and its Agents*

de Leon in contact with his Parisian connections as well as with Spence, "the most efficient and able advocate here [England], through the press, of Southern interests," and who soon thereafter also became the principal cotton agent of the Confederacy. Owing to de Leon's work, dozens of newspapers in France correspondingly printed articles amicable to the South, especially Paris's *Patrie*, which became the French version of Hotze's *Index*.[44]

In Parliament, southern sympathizers like William Lindsay and William Gregory continued to call for recognition of the free-trading Confederacy in order to end the violence. Lindsay called for peaceful separation, and claimed that the war had been caused by unjust and injurious northern protectionist taxation upon the South, culminating in the Morrill Tariff. Gregory called for southern recognition and declared: "By the new tariff the rulers of the United States have virtually proclaimed that the great American Continent is to be closed to the products of Europe." When another member of Parliament eloquently responded as to why he believed "that slavery was the real cause of the issue," he was forced to speak over shouts of "No, no!" and "The tariff!"[45]

Such Confederate editorial and parliamentary efforts seemed to have paid off with propagandistic dividends, as recognized by American Cobdenites Charles Sumner and John Bigelow, close friends of Richard Cobden and John Bright. In October 1862, for instance, Sumner expressed his frustration to John Bright at the general lack of northern support in England.[46] Transatlantic Cobdenites were fast realizing they would have to go on the offensive to subvert southern free-trade diplomacy.

Although no fans of the Morrill Tariff, Anglo-American Cobdenites like John Bright were nevertheless among the most vocal in defending the North's position in England. Bright continued to give speeches

---

Abroad, ed. by Wm. Stanley Hoole (Tuscaloosa: University of Alabama Press, 1963), 38, 41, 66.

[44] Dispatch 14, July 31, 1862; Benjamin to Mason, October 28, 1862; Mason to Benjamin, December 10, 1862; Benjamin to Mason, January 15, 1863, in Virginia Mason, *The Public Life of and Diplomatic Correspondence of James M. Mason, with Some Personal History* (Roanoke, VA: Stone Printing and Manufacturing Co., 1903), 314, 338–339, 355–356, 350–351; De Leon, *Secret History*, xvii.

[45] *Parliamentary Debates*, July 18, 1862, Vol. 168, 512–517, 553–554, 534–538, 541. On Confederate supporters in London, see John D. Bennett, *The London Confederates: The Officials, Clergy, Businessmen and Journalists Who Backed the America South During the Civil War* (Jefferson, NC: McFarland & Company, Inc., 2008).

[46] Richardson, *Greatest Nation on Earth*, 114; David Donald, *Charles Sumner and the Coming of the Civil War* (New York: Alfred A. Knopf, 1960), 45–69, 78–81; Edward L. Pierce, ed., *Memoir and Letters of Charles Sumner*, 4 vols. (Boston, MA: Roberts Brothers, 1893), IV, 48–49; Bigelow to Bright, February 16, 1863, Add. 43390, Vol. VIII, Bright Papers.

undermining the prominent tariff argument. Cassius M. Clay, the Union's Russian minister, having just read Bright's recent Rochdale speech, complimented him for showing "so forcibly" that "the tariff had nothing to do with our revolt." Bright's radical and polarizing pro-Union arguments had some influence in eventually turning British opinion.[47] His efforts were bolstered when US Cobdenite abolitionist William Lloyd Garrison started working closely with his British friend George Thompson in the spring of 1862 to help shift English public sympathy away from the South.[48]

But it was J. S. Mill who would offer the best refutation of the tariff thesis in England. By 1862, the tariff argument had gained enough public traction to earn Mill's attention, and he proved quite effective at voicing his opinion concerning slavery's centrality to the conflict. He sought to refute "a theory in England, believed by some, half believed by many more ... that ... the question is not one of slavery at all." Assuming this to be true, he asked, then what is the South fighting for? "Their apologists in England say that it is about tariffs." Yet the Southerners "say nothing of the kind. They tell the world ... that the object of the fight was slavery." Mill noted how "slavery alone was thought of, alone talked of ... the South separated on slavery, and proclaimed slavery as the one cause of separation." He also predicted that the Civil War would soon placate the abolitionists on both sides of the Atlantic; as the war progressed, "the contest would become distinctly an anti-slavery one."[49]

Mill's argument was effective. It was echoed in J. E. Cairnes's publication, *The Slave Power* (1862). Cairnes was "at some pains" to explain that the central issue of the American Civil War was "not one of tariffs," a view which had "pertinaciously" been "put forward by writers in the interest of the South."[50] London's *Daily News* followed Mill's counterattack with an anti-tariff argument of its own, observing that, as to the question of why

[47] Clay to Bright, December 13, 1861, Add. 43390, Vol. VIII, Bright Papers; Stanford P. Gwin, "Slavery and English Polarity: The Persuasive Campaign of John Bright against English Recognition of the Confederate States of America," *Southern Speech Communication Journal* 49 (Summer 1984): 406–419; Roman J. Zorn, "John Bright and the British Attitude to the American Civil War," *Mid America* 38 (July 1956): 131–145; Hugh Dubrulle, "'We are Threatened with... Anarchy and Ruin': Fear of Americanization and the Emergence of an Anglo-Saxon Confederacy in England during the American Civil War," *Albion* 33 (Winter 2001): 583–613; Campbell, *Unlikely Allies*, 99–101, 166.

[48] Henry Mayer, *All on Fire: William Lloyd Garrison and the Abolition of Slavery* (New York: St. Martin's Press, 1998), 535–537; In the fall of 1861, London-based Karl Marx also began arguing against the tariff argument that had become so prevalent in England. See "The North American Civil War," *Die Presse* (Vienna), October 20, 1861.

[49] *Daily News*, January 31, 1862; John Stuart Mill, "The Contest in America," *Fraser's Magazine* (February 1862), 12–13.

[50] J. E. Cairnes, *The Slave Power* (London: Macmillan and Co., 1863 [1862]), viii–ix, 2–14.

the South seceded, "the partisans of secession here, being crafty in their generation, are ready with an answer calculated to find its way to the English heart. They at once reply, 'A protectionist policy, a hostile tariff,'" even though "the Morrill tariff had virtually" nothing to do with secession. "'The eternal nigger' stands in bold relief in the front of this horrible offending," the *Daily News* concluded, and "there is no hustling him out of the way, he crops up everywhere. Tariffs only hide him for a moment."[51]

The antislavery counteroffensive would gain further transatlantic attention following Lincoln's preliminary Emancipation Proclamation of September 22, 1862. He did so in part hoping to garner moral support from those in Britain who still thought there was little difference between the governments of the North and South regarding American slavery. It soon helped in turning the transatlantic debate from tariffs to slavery. The tariff argument steadily lost editorial and public support, and Mill's abolitionist prophecy began to bear fruit by 1863, owing to numerous nongovernmental northern propagandistic efforts in England; the Union victory at Antietam in September 1862; and a growing acceptance of the sincerity of Lincoln's proclamation.[52]

Strong Anglo-Union financial investments complemented the proclamation's long-term effects upon Great Britain. Jay Sexton has drawn attention to the Civil War era's increased Anglo-American financial ties and the ensuing American "debtor diplomacy." In similar fashion, and on the heels of Lincoln's September proclamation, the *Charleston Mercury* petulantly reported that "Northern bonds and stocks, held in England, may be regarded as so numerous and important as to neutralize the temptations of free trade with the Confederate states."[53] Pro-Confederate tariff arguments were noticeably beginning to lose out, not only to concerted transatlantic antislavery efforts that enunciated slavery's centrality, but also to Anglo-Union investment.

The antislavery argument gained more transatlantic traction as Cobdenites redoubled their efforts. Oxford's Regius Professor Goldwin Smith became an active supporter of the North as a member of the Manchester Union and Emancipation Society. He correspondingly took

[51] *Daily News*, February 6, 1862.
[52] Kinley J. Brauer, "The Slavery Problem in the Diplomacy of the American Civil War," *Pacific Historical Review* 41 (August 1977): 442; Robert Douthat Meade, *Judah P. Benjamin: Confederate Statesman* (New York: Oxford University Press, 1943), 265; Frank Merli and Theodore A. Wilson, "The British Cabinet and the Confederacy," *Maryland Historical Magazine* 65 (Fall 1970): 239–262; Amos Khasigian, "Economic Factors and British Neutrality, 1861–1865," *Historian* 25 (August 1963), 453; Wright and Wright, "English Opinion on Secession," 153.
[53] *Charleston Mercury*, December 3, 1862.

on the various tariff-related arguments of southern sympathizers in Britain.[54] Richard Cobden now also gave his wholehearted endorsement to the northern cause, overcoming his earlier misapprehensions about the North's tariff and blockade. He wrote to Sumner in February 1863 that the Emancipation Proclamation had aroused "our old anti-slavery feeling ... and it has been gathering strength ever since." The proclamation also led to meetings, the result of which "closed the mouths of those who have been advocating the side of the South." Bright seconded Cobden's observation, writing to his American friend Cyrus Field: "Opinion here has changed greatly. In almost every town great meetings are being held to pass resolutions in favor of the North, and the advocates of the South are pretty much put down."[55] George Thompson, founder of the Garrison-inspired London Emancipation Committee, and British Cobdenite Thomas Bayley Potter, founder of the Manchester Union and Emancipation Society, also started seeing noticeable success by December 1862. Frederick Douglass's African American newspaper observed the change in England; thanks to the efforts of men like Bright, Thompson, and Cobden, the Confederacy could no longer hide their reason for rebellion behind phrases like "independence," "self-government," or "free trade." In doing so, "the sheep's clothing is removed and the devouring wolf appears."[56]

Pro-South advocates hoped to combat this mounting abolitionist counterattack through mobilization of their own, but with little success. In desperation, the Manchester Southern Club and Southern Independence Associations in Lancashire and London sought to emphasize instead that the Confederacy would never reopen the slave trade and would ultimately emancipate its slaves. Failed attempts were also made by John Roebuck in Parliament to recognize the South, arguing that the North was hypocritical on the slavery issue and "the South offers to us perfect free trade."[57] By 1863, such pro-Confederate arguments were becoming overwhelmed by northern antislavery propaganda, even as African American and other pro-North advocates gained greater success

---

[54] Worthington Chauncy Ford, "Goldwin Smith in 1864," *Proceedings of the Massachusetts Historical Society* 44 (October 1910): 3–13; Smith, *Letter to A Whig Member of the Southern Independence Association*, esp. 47–48; Goldwin Smith, letter of October 10, 1863, in *Speech of Mr. W. E. Forster, M. P., on the Slaveholders' Rebellion; and Professor Goldwin Smith's Letter on the Morality of the Emancipation Proclamation* (Manchester: Union and Emancipation Society's Depot, 1863).

[55] Adams, *Cobden Centennial*, 2; Cobden to Bright, December 29, 1862, Add. MS 43, 652, Cobden Papers; Cobden to Sumner, February 13, 1863, reel 27, Sumner Papers; Bright to Field, quoted in Samuel Carter III, *Cyrus Field: Man of Two Worlds* (New York: G. P. Putnam and Sons, 1968), 204; Campbell, *Unlikely Allies*, 164–165.

[56] Lorimer, "Role of Anti-Slavery Sentiment," 419; *Douglass' Monthly*, March 1863.

[57] *Parliamentary Debates*, June 30, 1863, vol. 171, 1771–1777.

in their attempts to persuade the British working class to favor the Union.[58]

American abolitionists like Henry Ward Beecher toured England calling for northern support and flipping the tariff argument on its head. In October 1863, Beecher told a Liverpool audience "foaming" with "madness" that the Morrill Tariff had in fact been passed "to pay off the previous Democratic [Buchanan] administration's debt .... It was the South that obliged the North to put the tariff on." Cobdenite Beecher even promised an end to northern protectionism: "There is nothing more certain in the future than that America is bound to join with Great Britain in the worldwide doctrine of free trade." In March 1864, radical pro-North Chartist Ernest Jones gave a popular speech in Bright's hometown of Rochdale, wherein he noted how "some gentlemen here tell you that the rebellion is for free trade – that it was a revolt against the Morrill tariff." Why then had the Crittenden Compromise, proffered unsuccessfully in December 1860, not contained "one word about free trade" or the Morrill Tariff? "It is slavery in the beginning, slavery to the end," Jones concluded.[59]

Under the growing onslaught of the slavery argument, coupled with Beecher's own tantalizing promises of future free trade with the Union, the South's own free-trade argument correspondingly lost ground. The *Leeds Mercury* noted this trend. In early 1864, it recalled "that during the first year of the war slavery was entirely ignored as a cause .... and the 'Morrill Tariff' was held to be the key to the whole affair." Now "when the British public ... casts its eyes northwards, it sees ... that slavery has a great deal to do with the object of the war, whatever it had to do with the cause of the war. Nominally the war is a war against rebellion: practically it is a war against slavery." Similar arguments were appearing in ever greater numbers in British publications.[60]

In 1865, Goldwin Smith, hoping to stem the rising tide of Anglophobia in the United States, attempted to explain initial British acceptance of the tariff argument to a Boston audience. Had the North stated plainly from

---

[58] J. M. Blackett, "Pressure from Without: African Americans, British Public Opinion, and Civil War Diplomacy," in *The Union, the Confederacy, and the Atlantic Rim*, ed. by Robert E. May (West Lafayette, IN: Purdue University Press, 1995), 69–100; Foner, *British Labor*, 67–78; Lorimer, "Role of Anti-Slavery Sentiment," 410–416; Campbell, *Unlikely Allies*, 163.

[59] Henry Ward Beecher, *Patriotic Addresses in America and England* (New York: Fords, Howard, & Hulbert, 1887), 640, 529; *Papers Relating to Foreign Affairs, Accompanying the Annual Message of the President to the Second Session Thirty-Eighth Congress*, Part I (Washington, DC: Government Printing Office, 1865), 337.

[60] *Leeds Mercury*, January 25, 1864. See, also, *Preston Guardian*, February 27, 1864; *York Herald*, April 23, 1864.

the beginning that their fight was "against Slavery, the English people would scarcely have given ear to the cunning fiction ... that this great contest was only about a Tariff." Smith had "heard the Tariff Theory called the most successful lie in history." And he conceded that it had indeed been influential in misleading Britain "and ought not to be over-looked. It was propounded with great skill, and it came out just at the right time, before people had formed their opinions, and when they were glad to have a theory presented to their minds."[61]

The tariff argument would prove not only influential, but also tenacious. While nearly muted from 1863 onward, it somehow survived the war itself. As late as January 1866, the *Blackburn Standard* yet touted the Morrill Tariff as "the last straw breaking the camel's back ... which produced the late civil war." Foreshadowing the conspiracy-theory-laden Anglophobic tariff debate of the American Gilded Age, the *Standard* concluded by expressing its hope, now that "the American people have shed blood in the cause of protection," that they might next "become converts to the free-trade principle."[62]

Conclusion

Alongside the diplomacy of King Cotton, historians need to remember as well the South's diplomacy of free trade. Compounded by various other transatlantic crises in the first years of the conflict, the Morrill Tariff heightened anti-northern and pro-southern sentiment across the Atlantic – and with it the prospect of European recognition of the Confederacy. The belief that slavery was the central cause of the conflict would not effectively permeate the British political landscape until well into the war. It took a few months after Lincoln announced his preliminary Emancipation Proclamation in September 1862 before the North and its antislavery allies – particularly J. S. Mill, Richard Cobden, and Anglo-American Cobdenites like John Bright, T. B. Potter, Goldwin Smith, George Thompson, William Lloyd Garrison, and Henry Ward Beecher – effectively began to counteract the tariff argument with their own moralistic propaganda as the war openly turned into a war over slavery.[63] Until then, the Confederate State Department and Confederate sympathizers in Great Britain skillfully used the tariff debate to their advantage.

The Morrill Tariff also created domestic cracks in the brittle Republican coalition by further alienating its minority of northeastern

[61] Goldwin Smith, *England and America* (Manchester: A. Ireland, 1865), 27–28.
[62] *Blackburn Standard*, January 24, 1866.
[63] Charles Francis Adams, Jr. would later single out Cobden's efforts as "the most influential" in snuffing out the European interventionist fuse. Adams, *Cobden Centennial*, 1.

Cobdenite cosmopolitans. These party fissures would only grow as the Republican party continued to promote its postbellum protectionist policies and as it became ensconced in charges of cronyism and corruption. The party's breaking point, however, lay in the decades ahead, an era that notably lacked the antislavery cause or a civil war to maintain Republican cohesion.

These mounting Republican tensions would become exacerbated following the death of Richard Cobden on April 2, 1865, within days of the fall of Richmond. A telegram of Cobden's passing made its speedy way to Egypt, where the driving force behind the transatlantic telegraph, American Cobdenite Cyrus Field, and French developer of the Suez Canal (1869) Ferdinand de Lesseps were feasting with one hundred European gentlemen. Field grimly handed the telegram to de Lesseps, who read it aloud over the din of the dinner's boisterous assemblage. Silence fell. Every man, representing every nation of Europe, immediately got up and left, "feeling as if he had lost a personal friend." In homage, Field thereafter placed a signed portrait of Richard Cobden on one side of his library and a portrait of John Bright on the other.[64]

Five days after Cobden's death, Charles Francis Adams, Sr., Union minister to England, walked through Midhurst in Sussex, in the trail of Cobden's funeral procession. It was a quiet, picturesque setting. Adams stood in the back, while various members of Parliament and close relatives filled the front. Bright himself openly wept, and Adams felt his own eyes swelling. With Cobden's support for democracy, "he becomes the founder of a new school, the influence of which is only just beginning to be felt," Adams presaged.[65] But the new economic nationalist school of Friedrich List would also prove influential in the coming decades. On his deathbed, Cobden reportedly had decried J. S. Mill for having "done more harm by his sentence about the fostering of infant industries, than he had done good by the whole of the rest of his writings."[66] Perhaps if Cobden had lived a decade longer, he would have regretted even more his inability to convert List during their chance London meeting in 1846. Although Cobden could not have guessed it, the global ideological battle between Cobdenite cosmopolitans and

[64] Cobden Club, *Report of the Proceedings at the Dinner of the Cobden Club, July 11, 1874* (London: Cassell Petter & Galpin, 1874), 28–29.

[65] Entry, April 7, 1865, in Charles Francis Adams, Jr., *American Statesmen: Charles Francis Adams* (Boston, MA, and New York: Houghton, Mifflin and Co., 1900), 371–373; Adams to Seward, April 7, 1865, *FRUS: Great Britain* (Washington, DC: Government Printing Office, 1865), 306.

[66] Donald Winch, "Between Feudalists and Communists: Louis Mallet and the Cobden Creed," in *Rethinking Nineteenth-Century Liberalism*, ed. by Howe and Morgan, 253–254.

Listian nationalists was just beginning. The Morrill Tariff had not only influenced the diplomacy of the Civil War, it had established the foundational protectionist policy of the Republican party for decades to come: a policy that would ultimately help drive the Cobdenite wing from the Republican party. Anglophobic charges of a British free-trade conspiracy would duly follow.

3 Mobilizing free trade
The postbellum American free-trade movement, foreign policy, and "conspiracy," 1866–1871

> The Rebellion failed to open up our markets for British goods, and the Free-Trade Cobden Club was immediately formed.
>
> *Tariff League Bulletin* (New York).[1]

> Mr. T. B. Potter presides at the London end of the line, and Mr. David A. Wells manages the Connecticut end. The lever with which these gentlemen will soon attempt to wag the world is to be free-trade. The Cobden Club is to furnish the muscle and Mr. Wells the brain .... In a very short time we shall have Cobden Clubs all over this country.
>
> *North American* (Philadelphia), September 14, 1877.

On Friday, July 27, 1866, 45-year-old Cyrus W. Field took a small boat and pushed off from the magisterial vessel christened the *Great Eastern*, and headed toward the docks of Heart's Content, Newfoundland. Field's boat pulled away as the last feet of gutta-percha cable spilled forth from the *Great Eastern*'s hulking frame. The Atlantic cable was finally laid. Field had spent more than a decade connecting the North American continent by rail and wire. Now, after a multitude of setbacks and failures, he and his British financial backers – among them the British government upon the urging of Field's recently deceased friend Richard Cobden – had indelibly joined Europe with North America. John Bright considered Field a hero, "the Columbus of our time," whose accomplishment marked the beginning of a new era of Anglo-American relations. To speak from the United Kingdom to North America "now is but the work of a moment of time, and it does not require the utterance even of a whisper. The English nations are brought together, and they must march on together."[2] At a subsequent Cobdenite banquet in England, Sir Louis Mallet honored Field's having "annihilated time and space between England and America ... in the

---

[1] "Does This Look Like Free Trade?" *Tariff League Bulletin*, July 27, 1888, 29.

[2] Bright to Sumner, August 16, 1866, in William Roscoe Thayer, "Bright–Sumner Letters, 1861–1872," *Proceedings of the Massachusetts Historical Society* 46 (October 1912–June 1913), 151; Isabella Field Judson, ed., *Cyrus W. Field: His Life and Work* (New York: Harper & Brothers Publishers, 1896), 206, 228, 272.

cause of Free Trade."[3] Although the world was by no means flat, thanks to the efforts of Field, its geographical and temporal distances were certainly shrinking at an astounding rate. Merchants and diplomats in New York and London could now reach each other in a matter of minutes with but a few clicks of a telegraph key. Certainly, this was a defining moment in the history of Anglo-American relations and of modern globalization.

The laying of the cable dovetailed with the transatlantic free-trade movement. Within a year of Cyrus Field's accomplishment, classical liberal reformers would create the Cobden Club in London and the AFTL in New York. Field himself was part of this elite group of radical transatlantic advocates of Cobdenism: the belief that international free trade and a foreign policy of non-interventionism would bring prosperity and peace to the world. Heralded by some of the most prominent ante-bellum abolitionist crusaders, the postbellum American free-trade movement maintained close ties with British free traders. Ties were strengthened further following the Cobdenite conversion of US economist David Ames Wells, and the peaceful settlement of the *Alabama* claims, a dispute stemming from the British supplying of warships to the Confederacy during the Civil War. Anglo-American free traders thus worked closely together in their attempt to make Cobdenism the ideology of American foreign policy.

But these same free-trade connections and designs would also bring with them Anglophobic protectionist charges of a transatlantic conspiracy. American protectionists claimed that the British were practicing informal aspects of free-trade imperialism by attempting to prize open American markets through the insidious influence of various transatlantic free-trade propagandists among the press, professors, and politicians. American members of London's Cobden Club (1866–1982) were their prime suspects. The controversy surrounding the spread of Cobden's Victorian cosmopolitan ideology, the American protectionist response, and the effect of an influential international nongovernmental organization – the Cobden Club – therefore offer new avenues for revisiting the contentious debate over American foreign market expansionism in the late nineteenth century.

The mid-century transatlantic arrival of Cobdenism began a new chapter in the history of American free trade, party politics, and foreign relations. The Democratic party of course contained numerous adherents to the Jeffersonian free-trade tradition throughout the long nineteenth

---

[3] Cobden Club, *Report of the Proceedings at the Dinner of the Cobden Club, July 11, 1874* (London: Cassell Petter & Galpin, 1874), 20–21.

century, and postbellum Jeffersonians would continue to criticize stringent "war" tariffs for hurting agricultural exports, for artificially inflating the price of consumer goods, and for frequently creating national budget surpluses that many Americans considered unnecessary. Yet, Cobdenism sprouted its American roots not within the Jeffersonian South, but in the Northeast, where more than three-quarters of its US adherents resided.[4] Whereas Jeffersonianism had become the antebellum ideology of American slave owners, Cobdenism would become the free-trade ideology of numerous American abolitionists. In further contrast to the South's Jeffersonian tradition, America's Cobdenites first began to promulgate their free-trade philosophy not as Democrats, but as Republican independents. The influence of Cobdenism within the Republican party, however, has until now gone neglected.[5] As a result, historians have precipitously downplayed the role of the conspiratorial accusations that followed, and have glossed over the ideological battle brewing between the postbellum Republican party's economic nationalist majority and its small contingent of Cobdenite cosmopolitans over the proper course of American industrial development and global economic integration.[6] Even if historians have overlooked the influence of Cobdenism in the United States, postbellum American protectionists – aligning themselves

---

[4] The Cobden Club's American membership was comprised primarily of Northeasterners, a roughly equal measure of professors, intellectuals, politicians, newspaper editors, manufacturers, financiers, and railroad men. Its notable American membership totaled over 200. Of them, 162 hailed from the Northeast (74 percent), 41 from the West (19 percent), and 16 from the South (7 percent). More than half lived in New York City and the Boston area, the twin hubs of the postbellum American free-trade movement. Among the first generation of Cobdenites alone, at least twenty-six were active leaders in the antislavery cause. See the online Appendix for a full membership list.

[5] For rare exceptions, see David M. Tucker, *Mugwumps: Public Moralists of the Gilded Age* (Columbia: University of Missouri Press, 1998), 91–94, 107–108, 113; Frank Ninkovich, *Global Dawn: The Cultural Foundation of American Internationalism, 1865–1890* (Cambridge, MA: Harvard University Press, 2009), 63–65; E. Berkeley Tompkins, *Anti-Imperialism in the United States: The Great Debate, 1890–1920* (Philadelphia: University of Pennsylvania Press, 1970), 66–67, 148–149; Nancy Cohen, *The Reconstruction of American Liberalism, 1865–1914* (Chapel Hill: University of North Carolina Press, 2002), 92; Ernest R. May, *American Imperialism* (New York: Atheneum, 1968); May, "Robinson and Gallagher and American Imperialism," in *Imperialism: The Robinson and Gallagher Controversy*, ed. by Wm. Roger Louis (New York: New Viewpoints, 1976), 227; Alfred Eckes, Jr., *Opening America's Markets: U.S. Foreign Trade Policy Since 1776* (Chapel Hill: University of North Carolina Press, 1995), 35.

[6] Edward Crapol, *America for Americans: Economic Nationalism and Anglophobia in the Late Nineteenth Century* (Westport, CT: Greenwood Press, 1973), 16; Anthony Howe, "Free Trade and the International Order: The Anglo-American Tradition, 1846–1946," in *Anglo-American Attitudes: From Revolution to Partnership*, ed. by Fred M. Leventhal and Roland Quinault (Aldershot: Ashgate, 2000), 150. The controversy goes unmentioned in Tom E. Terrill, *The Tariff, Politics, and American Foreign Policy 1874–1901* (Westport, CT: Greenwood Press, 1973).

increasingly under the intellectual leadership of the country's more progressive Listian nationalists – certainly did not. The tariff question came to dominate the American political arena as protectionists and free traders struggled over the proper course for US economic globalization.

David A. Wells and the rise of the American free-trade "conspiracy"

The Atlantic's temporal and geographical distances had been bridged with Cyrus Field's telegraph, but despite high expectations, this historic global development at first did little to ameliorate Anglo-American tensions. Relations remained tumultuous following the Civil War, even after the 1871 Treaty of Washington, which would settle many long-standing and contentious disputes between the two countries, and even with the strengthening of Anglo-American financial ties as the US Treasury Department sought British funding for the country's massive Civil War-related debts.[7] Britain's policy of free trade was held under particular suspicion within America's powerful protectionist political circles. One student of Listian nationalist Henry Charles Carey summarized this position in 1865 by elucidating American fears of British free-trade imperialism and by expressing the lingering anger over perceived British support for the Confederacy: "[Free trade] is largely a cry raised by British capitalists and manufacturers, to unsettle our policy, and that of the world, that they may reap the benefit, by making England the workshop for the world ... all will remember how the majority of the trading and manufacturing classes in England, and the tory aristocracy, sympathized with rebellion here." The "lies" of the *London Times*, the fitting out of the *Alabama*, and its escape "from their docks through the feeble meshes of 'British neutrality,' to prey upon our commerce, are all fresh in mind."[8] The label of "free trader" was now equivalent to "traitor" among American hardline high tariff proponents and Anglophobes.

Protectionist ire was directed particularly upon London's Cobden Club, established in England in 1866 by Thomas Bayley Potter, a British politician and abolitionist. Potter created the club in memory of his friend Richard Cobden, who had successfully fought for the repeal of Britain's Corn Laws in 1846, and who had dedicated much of his life to the global eradication of protectionism and war. One of the club's underlying goals was admittedly to undermine protectionist preeminence in the

---

[7] For the latter, see Jay Sexton, *Debtor Diplomacy: Finance and American Foreign Relations in the Civil War Era, 1837–1873* (Oxford: Clarendon, 2005); Sexton, "The Funded Loan and the *Alabama* Claims," *Diplomatic History* 27 (September 2003): 449–478.

[8] Giles Stebbins, *"British Free Trade," a Delusion* (Detroit: s.p., 1865), 1.

United States. But more generally the club desired world peace through international arbitration, non-interventionism, and free trade. The Cobden Club's avowed altruism was stated in its motto, "Free Trade, Peace, and Goodwill among Nations."[9]

Although the Cobden Club's meetings were always held in England and the majority were British members of Parliament, its membership was global, with honorary (non-due paying) members fighting for freer trade and sound money in their home countries, from western Europe to South Africa, Egypt, Fiji, Ceylon, India, and Japan. Membership was attained first through nomination by an existing member; followed by a vote of acceptance by the Cobden Club Committee in London in recognition of the nominee's advocacy of free trade and sound money principles in their home country; and finalized upon the nominee's acceptance of membership. As a later chairman of the Cobden Club noted, however, most of its members especially had "advocated Free Trade for this country [Britain], and brought it about, because they believed and proved it to be for the advantage of British trade." Although the club's aims were pacific and international in scope, its primary goal thus was the promotion of peace and prosperity for England. To England's Cobdenites, the idea of freer Anglo-American trade and peace also appeared attainable in the aftermath of the bloody and costly Civil War. The idea was further strengthened owing to the espousal of Cobden's peaceful doctrine among his American friends – American membership in the Cobden Club became second in number only to England (see Appendix).[10]

American Anglophobia and mounting opposition from economic nationalists made the Cobden Club's efforts extremely difficult. As American Cobdenite and antebellum abolitionist Joshua Leavitt noted in his 1868 essay on how best to establish closer political and commercial ties between the United States and Great Britain: "No man of prominence in America can support even a partial relaxation of the rigours of Protection without bringing upon himself the stigma of being a partisan, and probably a pensioner, of 'British Free Trade.'" So long as protectionism remained in the United States, Leavitt added, "it will remain an expression of unabated and unalterable hostility, in

---

[9] Anthony Howe, "Richard Cobden and the Crimean War," *History Today* 54 (June 2004): 46–51; Oliver MacDonagh, "The Anti-Imperialism of Free Trade," *Economic History Review* 14 (April 1962): 489–501.

[10] April 23, 1868, *Cobden Club Committee Report*, CC MSS; *London Times*, July 12, 1880, 11; Lord Rhayader, "Letter to the Editor," *Daily Telegraph*, March 9, 1937; H. B. Jackson, *History of the Cobden Club* (London: Cobden-Sanderson, 1939), 19, 21–22, 30, 39; Chairman of the Cobden Club, July 1, 1893, *The Cobden Club Dinner* (1893), 4–5. For the Cobden Club's influence in Britain, see Anthony Howe, *Free Trade and Liberal England, 1846–1946* (Oxford: Clarendon Press, 1997), 116–141.

the face of which it is in vain to expect any considerable amelioration in the political and commercial relations of the two countries."[11] Spreading Cobdenism to the United States would prove to be a difficult task.

The twin antebellum legacies of antislavery and the ACLL provided the much-needed inspiration to the postbellum American free-trade movement. American Cobdenite cosmopolitans observed in abolitionist language that protectionist politicians like Ohio's General Schenck – a man whom they vainly hoped would "follow the illustrious example of Sir Robert Peel, and proclaim himself a convert to the truths of Free Trade" – and Pennsylvania's William "Pig Iron" Kelley had shackled an "iron collar around the neck of the nation. At the crack of Kelley's whip is the whole nation forever hereafter to bow in unison to Pennsylvania's black idol." To free traders, the protective system was one of conscription, making the workingmen "semi slaves," coercing them through "odious laws to contribute toward supporting monopolies under the false title of 'the American System.'"[12]

The hostility was mutual. The founder of an anti-Cobden Club in Troy, New York, derisively described the American Cobden Club member as "a very small man with a very small head, very large ears, and a fearfully large mouth. The ear is a transatlantic ear, so constructed that it can hear the faintest whisper from London. The mouth of this odd specimen of humanity is in perpetual motion, but it never utters a sound which is not first heard in London." In order to counteract the growing influence and perceived threat of the Cobden Club's efforts to bring free trade to America throughout the last decades of the century, anti-Cobden Clubs were founded in New York and Pennsylvania, the long-standing industrial protectionist heartland. The American Protective Tariff League, for instance, was established in New York City largely to break the "fatal spell of the Cobden club," and to "out-Cobden" the Cobden Club's propaganda. According to its charter, Philadelphia's aptly named Anti-Cobden Club would be founded in the 1880s to protect against the "threatening danger" of an organization whose "sole purpose" was to engraft "upon our country the noxious and enervating doctrine of free trade." The Anti-Cobden Club's meetings were "filled to overflowing" within Philadelphia's Anti-Cobden Hall,

---

[11] Joshua Leavitt, *An Essay on the Best Way of Developing Improved Political and Commercial Relations Between Great Britain and the United States of America* (London: Macmillan and Co., 1869), 32–33.

[12] *Free-Trader* (May 1870), 199; (June 1870), 4, 20; Wells to Atkinson, August 7, 1868, folder 3, carton 13, Atkinson Papers, MHS.

where the club's founder, David Martin, worked to stymie free trade and civil service reform.[13]

In an inverted reflection of Free Trade England, protectionism proved politically popular in late-nineteenth-century America, and economic nationalists from within Pennsylvania's pig iron and steel manufacturing centers provided the intellectual leadership, as well as many of the charges of a British free-trade conspiracy.[14] Listian nationalist Henry Charles Carey of Philadelphia notably led the postbellum polemical and ideological vanguard. For many years he held court at his home on Sunday afternoons. These meetings famously became known as "Carey's Vespers," where all things political and economical were discussed, and where issues were hotly debated over chilled glasses of dry white hock wine imported from Germany's Rhine area, apparently without any sense of irony. Among its attendees were Ulysses S. Grant, Salmon P. Chase, Joseph Wharton, William "Pig Iron" Kelley, James G. Blaine, and Carey's nephew, Henry Carey Baird. The Cobdenite opposition was also invited to attend on occasion. Goldwin Smith, Cornell professor and émigré from Oxford, for example, once accepted an offer to attend "Carey's Vespers" in 1870. Having already given the Cobden Club its motto "Free Trade, Peace, Goodwill among Nations," after attending "Carey's Vespers," Smith then proffered to the protectionist city of Philadelphia a contrary one: "Monopoly, war, ill-will among nations."[15] From among Carey's ranks would arise notable Listian leaders, including Maine's famous "Plumed Knight," Republican politician James G. Blaine.

The influence of Victorian free trade ironically began to pervade Republican political circles by way of one of Carey's own protectionist

---

[13] *Chicago Inter Ocean*, January 4, 1888, quoting the founder of the Anti-Cobden Club, "Thousand Defenders of American Industry" of Troy, New York; *North American*, March 21, 1888; October 8, 1889; "The Annual Dinner of the American Protective Tariff League," *Erie County Independent*, January 18, 1889; *Syracuse Standard*, June 4, 1887; *Auburn Bulletin* (NY), September 18, 1889; *New York Evening Post*, September 24, 1889; *New York World*, September 23, 1892. For more on Philadelphia's "Anti-Cobden Club," see *North American*, August 27, 1890; July 21, 1892, 6; May 28, 1896, 2; December 12, 1896, 3.

[14] For more on protectionism's popularity, see Douglas A. Irwin, "Tariff Incidence in America's Gilded Age," *National Bureau of Economic Research Working Paper Series*, No. 12162 (April 2006): 1–34.

[15] Jackson, *History of the Cobden Club*, 21; Henry Carey Baird, *Recollections of General Grant at the "Carey Vespers," June 25, 1865* (Philadelphia [unpublished], 1889), 1, 19, folder 4, box 21; Henry C. Carey Section, Edward Carey Gardner Papers, Historical Society of Pennsylvania, Philadelphia, PA; Arnold W. Green, *Henry Charles Carey: Nineteenth-Century Sociologist* (Philadelphia: University of Pennsylvania Press, 1951), 36; Goldwin Smith to Potter, February 1, 1870, Add. 43663, Vol. XVII, Richard Cobden Papers, British Library, London, England.

disciples, David Ames Wells (1828–1898). As historian John Sproat has noted, Wells would exert "more 'potent influence' on American tariff thought in the late nineteenth century than any politician or academic economist of his time."[16] Born in Springfield, Massachusetts, Wells was raised upon the protectionist doctrine common among Massachusetts manufacturers' sons. After attending and excelling in the Lawrence Scientific School at Harvard University, he moved to Philadelphia in 1851, a city he once described "as the central sun of political economy and science, as there I could get the advice of Mr. Henry C. Carey." He thus became an adherent to the "strongest" school of protectionism while sitting "at the feet" of Carey. Wells kept up a regular correspondence and visitation with him for years thereafter. Wells then joined Abraham Lincoln's Treasury Department in 1865 as Special Commissioner, for a short time becoming the most important economist in government.[17] Entering political office under the protectionist persuasion, Wells would leave a Victorian free trader.

While Wells's personal doubts regarding the tariff arose as early as 1866 owing to the efforts of US Cobdenites Edward Atkinson and J. S. Moore, he covertly converted from protection to free trade following his visit to England as Special Commissioner in 1867. Republican Secretary of the Treasury Hugh McCulloch had written to Wells that perceptive high tariff men in the United States feared that Wells would "become too much indoctrinated with free-trade notions by a visit to England" – especially from London's Cobden Club. Apparently they were right to worry. Wells, coming to the belief that free trade would benefit the United States as well as Britain, became an ideologically changed man during his time in England, following an illuminating dinner with the Cobden Club and tours of Lancashire cotton mills, where Wells "learned many things which still further shook" his "faith in the doctrines of Protection." Yet, according to Wells, what completed his free-trade conversion was a conversation with Carey himself. The two were discussing Cobden's recent death, whereupon Carey remarked that "among the many mercies since the war," Cobden's passing was the greatest. "How is that?" Wells asked. "Why, don't you see," Carey replied, "he was such a friend of this country

---

[16] John Sproat, *"The Best Men": Liberal Reformers in the Gilded Age* (New York: Oxford University Press, 1968), 179. For Wells's influence, see Cohen, *The Reconstruction of American Liberalism 1865–1914*, 88–94; Joseph Dorfman, *The Economic Mind in American Civilization*, 5 vols. (New York: Viking Press, 1946), II, 969–970; Dorfman, *Economic Mind*, III, 134–135.

[17] F. B. Sanborn to the Cobden Club, *Official Report of the Annual Meeting of Members, 1898*, 6; *Free-Trader* (December 1870): 123; Tucker, *Mugwumps*, 28; Michael Perelman, "Retrospectives: Schumpeter, David Wells, and Creative Destruction," *Journal of Economic Perspectives* 9 (Summer 1995): 190.

that if he had come over here the people would have all gone to hear him, and he would have taken the occasion to indoctrinate them with Free-Trade." Carey's response unnerved Wells. Seemingly in anticipation of what was inevitably to follow, he attempted to mislead his former mentor about his conversion, assuring Carey in mid-September 1867 that he had "not turned free trader" upon returning from England. All the while, Wells linked up with the burgeoning American free-trade movement. Within a few years, he was made a member of the Cobden Club, and he would afterwards be appointed the club's secretary for the United States.[18]

Against the protectionists' realist argument that national commercial independence alone would guarantee American economic security, Wells would continue to elaborate upon his idealistic free-trade views. For him, the universal free exchange of goods was "in accordance with the teachings of nature," and, echoing Cobden, that free trade was "most conducive to the maintenance of international peace and to the prevention of wars." To Wells, protectionism was but another form of slavery as it prohibited individuals from freely utilizing the products of their labor.[19]

During the 1860s Wells not coincidentally befriended and gained the support of an outspoken and influential group of American Cobdenites, who had aided in his free-trade conversion. Republican Congressman James Garfield, an antebellum abolitionist from Ohio, Wells reminisced, "was in principle as radical a free trader as ever lived . . . he was a member of the Cobden Club [1869]," and "helped make me a free trader"; Garfield's "logic and his wit were always antagonistic to the theory of protective duties." Abolitionist, Boston cotton manufacturer, and intimate friend of Wells, Edward Atkinson considered Cobden "among the

---

[18] Wells to Atkinson, July 14, 1866, folder 1; July 6, 1867, folder 2; November 17, December 24, 1867, folder 3, carton 13, Atkinson Papers; Sproat, *"The Best Men,"* 192; *Free-Trader* (December 1870), 123; Wells to Carey, September 17, 1867, Folder 3, Box 19, Carey Papers; Herbert Ronald Ferleger, "David A. Wells and the American Revenue System 1865–1870" (PhD diss., Columbia University, 1942), 68; McCulloch to Wells, July 12, 1867, reel 1, David Ames Wells Papers, LOC; Minutes of February 21, 1871, Committee and Annual Meetings of the Cobden Club July 1866–August 1886, CC MSS; Ferleger, "Wells," 186; Tucker, *Mugwumps,* 28–33; Minutes of February 18, 1870, CC MSS. On J. S. Moore and Edward Atkinson's role in his free-trade conversion, see, respectively, Moore to Atkinson, March 19, 1869, carton 1, Atkinson Papers; Stephen Meardon, "Postbellum Protection and Commissioner Wells's Conversion to Free Trade," *History of Political Economy* 39 (Winter 2007): 571–604.

[19] "In Times of Peace, etc.," *Free-Trader* (May 1870): 207; David Ames Wells, *Free Trade* (New York and Milwaukee: M. B. Cary and Co., 1884), 294; Wells, "The Creed of Free Trade," *Atlantic Monthly* (August 1875), 15; Wells, *A Primer on Tariff Reform* (London: Cassell & Company, Limited, 1885), 9; Wells, *Freer Trade Essential to Future National Prosperity and Development* (New York: Wm. C. Martin's Steam Printing House, 1882), 3–4.

greatest of men in the service to mankind" and became a well-known proponent of introducing free trade to America in the manner of the ACLL. Atkinson also was an economic advisor to Charles Sumner, James Garfield, and the Cleveland administrations, as well as a leading American Cobden Club member (1869). Abolitionist Horace White, editor of the *Chicago Tribune*, frequently corresponded with J. S. Mill and Cobden's free-trade ally John Bright, subscribed to the Manchester School's anti-imperial critique of foreign policy, became a member of the Cobden Club in 1872, and sought to eradicate protectionism just as the Republican party had once dealt with slavery. For White, "Free Trade" was but an obvious addition to the slogan of "Free Soil, Free Labor, and Free Speech." Finally, the "Nestor of Free Trade," William Cullen Bryant, prominent poet and editor of the *New York Evening Post*, had attended ACLL meetings in London during the 1840s, used his popular newspaper to espouse free-trade principles, edited the American edition of Cobden's *Political Writings* in 1865, and became a member of the Cobden Club in 1869. The influence of these men upon Wells and their shared subscription to Cobdenism invariably led to further conspiratorial conjecture.[20]

Adding to the conspiracy theories surrounding Victorian free-trade ideology in the United States, leading members of London's Cobden Club did indeed work closely with these and other prominent American free traders in a concerted propaganda campaign. They disseminated well over 15 million Cobden Club leaflets and nearly 2.5 million books and pamphlets throughout the final decades of the nineteenth century.[21] Alongside its various political and economic propagandistic activities,

---

[20] David Wells, quoted in Ferleger, "Wells," 196; Minutes of June 10, 1869; David Ames Wells, "Tariff Reform: Retrospective and Prospective," *Forum* (February 1893): 701; Minutes of May 10, 1869, CC MSS; F. B. Sanborn to the Cobden Club, *Official Report of the Annual Meeting of Members, 1898*, 6; Atkinson to Wells, November 11, 1875, reel 3, Wells Papers; Atkinson to Wells, February 21, 1884, carton 16; Atkinson to R. R. Bowker, October 16, 1885, carton 17, Atkinson Papers; Atkinson, "Address to the American Free Trade League on the Hundredth Anniversary of Richard Cobden's Birth, June 3, 1904," in Edward Atkinson, *Facts and Figures* (Boston, MA and New York: Houghton, Mifflin and Company, 1904), 138; Harold Francis Williamson, *Edward Atkinson: The Biography of an American Liberal, 1827–1905* (Boston, MA: Old Corner Book Store, 1934), 4–7, 64; Joseph Logsdon, *Horace White, Nineteenth Century Liberal* (Westport, CT: Greenwood, 1971), 174, 357–358; *Chicago Tribune*, November 12, 1870; Tucker, *Mugwumps*, 6; Minutes of February 9, 1872, CC MSS; *Free-Trader* (December 1870), 118, 125–126; John Bigelow, *William Cullen Bryant* (Boston, MA: Houghton, Mifflin, 1890), 182–183; George Haven Putnam, *Memories of a Publisher, 1865–1915* (New York: G. P. Putnam's Sons, 1916), 40; Minutes of March 23, 1869, CC MSS.

[21] *List of Members and Committee Reports, 1898* (London: Cassell and Co., 1898), 198. Et al., see Thomas B. Potter to Wells, July 7, 1871; and James Caird [Cobden Club committee member] to Wells, August 13, 1871, Carton 1, Atkinson Papers.

the club also gave out prizes to free-trade scholars at American universities, and maintained close ties with the AFTL. These actions and connections, while not nefarious, definitely were motivated in part by British national interests and raised the alarm among American protectionist circles, as shown upon Wells's return from England. To friends and foes alike, it was clear that American free traders were now fighting their battles "under the banner of Cobdenism."[22]

Wells, backed by his clique of Cobdenites and bolstered by his recent conversion to free trade, published a scathing indictment of the present American tariff and currency system in his 1869 Treasury Department report. It concluded that the domestic market would not be able to soak up the country's agricultural surplus, and called for a revenue tariff and increases to the free list. New York Cobdenite Mahlon Sands believed Wells's report to be a "standard ... we can fight under," promising that the AFTL would bring Wells on board with a yearly salary of $5,000 once he broke ties with the Philadelphia protectionists once and for all. Horace White wrote Wells that it was "the most important and valuable state paper ever produced in this country on any financial or economical subject. The high tariff gentry will *never get over it*." The Cobden Club promptly made 3,750 copies for distribution and the AFTL included the report as a supplement to its January edition of the *Free-Trader* in 1870. Wells's American free-trade friends rejoiced, proclaiming that Wells "will be the Cobden of America ... you will win for our country the same victory and honor he won for his." Mahlon Sands noted: "Once he was Saul, now he is their chief apostle to the Gentiles." Maine's youthful, bearded, and magnetic Republican Congressman James G. Blaine had urged Wells to "be very cautious" in his report, but Wells opted instead for striking "very heavy blows," even if it cost him his job. He did not think, however, that the protectionists would "dare openly attack" him.[23]

Wells was wrong. His protectionist enemies, particularly his spurned mentor Henry Carey and *New York Tribune* editor Horace Greeley, charged that Wells had been bribed with British gold. Greeley's *Tribune* responded that "we do most surely believe that the scope and drift of

---

[22] George B. Curtis, *Protection and Prosperity: An Account of Tariff Legislation and its Effect in Europe and America* (New York: Pan-American Publishing Co., 1896), 617.

[23] *Report of the Special Commissioner of the Revenue*, 40 Cong., 3 Sess., January 5, 1869, Document 16, pp. 1–11, 47, 69–76; Sands to Atkinson, March 12, 1869; December 1869, carton 1, Atkinson Papers; White to Wells, December 24, 1869, reel 1, Wells Papers; *Free Trade and the European Treaties of Commerce, Including a Report of the Proceedings at the Dinner of the Cobden Club, July 17, 1875* (London: Cassell, Petter, and Galpin, 1875), 128; *Free-Trader. Supplement* (January 1870); Elihu Burritt to Wells, May 14, 1869, reel 1, Wells Papers; Crapol, *America for Americans*, 24–26; *Free-Trader* (March 1870), 169; Wells to Atkinson, October 29, 1868, folder 5, carton 13, Atkinson Papers.

Mr. Wells's late Report was influenced by the money of foreign rivals," and that Wells, as revenue commissioner, had been "bought and paid for" by the British. Carey, in a series of thirteen open letters to the *Tribune*, in turn asked why Wells's report aligned itself "so precisely in accordance with the views and wishes of those great British 'capitalists,'" who, "in their efforts to gain and keep foreign markets," distributed "money so freely among those of our people who are supposed to be possessed of power to influence public opinion?" In the House of Representatives, Republican Congressman "Pig-Iron" Kelley of Pennsylvania, Carey's most avid congressional disciple, attacked Wells for moving "stealthily toward his sinister objects." Kelley charged that Wells's report advocated on behalf of the British "whose interest is to hold us in commercial and maritime dependence," and that he had been bribed by his "Sheffield employers." Kelley also drew attention to the suspicious timing of Wells's 1867 trip to England and his conversion from protection to free trade. The charges of a British conspiracy had begun, and Wells strengthened such charges through his years of dissimulation among his former protectionist allies regarding his Cobdenite conversion.[24]

As a result of his controversial revenue report, Wells's career within mainstream Republican politics came to an abrupt end, foreshadowing the long, difficult road stretching before the reformers of the civil service and the tariff. Young Cobdenite Henry Adams noted as much to Edward Atkinson: "Our coming struggle is going to be harder than the anti-slavery fight."[25] The Republican mainstream's adverse reaction to Wells's report called for a change of Cobdenite tactics.

Mobilizing free trade: the AFTL and liberal republicanism

Disgusted by cronyism, corruption, and Republican protectionist orthodoxy, David Ames Wells and his fellow reformists crafted the message of the Liberal Republican movement. This predominantly free-trade and civil-service reform movement voiced its concerns primarily through print: American Cobden Club members Wells and Edward Atkinson in

---

[24] *New York Tribune*, March 9, 1869, 5; March 23, 1869, 4; June 8, 1869, 4; *Congressional Globe*, 41 Cong., 2 Sess., January 11, 1870, 371, 373; Crapol, *America for Americans*, 33.

[25] Adams to Atkinson, February 1, 1869, carton 1, Atkinson Papers. The Brooklyn Free Trade League was also founded in 1869, with Joshua Leavitt its president, and R. R. Bowker as secretary. See *Platform and Constitution of the Brooklyn Free Trade League* (New York: Hosford & Sons, 1869). For Kelley's free-silver proclivities, see Jeannette P. Nichols, "Silver Diplomacy," *Political Science Quarterly* 48 (December 1933): 570–571. On the civil service reform movement, see Ari Hoogenboom, *Outlawing the Spoils: A History of the Civil Service Reform Movement, 1865–1883* (Urbana: University of Illinois Press, 1961).

the *North American Review*; Samuel Bowles in the *Springfield Republican*; William Cullen Bryant in the *New York Evening Post*; Horace White in the *Chicago Tribune*; William M. Grosvenor in the *Missouri Democrat*; and Henry Adams, himself holding "a warm feeling of good-will to England," joined the Cobdenite camp in the pages of the *North American Review*. Adams had known Cobden well during his years in England, and drew inspiration from John Bright and "Mr. Cobden" regarding "the free-trade issue and our outrageous political corruption." While Henry Adams's free-trade position might have been unpopular, he wrote Bright in 1869, "I know what to say and I shall say it without much caring whose toes I tread upon." His brother, Charles Francis Adams, Jr., was also an admitted free trader: "One who believes in the economic dispensation of Adam Smith, as developed by Richard Cobden." Oxford Professor Goldwin Smith's 1869 arrival in Ithaca, New York, provided the trans-atlantic free-trade movement with further intellectual and editorial firepower.[26]

In 1865, Bryant, Jacob D. Cox, White, and Atkinson founded the AFTL, with the success of Cobden and Bright's ACLL as inspiration. Bryant was its inaugural president through 1867, replaced by Cyrus Field's brother, the jurist and peace activist David Dudley Field, followed by David Wells in 1871.[27] The AFTL commenced upon an active pro-paganda campaign, aided further when, after some coaxing on Atkinson's part, Reverend Henry Ward Beecher officially joined the free-trade fray. Beecher, General Roeliff Brinkerhoff, Professor Arthur Latham Perry of Williams College, Edward Atkinson, William Lloyd Garrison, and David Dudley Field went on speaking tours throughout the country on the AFTL's behalf from 1869 to 1870. Dozens of meetings were held and thousands of pamphlets were distributed. Other prominent AFTL mem-bers included Ralph Waldo Emerson, Joshua Leavitt, former New York Governor Samuel Tilden, former Ohio Governor George Hoadley, a young publisher by the name of Henry George, Congressman Samuel "Sunset" Cox, Carl Schurz, E. L. Godkin, Robert B. Minturn, and

---

[26] Henry Adams to Carl Schurz, October 27, 1870, in Henry Adams, *The Letters of Henry Adams*, ed. by J. C. Levenson, et al., 6 vols. (Cambridge, MA: Belknap Press, 1982), II, 86; Adams to Carl Milnes Gaskell, January 29, 1882, in ibid., 448; Adams to Bright, February 3, 1869, Add. 43391, Vol. IX, John Bright Papers, British Library, London, England; Charles Francis Adams, Jr., *The Richard Cobden Centennial. Speech of Charles Francis Adams at the Dinner of the Free Trade League at the Hotel Vendome, Boston, on the Evening of June 2, 1904*, 3; Goldwin Smith to T. B. Potter, November 1, 1869, Add. 43663, Vol. XVII, Richard Cobden Papers, British Library, London, England.

[27] For David Dudley Field's internationalism, see Lawrence Goldman, "Exceptionalism and Internationalism: The Origins of American Social Science Reconsidered," *Journal of Historical Sociology* 11 (March 1998): 1–30.

William M. Grosvenor. Charles M. Marshall was the AFTL's treasurer, and Mahlon Sands its secretary.[28]

The AFTL organized a propaganda campaign to spread Cobdenism to the United States. It began publishing a monthly, *The League*, from June 1867 to October 1868. The newspaper was named after the ACLL's own popular circular, and its motto was a quote from Richard Cobden: "Free-Trade: The International Common Law of the Almighty." With the increasing popularity of protectionist publications containing "league" in their titles, however, in 1868 *The League* was renamed *The Free-Trader* (1868–1871), which jumped in publication from 4,000 to 16,000 between 1869 and 1870 alone, making its way to "nearly every newspaper in the United States," and even noting its first female subscriber in December 1869.[29]

The AFTL maintained close ties with the Cobden Club and the Free Trade Association of London, with the latter writing the AFTL upon its inception that its endeavor to secure free trade for free labor was but the "consummation of the task" that had been "commenced in the abolition of slavery. Free Trade is the vital element of Free Labour: without the former the latter cannot healthfully exist." The AFTL's "Declaration of Principles" advocated "Free Trade, the natural and proper term in the series of progress after Free Speech, Free Soil and Free Labor." The Cobden Club's membership roles swelled with the addition of large numbers of AFTL members, further strengthening transatlantic free-trade ties.[30]

The American free-trade movement gained ever more momentum as its onetime abolitionist leadership sought to move past the Civil War's

[28] *League* (September 1867), 40; Atkinson to Beecher, June 25, 1867, carton 14, Atkinson Papers; Mahlon Sands, *The Free Trade League to its Subscribers and the Public* (1869); Charles DeBenedetti, *The Peace Reform in American History* (Bloomington: Indiana University Press, 1980), 63, 64; Mahlon Sands to Atkinson, March 1, 1869; March 12, 1869; March 29, 1869; April 8, 1869; April 22, 1869; April 29, 1869, carton 1, Atkinson Papers; Caro Lloyd, *Henry Demarest Lloyd, 1847–1903, A Biography*, 2 vols. (New York: G. P. Putnam's Sons), I, 24–25; Tilden to Thomas Bayley Potter, August 23, 1877, folder 41, Samuel Tilden Papers, NYPL. Other founders of the AFTL included Alfred Pell and Parke Godwin. See *Constitution of the American Free Trade League and List of Members* (1865).

[29] *League* (June 1867); *Free-Trader* (June 1868), 1; *Free-Trader* (January 1870), 125; *Free-Trader* (March 1870), 168. The December issue was sent to its first known female subscriber, unnamed, residing in Fairfield, Vermont. *Free-Trader* (January 1870), 127.

[30] Earl Dudley Ross, "Liberal Republican Movement" (PhD thesis, Cornell University, 1910), 3–5; Michael McGerr, *The Decline of Popular Politics: The American North, 1865–1928* (New York: Oxford University Press, 1986), 59; Howe, "Free Trade and the International Order," 145; *Constitution of the American Free Trade League and List of Members* (1865); *Address of the Free Trade Association of London, to the American Free Trade League, New York* (London: P.S. King, 1866), 4.

problematic legacy of Reconstruction. In 1869, for instance, former abolitionist Horace White's *Chicago Tribune* gave its endorsement to the following sentiment: "The negro, having secured all his rights, including a seat in the United States Senate, has ceased to be an object of interest." Atkinson expressed a similar attitude: "Let the reconstruction matters be once settled, and the fight between Protection and Free Trade will be upon us, and Free-Trade views will win." While the rhetoric of antislavery permeated the coming free-trade debates, the former southern slaves themselves would increasingly become marginalized both in national politics and in the minds of American Cobdenite abolitionists in the decades following the Civil War. Historian Andrew Slap has even argued that by 1872 the Liberal Republican movement itself would doom Reconstruction.[31]

The AFTL's free-trade insurgency did not go unnoticed or unchallenged. Immediately upon the league's founding, a spokesman for Cincinnati's Society for the Encouragement of American Industry observed "that British agents in this country are already at work to reduce the tariff." Economic nationalist Giles Stebbins of Detroit stated without reserve that the AFTL "is 'run' in the interest of foreign manufacturers and their importing agents – who want control of our markets – and of political demagogues." In Congress, protectionist representative and iron mill owner John A. Griswold of Troy, New York, expressed his own suspicions about the AFTL's strong transatlantic relationships. He also read a letter from the former American consul at Liverpool, Thomas H. Dudley, who warned that the British were "making great efforts on this side to repeal our tariff and admit British goods free of duty . . .. Their plan is to agitate in the Western States, and to form free-trade associations all over the country."[32]

---

[31] *The League* 1 (June 1867), 5; *Chicago Tribune*, April 4, 1870; Williamson, *Atkinson*, 81; Andrew L. Slap, *The Doom of Reconstruction: The Liberal Republicans in the Civil War Era* (New York: Fordham University Press, 2006). See, also, Richard O. Curry, "The Abolitionists and Reconstruction: A Critical Appraisal," *Journal of Southern History* 34 (November 1968): 527–545; William Gillette, *Retreat from Reconstruction, 1869–1879* (Baton Rouge: Louisiana State University Press, 1979); James M. McPherson, *The Struggle for Equality: Abolitionists and the Negro in the Civil War and Reconstruction* (Princeton, NJ: Princeton University Press, 1964); McPherson, *The Abolitionist Legacy: From Reconstruction to the NAACP* (Princeton, NJ: Princeton University Press, 1976); Heather Cox Richardson, *The Death of Reconstruction: Race, Labor, and Politics in the Post-Civil War North, 1865–1901* (Cambridge, MA: Harvard University Press, 2001); and Charles W. Calhoun, *Conceiving a New Republic: The Republican Party and the Southern Question, 1869–1900* (Lawrence: University Press of Kansas, 2006).

[32] Edward D. Mansfield, *The Tariff – British Imposture and Political Humbug* (Cincinnati, OH: Society for Encouragement of American Industry, 1865), 1; Giles B. Stebbins, *Read and Circulate! The Free Trade Falsehood that "A Tariff is a Tax" Exposed* (Detroit: Self-published, 1871), 1; *Congressional Globe*, 39th Cong., 1st Sess. (Washington, DC: Government Printing Office, 1866), 3689.

Dudley's observation proved rather accurate. Free-trade leagues closely associated with the AFTL and the Cobden Club began sprouting up throughout the country in subsequent years, predominantly in the Northeast and West. The South, undergoing its own vast economic, political, and social upheaval, had ample issues besides that of free trade to keep its attention. Struggling post war southern development of infant industries, internal improvements, the flight of former slave labor to the North and West, initial Democratic political impotence, and corresponding political and racial violence were gradually bringing about, among other changes, a reorientation of the South's outlook on the tariff question during Reconstruction and afterward. Mining and manufacturing interests in Virginia, West Virginia, Alabama, and Tennessee were "more zealous" for protectionism, for example, as were struggling southern textile industries, Louisianan sugar interests, and Kentucky's hemp growers.[33] Aside from a handful of laissez-faire "Bourbon" Democrats, free-trade advocacy was finding its most vocal postwar adherents outside of the Jeffersonian New South.[34]

During this period that historian Morton Keller describes as "the triumph of organizational politics," the process of creating local free-trade (and protectionist) leagues was systematized. The *Chicago Tribune* explained how simple it was to form one, giving the following suggestions to local clubs: hold monthly meetings and debates between protectionists and revenue reformers; supply traveling lecturers; and that "good could be done – as Cobden's example shows – by catechizing candidates for Congress and for Legislatures which were to elect Senators, on their views of revenue reform."[35]

---

[33] *New York Tribune*, April 5, 1881, 4; Eric Foner, *A Short History of Reconstruction, 1863–1867* (New York: Harper & Row, 1990), esp. 148–179; Edward L. Ayers, *The Promise of the New South: Life after Reconstruction* (New York: Oxford University Press, 1992), 104–131; Howard K. Beal, "The Tariff and Reconstruction," *American Historical Review* 35 (January 1930): 276–294; Richard Franklin Bensel, *The Political Economy of American Industrialization, 1877–1900* (Cambridge: Cambridge University Press, 2000), xxi, 8; Carter Goodrich, "Public Aid to Railroads in the Reconstruction South," *Political Science Quarterly* 71 (September 1956): 407–442; William Appleman Williams, *The Roots of the Modern American Empire: A Study of the Growth and Shaping of Social Consciousness in a Marketplace Society* (New York: Vintage Books, 1969), 14. See, also, Gavin Wright, *Old South, New South: Revolutions in the Southern Economy Since the Civil War* (New York: Basic Books, 1986).

[34] Allen Johnston Going, *Bourbon Democracy in Alabama, 1874–1890* (Tuscaloosa: University of Alabama Press, 1951); Willie D. Halsell, "The Bourbon Period in Mississippi Politics, 1875–1890," *Journal of Southern History* 11 (November 1945): 519–537; Judson C. Ward, Jr., "The Republican Party in Bourbon Georgia, 1872–1890," *Journal of Southern History* 9 (May 1943): 196–209.

[35] Morton Keller, *Affairs of State: Public Life in Late Nineteenth Century America* (Cambridge, MA: Belknap Press, 1977), 238–273; *Tribune* reprinted in "The Organization of Free Trade Clubs," in *New Century* (New York: International Free-Trade Alliance, 1876), 91.

With the legacy of the ACLL in mind, the AFTL's principal goals were to send out lecturers and distribute free-trade tracts throughout the West and North, alongside organizing "Revenue Reform societies in all the large towns." The Chicago Free Trade League held its first meeting early in 1866, with Horace White a member of its constitutional committee and a vice president. Western agrarian communities appeared ripe for harvesting free-trade feeling. After all, asked Cobdenite Congressman Samuel "Sunset" Cox, "who should ponder the lesson of the English corn laws, if not the American farmer?"[36] The Chicago branch proposed to fight against exorbitant railway rates and the present national tariff, which at once "distinguishes and damns the name of [Justin] Morrill," Republican author of the 1861 protective tariff.[37] Over in Boston, Atkinson, Charles Francis Adams, Jr., and William Lloyd Garrison organized the Reform League in April 1869, which focused on civil service reform and tariff reductions. Atkinson, Wells, William Grosvenor, Sands, White, and Jacob Cox also formed the Taxpayers' Union in November 1871 to act as a lobbying group in Washington, DC, in order to more effectively influence legislation for a revenue-only tariff. The AFTL's Henry Demarest Lloyd headed the publication of a new monthly, *The People's Pictorial Taxpayer*. In coordination with Sands at the AFTL, William Grosvenor was made the Taxpayer Union's Washington "Free Trade lobbyist," with free-trade radical J. S. Moore his secretary. Grosvenor himself began developing a secret grassroots list of the country's tariff reformers. Their efforts in the West and Northeast paid noticeable dividends. The *Nation* observed in 1870 that "a great change" had come over public opinion over the last few years concerning the tariff. "Newspapers all over the country, and particularly in the West ... have become decidedly free-trade."[38]

In what would become a predictable and effective response throughout the United States, protectionists regrouped in these same areas of agitation to save industries from what they viewed as a rapidly spreading Cobdenite threat. To thwart Horace White's determination to access "the markets of the world," the *Chicago Tribune*'s former protectionist

[36] Samuel S. Cox, *Free Land and Free Trade: The Lessons of the English Corn Laws Applied to the United States* (New York: G. P. Putnam's Sons, 1880), 117.

[37] *Chicago Tribune*, January 10, 1866, 2.

[38] Mahlon Sands to Atkinson, February 13, 1869; March 1, 1869; March 8, 1869; March 10, 1869; March 12, 1869; March 16, 1869; March 18, 1869, carton 1, Atkinson Papers; first *Tax-Payers' Union Circular*, dated November 29, 1871; Grosvenor to Atkinson, December 21, 1871, carton 1; Grosvenor to Atkinson, January 2, 1872, Sands to Atkinson, January 4, 1872, Grosvenor to Atkinson, January 13, 1872; January 29, 1872, carton 2, Atkinson Papers; Williamson, *Atkinson*, 87–89; Slap, *Doom of Reconstruction*, 129; *Nation*, March 3, 1870, 132.

editor, Joseph Medill, for instance, encouraged "the friends of the 'American System' to organize also, and meet sophistry with facts." In Detroit, Carey disciple Giles Stebbins directly connected and attacked British free trade and the AFTL's efforts in the western United States. In New York, the journal *The Protectionist* announced in early 1870 that it would begin issuing its paper weekly rather than monthly "in order to counteract more effectually the increasing dissemination of the pernicious Free-Trade doctrines of the Free-Trade press of the country." Henry Carey's nephew, Philadelphia publisher Henry Carey Baird, in turn took up his aging uncle's progressive protectionist mantle, and began to spar with the leading free traders of the day on the stump and in print so as to block the "nefarious schemes" of the AFTL, that "foreign importers' British Free-Trade League of New York."[39]

Stoking conspiratorial embers to white hot, allegations of the AFTL's transatlantic ties came out into the open in 1869 when, upon receiving a copy of the AFTL's financial records, *New York Tribune* editor Horace Greeley uncovered that three-fourths of the League's funds "came either directly from foreign houses" or "their recognized agencies" in New York, particularly from the wealthy Baring family in England. The AFTL was by no means a national movement, the *Tribune* asserted, but was "Foreign in the incitement of its organization, Foreign in the interests it is intended and calculated to promote, and Foreign in much the larger portion of the contributions whereby it is supported and rendered efficient." The *Tribune* also noted that these were not merely financial ties, but familial; AFTL member Robert B. Minturn, the *Tribune* pointed out, was the brother-in-law of Baring himself.[40]

Instead of responding in the defensive to the *New York Tribune*'s discovery, the AFTL welcomed the revelation. It found the *Tribune*'s findings encouraging, particularly because they pointed out that the league had been able to raise a whopping $50,000 in just nine months. Such rapid fundraising suggested that the AFTL "shall not have to wait so long ... as the anti-corn-law men of England did for Free-Trade in corn." As to the *Tribune*'s discovery that the majority of funding came from

[39] *Chicago Tribune*, January 5, 1866; Bessie Louis Pierce, *A History of Chicago, From Town to City, 1848–1871*, 2 vols. (New York: Alfred A. Knopf, 1940), II, 293; *Chicago Tribune*, January 11, 1866; Stebbins, *"British Free Trade," a Delusion*; Stebbins, *Western Campaign of the Agents of the "American Free Trade League"* (Detroit: American Industrial League, 1869); Stebbins, *Read and Circulate!*, 184–189; *Protectionist*, quoted in *Free-Trader* (April 1870), 181; Henry Carey Baird, *The Rights of American Producers, and the Wrongs of British-Free-Trade Revenue-Reform* (Philadelphia, PA: Collins, Printer, 1872), 8, 1. See, also, Henry Carey Baird, *Some of the Fallacies of British-Free-Trade-Revenue-Reform* (Philadelphia, PA: Collins, Printer, 1871).

[40] *New York Tribune*, May 28, 1869, 4; June 8, 1869, 4; May 22, 1869, 7.

"importers, foreign bankers, or ship-owners," this the AFTL also did not deny. After all, the league observed, "we doubt if anybody will think the worse of Free-Trade because men who own ships and men who use them believe their business honorable and honest, and who ask that the laws of trade shall have free course, untrammeled, except for the necessary purpose of revenue." As to the "foreign bankers," there were only a couple, unless foreign bankers included anyone dealing in foreign exchange. Such appeals to "petty prejudice," the AFTL countered, were "always the resort of knaves and fools when argument fails them."[41] The protectionists, it seemed, had proven unsuccessful at derailing the AFTL's early momentum.

The fervor that once drove antebellum antislavery soon found renewed rhetorical expression among Cobdenites on both sides of the Atlantic. In the pages of the AFTL's *Free-Trader*, for instance, William Grosvenor asked: "What is the difference of principle between that slavery which took the whole of the earnings of labor for the benefit of another and that slavery which takes any part of its earnings for the benefit of another? We are all anti-slavery men to-night." In England, John Bright considered it "strange that a people who put down slavery at an immense sacrifice, are not able to suppress monopoly which is but a milder form of the same evil. Under slavery the *man* was seized and his labor was stolen from him, and the profit enjoyed by his master and owner." Likewise, under protection-ism "the *man* is apparently free, but he is denied the right to exchange the produce of his labor except with his countrymen, who offer him less for it than the foreigner would give."[42] Abolitionist agitators had found a ready rhetorical outlet for their political economic reformation.

From December 1870 to June 1871, the American free-trade move-ment saw sizeable propagandistic gains. Local AFTL meetings increased, spanning from Maine to Minnesota, and the distribution of the league's free-trade tracts in this period alone numbered more than 245,000. Following the 1870 elections, the AFTL had also unsuccessfully sug-gested a secret conference that would join "Western Revenue Reform Republicans with democrats" to start the new reform movement and control the House of Representatives. Horace White was subsequently castigated for suggesting a bipartisan anti-protectionist union with the Bourbon Democrats in Congress. He was taken to task for such an ill-timed idea, put forward just as the Klan began ratcheting up its violence

---

[41] *Free-Trader* (November 1870), 104.

[42] Grosvenor, quoted in *Free-Trader* (December 1870), 125; Bright, quoted in Herman Ausubel, *In Hard Times: Reformers Among the Late Victorians* (New York: Columbia University Press, 1960), 221.

and intimidation in the South, thereby forcefully reminding the country of the Democratic party's ongoing racist, bloody legacy.[43]

In spite of White's bipartisan backfire, the AFTL soon began to gain adherents among American blacks. Joseph H. Perkins of Cincinnati, for instance, made a name for himself stemming from his free-trade advocacy, as did the Colored Young Men's Christian Association of Washington. Owing to such cross-racial momentum, William Cullen Bryant half-predicted and half-hoped that the American System would not maintain such a strong hold upon the Republican party as it had on the Whigs.[44]

The growth of the free-trade movement caught the eye and ire of Pennsylvania's William "Pig-Iron" Kelley, who as a youth had subscribed to the "cosmopolitanism of free trade" and zealously had given his support to the 1846 Walker Tariff. In 1859, however, he had arrived at the Listian belief that "the protective system is the only road to really Free Trade." Kelley also observed how "Free-Trade principles are spreading through the North like wildfire, just as secession principles once overran the South."[45] Cobdenites were not the only ones retooling the rhetoric of antislavery for the postbellum tariff debate.

The increasing power of the Liberal Republicans' Cobdenite leadership was being felt in national as well as local politics. Speaker of the House James G. Blaine (R-ME) had been warned in late 1870 that free-trade sentiment was becoming more popular among northwestern Republicans. Blaine correspondingly began to view the Liberal Republican free-trade reach within Congress with enough trepidation that he made a duplicitous deal, ostensibly offering them control of the House Ways and Means Committee in return for continued party loyalty. American free traders thereafter tried to have Republican Congressman James G. Garfield – who had by now "lost the good-will of the Protectionists" owing to his warning that protectionism would be the ruin of the Republican party – appointed chairman of the committee, only to be thwarted in the end by Blaine.[46]

---

[43] Mahlon Sands to Carl Schurz, November 10, 1870, reel 4, Carl Schurz Papers, LOC; Logsdon, *White*, 183.

[44] *Free-Trader* (December 1870), 121.

[45] William D. Kelley, *Reasons for Abandoning the Theory of Free Trade, and Adopting the Principle of Protection to American Industry. Addressed to the Farmers and Working Men of the United States* (Philadelphia, PA: Henry Carey Baird, 1872), 4, 22, 26.

[46] R. C. Cook to Blaine, November 17, 1870, reel 7, James Gillespie Blaine Family Papers, LOC; *Free-Trader* (May 1870), 202; (April 1870): 180; (June 1870), 5; Ida Minerva Tarbell, *The Tariff in our Times* (New York: The Macmillan Company, 1915), 70; Logsdon, *White*, 183–184.

In 1870, some of these same liberals decided to get more politically engaged. Under the leadership of Cobdenites Carl Schurz and William Grosvenor, they formed an independent ticket – a Liberal Republican party ticket – "in favor of tariff reform" in Missouri. A similar association seeking universal amnesty, civil service reform, and free trade was developed in Cincinnati the following year, led by AFTL leaders Jacob Cox and George Hoadley.[47]

Alongside such political organizing, the Liberal Republican movement in turn found strong journalistic support. Cobdenite editors such as Horace White of the *Chicago Tribune*, Manton Marble of the *New York World*, Samuel Bowles of the *Springfield Republican*, and Murat Halstead of the *Cincinnati Commercial* took up the cause in their respective newspapers. Listian Henry Carey Baird began describing the *New York Evening Post* as "the special organ, advocate, and friend of the British free-trade revenue reformers," which was now under the editorship of Charles Nordhoff. In May 1870, these same free traders met privately in Washington, DC, with David Wells; the AFTL's Taxpayer Union lobbyist William Grosvenor of the *St. Louis Democrat* (and representative of the Missouri party); E. L. Godkin of the *Nation*, who Oswald Garrison Villard described as "a devoted adherent of the Manchester School" and a subscriber to the "lofty idealism of Cobden and Bright"; Charles Francis Adams, Jr.; Henry Adams; Amasa Walker; his son Francis Walker; and Mahlon Sands. At this private meeting, they resolved to ask President Grant for a renewal of Wells's term as Special Commissioner of the Revenue, and decided "that action outside of the Republican Party would become necessary" if the Republican party did not seek "repentance" for its protectionist past and "remove the crushing shackles" of the current high tariff system. This meeting was followed by a larger one in late November at the invitation of the AFTL. The Liberal Republican movement's national phase had commenced.[48]

The summer of 1870 then witnessed two occurrences that significantly enhanced growing Republican intraparty dissent: David Wells was forced to step down from his Treasury Department position; and, in Cobdenite fashion, Charles Sumner successfully halted the Grant administration's

---

[47] Roeliff Brinkerhoff, *Recollections of a Lifetime* (Cincinnati, OH: The Robert Clarke Co., 1900), 214–215; Joyner, *Wells*, 123; Slap, *Doom of Reconstruction*, 129–130.

[48] Baird, *Rights of American Producers*, 4; *Free-Trader* (May 1870), 204; Oswald Garrison Villard, *Some Newspapers and Newspaper Men* (New York: A. A. Knopf, 1923), 297; Slap, *Doom of Reconstruction*, 128; Leslie Butler, *Critical Americans: Victorian Intellectuals and Transatlantic Liberal Reform* (Chapel Hill: University of North Carolina Press, 2007), 225–226.

attempt to annex Santo Domingo.[49] As a result, Grant turned against the independents for thwarting his expansionist scheme, and proceeded further down the path of cronyism and political patronage in order to gain temporary congressional allies. Grant thereby also garnered further animosity from civil service reformers. Yet around this time a growing Anglo-American crisis was also reaching its breaking point, temporarily overshadowing these ever more visible Republican rifts.

"Messages of peace and goodwill": free-trade transatlanticism and the 1871 Treaty of Washington

With the presidential election of 1872 on the horizon, transatlantic Cobdenite efforts turned toward foreign policy. Anglo-American tensions had heightened throughout the 1860s. Anglophobia did not just spill over from the Civil War; it flooded the American political landscape. By 1870, for its part, the British government was rather eager to bring an end to transatlantic ill will as its political leaders peered with anxiety across the English Channel at the outbreak of war between France and Prussia. Many US Northerners, however, held a lingering resentment over seeming British support for the South during the Civil War, particularly over the British selling of warships like the *Alabama* to the Confederacy. The British-made vessels had proven effective against northern ships, and the US federal government now sought indemnities from Britain over its role in these so-called *Alabama* Claims. The possibility of war between Britain and the United States loomed large – an ominous speculation that was commonly batted about on both sides of the Atlantic. "There is to be a war of some kind with England," Henry Carey observed in 1869, "either of tariff or of gunpowder."[50]

The postbellum prospect of Anglo-American strife spurred proponents of peace to encourage instead global Anglo-Saxon political union in order to avoid further disagreement. Cobdenite Goldwin Smith, having just left his post as Oxford University's Regius Professor in order to teach in the

[49] For further Cobdenite opposition, see Robert L. Beisner, "Thirty Years Before Manila: E. L. Godkin, Carl Schurz, and Anti-Imperialism in the Gilded Age," *Historian* 30 (August 1968): 561–577.

[50] Carey to Charles Sumner, May 3, 1869, reel 46, Sumner Papers; *Extension of Peace: Proposal for the Amalgamation of Great Britain and the United States* (London: Hammond & Co., 1873 [1871]). See, also, Adrian Cook, *The Alabama Claims: American Politics and Anglo-American Relations, 1865–1872* (Ithaca, NY: Cornell University Press, 1975); Allan Nevins, *Hamilton Fish: The Inner History of the Grant Administration* (New York: Dodd, Mead, 1936); Sexton, "The Funded Loan and *Alabama* Claims"; Duncan Andrew Campbell, *Unlikely Allies: Britain, America and the Victorian Origins of the Special Relationship* (London: Hambledon Continuum, 2007), 182–188.

United States, held out hope that the *Alabama* dispute would not lead to violence. He wrote the Cobden Club's founder, Thomas Bayley Potter, that the club might even lend its aid to ending the "Alabama case" as it was "just the sort of thing for the Club to do ... if we could once get rid of this wretched quarrel ... a great obstacle to Free Trade principles in America will be removed." But Smith also warned Potter that "any direct efforts on the part of Englishmen to propagate Free Trade here by supporting Free Trade associations" needed to be avoided, as "they put a weaker and fatal efficacy into the hands of Carey & Co."[51]

Smith and Potter's desire to see the Cobden Club play a part in the proceedings was not all that farfetched. Anglo-American Cobdenites would play crucial roles throughout the dispute. The showdown already was appearing less dangerous with Cobdenite Charles Francis Adams, Sr. as American arbiter, and with Cobdenite William Gladstone as Britain's prime minister.[52] Cyrus Field played a key role, as well. As dangerous as it was, he had long found himself acting as an unofficial American ambassador between the two countries. He had already diffused a difficult situation during the Civil War when Confederates had attempted to draw Canada into the conflict by staging a Canadian raid upon St Albans, Vermont. Indeed, throughout the Civil War, Field had maintained close ties with England. Perhaps too close; charges of treason were brought against him in 1862 owing to his intimate transatlantic correspondence. A decade later, riding high upon his transatlantic cable, Field would prove integral in bringing a peaceful end to the *Alabama* controversy. In an era where the US Foreign Service was less than professionalized, Field – alongside the efforts of international bankers wary of an upset financial market – epitomized the importance of nongovernmental actors in late-nineteenth-century foreign relations.[53]

Field found himself in London when the *Alabama* Claims dispute broke out in the late 1860s. It was further fortuitous that his friend William Gladstone had returned to the British premiership, compounded by Field's close contact with President Grant and his cabinet, as well as strong ties to the British legation in Washington. Field first encouraged

---

[51] Smith to Potter, November 1, 1869; Smith to Potter, December 7, 1869; Smith to Potter, February 1, 1870, Add. 43663, Vol. XVII, Cobden Papers. On the Irish issue, see especially David Sim, *A Union Forever: The Irish Question and U.S. Foreign Relations in the Victorian Age* (Ithaca, NY: Cornell University Press, 2014).

[52] Early in his career, William Gladstone had been a Tory opponent of Cobden, but converted to Cobdenism by around 1860. See Anthony Howe, "Gladstone and Cobden," in *Gladstone Centenary Essays*, ed. by David Bebbington and Roger Swift (Liverpool: Liverpool University Press, 2000), 113–132.

[53] Samuel Carter III, *Cyrus Field: Man of Two Worlds* (New York: G. P. Putnam's Sons, 1968), 217–218, 198–203; Sexton, "The Funded Loan and the *Alabama* Claims."

John Bright to offer his own pacific opinion on the *Alabama* matter in order to thaw the sudden chill in relations. Field then held a banquet for the English High Commissioners, where his guests gave their "unofficial and cordial ratification" to the Treaty of Washington, and where William Cullen Bryant and Henry Ward Beecher gave speeches on the future of Anglo-American peace and friendship.[54]

No matter how many letters were exchanged, however, Bright's old friend Charles Sumner, in his usual uncompromising and principled manner, proved intransigent on the subject of reparations. In initial agreement with President Grant and Hamilton Fish, Sumner demanded that Canada and the West Indies be handed over to the United States both as payment for Britain's transgressions, and so as to avoid any future conflicts between the North American neighbors. Such a desire to join the United States with Canada was concurrently shared by Goldwin Smith, an idea that he would advocate for many years to come, although never in the outraged spirit in which it was promulgated by Sumner.[55]

Sumner's vituperative response, exaggerated as it was in the British press, has since been portrayed as one stemming from some combination of Anglophobia, jingoism, and an unhappy marriage. Yet it was not fear of the British, militarism, or his estranged wife that motivated him, although his actions might metaphorically be viewed as those of a spurned lover. Sumner's was the anger of an Anglophile upset that the British government and people had not lived up to his high expectations during the Civil War. It was also the reaction of a Cobdenite peace advocate seeking an end to any further disputes between the two countries on the North American continent. Sumner was flummoxed to find that his emotive message had been so misconstrued in Britain; the transatlantic hysteria that followed was entirely unintentional.[56]

---

[54] Justin McCarthy, ed., *The Settlement of the Alabama Question. The Banquet Given at New York to Her Britannic Majesty's High Commissioners by Mr. Cyrus W. Field* (London: Tinsley Brothers, 1871), ix; *London Times*, March 4, 1872, 12; Field to Vice-President Schuyler Colfax, February 24, 1872; Francis Wells to Field, April 16, 1872; Edward Thornton to Field, April 17, 1872, folder 2, box 1, Cyrus W. Field Papers, NYPL; Carter, *Field*, 198–203.

[55] Goldwin Smith, *America & England Their Present Relations. A Reply to Senator Sumner's Recent Speech* (London: John Cambden Hotten, 1869); D. H. Chamberlain, *Charles Sumner and the Treaty of Washington* (New York: Riverside Press, 1901), 32–33. For French-Canadian support for annexation at this time, see Hector Fabre, *Confederation, Independence, Annexion: Conference faite a l'Institut Candien de Quebec* (Quebec: Imprime au bureau de l'Evenement, 1871).

[56] Campbell, *Unlikely Allies*, 184; David M. Pletcher, *The Diplomacy of Trade and Investment: American Economic Expansion in the Hemisphere, 1865–1900* (Columbia: University of Missouri Press, 1998), 53; Cook, *The Alabama Claims*, 89–102.

Sumner's Canadian agitation also had a strong connection to Richard Cobden, as it stemmed from Cobden's own "loose the bond and go" approach to the British colonies. In response to Sumner's enthusiastic reaction to Montreal's agitation in favor of American annexation in 1849, Cobden had written to Sumner: "I agree with you that nature has decided that Canada and the United States must become one ... if the people of Canada are tolerably unanimous in wishing to sever the very slight thread which now binds them to this country, I see no reason why ... it should not be done amicably." As Charles Francis Adams, Jr. noted in his study of the event: "These words of Cobden furnished the key of the situation as it lay in his essentially doctrinaire mind. He, accordingly, looked forward with confidence to the incorporation of British Columbia into the American Union; but he always insisted that it 'should be made by peaceful annexation, by the voluntary act of England, and with the cordial assent of the colonists.'" To support his uncompromising stance, Sumner would repeat Cobden's words as late as April 1869.[57]

But Sumner misread the situation in Canada and in England. Unfortunately for him, although one failed Canadian proposal for a North American Zollverein was briefly put forth in 1870, the annexationist sentiment that had been popular between 1849 and 1854 had subsided in Canada. Goldwin Smith observed at the time that London also was "beginning to turn away from the tenets of the Manchester school," as demands arose for greater imperial consolidation rather than devolution.[58] Sumner had effectively misunderstood the rise of Canadian nationalism that had followed confederation in 1867. Unlike in the American case, Canadian nationalism "never meant separation" from the motherland. Thus, when Sumner was told that English sentiment was decidedly against letting Canada go, Sumner stubbornly replied that "he knew ... that England was willing; with the sentiment so strong in England the Canadians could be dealt with." Goldwin Smith admitted afterward that Sumner had been misled by his years of correspondence with Cobden, Bright, and the Duke of Argyle. Much of this international crisis therefore stemmed from Sumner's misunderstanding of Canadian nationalism and the dampening of Cobdenite sentiment in Britain. Sumner's Cobdenite misreading of the situation perplexed more than

[57] Sumner to Cobden, May 2, 1849, reel 68; Cobden to Sumner, November 7, 1849, microfilm, reel 7, Charles Sumner Papers, Houghton Library, Harvard University, Cambridge, MA; Goldwin Smith, *Treaty of Washington: A Study in Imperial History* (Ithaca, NY: Cornell University Press, 1941), 19, 20, 29, 29n; Charles Francis Adams, Jr., *Before and After the Treaty of Washington: The American Civil War and the War in the Transvaal* (New York: New York Historical Society, 1902), 103–104.

[58] Smith, *Treaty of Washington*, 19, 20, 29, 29n; Marc-William Palen, "Adam Smith as Advocate of Empire, c. 1870–1932," *Historical Journal* 57 (March 2014): 179–198.

the British press. Henry Adams expressed his own incomprehension of Sumner's pro-annexationist motivation to John Bright, and even urged Edward Atkinson to bring Sumner to his senses by giving his support to the Treaty of Washington.[59]

In 1871, a settlement was ultimately reached through international arbitration, in no small part owing to the efforts of Cyrus Field. Seeing friends Grant and Sumner as the crux and key to peaceful settlement, Field sent a torrent of letters to the two of them throughout 1869, anxious as he was "to keep good feeling between England and America."[60] Following the successful *Alabama* settlement, Field invited his transatlantic friends to his regularly held Thanksgiving dinner at the Buckingham Palace Hotel in London, complete with sweet potatoes, pies, and roast turkey. Prime Minister Gladstone, sitting on Field's right at the dinner, commented that Field had been "the most efficient promoter of the settlement of the *Alabama* question," and that Cyrus was like "a telegraph wire, so often has he crossed the Atlantic, and always charged with messages of peace and good will from nation to nation."[61]

The 1871 settlement's possible positive implications for Anglo-American friendship were not lost on transatlantic Cobdenites. In 1873, Wells remarked at the annual Cobden Club dinner that the Treaty of Washington had marked "one of the most important epochs in the history of our time." It was also a good step in the direction of free trade through its liberalization of the Anglo-American fish trade. While the world was still far from attaining universal peace, "this is but one more reason for seeking the means of preventing war." He concluded, amid boisterous cheers, with a toast to international arbitration, peace, friendship, and transatlantic brotherhood.[62]

Such an amicable relationship, however, remained a long way off. Listian Henry Carey strongly opposed the treaty. With considerably less enthusiasm, Carey agreed with Wells that the treaty "is really one of free trade with the British Empire." Playing upon fears of the British, Carey

[59] Adams, *Before and After the Treaty of Washington*, 103–104; Smith, *Treaty of Washington*, 29; Henry Adams to John Bright, February 3, 1869, Add. 43391, Vol. IX, Bright Papers; Henry Adams to Edward Atkinson, February 1, 1869, carton 1, Atkinson Papers. For the Canadian proposal for a Zollverein stemming from the *Alabama* dispute, see *New York Times*, March 30, 1870, 2.

[60] Carter, *Man of Two Worlds*, 281–282.

[61] Carter, *Man of Two Worlds*, 299; *Proceedings at the Banquet given by Mr. Cyrus W. Field, at the Palace Hotel, Buckingham Gate, London, on Thursday the 28th November, 1872* (London: R. Clay, Sons, and Taylor, 1872), 6–7, 11. See, also, *Report of the Proceedings at the Dinner of the Cobden Club, July 11, 1874* (London: Cassell Petter & Galpin, 1874), 15.

[62] David Ames Wells, *Free Trade and Free Enterprise: Report of the Proceedings at the Dinner of the Cobden Club* (London: Cassell, Petter & Gilpin, 1873), 63, 72, 73.

wrote to Grant that the treaty's softening of US trade relations with Canada merely allowed the British to side-step American protectionist walls and would allow a British fleet to float with ease into the Great Lakes, placing US cities in imminent danger.[63] While transatlantic Cobdenism played an important role in settling the *Alabama* dispute and ameliorating Anglo-American relations, economic nationalists like Carey showed that their Anglophobic outlook was far from softened by the dispute's settlement.

Conclusion

Cyrus Field's laying of the Atlantic cable in 1866 dangled the tantalizing prospect of better Anglo-American relations. Aided by the speeding up of transatlantic communications alongside various propagandistic efforts of the Cobden Club and the AFTL, British and American Cobdenites were increasingly making their presence felt in foreign and domestic affairs. Their influence manifested itself through the peaceful settlement of the *Alabama* claims, the burgeoning American free-trade movement, and the corresponding Anglophobic charges of a vast free-trade conspiracy. Conspiratorial charges were leveled against the real and perceived American influence of the Cobden Club, which had become closely tied to the AFTL. Indeed, US Cobden Club members took charge of the postbellum free-trade movement, and gained further intellectual leadership following the Cobdenite conversion of David Ames Wells, a onetime protectionist disciple of Henry Charles Carey.

American free traders found further postbellum inspiration from the antebellum abolitionist movement and the earlier successes of the ACLL in England. For independent Republicans like Wells, Horace White, and Edward Atkinson, protectionism was but a further shackle enslaving Americans; rather than having the freedom to trade with all the world, Americans were instead being coerced into buying foreign and American-made goods at artificially high prices by order of the US government. American Cobdenites also believed that cronyism, political corruption, monopoly, and war invariably followed in protectionism's wake.

The Republican party all the while was fast moving away from its antebellum antislavery ideological foundations and was rebranding itself as the party of protectionism and imperial expansion. Like their Cobdenite counterparts, Republican economic nationalists used antislavery language.

[63] Carey to Grant, November 23, 1874, in Henry C. Carey, *Miscellaneous Papers on the National Finances, the Currency, and Other Economic Subjects* (Philadelphia, PA: Henry Carey Baird & Co., 1875), 17–20.

But they instead associated free trade with slavery, suggesting that premature adoption of free trade would enslave American markets and infant industries to the more advanced British manufacturers. The party's Listian wing would also begin to coercively seek access to Latin American and Pacific markets, in part to undermine British influence in those regions.

In desperation, the Republican Cobdenite minority worked to alter the party's economic nationalist course through political action. With the establishment of the Liberal Republican movement, they sought to remake the Republican party into one of free trade, anti-imperialism, and civil service reform. By doing so, they found themselves directly involved in halting Republican imperial ventures and in shaping the outcome of various political contests, from the 1872 presidential elections to the 1884 election of Grover Cleveland.

4   Fighting over free trade
Party realignment and the imperialism of economic nationalism, 1872–1884

[Henry Carey] has over and over again expressed the opinion that the death of Richard Cobden was one of the crowning mercies for which the United States had cause for gratitude.

> David Ames Wells, speaking at the 1873 Cobden Club banquet.[1]

Mr. Wells would gladly have repeated in America the career of Cobden.   J. Laurence Laughlin.[2]

The tariff issue dominated late-nineteenth-century American politics like no other. The Republican party's Cobdenite independents, believing that free trade and non-interventionism would bring prosperity and peace to the world, found themselves outnumbered by Republicans who instead believed that nations were locked in a perpetual state of war. For the latter, protectionism was viewed as both a defensive and an offensive weapon for sheltering American infant industries from unfettered global market competition, especially from Free Trade England. Protectionism's extraordinary ability to indirectly redistribute wealth between and within sections also made it a fixture of congressional policy-making. With the exception of the Democratic party's Randall faction, a majority of congressional Democrats tended to champion Jeffersonian free trade. In contrast, a majority of the Republican party favored protectionism, despite the ongoing efforts of its Cobdenite wing. And with Democrats usually controlling the Senate and Republicans the House, any significant tariff revisions usually occurred only on the rare occasions in which one party gained control of both congressional houses (Republicans in 1890 and 1897; Democrats in 1894). Congressional voting data also suggests that the parties generally remained intractable concerning the tariff issue throughout the era. Minority protectionist elements in the New South had little tangible success in turning their

---

[1] David Ames Wells, *Free Trade and Free Enterprise: Report of the Proceedings at the Dinner of the Cobden Club* (London: Cassell, Petter & Gilpin, 1873), 45.

[2] J. Laurence Laughlin, "David Ames Wells," *Journal of Political Economy* 7 (December 1898): 93–94.

section away from its Jeffersonian ideological roots, for example, and America's Cobdenites in the North and West had little to show for their attempts to turn the Republican party away from its economic nationalist course from the mid-1860s to mid-1880s.[3]

Owing in no small part to the growing importance and divisiveness of the tariff issue, the 1870s ushered in an era of national party crisis. The Democratic foundations were cracked, its southern wing seeking Redemption through black disenfranchisement, political intimidation, and Klan terrorism. The Republican party found itself riven by factionalism as its powerful old-guard "Stalwart" pro-Grant political machinery led by Roscoe Conkling squared off against its younger "Half-Breed" rivals, who instead supported James G. Blaine, John Sherman, or George Frisbie Hoar.[4] A third group, the party's Liberal Republican independents, found themselves at loggerheads with the Republican faithful in attempting to end the party's corruptive political machines, its spoils system, its protectionist policies, and Reconstruction. Black Republicans became ever more disillusioned while they watched the onetime antislavery party shift toward these other issues, and away from African American civil rights.[5] Following the 1870 ratification of the

---

[3] Richard Franklin Bensel, *The Political Economy of American Industrialization, 1877–1900* (Cambridge: Cambridge University Press, 2000), 506, 468–509. See especially Tables 7.1 and 7.2, pp. 470–471. Sharyn O'Halloran, for example, suggests that congressional trade voting patterns aligned one-to-one with partisan affiliation, whereas Judith Goldstein has shown that ideology at times trumped sectional and party interests. Sharyn O'Halloran, *Politics, Process, and American Trade Policy* (Ann Arbor: University of Michigan Press, 1994), 51; Judith Goldstein, *Ideas, Interests, and American Trade Policy* (Ithaca, NY: Cornell University Press, 1993).

[4] Charles W. Calhoun, *Conceiving a New Republic: The Republican Party and the Southern Question, 1869–1900* (Lawrence: University Press of Kansas, 2006); Frank B. Evans, "Wharton Barker and the Republican National Convention of 1880," *Pennsylvania History* 27 (January 1960): 28–43; Richard E. Welch, Jr., *George Frisbie Hoar and the Half-Breed Republicans* (Cambridge, MA: Harvard University Press, 1971); Allan Peskin, "Who Were the Stalwarts? Who Were Their Rivals? Republican Factions in the Gilded Age," *Political Science Quarterly* 99 (Winter 1984–1985): 703–716.

[5] Richard A. Gerber, "The Liberal Republicans of 1872 in Historiographical Perspective," *Journal of American History* 62 (June 1975): 40–73; Matthew T. Downey, "Horace Greeley and the Politicians: The Liberal Republican Convention in 1872," *Journal of American History* 53 (March 1967): 727–750; Earle D. Ross, *The Liberal Republican Movement* (New York: H. Holt and Co., 1919); Patrick W. Riddleberger, "The Break in the Radical Ranks: Liberals vs. Stalwarts in the Election of 1872," *Journal of Negro History* 44 (April 1959): 136–157. On black disillusionment, see August Meier, "The Negro and the Democratic Party, 1875–1915," *Phylon* 17 (2nd Qtr. 1956): 173–191; Lawrence Grossman, *The Democratic Party and the Negro: Northern and National Politics, 1868–92* (Urbana: University of Illinois Pres, 1976); Peter D. Kingman and David T. Geithman, "Negro Dissidence and the Republican Party, 1864–1872," *Phylon* 40 (2nd Qtr. 1979): 172–182. On the Gilded Age national party system, see Daniel Klinghard, *The Nationalization of American Political Parties, 1880–1896* (Cambridge: Cambridge University Press, 2010).

Fifteenth Amendment guaranteeing voting rights irrespective of race or color, for example, laissez-faire Liberal Republicans speculated that the federal government arm had been extended far enough – maybe even too far – to protect freedmen and women.[6] And the Republican party as a whole began to turn away from issues of antislavery toward those of political economy: tariff and monetary reform.[7] The intraparty conflict and ideological reformation that followed would culminate between the presidential contests of 1872 and 1884.

The results of the 1872 presidential campaign reverberated across national politics, the transatlantic free-trade movement, and US foreign relations for years to come. Liberal Republican Cobdenites encountered intense opposition to their attempts to reconfigure the party's dominant economic nationalist ideology in the North and West. Along the way, these free-trade Republican independents became vocal anti-imperial critics of the Republican party's early implementation of the imperialism of economic nationalism. This embryonic imperial policy would grow as Listian nationalists like James G. Blaine (R-ME) began having their way in domestic and foreign affairs. Their progressive Listian global vision sought to reform American imperialism by forcing open new markets for American goods while maintaining protectionism at home, thereby promising higher prices for American goods and, correspondingly, higher wages for American laborers. Whereas in England free trade coexisted with empire and civil society, within the less industrially developed United States economic nationalism and empire were instead starting to align. Listian nationalism was beginning to find an accepting home market.

Republican imperialism of economic nationalism would start to become more politically palatable owing to the onset of a global economic depression in 1873. The depression led to severe lay-offs and business failures in the United States. Added to this, the federal government's *de facto* deflationary turn to the gold standard that same year – the "Crime of '73" – constricted the money supply, making it harder for indebted Americans to pay back their loans. Populist distrust of the British-led

---

[6] This retreat from civil rights coincided with a broader anti-democratic turn among some northern elites. See Sven Beckert, "Democracy and its Discontents: Contesting Suffrage Rights in Gilded Age New York," *Past and Present* 174 (February 2002): 116–157.

[7] Andrew L. Slap, *The Doom of Reconstruction: The Liberal Republicans in the Civil War Era* (New York: Fordham University Press, 2006); Wilbert H. Ahern, "Laissez Faire vs. Equal Rights: Liberal Republicans and Limits to Reconstruction," *Phylon* 40 (Spring 1979): 52–65; Patrick W. Riddleberger, "The Radicals' Abandonment of the Negro during Reconstruction," *Journal of Negro History* 45 (April 1960): 88–102. Many southern black Republicans were also staunch supporters of government-backed internal improvements. Kingman and Geithman, "Negro Dissidence," 177–178.

gold standard and its American adherents grew throughout the decade, an Anglophobic sentiment that would be used against Anglo-American "goldbug" advocates of free trade and anti-imperialism. For their part, Cobdenite critics of American imperialism strengthened their transatlantic ties in response to the protectionist and imperialist proclivities of the postbellum Republican party. And these same American free traders continued to draw inspiration from England's ACLL, its free-trade successes now thirty years past, alongside contemporary support from London's hyperactive Cobden Club.

An examination of the domestic and international dimensions of the American free-trade movement offers a new ideological approach to postbellum party politics and foreign policy. US Cobdenites – under the direction of David Ames Wells, Horace White, William Cullen Bryant, Edward Atkinson, and R. R. Bowker – worked to halt the Republican party's sharp economic nationalist turn and to undermine its incipient imperialist impulse. Republican intransigence to these attempts would gradually encourage the Liberal Republican Cobdenites to shift their support to reformist elements within the Democratic party. This party realignment would reach fruition during the pivotal presidential elections of 1884 – with long-term consequences for American global economic integration for decades to come.

The disastrous 1872 elections

The 1872 Liberal Republican Convention in Cincinnati garnered support from disaffected Republicans and a growing number of Bourbon Democrats, but the convention's faction of Liberal Republican free traders stood out as the most zealous. David Ames Wells, George Hoadley, and Horace White were on the committee that framed the Liberal Republican national platform, and William Grosvenor laid out the intended goals of this "meeting of Republican reform friends": first, restore local self-government in the South; second, establish a tariff for revenue only; third, bring about "hard money" currency reform; and fourth, institute proper reform of the civil service. Grosvenor himself was instructed to remain in the capital as the "Washington agent" of the AFTL.[8]

---

[8] Caro Lloyd, *Henry Demarest Lloyd, 1847-1903, A Biography*, vol. I (New York: G. P. Putnam's Sons), 26–30; *New York Tribune*, March 16, 1872, 4; Grosvenor to Atkinson, December 21, 1871; March 28, 1872, Jacob D. Cox to Atkinson, April 5, 1872, Grosvenor to Atkinson, April 6, 1872, carton 2; Atkinson to Charles Sumner, April 3, 1872, carton 14, Atkinson Papers.

With the endorsement of Wells and the AFTL, Charles Francis Adams, Sr. initially stood out as a strong, albeit reluctant, favorite for the convention's presidential nomination. Yet the free traders quickly lost control of the convention. This happened in part because the convention contained a motley mixture of free-trade and protectionist elements, as well as some men focusing solely on civil service reform or on a more liberal policy in the New South that included amnesty for ex-Confederates. Another reason for their loss of control resulted from the free-trade faction's lack of political talent. They were outmaneuvered by protectionist *New York Tribune* editor Horace Greeley, who had become involved in the Liberal Republican political movement. Greeley's sudden interest in the movement evoked distrust from Atkinson and other free-trade leaders. They did not believe Greeley "to be honest as to the tariff" or civil service reform. Soon confirming their suspicions, Greeley threatened to withdraw the *Tribune*'s powerful support if the Liberal Republican platform included a free-trade plank: "If it should be decided to make Free Trade a cornerstone of the Cincinnati Movement," he and his newspaper would "ask to be counted out." In an ironic twist of political fate and maneuvering, the Cobdenites' same economic nationalist enemy Greeley thereafter obtained the convention's presidential nomination, as well as the national Democratic party's subsequent half-hearted endorsement.[9]

Cobdenite apprehension of Greeley's machinations turned into paranoia when it was suspected that key Liberal Republican leaders had sacrificed the free-trade cause upon Greeley's protectionist alter. The AFTL leadership was concerned about rumors that William Grosvenor, their own Taxpayers' Union lobbyist in Washington, might have switched sides. As a result, the AFTL leadership feared that Grosvenor's secret list of American free traders might "fall into the hands of the Greeley men," as AFTL Secretary Mahlon Sands explained to Edward Atkinson. With Atkinson's cautious authorization, AFTL officers Sands, Henry D. Lloyd, and Robert Minturn correspondingly had Grosvenor's rooms in Washington, DC, ransacked while he was away. His books and papers were confiscated and taken to AFTL headquarters in New York for further inspection. An embarrassing volley of charges and countercharges followed this act of internal espionage. Grosvenor, indignant, explained

---

[9] Gerber, "The Liberal Republicans of 1872"; Slap, *Doom of Reconstruction*, 126–163; Downey, "Horace Greeley and the Politicians"; Ross, *Liberal Republican Movement*; Riddleberger, "Break in the Radical Ranks"; John G. Sproat, *"The Best Men": Liberal Reformers in the Gilded Age* (New York: Oxford University Press, 1968), 82. On the "ideological confusion" of mid-nineteenth-century Republican politics, see, also, Adam-Max Tuchinsky, *Horace Greeley's New-York Tribune: Civil War-era Socialism and the Crisis of Free Labor* (Ithaca, NY: Cornell University Press, 2009), 215, chap. 7.

his innocence in the matter. With AFTL faces red over the affair, tempers soon cooled, and the decision was made to pay Grosvenor's remaining debts in Washington and to dissolve the Taxpayers' Union.[10]

This episode hints at the distrust and disunity that followed in the wake of the disastrous 1872 Liberal Republican Convention. America's Cobdenites thereafter had a poor choice of backing either Grant or Greeley for president.[11] Lacking an acceptable presidential option, in desperation William Lloyd Garrison lashed out at Charles Sumner and Horace White, and White's *Chicago Tribune* defended itself against editorial barrages from Garrison, Bryant's *New York Evening Post*, and Godkin's *Nation*. Adding to the growing disconnect between the Cobdenites and the mainstream Republican party, the pro-free-trade *Chicago Tribune* found itself replaced by the newly christened protectionist *Chicago Inter-Ocean* as the Republican party's official Illinois news organ.[12] Upon Grant's reelection, the *Chicago Tribune* summed up the situation: "Grant, the practical protectionist, has triumphed over Greeley, the theoretical protectionist, who suffered himself to be made the figure-bearer of a free trade party."[13] The fallout from the convention had a further important result. Greeley's nomination and his subsequent loss to Grant further weakened the tenuous ties binding the minority Cobdenite faction to the Republican party mainstream.

Although maintaining their independent status and free-trade proclivities, Wells's Cobdenites dissolved the Liberal Republican movement in despair. The independent Republican free traders were once again left directionless, floundering in relative political impotence. They looked helplessly on as the Panic of 1873 struck. Grant and the Stalwarts took the brunt of the blame, paving the way for a Democratic takeover of the House of Representatives the following year. Atkinson took the 1872 convention debacle particularly hard, and thereafter developed a more patient, long-term view toward tariff reform. He afterward wrote to Wells

---

[10] Carl Schurz to Horace Greeley, May 6, 1872, Box 4, Horace Greeley Papers, NYPL; Minturn to Atkinson, May 9, 1872; Sands to Atkinson, May 10, 1872; Grosvenor to Atkinson, May 12, 1872; Sands to Atkinson, May 13, 1872; Sands to Atkinson, May 22, 1872, carton 2; Atkinson to Sands, May 10; May 11; May 14, 1872; Atkinson to Grosvenor, May 11; May 14, 1872; Atkinson to Minturn, May 13; May 15; May 21, 1872, carton 14, Atkinson Papers.

[11] E. L. Godkin to Atkinson, May 29, 1872; Lloyd to Atkinson, June 4, 1872; S. L. Taylor to Atkinson, June 24, 1872; Jacob D. Cox to Atkinson, July 2, 1872; J. S. Moore to Atkinson, July 6, 1872, carton 2, Atkinson Papers.

[12] Slap, *Doom of Reconstruction*, 172–182; Joseph Logsdon, *Horace White, Nineteenth Century Liberal* (Westport: Greenwood, 1971), 238–275.

[13] Sproat, *"The Best Men,"* 75–82. In 1866, Horace White had attempted to educate Grant on the subject of free trade, sending him a copy of the *Catechism on the Corn Laws*, a volume that was duly shelved, unread, in Grant's library. Logsdon, *White*, 169–170.

that "we must . . . remember that England took from 1824 to 1846 before the corn laws were repealed, and it took 20 years more to perfect their work." It might take a while, but he was confident free trade would win out.[14]

Also with optimism, the *Chicago Tribune* and David Wells looked upon the tens of thousands of mobilizing western Granger farmers. White's *Tribune* offered editorial aid to those farmers who were showing free-trade colors.[15] White and the AFTL became influential enough among the Grangers that one protectionist journal noted suspiciously how the "cunning" AFTL was working "to deceive the farmers into the belief that the country, owing to the protective features of the tariff, is about to enter upon a period of serious embarrassment, from which it can escape only by the early adoption of a free-trade tariff." New York City's Cobdenite news organ *New Century* noted that the Grangers themselves appeared "ripe for the enlightenment" of free trade.[16]

Such optimistic free-trade designs for the Granger movement, however, proved rather precipitous. Rapid economic growth coupled with a restricted currency led to deflation and declining crop prices from 1873 to 1896. Grangers, suffering from the deflationary policy, sought an expansion of the money supply to counter this trend; and the adoption of national bimetallism – the national coinage of silver and gold – seemed like an effective way to do so. This upsurge in silverite sentiment in the wake of the 1873 panic led goldbug AFTL leader Robert Minturn to write Atkinson in 1878 that he had at first hoped that economic "hard times" would have turned Westerners to the principles of free trade. Instead, the West had moved toward national bimetallism.[17]

To counter this move, America's pro-gold-standard Cobdenites regrouped to oppose the Bland–Allison Act of 1878. In doing so, they unwittingly placed themselves at the transatlantic center of further conspiratorial charges – this time surrounding monetary policy. The passage of the Bland–Allison Act ended up being a slight victory for American silverites as it provided that the US government would make monthly purchases of western silver. Cobdenite opposition to the bill also caused these "enemies of silver" to be characterized afterward as co-conspirators with the gold-standard bearers of the City of London, as they jointly connived to keep

---

[14] Atkinson to Wells, November 11, 1875, reel 3, Wells Papers.
[15] Wells, *Free Trade and Free Enterprise*, 62; *Chicago Tribune*, January 16, 1873, 4; January 18, 1873, 2; March 18, 1873, 4; March 28, 1873, 2; April 3, 1873, 1; April 17, 1873, 2; April 19, 1873, 2; July 4, 1873, 2.
[16] "The Granges and the Free-Trade League," *Republic* (November 1873): I, 513; *New Century* (February 1876): 67.
[17] Minturn to Atkinson, July 3, 1878, carton 2, Atkinson Papers.

Figure 4.1 "Cobdenite Insignias." The International Free-Trade
Alliance's [center] and the New York Free Trade Club's [right] insignias
were nearly identical to the Cobden Club's [left].

"up their Cataline assemblages" with "their daggers ever ready to strike
down the silver dollar," or so Elihu Farmer recounted in *The Conspiracy
against Silver* (1886). The US goldbug "priests to this golden Juggernaut . . .
smile to see the wreck and ruin its gilded wheels have wrought; while
around this car may be seen the bloody footprints of the British lion."[18]

While this sanguine battle over silver played out throughout the 1870s,
American Cobdenites continued to mobilize. Free-trade agitation in New
England led to the creation of the Boston Free Trade Club, which the
Nation described as "one of the most active and rapidly growing organiza-
tions of the kind." In New York City, Abraham Earle, R. R. Bowker,
William Cullen Bryant, William Graham Sumner, and Parke Godwin
established the International Free Trade Alliance (IFTA), which once
again turned to the free-trade efforts of Richard Cobden for inspiration.
The alliance's transatlantic energy was doubly useful, with the AFTL still
reeling from the 1872 election fallout. Along with using the ACLL as a
blueprint for American agitation, the new alliance also borrowed the
Cobden Club's insignia [figure 4.1] and its mantra: "Free Trade, Peace
and Good Will among Nations." The IFTA's members numbered throughout the United States, and stretched as far north as Quebec and as far west
as Japan, giving some credence to its titular claim to internationalism.[19]

---

[18] E. J. Farmer, *The Conspiracy against Silver, or a Plea for Bi-Metallism in the United States*
(Cleveland, OH: Hiles & Coggshall Printers and Binder, 1886), 8.
[19] *Nation*, December 28, 1876, 377; Abraham L. Earle, *Our Revenue System and the Civil
Service, Shall They be Reformed?* (New York: International Free Trade Alliance, 1874);
First Report and Circular Address of the International Free Trade Alliance (1874); *New
Century* (December 1875): 9–11, 17; *New Century* (January 1876): 43.

Where Edward Atkinson moderated his Peelite approach to ending American protectionism, David Wells strengthened his radical subscription to Victorian free-trade ideology.[20] Wells returned to England in 1873 to speak at the Cobden Club's annual dinner then being held in Greenwich. Introduced at the banquet as "the leader of the Free Trade party in that country," he highlighted the outspoken economic nationalist opposition to Cobdenite principles in the United States. Fear of Victorian free trade remained strong among his countrymen who subscribed to "the old, selfish, and Pagan principle" of protectionism. Wells, quite aware of the suspicion his trip would arouse at home, also acknowledged that some among them would consider his attendance at the dinner "sufficient evidence of a conspiracy and a reward for the betrayal of their industrial interests."[21]

Unlike the charges of conspiracy, the cosmopolitan flattery bestowed upon Wells was well deserved. Like Cobden before him, Wells was indeed becoming the "International Man," accepting honorary membership in the Royal Statistical Society in 1871; filling J. S. Mill's now vacant position in the French Academy of Political Science in 1874; joining the *Regia Accademia dei Lincei* of Italy in 1877; and presiding over the AFTL in 1871, the American Social Science Association in 1875, and the New London Historical Society in 1880.[22] America's Listians had certainly found a formidable intellectual opponent in Wells. Although beset by continued charges of a transatlantic conspiracy and political setbacks, Wells and his Cobdenite coterie were starting to regain some of their lost momentum and to strengthen their transatlantic ties.

Peelite politics and the 1876 elections

Outnumbered in their own party, independent Republican free traders were not afraid of reaching across the aisle when the opportunity arose. In 1876, Wells and J. S. Moore worked privately with his ally Congressman William R. Morrison (D-IL), the Chairman of the House Committee on Ways and Means, and a founding member of the recently created Illinois Free Trade League. Their 1876 efforts evolved into the first serious attempt to lower US tariffs following the Civil War. The proposed Morrison Tariff bill ultimately ended up "conservative" rather than

[20] Louis Mallet to Thomas Bailey Potter, November 18, 1872, Cobden Papers, Add. 43663, Vol. XVII.
[21] Minutes of May 8, 1873, CC MSS; *London Times*, June 30, 1873, 9; Wells, *Free Trade and Free Enterprise*.
[22] Terrill, "David A. Wells"; Worthington Chauncey Ford to Wells, October 23, 1880, folder "1880," box 1, Worthington Chauncey Ford Papers, NYPL.

"extreme" in its tariff reductions, upon the request of Democratic Speaker of the House Michael Kerr. Coinciding as it did amid the era's nascent ideological conflict over American economic globalization, Anglophobic Republicans and the protectionist press labeled it "an English measure – a Cobden Club measure ... designed to subserve British at the expense of American interests." The Morrison bill would become the first among many unsuccessful attempts to reduce import tariffs and thereby more liberally open up the American market to the global economy in the last years of the 1870s.[23]

Less than three weeks later, rumors began to circulate that Wells was receiving payments of $10,000 a year from the Cobden Club. Although lacking a smoking gun, *Inter Ocean* and other protectionist papers thought it probable, since "he is known to have been its active, energetic, thorough-going propagandist in this country for a number of years." Such an opinion "has diffused itself widely among the people that Mr Wells is an agent – a paid agent – a well-paid agent – of the Cobden Club."[24]

Unbeknownst to the *Inter Ocean*, evidence does suggest that Wells may occasionally have been able to obtain modest sums from the Cobden Club to help fund free-trade leagues in the United States, despite his denials. In 1876, Alfred B. Mason, for instance, wrote to Wells for financial support in order to start up a free-trade league in Illinois. In it, he inquired whether "a cable dispatch to the Sec. of the Cobden Club" might "bring £1,000." R. R. Bowker in turn coyly beseeched Wells in the summer of 1880 to ask "the gentlemen who ... are always ready to back you in good works (those outside of New York I mean)," for $1,000 to support the New York Free Trade Club. That Wells was a "well-paid agent," however, was unproven and highly unlikely considering that the Cobden Club was not nearly as wealthy as its detractors claimed.[25] With or without token British financial support, Wells's desired Morrison bill also came to naught, pushed to the

---

[23] *New York Times*, August 2, 1877, 5; David Earl Robbins, "The Congressional Career of William Ralls Morrison" (PhD dissertation, University of Illinois, 1963), 59–60, 64–65; Michael C. Kerr to Wells, December 31, 1875; January 12, 1876; Anson Phelps Stokes to Wells, January 17, 1876; Morrison to Wells, February 20; March 9; March 16, 1876; *Illinois Free Trade League, Circular No. 1*, September 1, 1876, reel 4, Wells Papers; Tom E. Terrill, "David A. Wells, the Democracy, and Tariff Reduction, 1877–1894," *Journal of American History* 56 (December 1969): 549; Cobden Club, *Report and List of Members for the Year 1903* (London, 1904); Terrill, *Tariff, Politics, and American Foreign Policy*, 29–34; Bensel, *Political Economy of American Industrialization*, 468–488. For similar charges, see, also, *Chicago Inter Ocean*, February 9, 1876, 4; February 7, 1876, 4.

[24] *Chicago Inter Ocean*, February 29, 1876, 4. No such proof ever surfaced.

[25] Mason to Wells, October 2, 1876, reel 4; and Bowker to Wells, June 12, 1880, reel 6, Wells Papers. Similar charges were laid against Horace White in 1876. See Philip Kinsley, *The Chicago Tribune, Its First Hundred Years* (Chicago, IL: The Chicago Tribune, 1945), 231. Wells refuted the conspiracy charges. See *New York Times*, May 11, 1883, 3.

political wayside owing to the 1870s depression, mounting government debt, and the upcoming presidential elections.

During the 1876 elections, Cyrus Field entertained the idea of having a hand in shaping the Republican presidential ticket. He asked John Bright for his opinion on the matter, and expressed his own hope for a Republican ticket that included Charles Francis Adams, Sr. as president, Carl Schurz as secretary of state, and David Wells as secretary of treasury, since they were "all sound on the currency question, Civil Service Reform, and the Tariff." Bright likewise hoped Adams would become the next president.[26] Although the independent Republican vote played a prominent part in the run-up to the election, once again transatlantic Cobdenites like Field and Bright would be disappointed. The Republicans chose Rutherford B. Hayes to run against Democratic candidate Samuel Tilden of New York in what became one of the most contentious elections in American history, with Tilden winning the popular vote and possibly the electoral, as well. Yet his victory was by no means assured, as swing votes in various southern states remained in dispute owing to rampant violence, fraud, and voter intimidation, particularly against southern blacks. Although the independent vote was split, David Wells, Henry Adams, and Henry's father, Charles, at least, found Tilden to be the clear choice, with Henry admitting that Tilden was "the best man without regard to party."[27] The political compromise the following year – which included granting southern states federal funds for the development of various internal improvement schemes – ended with Republican Hayes occupying the White House and Democratic "Redeemers" brutally reoccupying state governments throughout the south. The compromise signaled a violent resurgence of the southern wing of the Democratic party, a development that not only brought a tragic end to Reconstruction, but would further reshape the local and national political landscape for years to come.[28]

---

[26] Field to Bright, December 10, 1875, Add. 43391, Vol. IX, Bright Papers; Bright to Field, November 1, 1875, folder 2, box 1, Field Papers.

[27] Henry Adams to David Ames Wells, July 15, 1876; Watson R. Sperry to Wells, September 20, 1876, reel 4, Wells Papers. Both parties were strategically motivated to garner the Liberal Republican vote. See Michael F. Holt, *By One Vote: The Disputed Presidential Election of 1876* (Lawrence: University Press of Kansas, 2008).

[28] For more on the 1876 elections, see Marc-William Palen, "Revisiting the Election of 1876 and the Compromise of 1877," in *A Guide to Reconstruction Presidents, 1865–1881*, ed. by Edward O. Frantz (London: John Wiley & Sons, 2014), 415–430; C. Vann Woodward, *Reunion and Reaction: The Compromise of 1877 and the End of Reconstruction* (Boston, MA: Little, Brown, 1951); Holt, *By One Vote*; Keith Ian Polakoff, *The Politics of Inertia: The Election of 1876 and the End of Reconstruction* (Baton Rouge: Louisiana State University Press, 1973); Ari Arthur Hoogenboom, *The Presidency of Rutherford B. Hayes* (Lawrence: University Press of Kansas, 1988).

Following Hayes's "election," his Republican administration would thereafter support various expansionist endeavors, such as the Samoan treaty of 1878 (gaining access to Pago Pago) and the development of a US-controlled Central American isthmian canal. The Hayes administration also made tentative steps toward accessing Latin American markets, steps toward regional economic integration that James G. Blaine would work to continue as secretary of state both under James Garfield and Benjamin Harrison.[29]

The fateful year of 1876 also marked the centenary of Adam Smith's *The Wealth of Nations*. In December, Wells and his fellow American "disciples of free trade theory" gathered together in New York to celebrate the anniversary. It was a "grand assemblage," and one that Wells, R. R. Bowker, and Parke Godwin – son-in-law of William Cullen Bryant – had been planning for nearly a year. Yet for more than a few of the one-hundred free traders and reformers attending the dinner, their once-shining optimism appeared tarnished following the setbacks of 1872 and the onset of a nationwide depression in 1873.[30]

American free traders once again gathered moral support from across the Atlantic. Edward Atkinson, speaking before the Cobden Club Committee in London a few months later, opined that, although at times counterproductive, continued cooperation between the Club and "Free Trade Associations in the United States" were "undoubtedly of great value and importance." Less than two months later, the Cobden Club Committee in London unanimously appointed Wells to be the club's honorary secretary in the United States in order to more effectively spearhead the American free-trade movement "in cooperation" with the club. The *New York Tribune* was quick to ridicule the appointment and Wells himself for being "an American Cobden . . . who accepts a subordinate post" within an English club whose mission was to give "British control over American markets."[31]

Rather than be cowed, American Cobdenites increased their numbers. William R. Morrison (D-IL), upon receiving notification of his election to

[29] Terrill, *Tariff, Politics, and American Foreign Policy*, 20–41.
[30] Bowker to Wells, January 11, 1876, reel 4, Wells Papers; Wells to Bowker, January 13, 1876, Box 11, R. R. Bowker Papers, LOC; "The Adam Smith Centennial," in *New Century* (New York: International Free Trade Alliance, 1876), 169–215; *New York Times*, December 13, 1876, 5; Cyrus W. Field to Parke Godwin, November 27, 1876, Box 6, Bryant-Godwin Papers, NYPL; Minutes of February 14, 1873, CC MSS; *Report of the Proceedings at the Annual Dinner of the Cobden Club, June 24th, 1871* (London: Cassell, Petter, and Galpin, Ludgate Hill, E.C., 1871); *Report and List of Members for the Year 1903*; E. McClung Fleming, *R. R. Bowker: Militant Liberal* (Norman: University of Oklahoma Press, 1952), 94; Tucker, *Mugwumps*, 76; Minutes of September 22, 1877, CC MSS.
[31] *New York Tribune*, October 25, 1877; September 12, 1877.

the Cobden Club in April 1877, wrote Wells that he was "glad to aid in the free trade movement."[32] Free-trade efforts were further bolstered when energetic R. R. Bowker of New York returned from London to the American free-trade battleground. Bowker had been an active and influential reformer since 1869 as secretary of the Brooklyn Free Trade League. In 1875, he helped set up the IFTA, and edited its free-trade journal, the *New Century*. In 1877, he thereafter helped establish the New York Free Trade Club, what critics referred to as "The New York branch of the Cobden Club." Bowker also formed the Council for Tariff Reform, which united younger free-trade elements with the older AFTL. In 1879, he thereafter helped create the Society for Political Education, which sought regulation of corporations, public discussion of the tariff issue, and a tariff for revenue only. Under Bowker's supervision the society disseminated publications up to the 1890s.[33]

Bowker's advocacy for free trade turned to zealousness upon his election to membership in the Cobden Club in 1880, his continued attendance at its London dinners, and correspondence with its leaders. His letter of acceptance to the Cobden Club was considered important enough on the subject of free trade that 25,000 copies were immediately produced for dissemination in the United States. He thereafter helped Wells breathe new life into the ailing AFTL in 1883, which had lain largely dormant ever since "the *fiasco* of the Greeley campaign of 1872," as Bowker described it.[34]

A visit to the United States by the founder of the Cobden Club, Thomas Bayley Potter, in late 1879 further connected the transatlantic free-trade movement. He promptly made contact with the American heads of the Cobden Club, Wells and Atkinson, whereupon Potter asked them to make sure the upcoming 1880 list of American Cobden Club members was up to date. He also requested that they beef up their distribution of the club's pamphlets, and asked that they might inform

---

[32] Minutes of June 16, 1877, CC MSS; Morrison to Wells, April 5, 1877; Potter to Wells, August 1, 1877, reel 4, Wells Papers.

[33] *New York Times*, November 9, 1880, 5; Joyner, *Wells*, 147–150; George Haven Putnam, *Memories of a Publisher, 1865–1915* (New York and London: G. P. Putnam's Sons, 1916), 171–173; Dugdale to Ford, April 9, 1881, folder 1881, box 1, Ford Papers.

[34] George B. Curtiss, *Protection and Prosperity: An Account of Tariff Legislation and its Effect in Europe and America* (New York: Pan-American Publishing, 1896), 627; Fleming, *Bowker*, 93–94, 198; Wells to McAdam, 1880; Potter to Bowker, May 21, 1881, Box 51; [draft copy] Bowker to Ostrogorski, January 15, 1898, Box 89; *The American Free Trade League. Constitution. Provisionally Adopted by the Executive Committee, June 18, 1883*, Box 90, Richard Rogers Bowker Papers, NYPL. In 1885, Bowker undertook to dispel charges that the Cobden Club was funding the American free-trade movement owing to the club's lack of wealth in *The Economic Fact-Book and Free-Traders' Guide* (New York: New York Free Trade Club, 1885), 13–16.

Harvard and Yale of the club's new silver medal award for the best student scholarship on the subject of political economy. The protectionist *Western Manufacturer* of course immediately assumed that he had arrived in New York City to "do a little legislating in the interest of English manufacturing."[35]

In celebration of Potter's arrival, the New York Free Trade Club threw him an opulent banquet at Delmonico's. The luxurious restaurant was decorated that night with various Anglo-Saxon ephemera: the walls covered in both British and American flags, the tables decorated with a shield depicting Brother Jonathon and John Bull shaking hands over the Atlantic Ocean. Potter commented on what he saw as good progress toward bringing free trade to the United States. He then announced his hope for curbing imperialism throughout the globe, and "an alliance, perhaps even a confederation, of the English speaking race which may have a power and influence over the whole world" and which would act as "a final check to selfish and aggressive war."[36]

While Anglo-American Cobdenites were calling for Anglo-Saxonism, free trade, and anti-imperialism, protectionists turned some of their attention to the growing numbers of Irish immigrants pouring onto US shores, seeing in them a potential Republican voting bloc and an Anglophobic ally against the growing Cobdenite influence of Free Trade England. Listian John F. Scanlan, a Carey disciple and secretary of Chicago's Industrial League of America, wrote a pamphlet in 1880 discouraging Irishmen from voting for free trade and the Democratic party. Scanlan charged that both the Democrats and England, "through the Cobden Club," were making war on American industry. "It becomes treason doubly odious" to discover Irish Americans working for English interests "just as effectively as if they were neath [sic] the blood stained cross of St George, with the Cobden Club playing Rule Britannia, marching to the ballot box to introduce into this country that blighting system of free trade, which drove us from our native land with the 'vengeance.'"[37]

In the midst of such anti-Cobdenite sentiment, the 1880 Republican party ironically ended up nominating Cobden Club member James Garfield for the presidency. Garfield himself had worked out an effective enough balancing act on the tariff issue to remain standing near the center

[35] Potter to Atkinson, December 22, 1879; January 16, 1880; January 20, 1880; February 15, 1880, carton 1, Atkinson Papers; *Western Manufacturer*, November 15, 1879, 148, quoted in Ralph Russell Tingley, "American Cobden Clubs" (MA thesis, University of Chicago, 1947), 32.

[36] *New York Tribune*, November 18, 1879, 1, 4; *Nation*, November 1879, 338.

[37] John F. Scanlan, *Why Ireland is Poor. Ripe Fruit from the Tree of British Free Trade* (Chicago, IL: McCann & O'Brien, 1880), 22.

of national Republican politics. Garfield's nomination deal was sweetened for Roscoe Conkling's Stalwart faction by having one of their own – Chester A. Arthur – made Garfield's vice-presidential running mate.[38]

Garfield's Republican nomination gave R. R. Bowker, Edward Atkinson, and their fellow Cobdenites an obvious choice for their votes. Atkinson's friend George P. Smith was exuberant that the country was soon to have a president that "will have you [Atkinson] at his hand – and go at things, ala Jackson, and R. J. Walker – the prosperity to follow will be as in 1847 to 1857," when lower tariffs had previously been enacted. Atkinson noted to president-elect Garfield how the manufacturers were coming on board and becoming "aware that they are no longer infant." And it very much looked as though Atkinson would have the new president's ear on economic matters. Thomas Bayley Potter expressed his pragmatic pleasure to Atkinson owing to Garfield's Cobden Club membership. "Of course I don't estimate the latter for more than its worth, as he must in the main adopt the programme of the Republican Party. Still, the question of Free Trade must surely have more fair play than it has had," Potter opined.[39]

Garfield's membership in the Cobden Club became "a matter of great importance" to the protectionist press. Bipartisan speculation spread about whether or not Garfield was secretly a free trader. Adding to this controversy, Potter defended to the president-elect the Cobden Club's continued propagandistic efforts in the United States. Potter impoliticly wrote to Garfield that his "triumphant election will seal forever the success" of the free-trade cause, and saw "no reason why I should not offer my good wishes on your election." After all, he continued, Republicans of all stripes had not minded when Potter had circulated

[38] Thomas C. Reeves, "Chester A. Arthur and the Campaign of 1880," *Political Science Quarterly* 84 (December 1969): 628–637; Peskin, "Who were the Stalwarts?" Following a strong defense of "hard money," Garfield, an advocate for freer trade for many years following the Civil War, was nominated by John Bright, unanimously elected (see Potter to Garfield, June 10, 1869, reel 16, Garfield Papers), and thereafter accepted his membership. Owing to his district's protectionist sentiments and the enforced protectionist orthodoxy of the Republican party, by the late 1870s Garfield found it necessary to outwardly moderate his position in order to remain active within mainstream Republican politics, and his public views on free trade mellowed as well. Wells wrote something very similar in his letter to the *New York Times* of May 2, 1886. Perhaps it also explains why Garfield wished to avoid the issue in the 1880 presidential elections. See *New York Times*, February 3, 1878, 10; Robert Caldwell, *James A. Garfield: Party Chieftain* (New York: Dodd, Mead and Company, 1931), 192–201, 210; and David M. Pletcher, *The Awkward Years: American Foreign Relations Under Garfield and Arthur* (Columbia: University of Missouri Press, 1962), 150.

[39] George P. Smith to Atkinson, June 3, 1880; Atkinson to Garfield, June 29, 1880, carton 15; Garfield to Atkinson, December 6, 1880; T. B. Potter to Atkinson, June 11, 1880, carton 2; Atkinson to Wells, November 7, 1880, carton 15, Atkinson Papers.

pamphlets in the antebellum United States on behalf of the antislavery cause. Where Potter once worked "for Cobden's principles" on behalf of "Union and Emancipation and for the repeal of the Corn Laws long ago," so now the American people could hardly hold a grudge in his "effort to influence by fair argument American political opinion in favor of 'Free trade, peace, Good will among nations.'"[40]

Quick to prove Potter wrong, the protectionist press showed that it could indeed hold a grudge. Garfield's alleged free-trade communiqués with Potter became a matter of public knowledge soon thereafter. The protectionist backlash was such that Garfield, in nearly his first act in the White House, was forced to deny publicly any "Cobden Club connection" and that he did not subscribe to "the principles of the Cobden Free-Trade Club."[41]

Whatever possible freer trade may have followed Garfield's election died with his assassination. The president was shot in the back while on his way to deliver a book to his friend Cyrus Field. The subsequent 1882 Tariff Commission of Chester Arthur, Garfield's presidential successor, came to naught, and the "Mongrel Tariff" of 1883 did little to change US tariff rates, while somehow finding a way to upset all parties involved. Secretary of State Frelinghuysen's Spanish treaty allowing for regional trade reciprocity with Cuba and Puerto Rico thereafter earned the support of Listian James G. Blaine and gained the moral and economic disdain of the New York Free Trade Club, which feared the treaty would undercut "true" revenue reform and, through its preferential limitations, impede the opening of all the world's markets to US goods. The treaty would be condemned by incoming Democratic President Grover Cleveland, and withdrawn in 1885.[42]

Aside from halting possible tariff reform, the assassination of President Garfield had larger repercussions at the national and international level. His death was a gruesome result of the Republican party's internal discord. By the election of 1880, the party had been riven by factionalism

---

[40] *New York World*, October 22, 1880; Potter to Garfield, November 14, 1880, reel 76, James A. Garfield Papers, LOC.

[41] *North American*, March 10, 1881. See, also, *Geneva Gazette* (New York), October 12, 1880; *New York Herald*, October 11, 1880; *New York Times*, March 10, 1881; *New York Times*, May 11, 1888.

[42] Lucretia R. Garfield to Field, November 7, 1881, folder 6, box 1, Field Papers; Thomas G. Shearman to Wells, November 23, 1880, reel 6, Wells Papers; Sproat, *"The Best Men,"* 193–194; Harold Francis Williamson, *Edward Atkinson: The Biography of an American Liberal, 1827–1905* (Boston, MA: Old Corner Book Store, 1934), 134; Blaine letter to Frye, *New York Tribune*, July 26, 1890, 1; J. Laurence Laughlin and H. Parker Willis, *Reciprocity* (New York: The Baker & Taylor Co., 1903), 114–126; *The Spanish Treaty Opposed to Tariff Reform. Report of a Committee of Enquiry Appointed by the New York Free-Trade Club* (New York: G. P. Putnam's Sons, 1885).

and lacked the cohesive antislavery underpinning that had helped bring the party into existence a quarter century before. Republican Stalwart supporters of Grant were now fighting with the party's younger Half-Breed supporters. Republican independents in turn continued to criticize the pervasive protectionism, patronage system, and corruption of mainstream politics. It took nothing less than Garfield's death to begin bridging the Republican divide. Deranged after not receiving a political appointment, Charles Guiteau had shot Garfield. Guiteau explained his mad act by saying: "I am a Stalwart and now Arthur is President." From his jail cell, Guiteau noted with morbid pragmatism: "The President's tragic death was a sad necessity but it will unite the Republican party." The assassination at once highlighted the divisiveness of the Republican party and the corruption of the spoils system. Guiteau's prophetic vision for Republican party solidarity, however deranged, would come to fruition, but not until 1884.

The imperialism of economic nationalism

With the Republicans controlling the executive in the aftermath of the Civil War, by the late 1860s the party began exhibiting imperial traits that bore little resemblance to its antebellum Whig roots. The economic nationalist American System complemented well the jingoistic expansionism of postbellum Republican protectionists. With protectionism firmly entrenched at home, William Seward and U. S. Grant could now look abroad with an eye toward formal imperial annexation of territory and informal imperial control of foreign markets. The imperial-minded Seward jumped at the chance to add Alaska to American ownership, chomped at the bit whenever he thought of Canada's fallow lands lying temptingly to the north, and sought to annex the Danish West Indies.[43]

British influence in the Western Hemisphere was a prime target of these more progressive Republican imperial policies. Listian nationalists like John A. Kasson and James G. Blaine frequently pointed to the massive growth of invested British capital and trade in Latin America throughout the last decades of the century, utterly dwarfing US trade and investment in the area, in order to emphasize the need for informal American imperial expansion there. Kasson wondered how much longer Congress would ignore "the demands for new markets for our already excessive and rapidly increasing products." Massive American investments and internal

---

[43] David E. Shi, "Seward's Attempt to Annex British Columbia, 1865–1869," *Pacific Historical Review* 47 (May 1978): 217–238; Halvdan Koht, "The Origins of Seward's Plan to Purchase the Danish West Indies," *American Historical Review* 50 (July 1945): 762–767.

improvements in Latin America would open up western-hemispheric markets. The American flag, not the Union Jack, they believed, should wave from atop Latin American ports. "The tradition against the policy of outlying possessions is, at this stage of our history," Kasson concluded, "simply imbecile."[44] Weak American influence (in comparison to the British) therefore stimulated the American Listian demand for western-hemispheric investments and government subsidies in Latin American telegraph, railroad, and steamship lines.

This progressive protectionist stimulus received a further geopolitical boost when the British-backed Western Telegraph Company established a cable between Rio and Portugal in 1874, and as the Germans also began to make an effort to rival Britain's informal empire in the region.[45] From the early 1880s to early 1890s, Blaine would develop a grand solution entailing a protectionist Pan-American trade union, with the principal goal of expanding American markets while excluding British influence throughout the hemisphere. Listian nationalist U. S. Grant himself had earlier been keen on seeing Santo Domingo under direct US influence in the name of the Monroe Doctrine, for the sake of national prestige and on behalf of "big business."[46] His secretary of state, Hamilton Fish, also played the Monroe Doctrine card when the European powers took excessive interest in a revolution that broke out in Cuba in 1875. Jay Sexton in turn has brought renewed attention to the Grant administration's mixture of Reconstruction-era antislavery ideology, limited internationalism, and an informal imperial approach toward ending Spanish–Cuban conflict from the late 1860s to the mid-1870s, with their sights set on establishing informal financial ties and restrictive trade reciprocity rather than formal annexation.[47] The 1873 economic depression further spurred on

---

[44] John A. Kasson, "The Monroe Doctrine in 1881," *North American Review* 133 (December 1881): 532–533.

[45] David M. Pletcher, *The Diplomacy of Trade and Investment: American Economic Expansion in the Hemisphere, 1865–1900* (Columbia: University of Missouri Press, 1998), 180–215; Howard B. Schonberger, *Transportation to the Seaboard: The Communication Revolution and American Foreign Policy, 1860–1911* (Westport, CT: Greenwood Press, 1971), 178–179; Ian D. Forbes, "German Informal Imperialism in South America before 1914," *Economic History Review* 31 (August 1978): 384–398; Nancy Mitchell, *The Danger of Dreams: German and American Imperialism in Latin America* (Chapel Hill: The University of North Carolina Press, 1999).

[46] Merline Pitre, "Frederick Douglass and the Annexation of Santo Domingo," *Journal of Negro History* 62 (October 1977): 390–400; Harold T. Pinkett, "Efforts to Annex Santo Domingo to the United States, 1866–1871," *Journal of Negro History* 26 (January 1941): 12–45; Charles C. Tansill, *The United States and Santo Domingo, 1798–1873, A Chapter in Caribbean Diplomacy* (Baltimore: The Johns Hopkins University Press, 1938), 344–406.

[47] Jay Sexton, "The United States, the Cuban Rebellion, and the Multilateral Initiative of 1875," *Diplomatic History* 30 (June 2006): 335–366. For Grant and Fish's informal imperialism, see, also, Walter LaFeber, *The New Empire: An Interpretation of American*

aggressive expansionist speculation over how to solve the problems of perceived American overproduction. In a way, these imperial designs might be viewed as an attempted "Scramble for the Americas," a regional reflection of contemporaneous European activities in Africa. Such Republican agitation also represented the early stirrings of the postbellum era's imperialism of economic nationalism.

For their part, America's Cobdenite leadership was also noticing the increased attention given to the problem of overproduction, particularly the need for new markets. Just before Garfield's assassination, Wells had written to him about how Wells had noticed a speculative shift over the cause of the 1873 depression: "One argument had risen to prominence since the mid-seventies that America was shifting too fast from the production of raw materials to a manufacturing economy, and that she would have no market for the goods that poured from her factories." Wells was in partial agreement, while at the same time remaining quite critical of the Republican party's early Listian efforts to establish an expansive US closed-door empire in the Western Hemisphere. The desire for foreign markets was certainly growing in popularity, albeit with disparate proposals for gaining them.[48]

Alongside this growing acceptance of the theory of overproduction, French meddling in Mexico and British expansion in the Caribbean during the Civil War era remained fresh in American minds, and geopolitical fears of undue European influence in the Western Hemisphere rebounded.[49] British influence was particularly worrying. Economic competition with Britain was a driving force behind such conjecture, and prodded forward US imperial projects. Partly owing to growing British trade interests in the Sandwich Islands, for instance, in 1875 the Grant administration had signed a restrictive reciprocity treaty with Hawaii. Behind closed doors, a clause was added to the treaty at the behest of Senator Justin Morrill (R-VT) that would forbid Hawaii from making "any treaty by which any other nation shall obtain the same

Expansion, 1860–1898 (Ithaca, NY, and London: Cornell University Press, 1963), 32–39; James Chapin, "Hamilton Fish and American Expansion," in *Makers of American Diplomacy: From Benjamin Franklin to Henry Kissinger*, ed. by Frank J. Merli and Theodore A. Wilson (New York: Charles Scribner's Sons, 1974), 223–251. For the Monroe Doctrine, see especially Jay Sexton, *The Monroe Doctrine: Empire and Nation in Nineteenth-Century America* (New York: Hill and Wang, 2011).

[48] Wells quoted in Pletcher, *Awkward Years*, 5. W. A. Williams suggested that the early 1880s boom in agricultural exports helped shape Blaine's views, "making overseas economic expansion a central element" in his Republican program. Williams then lumps this expansionist outlook with that of David Wells. William Appleman Williams, *The Roots of the Modern American Empire: A Study of the Growth and Shaping of Social Consciousness in a Marketplace Society* (New York: Vintage Books, 1969), 21.

[49] Pletcher, *Awkward Years*, 144.

privileges" as the United States. The treaty effectively turned the islands into a closed American market, making it, according to Blaine, "essentially a part of the American system of states" by giving "to our manufacturers therein the same freedom as in California and Oregon." Henry Carey, in proper progressive Listian fashion, had also warmed up to the reciprocity idea as the next step toward ultimate "perfect freedom of trade," so long as American reciprocity yet bore the trappings of protectionism and did not include British Canada.[50]

The free-trade response to the Hawaiian treaty was mixed. American Cobdenites were torn between pragmatism and being true to their ideals. William Cullen Bryant's *New York Evening Post* reluctantly gave the treaty its support as Bryant, in "his zeal for Free Trade," was "extremely anxious to have the paper support everything which wears the appearance of Free Trade." Wells, however, looked askance upon the reciprocity treaty, seeing it as little more than protectionism hidden under the guise of free trade. Congressmen Roger Q. Mills and William R. Morrison were similarly "soured" on the treaty. But then-Congressman Garfield pragmatically pointed out to Wells that opposition to this reciprocity treaty would make any future (and more liberal) reciprocity with Canada – which Wells and various other Cobdenites greatly desired – nearly impossible. In the end, with Wells as advisor, Morrison crafted a strong case against the formal imperial acquisition of Hawaii; dismissed the British bogeyman; and encouraged neutral and equal access to Hawaiian ports for all nations instead of Republican-style reciprocity.[51]

Arch-Anglophobe Blaine was fast becoming a proponent of protectionism mixed with restrictive reciprocity, as illustrated by his Listian support for Hawaiian reciprocity and Latin American interventionism. In 1881, British merchants in Hawaii once again argued that they should receive the same favored treatment that US goods were receiving under the 1876

---

[50] R. S. Kuykendall, *The Hawaiian Kingdom: 1874–1893* (Honolulu: University of Hawaii Press, 1967), 28; Stephen Meardon, "Reciprocity and Henry C. Carey's Traverses on 'The Road to Perfect Freedom of Trade,'" *Journal of the History of Economic Thought* 33 (September 2011): 329–330.

[51] Pletcher, *Awkward Years*, 139; Morrison to Wells, February 20, 1876; Watson R. Sperry [editor of *Evening Post*] to Wells, February 11, 1876; Mills to Wells, February 29, 1876; James Garfield to Wells, February 24, 1876; Morrison to Wells, February 20, March 9, March 16, 1876, reel 4, Wells Papers; "Reciprocity Comes too High," *Million*, January 17, 1885, 363–364; Terrill, *Tariff, Politics, and American Foreign Policy*, 19–20; Merze Tate, *Hawaii: Reciprocity or Annexation?* (Lansing: Michigan State University Press, 1968), 108–117; Sylvester K. Stevens, *American Expansion in Hawaii, 1842–1898* (Harrisburg: Archives Publishing Co. of Pennsylvania, 1945), 108–140; David M. Pletcher, *The Diplomacy of Involvement: American Economic Expansion across the Pacific, 1784–1900* (Columbia: University of Missouri Press, 2001), 54–56. See, also, Donald Marquand Dozer, "The Opposition to Hawaiian Reciprocity, 1876–1888," *Pacific Historical Review* 14 (June 1945): 157–183.

reciprocity treaty. Blaine, as Republican secretary of state, moved quickly to counter the British claims and to make sure that Hawaii remained within the regional economic sphere of the United States. He subsequently warned the Hawaiian king that only the United States was allowed such favorable economic inroads in Hawaii. Blaine similarly showed his Listian colors as a strong supporter of government-supported internal improvements, by meddling in the War of the Pacific (1879–1883) in South America, and even by trying to find a way around the limitations of the Clayton–Bulwer Treaty in order to secure an American-controlled isthmian canal.[52] From the mid-1870s to early 1880s, Blaine had begun seeking his progressive protectionist vision for regional economic integration.

Nor was Blaine alone. The subsequent Republican Arthur administration sought a similar hemispheric integration. In 1883, the Arthur administration asked former President Grant to take the lead on a restrictive reciprocity treaty with Mexico in order to not only undercut European influence in that country, but also to impose the Monroe Doctrine and to stimulate southern business. Mexican railroad promoters were particularly supportive of the plan, as were Listians like Grant, who, it should be noted, was himself a partner in a southern Mexican railroad scheme. Strong opposition arose, however, especially from Louisiana sugar producers, and the bill ended up tied together with Arthur's restrictive reciprocity treaty proposals with Cuba, Puerto Rico, and the Dominican Republic, as well as the proposed Nicaraguan canal. All these proposals came to an anticlimactic end following Grover Cleveland's election, as he disapproved of Republican imperialism and its coercive policy of restrictive reciprocity.[53] Regardless of their success or failure, these Republican Listian policy prescriptions for maintaining high protective tariff walls at home and prying open new markets abroad through either formal annexation or informal restrictive reciprocity were not the imperialism of free trade, but the early stirrings of the imperialism of economic nationalism.

---

[52] Eric T. L. Love, *Race over Empire: Racism and U.S. Imperialism, 1865–1900* (Chapel Hill: University of North Carolina Press, 2004), 89–90; Tom E. Terrill, *The Tariff, Politics, and American Foreign Policy, 1874–1901* (Westport, CT: Greenwood Press, 1973), 45.

[53] Terrill, *Tariff, Politics, and American Foreign Policy*, 68–92; Pletcher, *Awkward Years*, 185–188; Pletcher, *Diplomacy of Trade and Investment*, 110–112, 148–179; Osgood Hardy, "Ulysses S. Grant, President of the Mexican Southern Railroad," *Pacific Historical Review* 24 (May 1955): 111–120. These treaties were under the direction of John W. Foster, who believed that the proposed treaty with Spain "will be annexing Cuba in the most desirable way." In 1892, he would replace James G. Blaine as secretary of state in the Harrison administration. The Cleveland administration instead supported more liberal reciprocity policies with Mexico, Canada, and Hawaii. Terrill, *Tariff, Politics, and American Foreign Policy*, 79, 92.

This regionalized Listian approach to American economic integration met opposition not only from American free traders but also from protectionist purists like Republican Senator Justin Morrill and Philadelphia's Joseph Wharton who yet put all their faith in the home market and often belittled foreign traders. Nevertheless, some hardline protectionists were gradually being swayed by the idea that high tariffs mixed with restrictive reciprocity would protect the home market *and* open foreign markets – that this protectionist double dose might provide a proper cure to American overproduction, especially with the frequent onset of economic panics throughout the last decades of the century. Blaine's own Listian calls were being further amplified by his right-hand man – and Greeley's *Tribune* editorial successor – Whitelaw Reid.[54] Thus, by the early 1880s, more and more people in government and business were warming up to the Listian idea that the key to prosperity lay in maintaining protection of the home market while increasing foreign commerce through protectionist reciprocity: that it was the best solution to the problem of American overproduction.[55]

Free trade West and South

While Listians started to gain imperial sway in the realm of US foreign policy, Cobdenites continued their work at thwarting the Republican protectionist machine. For example, the year 1883 witnessed a strong, albeit unsuccessful, gubernatorial run in Iowa by pro-free-trade Democratic candidate George Kinne, who had the attentions of the AFTL in New York and the Cobden Club in England. The year 1883 also saw the appearance of the first independent candidate, Cobdenite William Brownlee of Detroit, run for office on the sole issue of free trade, with the endorsement of Wells and Bowker.[56]

Just a few years before, and amid great controversy, the Cobden Club also mass-disseminated a pamphlet, *The Western Farmer of America* (1880), written by an Englishman, Augustus Mongredien. The tract

---

[54] Terrill, *Tariff, Politics, and American Foreign Policy*, 80–84. Henry Carey had begun requesting Reid to attend his Sunday "Vespers" in 1874. Henry Carey to Whitelaw Reid, January 9, 1874, Folder 1, Box 20, Carey Papers.

[55] Williams, *Roots of Modern American Empire*, 27–29.

[56] Article extract in Philpott to Bowker, August 20, 1883; Philpott to Bowker, September 13, 1883; George Peabody to Bowker, September 14, 1883; Thomas G. Shearman to Bowker, September 26, 1883; J. Sterling Morton to Bowker, September 24, 1883; Brownlee to Bowker, July 5, August 1, 1883, Box 89, Bowker Papers, NYPL; New York Free Trade Club, *National Conference of Free Traders and Revenue Reformers. Chicago, November 11 and 12, 1885* (New York: New York Free Trade Club, 1885), 18; Brownlee to Wells, October 5, 1882, reel 6, Wells Papers.

encouraged western farmers to support free trade over protectionism in the upcoming 1880 presidential election. Thomas Bayley Potter, just a week before the pamphlet's release, begged Edward Atkinson not to be "very cross" with him, as Atkinson and fellow American Cobden Club member George Plumer Smith had strongly urged the club not to publish it, fearing the Anglophobic protectionist response. The Cobden Club Committee nevertheless had decided to overrule Atkinson since Wells "strongly recommended the publication, which he said would be severely criticised but would do good. All our other friends ... approved."[57]

In hindsight, Potter likely regretted not heeding Atkinson's advice. Mongredien's pamphlet created quite a splash in the United States, but not of the kind hoped for by the Cobden Club. The protectionist counter-attack was impressive indeed. The publication was portrayed as an obvious English attempt to influence the upcoming 1880 elections, authorized by a British association with the power equal to a "hostile national power." The Cobden Club at least felt chastened enough to be more circumspect thereafter about its pamphleteering efforts in the United States.[58]

For Atkinson, the publication of Mongredien's pamphlet and the protectionist response only solidified the hard lessons learned in 1872 regarding direct meddling in national politics.[59] In Atkinson's eyes, the younger more radical free-trade elements, particularly Professors William Graham Sumner and Arthur Latham Perry, were "doing mischief." Atkinson himself had once "indulged" in what he called "the vituperative method," he later confessed to Bowker. But Atkinson, at least, had learned his lesson. He continued to express his dissatisfaction with the extreme approach of the more radical free-trade fringe for years to come.[60]

---

[57] T. B. Potter to Atkinson, June 11, 1880, carton 2, Atkinson Papers.

[58] Jonathan B. Wise, *The Farmer's Question: Being a Reply to the Cobden Club Tract Entitled "The Western Farmer in America"* (Cambridge: University Press, John Wilson and Son, 1880), 5. See, also, *Boston Daily Advertiser*, October 27, 1880; *North American*, October 11, 1880; *Chicago Inter Ocean*, October 13, 1880, 9; "Who is Augustus Mongredien?," *Bulletin of the American Iron and Steel Association* 4 (July 1880); Thomas Haines Dudley, *Reply to Augustus Mongredien's Appeal to the Western Farmer of America* (Philadelphia, PA: Allen, Lane & Scott's Printing House, 1883).

[59] Atkinson to Poultney Bigelow, February 13, 1882, carton 16, Atkinson Papers. Poultney, as both secretary of the New York Free Trade Club and as Corresponding Member for the Cobden Club, frequently distributed Cobden Club publications, and wrote his correspondence on Cobden Club letterhead. See Poultney Bigelow to William Graham Sumner, January 6, April 10, May 12, 1880, April 27, 1881, n.d. [Summer 1881], March 6, 1883, Box 2, Folder 41, William Graham Sumner Papers, Sterling Manuscripts and Archives, Yale University, New Haven, CT.

[60] Atkinson to Wells, September 21, 1882, carton 16, Atkinson Papers; Atkinson to Charles S. Fairchild, May 16, 1887, carton 3; Atkinson to Bowker, January 11, 1890, carton 19, Atkinson Papers.

As late as 1888, Atkinson recollected to Potter that Mongredien's pamphlet did "more harm than good," and nearly cost Garfield the 1880 election: "The election of Gen. Garfield turned on a very narrow margin, that pamphlet by the Cobden Club was one of the forces which created that narrow margin at that time."[61]

The free-trade movement also began making more inroads in the US South. American Cobden Club member, sometime congressman, and editor of the *Louisville Courier-Journal* Henry Watterson perhaps best exemplified the rare confluence of southern Jeffersonianism and northern Cobdenism. Much as Atkinson took special interest in the development of postbellum Southern cotton production as when he brought the International Cotton Exhibition to Atlanta in 1881, Watterson called for the expansion of foreign markets to spur southern economic recovery in a speech entitled "The New South." At around the same time that Wells was calling for free trade with Mexico, Watterson was encouraging commercial, and eventual political, union between the United States and Mexico as a viable solution to southern economic ills.[62] His southern roots also opened him up to attack. Protectionist Republicans frequently and rather effectively waved the "bloody shirt," and Watterson found himself castigated for his past Confederate ties and his present free-trade proclivities.[63]

But American protectionists did not stop at the "bloody shirt." They began organizing nationally. In November 1881, the various protective tariff leagues throughout the country held national conventions in Chicago and New York. At the former, a young high-tariff enthusiast from Ohio named William McKinley was particularly outspoken on behalf of a protective tariff. It was at about this time as well that protectionist leagues took further aim at the activities of the Cobden Club and what they saw as the disturbing growth in public opposition to high tariffs. The Metropolitan Industrial League, for instance, was created in New York City to combat such "persistent efforts of the theorists in political

---

[61] Atkinson to Potter, October 3, 1888, carton 19, Atkinson Papers.

[62] David A. Wells, *Freer Trade Essential to Future National Prosperity and Development* (New York: Wm. C. Martin's Steam Printing House, 1882); Wells, "An Economic Study of Mexico," *Popular Science Monthly* 28 (April 1886): 721–736; 29 (May 1886): 11–29; Williamson, *Atkinson*, 169–170; Daniel S. Margolies, *Henry Watterson and the New South: The Politics of Empire, Free Trade, and Globalization* (Lexington: University Press of Kentucky, 2006), 44–45. On the New South and US foreign policy, see Patrick J. Hearden, *Independence & Empire: The New South's Cotton Mill Campaign, 1865–1901* (DeKalb, IL: North Illinois University Press, 1982); Tennant S. McWilliams, *The New South Faces the World: Foreign Affairs and the Southern Sense of Self, 1877–1950* (Baton Rouge and London: Louisiana State University Press, 1988).

[63] *New York Tribune*, September 16, 1880, 1; October 22, 1880, 4; December 2, 1880, 4; January 17, 1881, 1; August 2, 1882, 4. Former Confederate L. Q. C. Lamar was another prominent Cobden Club member.

economy." In 1883, leading industrialists founded the Association for the Protection of American Industries with U. S. Grant its president, followed closely a couple years later by the creation of the American Protective League.[64]

Protectionists also took aim at colleges where Cobdenites proliferated as professors of political economy. Industrial magnate Joseph Wharton founded the Wharton School at the University of Pennsylvania in 1881 as a protectionist counterweight to academic free-trade theories. William Graham Sumner, ever following his "manly course" to tackle the protectionist system, even found his position at Yale threatened in 1883 after he mocked a recent speech given by William Evarts before the New York Association for the Protection of American Industry. Sumner was a highly talented teacher, but he was also what Edward Atkinson considered an extreme adherent to the tenets of laissez-faire, and not afraid to lash out at those "who dread the Cobden Club." Sumner also caustically argued that the protective tariff was an "arrant piece of economic quackery" and "a subtle, cruel and unjust invasion of one man's rights by another .... It is at the same time a social abuse, an economic blunder, and a political evil."[65] Sumner was outspoken about his free-trade principles both in and out of the classroom throughout the Gilded Age, and at Yale actively disseminated Cobden Club publications and bestowed a Cobden Club silver medal each year for the best paper on political economy.[66] His Cobdenite ideology complemented his adherence to what would become known as Social Darwinism, which for Sumner created an almost anarchic scientific belief in free-market principles as famously articulated by Britain's Herbert Spencer.[67] Sumner was thus much more antagonistic to

---

[64] *Proceedings of the National Tariff Convention Held at the Cooper Institute, New York, November 29 and 30, 1881* (Philadelphia, PA: American Iron and Steel Association, 1882), 49; *Chicago Tribune*, November 17, 1881, 4; *New York Tribune*, December 1, 1881, 5; Wilford J. Eiteman, "The Rise and Decline of Orthodox Tariff Propaganda," *Quarterly Journal of Economics* 45 (November 1930): 23–24.

[65] "The Month," *Penn Monthly* (November 1880): 883; William L. Phelps, "When Yale was Given to Sumnerology," *Literary Digest International Book Review* 3 (1925): 661–663; Sumner, "Protectionism: The –Ism which Teaches that Waste Makes Wealth," in *Essays of William Graham Sumner*, ed. by Albert Galloway Keller and Maurice R. Davie, 2 vols. (New Haven, CT: Yale University Press, 1934), II, 366–367, 435; Sumner, "Why I am a Free Trader," *Twentieth Century*, April 24, 1890, 8–10.

[66] Richard Gowing [Secretary of the Cobden Club] to Sumner, January 7, 1880; Potter to Sumner, July 17, 1880; Gowing to Sumner, August 8, 1883; July 14, October 31, 1885; January 26, September 14, 1886; January 10, 1889; September 30, 1890, Box 5, Folder 107, William Graham Sumner Papers, Sterling Manuscripts and Archives, Yale University, New Haven, CT.

[67] Sidney Fine, *Laissez Faire and the General-Welfare State: A Study of Conflict in American Thought, 1865–1901* (Ann Arbor: University of Michigan Press, 1956), 32–46, 80–81, 84–89.

protectionists than was the more moderate Atkinson, especially considering that, as a Yale professor, Sumner held a position that involved directly
shaping the minds of future generations of Americans. The *New York
Tribune* therefore attempted to cut short the career of Sumner and other
"shallow and one-sided" professors.[68]

Against such protectionist pushback, the American free-trade movement pressed on. In May 1883, Cobdenite Henry Adams wrote Carl
Schurz that now was the time for "radicalism." He asked Schurz how
the "Free Trade organization" might punish the Democrats in the
Northwest, if they shied away from free trade. Adams recommended
organizing "a free trade party, and if we had the strength to contest a
single State, make an independent nomination for the Presidency."[69]
Free-trade advocates like Adams would receive a further boost in popularity owing to an American economic boom coupled with a desperate
European market suffering from diseased crops and animals.

Nor would Adams's calls for free-trade radicalism go unheeded.
American free traders rallied to the Cobdenite cause, including a growing
number of women. Henry Ward Beecher – a firm believer in the moral
"virtue and manhood" of free trade – took a lead role as president of the
Brooklyn Revenue Reform Club.[70] The New York Free Trade Club in
turn sponsored a series of lectures. Beginning in the early 1880s, it also
began holding annual dinners, which received great attendance, including large numbers of women, drawn at once to Cobdenism's dual promise
of cheap products and world peace. Owing to such feminine interest in
the transatlantic free-trade movement, the Cobden Club went co-ed in
1885. Its first female member was none other than Florence
Nightingale.[71]

Much like American protectionist leagues, the more localized free-
trade clubs began organizing at the national level. Bowker's New
York Free Trade Club, along with William Brownlee's Michigan Free
Trade League and AFTL Western Secretary Henry Philpott's Iowa Free

[68] *New York Tribune*, February 11, 1883, 6; February 16, 1883, 5; February 25, 1883, 6;
March 11, 1886, 2; May 18, 1890, 18; February 3, 1897, 7.

[69] Adams to Schurz, May 20, 1883, in *Letters of Henry Adams*, II, 503.

[70] *New York Tribune*, December 9, 1881, 5; February 27, 1881, 2; April 5, 1881, 4; January
27, 1886, 8; Henry Ward Beecher to Ford, October 19, 1881, folder 1881; Beecher to
Ford, December 11, 1881, folder 1882, box 1, Ford Papers. Reform Club secretary
Thomas Shearman's subsequent publication of the correspondence between the
Brooklyn Revenue Reform Club and Cobden Club founder T. B. Potter was castigated
by the *New York Tribune*.

[71] Williams, *Roots of Modern American Empire*, 20; *New York Tribune*, April 15, 1882, 2;
November 23, 1883, 5; May 29, 1883, 5; March 16, 1884, 2; *Annual Meeting*, July 17,
1886, CC MSS; H. B. Jackson, *History of the Cobden Club* (London: Cobden-Sanderson,
1939), 38–39.

Trade League helped organize a conference held at Detroit's Opera House on May 31, 1883. Representative delegates from various state and local leagues totaled around seventy-five, and Wells arrived as the keynote speaker. Mayor Thompson of Detroit suggested "a movement in favor of a North American *Zollverein*," a suggestion that had also been called for by farmers of Cobden, Illinois, the year before as well as by Canadian Cobdenite Goldwin Smith throughout the previous decade. It was a public forum wherein women were "especially invited to attend." One hoped-for result was expressed by the young publisher and a future leader of the Progressive Era free-trade movement, publisher George Haven Putnam, who suggested that the conference might garner enough attention to be referenced by "some of our English Free-Trade friends" at the following month's Cobden Club dinner. Another result of this conference was the design of a national conference in Chicago to be held in two years' time. The free-trade movement's efforts even drew the interest of some in Montreal, where they founded a free-trade club based upon the AFTL style, with the long-term goal of creating a free-trade league that would represent the entire Dominion of Canada.[72]

The 1884 presidential elections and the end of Republican free trade

Following such bolstering to the free-trade circle, the final straw fell that broke the Cobdenites' Republican backing. In 1884, the Republican party nominated for president the corruption-laden Listian nationalist James G. Blaine of Maine. Blaine was a strong proponent of the American System, and Listian Henry Carey had a helping hand in shaping Blaine's forward-looking Anglophobic views on economic nationalism during Blaine's attendance at "Carey's Vespers" in the late 1860s.[73] Blaine

---

[72] "Instructions to Delegates to the Free Trade Conference"; Brownlee to Bowker, April 26, May 7, May 12, May 14, May 23, July 18, June 19, 1883; S. W. Emerson [Kings County] to Bowker, May 2; Poultney Bigelow [NYFTL] to Bowker, July 5, July 27, 1883; Putnam to Bowker, May 28, 1883, Box 89, Bowker Papers, NYPL; *Chicago Tribune*, June 1, 1883, 6; *Report of the Tariff Commission Appointed under Act of Congress Approved May 15, 1882*, 47th Cong., 2nd Sess., Misc. Doc. No. 6, Part 1 (Washington, DC: Government Printing Office, 1882), I, 968–970; *Chicago Tribune*, September 9, 1882, 7; John Redpath Dougall [Montreal] to Bowker, June 27, 1883. Cobden, Illinois, was named after Richard Cobden, as were Cobden, Ontario [Canada], Cobden, Victoria [Australia], and Cobden, Minnesota.

[73] Alexander Del Mar, "Henry C. Carey's Roundtable," *Gunton's Magazine* 13 (August 1897): 99; Edward Crapol, *America for Americans: Economic Nationalism and Anglophobia in the Late Nineteenth Century* (Westport, CT: Greenwood Press, 1873), 22. See, also, Mark Wahlgren Summers, *Rum, Romanism, and Rebellion: The Making of a President, 1884* (Chapel Hill: University of North Carolina Press, 2000).

would evolve into the most progressive of American Listian nationalists. A young, antislavery, Whig member of the Republican party in the 1850s, he had become a proponent of regional American expansion from the 1840s onward, although his nationalistic belief in such expansive Manifest Destiny had been tempered in the antebellum period stemming from his fear of the territorial expansion of southern slavery. Upon his entrance into politics, his ascent up the Republican political ladder was swift, and it is fair to say that he was probably the most famous politician of the Gilded Age, as well as one of the era's most unscrupulous. He was a particularly ambidextrous political matador, waving the "bloody shirt" before his Democratic opponents with one hand, while shaking a political red cape with the other in the hopes of goading John Bull into a calamitous charge. He was also a leader of the Half-Breed Republican patronage system. The prospect of Blaine as president was a difficult pill for any man desirous of civil service reform, peaceful Anglo-American relations, or freer trade to swallow.[74]

America's Cobdenites therefore had a difficult choice to make in 1884: remain loyal to the Republican party or to their free-trade principles. The vast majority decided to throw their support behind the Democratic civil service reformer Grover Cleveland, whereupon they received the new nickname of "Mugwump." However, a handful of Republicans independents chose to remain faithful to the party. Cyrus Field, worried that a Democratic administration would not be as open to the idea of his planned Pacific cable and with Blaine a long-time friend, voted Republican.[75] For more pragmatic political reasons, Henry Cabot Lodge followed suit, as did another rising Republican politician by the name of Theodore Roosevelt, who had earlier been exposed to the Cobdenite doctrine while attending Harvard.[76]

Since the late 1870s, Roosevelt had been a "howling academic free trader," according to Henry George, the radical American tax reformer and absolute free trader. George even recollected how, during his 1883 speech on free trade before "the Cobden Club of New York" (as he called it), "a young man who sat on the platform behind him . . . and applauded his most radical utterances with such tumultuous vehemence that the speaker almost lost the thread of his discourse in his wonder over who the

---

[74] Edward Crapol, *James G. Blaine: Architect of Empire* (Wilmington, DE: Scholarly Resources, Inc., 2000), 1–39.

[75] Field to Blaine, October 22, 1884, folder 8, box 1, Field Papers; Field to Blaine, November 18, 1884, reel 10, Blaine Papers; Carter, *Man of Two Worlds*, 334–336. For free-trade conspiracy charges leveled against Field, see *New York Evening Telegram*, October 4, 1884.

[76] Lodge to Carl Schurz, July 14, 1884, microfilm reel 3, Henry Cabot Lodge Papers, MHS.

young man with the eye-glasses and the big teeth could be. This was Theodore Roosevelt in the very early 80s."[77] A young Roosevelt believed that tariff reform was "the great question of the day." He joined the New York Free Trade Club in 1882, and became one of its financial officers. At the club's 1883 dinner, he even gave a speech, "The Tariff in Politics," wherein he encouraged and hoped for the success of free trade over protectionism, and called for a tariff for revenue only. His free-trade advocacy and admiration for Henry George were not the only actions considered anathema among most late-nineteenth-century Republicans – in 1883, Roosevelt became a member of the Cobden Club. So, too, had his friend and mentor Henry Cabot Lodge three years earlier, having just ended his professorship at Charles Eliot's Harvard College.[78]

Lodge and Roosevelt thus showed up to the 1884 Republican National Convention in Chicago as anti-Blaine free-trade reformers. Roosevelt himself had arrived as part of a delegation representing the New York Free Trade Club to demand the abolition of the "war tariff" from the Republican party platform. Yet Roosevelt and Lodge would end up throwing their support behind Blaine and the Republican banner of protection in the 1884 elections and beyond, and their names were thereafter stricken from the Cobden Club's list of members.[79]

Lodge's own protectionist turn appears to have been considerably more dramatic, no mere political posturing as Roosevelt's appears to have been. Lodge had early on expressed his independent streak, as seen in his support for presidential candidates Tilden in 1876 and Garfield in 1880, and continued to express his free-trade proclivities as late as 1884. Yet at the same time, as an academic, he was gradually becoming infatuated with the American System. Further illustrating his ideological transformation from Cobdenite to Listian, after his 1884 decision to back Blaine, he would become a staunch and vocal defender of protectionism and imperial expansion. Correspondingly, his former free-trade friends among the Republican independents successfully worked to see Lodge defeated in his own 1884 Republican congressional

---

[77] *Single Tax Review* (1909) IX, 56–57.
[78] Roosevelt to Bowker, May 24, 1883, Box 5, Bowker Papers; *The Members of the Cobden Club, with Dates of Entrance* (London: Cassell, Petter, Galpin & Co., 1880); *Organization of the New York Free Trade Club, 1882; New York Free Trade Club Annual Dinner. May 28, 1883. List of Toasts and Speakers*, Box 90, Bowker Papers, NYPL; Bowker, ed., *The Economic Fact-Book*, 14.
[79] *Million*, June 14, 1884, 118; *Petition of the New York Free Trade Club to the Republican National Convention*, May 29, 1884; Edward P. Kohn, "Crossing the Rubicon: Theodore Roosevelt, Henry Cabot Lodge, and the 1884 Republican National Convention," *Journal of the Gilded Age & Progressive Era* 5 (January 2006): 18–45.

run.[80] Lodge expressed his lingering animosity toward his former Cobdenite colleagues on various occasions following their 1884 fallout. In a later defense of Republican protectionism, for instance, he castigated his former free-trade friends as "devout followers of the Manchester School, and take all their teachings and practices with little discrimination. They are essentially imitative."[81]

Roosevelt thereafter leaned on Lodge's own high tariff arguments and sought his approval on the issue in subsequent years. Roosevelt also would end up later denying that he had ever been a member of the Cobden Club, and would make "a savage onslaught" on Grover Cleveland's attempts at tariff reform to make certain "the mugwump papers" did not think his attitude "in any way one of alliance with them."[82] His Anglophilia would resurface somewhat, but he made a habit of avoiding the tariff issue in the coming decades, and his early flirtation with free trade would come back to haunt him in later Republican political life.[83] Roosevelt's less than amicable split from the Mugwumps might also help explain much of his future disdain for American Cobdenites, who indignantly considered his and Lodge's 1884 choice one of political expediency rather than that of moral and ideological principle.

Conclusion

While both major postbellum political parties faced internecine conflict, protectionist and free-trade forces began mobilizing nationally. One

---

[80] "Henry Cabot Lodge as an Apostle of the Autocratic Money-Controlled Machine and the Foe of Popular Rule," *Arena* 36 (Nov. 1906): 534–535; Henry Cabot Lodge, *Speeches and Addresses, 1884–1909* (Boston and New York: Houghton Mifflin Company, 1909), 125; Claude Moore Fuess, "Carl Schurz, Henry Cabot Lodge, and the Campaign of 1884: A Study in Temperament and Political Philosophy," *New England Quarterly* 5 (July 1932): 461, 463, 467–482.

[81] Henry Cabot Lodge, "Protection or Free Trade – Which?" *Arena* 24 (November 1891): 653.

[82] *Boston Daily Advertiser*, October 29, 1884, in *Selections from the Correspondence of Theodore Roosevelt and Henry Cabot Lodge*, 2 vols. (New York: Charles Scribner's Sons, 1925), I, 20–21; Roosevelt and Lodge, January 17, 1888, ibid., I, 61–62; Roosevelt to Lodge, January 22, 1888, ibid., I, 62–65; Roosevelt to Lodge, September 27, 1902, ibid., I, 532–534.

[83] William N. Osgood, *An Open Letter to Hon. Henry Cabot Lodge, Relating to His Speech upon the Present Tariff Recently Delivered before the Harvard Finance Club* (Boston: Massachusetts Tariff Reform League, 1888); Theodore Roosevelt, *Campaigns and Controversies* (New York: C. Scribner's Sons, 1926), 52–53; Roswell A. Benedict, *Malefactors of Great Wealth!* (New York: American Business Bureau, 1907), 377–381; *Moody's Magazine* (February 1908): 157. See, also, James Anthony Rosmond, "Nelson Aldrich, Theodore Roosevelt and the Tariff: A Study to 1905" (PhD diss., University of North Carolina at Chapel Hill, 1974).

result was the national abandonment of black civil rights. Owing to their laissez-faire predilections, Cobdenite abolitionists effectively shifted their antislavery struggle to freeing American trade, and Republican economic nationalists similarly refocused the party's primary attention from antislavery to protectionism, all of which would have dire long-term consequences for Reconstruction and African American rights. Economic nationalists also renewed their conspiratorial attacks upon American free traders, suggesting that American Cobdenite advocacy, whether from professors, the press, or the public sphere, was part of a vast transatlantic free-trade imperial plot to undermine American industries and wages. Within this toxic environment, Listian nationalism was coming into its own at the national and international level, especially owing to the efforts of U. S. Grant and James G. Blaine. The charismatic and enigmatic Blaine in particular was fast becoming the most progressive of Gilded Age economic nationalists. Owing to European economic expansion in the Western Hemisphere and to the onset of the Great Depression in 1873, Blaine headed the vanguard of a new coercive closed-door Republican foreign policy of expansionism: the imperialism of economic nationalism.

Even as Republican Listians began implementing the imperialism of economic nationalism, the transatlantic ties of American Cobdenism – real and perceived – were strengthening the American free-trade movement following the political setbacks of the 1870s and early 1880s. The 1884 presidential election resulted in a political realignment of great import for future American domestic and foreign relations, and its outcome owed much to America's independent free traders. By tracing the impact of Cobdenism upon US political culture, this complex party realignment becomes clearer. With Blaine's 1884 presidential nomination, most Cobdenite Republican independents, now nicknamed Mugwumps, switched their support to the Democratic party's candidate, the civil service reform governor of New York, Grover Cleveland. On the issues of tariff reform and American expansionism, perhaps the most significant immediate result of the election was the Cobdenite abandonment of the Republican ship. With Republican free traders overboard, the party could finally claim what Henry Carey had searched for since the party's founding: a semblance of ideological cohesion not seen since the days of antebellum antislavery. Five years after Carey's death, it had finally become the Party of Protectionism *en bloc*.[84]

Cleveland won the presidential battle, despite Republican attempts to attract the Irish vote by laying the blame for Ireland's economic problems

---

[84] On Republican support for the tariff, see, also, Richard Bensel, *The Political Economy of American Industrialization*, 457–509.

upon British free trade.[85] Cleveland's victory stemmed in part from the Cobdenite support he received from among the Bourbon Democrats, the staunch laissez-faire wing of the party, and of course from the newly christened Mugwump independents.[86] The Mugwumps were further delighted upon Cleveland's election owing to his slight victory, taking the state of New York by only 1,149 votes. To the Mugwumps, whose area of control rested predominantly in the Northeast, this slim margin demonstrated to them that they had brought about Cleveland's success. E. L. Godkin, British-born Mugwump editor of the *Nation*, stated that the "independent Republicans of the country have elected Grover Cleveland President. That point is so clear in the result that nobody questions it."[87] Wells and his American Cobdenites had found their man in Cleveland; and they felt he owed his election to them.

[85] *New York Tribune*, August 2, 1884, 4.
[86] Horace Samuel Merrill, *Bourbon Leader: Grover Cleveland and the Democratic Party* (London: A. & C. Black, 1958); Merrill, *Bourbon Democracy of the Middle West, 1865–1896* (Baton Rouge: Louisiana State University Press, 1953). Cobdenite "Bourbon" Democrats included Thomas F. Bayard, John G. Carlisle, Lucius Q. C. Lamar, J. Sterling Morton, and Samuel Tilden.
[87] "The Week," *Nation* 39 (November 13, 1884), 407. See, also, *Million*, November 22, 1884, 303. Despite some disagreement concerning the accuracy of the claims, historians agree that the Mugwumps were influential in his election, owing to their strong political support in New York and Massachusetts. See for instance, Richard E. Welch, Jr., *The Presidencies of Grover Cleveland* (Lawrence: University Press of Kansas, 1988), 29–30; Fleming, *Bowker*, 203; Terrill, "David A. Wells," 548.

5   The Great Debate

The first Cleveland presidency, free-trade culture,
and the anti-imperialism of free trade, 1884–1889

> The Cobden Club found a willing ally in the Democratic party.
>
> George B. Curtiss.[1]

> The American members ... have combined to conquer and subdue
> American energy and enterprise. They shine out on the British
> Cobden Club list like apples of gold in pictures of silver. They ought
> to be preserved as relics for the reverential inspection of the rising
> generation of American workingmen.
>
> The Republican Campaign Text-book for 1888.[2]

> This Club is the most potent and dangerous of all the forces menacing
> our industries and therefore menacing our liberties – most potent
> because of the wealth and political influence back of it; most dangerous
> because of its stealthy methods. Let no man belonging to the Cobden
> Club or avowing any sympathy with it ever be trusted to office.
>
> Excerpt, "Address of the Irish-American Protection Union of New York,"
> December 3, 1884.[3]

Just days before the November 1884 presidential election, Thomas
Dudley, former US Consul in Liverpool, England, gave a rousing speech
to a Republican gathering in Astoria, New York. Although Grover
Cleveland, the Democratic presidential candidate, had pointedly avoided
serious discussion of the tariff on the campaign trail, Dudley emphasized
that it was the "great issue" before the nation. The approaching election
offered the country a clear-cut choice between "the American system of
protection" and "the English system of a tariff for revenue only." England
had formed the Cobden Club to undermine the American System,
Dudley conspiratorially observed. "And for wealth, for power, and for
the influence of its members," he knew of no other organization that came

---

[1] George B. Curtiss, *The Industrial Development of Nations and a History of the Tariff Policies of the United States, and of Great Britain, Germany, France, Russia and Other European Countries*, 3 vols. (Binghamton, NY: George B. Curtiss, 1912), III, 254.

[2] George Francis Dawson, *The Republican Campaign Text-book for 1888* (New York: Brentano's, 1888), 91.

[3] Reprinted in *Million*, December 13, 1884, 326.

close. "It has its agents all over this country with its pamphlets and other documents, and now has as its chief agent the Democratic party of this country to assist it in its work."[4]

Dudley also noted how Harvard's own president, Charles Eliot, had now brazenly taken to bragging that each and every one of his students favored free trade. The Cobden Club was further poisoning the minds of America's youth by offering silver medals to the students of Eliot's Harvard, William Graham Sumner's Yale, and Arthur Latham Parry's Williams College, all three men being themselves members of the club. And why does Reverend Henry Ward Beecher support Cleveland? Because of Beecher's "attachment to free trade and the Cobden Club," Dudley explained. The failed 1884 Morrison tariff bill had also recently been proposed by order of the club, Dudley charged, through the efforts of the club's American "minions," Congressmen Samuel "Sunset" Cox, John Carlisle, and William R. Morrison, the bill's author. Only by fighting the Cobden Club's efforts, Dudley concluded to loud and prolonged applause, would America "become the great manufacturing country of the world."[5]

However formidable, such Anglophobic Republican opposition in 1884 was unable to keep Cleveland and his Cobdenites from the White House. Correspondingly, as Dudley's speech and this chapter show, American economic nationalists spotted and attacked the alleged transatlantic free-trade enemies proliferating among Cleveland's advisors, cabinet members, and supporters.[6] And amid their ideological fencing over the proper approach to US economic globalization – whether it would integrate regionally through protectionism and imperialism or globally through free trade and non-interventionism – both economic nationalists and Cobdenite cosmopolitans would retool the rhetoric of antislavery to strike out at the opposition. The antebellum legacy of antislavery seeped into the postbellum struggle over American economic development and global economic integration, as would the legacy of Britain's ACLL. Faced with mounting inflationary calls for national bimetallism – the coinage of both silver and gold – Cleveland's cabinet, following the City of London's lead, would also work toward maintaining

---

[4] Thomas H. Dudley, *The Cobden Club of England and Protection in the United States: A Speech Made at a Republican Meeting, Held at Astoria, New York, October 23d, 1884*, 3, 5–7, 10–12. For the growing importance of the tariff issue, see, also, S. Walter Poulshock, "Pennsylvania and the Politics of the Tariff, 1880–1888," *Pennsylvania History* 29 (July 1962): 291–305.

[5] Dudley, *The Cobden Club of England and Protection in the United States*, 14–15, 32.

[6] Listian John A. Kasson also dedicated a speech in 1884 to attacking the teachings of Cobden in *Tariff Tract No. 3, 1884: Free Trade not the International Law of the Almighty* (Philadelphia, PA: American Iron and Steel Association, 1884).

the deflationary *de facto* US gold standard. Finally, in 1888 Cleveland himself would shift the nation's attention to the "Great Debate" over the proper course of American economic expansion, giving rise to more charges of a free-trade conspiracy as well as an outpouring of American free-trade culture within the literary work of Walt Whitman, Edward Bellamy, and Mark Twain.

The Gilded Age conflict over American economic globalization has long sat uneasily within the history of American imperialism. In attempting to describe the late-nineteenth-century rise of an American free-trade or open-door empire, a variety of influential US imperial histories have sought to downplay the substantial political and ideological conflict over American economic expansion. In seeking a bipartisan American open-door empire, they have instead conflated Grover Cleveland's non-consecutive Cobdenite administrations with those of his Democratic Jeffersonian predecessors and Republican Listian successors. However, incorporating the politico-ideological controversy over American economic globalization with that of Anglo-American imperial debates illuminates how the Cleveland administration's anti-imperialism of free trade stood far apart from both the antebellum imperial expansionism of the Democrats and the postbellum Republican imperialism of economic nationalism.

American Cobdenism had a demonstrable influence upon the administrations of Grover Cleveland, and controversially so.[7] Cleveland's administrations adhered to Cobdenite policies of freer trade, anti-imperialism, the gold standard, and generally amicable Anglo-American relations, and would temporarily upset the Republican party's imperial designs in Latin America, the Pacific, and Africa. The Cobdenite adherence of Cleveland's administration would also add fuel to the conspiratorial fire.

The American legacies of antislavery and the ACLL

A year after Grover Cleveland's 1884 presidential election, New York City's AFTL called its second national conference, this one in Chicago. Members of thirty-nine clubs and delegates from twenty states arrived to hear David Ames Wells – the current AFTL president and US secretary of the Cobden Club of London – and other leading free traders speak on the need for tariff reductions.[8]

---

[7] Marc-William Palen, "Foreign Relations in the Gilded Age: A British Free-Trade Conspiracy?," *Diplomatic History* 37 (April 2013): 217–247; Palen, "The Imperialism of Economic Nationalism, 1890–1913," *Diplomatic History* 39 (January 2015): 157–185.

[8] *New York Tribune*, November 13, 1885, 4. Atkinson himself notably abstained, still smarting from the 1872 debacle, and still "disgusted" by the free-trade movement's new

The twin legacies of the ACLL and antislavery manifested themselves at the conference. R. R. Bowker, AFTL secretary, beseeched the conference delegates to donate funds for the upcoming congressional elections, just as all of England had once come to the support of Richard Cobden and John Bright. About $20,000 was desperately needed despite, he wryly joked, "our unbounded resources of British gold." Where once the Republican party had stood as the "party of freedom" and had been created to "free our soil from the curse of negro slavery," Bowker suggested that the party now encouraged a system that tied Americans "down into a new slavery." In contrast, tariff reform and sound money represented the keys to prosperity and freedom. Hinting at the growing political influence of American labor, Bowker also paid tribute to American workers and trade unions. He urged free traders to target these men and women, and to explain to them the immorality and corruption inherent in the protective system. While he readily admitted the election had not been decided on the issue of the tariff, Bowker also had faith that the new reform-minded president, Grover Cleveland, would become "the champion of the tax-payers against the tax-eaters."[9] And J. Sterling Morton (D-NE), presiding over the conference, proclaimed that American commercial slavery could only be overcome through open and free global economic competition. He directly connected the free-trade movement's goals with those of abolitionism: "It has been said by many that the old Abolition party had accomplished its end, and that there was nothing more to be freed ... but we have an enslaved commerce ... the shackles will be stricken from American commerce."[10]

---

dogmatic doctrinaire leaders, Professors William Graham Sumner and Arthur Latham Perry. Atkinson to Bowker, October 16, 1885, carton 17, Atkinson Papers.

[9] New York Free Trade Club, *National Conference of Free Traders and Revenue Reformers. Chicago, November 11 and 12, 1885* (New York: New York Free Trade Club, 1885), 11–15; *Chicago Tribune*, November 13, 1885, 1–2. There remained a general disconnect between the middle- to upper- class free traders and the demands of American labor, eerily reminiscent of the divisions between the ACLL and the Chartist movement in England in the 1830s and 1840s. Former AFTL Secretary Henry Demarest Lloyd would become disillusioned with Cobdenism following the excesses of the railroads and the violent 1877 Great Railroad Strike. John L. Thomas, *Alternative America: Henry George, Edward Bellamy, Henry Demarest Lloyd and the Adversary Tradition* (Cambridge, MA: Belknap Press, 1983), 77–81. For attempts to sway laborers to support free trade, see *American Laborer's Political Manual. To which is Added the Laboring-Man's Interview with the Party Chiefs on the Great Issue of the Tariff. Both Platforms being Given* (Boston, MA: American Laborers Educational Society, 1884); and various issues of the *Free-Trader*.

[10] New York Free Trade Club, *National Conference of Free Traders*, 2–3. See, also, William Graham Sumner, "Tariff Slavery," *Million*, June 7, 1884, 106. On the South's capture of the national cotton textile market, see Gavin Wright, "Cheap Labor and Southern Textiles, 1880–1930," *Quarterly Journal of Economics* 96 (November 1981): 605–629.

Alongside antislavery and the ACLL, the New South also arose as a topic of some discussion at the conference. The former slave-based economy had come a long way since the Civil War, as had northern temperament. The South's economy had begun to rebound with infant industries of its own, so much so that "the fully developed matron of the North is asking protection against the infant-suckling of the South," a delegate from Ohio observed. Although only a handful of southern delegates were present, they made their voices heard. John Dargan of South Carolina, "fired" by the free-trade writings of William Graham Sumner, David Wells, and Henry George, admitted that he had at first been hesitant to speak up, fearing "the readiness with which you would suspect that I had come before you to advocate nullification as the best method . . . and I felt that you would think, if I failed in that I would say the next step, gentlemen, is secession." He was happy to report instead the warm reception from his "Northern friends." He could not wait to return home and say to his southern audiences "that under my eyes the bloody shirt has been torn to tatters, and its miserable rags swept out of sight forever."[11] The American free-trade movement now looked capable of cutting across long-standing sectional divisions.

David Ames Wells then rose to speak out against the more progressive elements within American protectionist circles. He granted that there were some "honest advocates of the protective system" who looked "to free-trade as an ultimate objective point." But unfortunately most "put this ultimatum a long way off in the future." Along with his denunciation of American Listian nationalism, Wells emphasized the American farmer's mounting need for foreign markets, as farmers yet outnumbered "all the mills, mines, fields, and factories." This sentiment was seconded by a farmer and wool grower from Ohio, who proclaimed that America's excess products "must find markets in foreign countries," and that only a policy of free trade could accomplish this. Others noted that the markets of South America might easily become available if only the United States were to "adopt a tariff as simple and liberal as that of Great Britain." While delegates disagreed over preferred methods of taxation or the degree of revenue tariff reductions, they all shared the desire for freer trade and access to global markets *sans* the coercive, restrictive, and protectionist market-seeking advocated by American Listians. And the free traders finally had a man in the White House who appeared amenable to tariff reform; when a gentleman from Flint, Michigan, suggested that the league send Cleveland an address

[11] New York Free Trade Club, *National Conference of Free Traders*, 57.

concerning the tariff, Wells responded confidently that on that issue "we can trust the President."[12]

American protectionists agreed. They claimed to have discovered hidden transatlantic ties connecting American free traders to the Cobden Club and Cleveland's election. Republican Congressman J. P. Dolliver of Iowa warned that "the Cobden Club is working here" in America. For the past ten years, the organization's free-trade tracts and pamphlets have fallen "among us like the leaves of autumn . . . . The Democratic Party is the tool of these Cobden Club members and their sympathizers." Former Congressman Thompson Murch of Maine noted that throughout his home state "the Cobden Club's influence is felt. Their pamphlets find their way into every farm house. There can be no disputing the fact that Democracy, free trade, and British interests are bound up together. The money and influence of English manufacturers play a much greater part in American politics than most persons would believe." At the behest of the British government, they charged, the club was bent upon destroying the American System.[13]

While such conspiratorial potshots were being leveled at the incoming Democratic administration, free traders returned fire with the rhetoric of antislavery. At a New York Free Trade Club dinner in early 1885, Reverend Henry Ward Beecher gave a fiery speech condemning protectionism for impeding the freedom of mankind to an enthralled audience of free traders as they sipped upon *sorbet a la Cobden*.[14] In *Industrial Slavery* (1885), so too did Frank H. Hurd ask: "Who is free who cannot control his own labor? What was the African slavery . . . but the ownership of the labor of one man by another man? Whoever owns my labor owns me." Hurd concluded that the high price wrought through protectionist legislation was nothing more than slavery for the American workingman. Free trade alternatively "strikes off the shackles and sets him upon his feet as a free man again."[15]

Hurd also hinted at the growing crisis of American overproduction and market expansion that would grip American foreign policy for decades to come. When protectionists cried about overproduction, he argued, they were really complaining about America's "limited market." What the

---

[12] New York Free Trade Club, *National Conference of Free Traders*, 5–9, 21, 32–33, 111, 127.
[13] *New York Tribune*, October 3, 1884, 5; October 29, 1884, 8. See, also, *San Francisco Evening Bulletin*, August 23, 1888, 4; *London Times*, July 12, 1880, 11; *Standard* (London), October 6, 1884, 3.
[14] *New York Times*, February 24, 1885.
[15] *New York Times*, November 14, 1885; Frank H. Hurd, *Industrial Slavery* (New York: New York Free Trade Club, 1885), 64. Hurd co-founded Toledo's Anti-Protective Tariff League with J. M. Osborne, head of the Ohio Free Trade League.

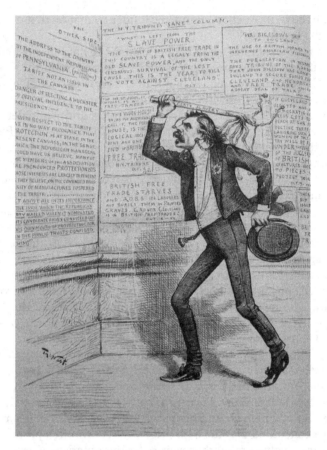

Figure 5.1 "Lashing Himself into Fever Heat." Thomas Nast mocks
Whitelaw Reid's *New York Tribune* editorial tactic of tying Cleveland to
British free trade and southern slavery in the lead up to the 1884
elections. "Lashing Himself into Fever Heat. Black-Law Reid, 'You are
British Free-Traders, Dudes, Pharisees, Frauds, and Mugwumps –
that's what you are!'" *Harper's Weekly*, October 18, 1884, 690

United States needed instead was access to all the markets of the world.
Mexico, South America, and Canada were ready; "Ah! the world is
ready .... Open the doors and let the world be free to come here and
buy, both from the Orient and the Occident, and the channels will be
bursting with the overflow that will come rushing through your streets."[16]

[16] Hurd, *Industrial Slavery*, 68. See, also, E. J. Donnell, *Slavery and "Protection": An
Historical Review and Appeal to the Workshop and the Farm* (New York: E. J. Donnell,

For American Cobdenites like Beecher and Hurd, free trade and equal access to the world's markets would free the "enslaved" working class, an argument that struck a chord with some among the burgeoning American labor movement. Labor leaders such as Ezra Heywood of the New England Labor Reform League found the Cobdenite argument persuasive indeed. He believed that the "tyrannous greed which held negroes slaves, now denies to workers freedom in exchange; as color lines fade out ... the same political party which helped abolish chattel-bondage" in the South "now insists that 'protective' slavery shall be perpetual in New England!"[17] Heywood's pro-free-trade labor sentiment was, it seems, the rare exception to the rule.

Such Cobdenite calls for free trade with all the world stood in stark contrast to both the autarky of more orthodox home-market protectionists and the coercive regionalized economic globalization espoused by American Listians. Republican protectionists parried with antislavery language of their own, pointing to the poverty of the British working class, the supposed glut of British goods, and the frequency of forced emigration from Free Trade England owing to British overproduction. According to high tariff proponents, the pauper laborer of England was thus shackled in servitude to its free-trade system of cheap products and cheap wages.[18] On one side, Americans were thus allegedly conspiring with British free traders to keep the United States dependent on British markets and cheap wages; on the other, industrial slave-masters were holding the United States back from its promised position as the manufacturing center of global trade. Such was the polemical political climate when Cleveland and his Cobdenite cabinet came into office.

Alongside the legacy of antislavery, the ACLL's earlier successes continued to play an inspirational role within the American free-trade movement, including an attempt at tariff reduction in 1884. General M. M. Trumbull's popular work, *The American Lesson of the Free Trade Struggle in England*, was republished within this toxic political and ideological milieu "to show that the moral of the contest is as applicable to the United States to-day as it was to England forty years ago." The new edition was replete with an introductory letter of prophetic praise from John Bright, who

---

1884), 14–15; and *Proceedings of the Annual Dinner of the New York Free Trade Club, March 15th, 1884* (New York: New York Free Trade Club, 1884), 17.

[17] Ezra H. Heywood, *Free Trade: Showing that Mediaeval Barbarism, Cunningly Termed 'Protection to Home Industry,' Tariff Delusion Invades Enterprise, Defrauds Labor, Plunders Trade, and Postpones Industrial Emancipation* (Princeton, MA: Co-operative Publishing Company, 1888), 1. Heywood was also a radical women's suffragist.

[18] *New York Tribune*, August 19, 1885, 4.

predicted that just as "the shackles have been struck from the limbs of the slave," so "they cannot remain to fetter the freedom of your industries."[19]

In 1884, Cobdenite Congressman William R. Morrison sought tariff reductions in a fashion similar to that taken by Sir Robert Peel in England. Morrison did so with the encouragement of the American free-trade "jackal" Edward Atkinson, and its "roaring lion" David Wells. Reeling from the aforementioned conspiratorial attacks and the small chance of the bill's ultimate success, however, Morrison himself was becoming disconsolate. Even as Philadelphia's Wharton Barker and Robert Ellis Thompson gave public notice of the publication of the seventh edition of Friedrich List's *National System of Political Economy*, Wells recommended that Morrison read a pamphlet entitled *History of the Free Trade Struggle in Great Britain* to "strengthen" his "soul."[20] The ACLL's antebellum efforts remained a source of inspiration for the postbellum American free-trade movement.

With Morrison's Peelite 1884 tariff bill hanging in political limbo, US free traders continued to educate and organize. In the West, far-traveling Henry Ward Beecher observed "a change of sentiment, in favor of free trade," a change that might lead to the destruction of "the very poisonous root" of protectionism.[21] Cobdenites also found fresh support from more moderate reform organizations like the Manufacturers' Tariff Reform League – a New York-based manufacturing lobby – and the Philadelphia Tariff Reform Club, a low-tariff group that popped up smack in the middle of the protectionist heartland. Aid also arrived from the more extreme free-trade press, particularly the *Million*, which started publishing in March 1884 in Des Moines, Iowa, under the editorship of the AFTL's western secretary, Henry Philpott. The paper was chock full of the writings of leading US Cobdenites, editorial defenses of the Cobden Club, and reprints of Cobden Club leaflets.

Philpott also took a growing interest in garnering African American support for free trade. In his *Belford's* article, "A Plea for the Negro," he was perplexed that no philosopher for or against free trade had

---

[19] M. M. Trumbull, *The American Lesson of the Free Trade Struggle in England* (Chicago, IL: Schumm and Simpson, 1884 [1882]), 7, 5. Similarly, see Bright's widely circulated letter of acceptance as an honorary member of the Boston Free Trade Club, reprinted in Free Trade League of Victoria, "Address to the People," in *Free Trade Papers* (Melbourne: Free Trade League of Victoria, 1876), 1–2.

[20] *The American*, March 1, 1884, 327; Atkinson to Morrison, December 28, 1882, carton 16, Atkinson Papers; Harold Francis Williamson, *Edward Atkinson: The Biography of an American Liberal, 1827–1905* (Boston, MA: Old Corner Book Store, 1934), 136; Atkinson to Wells, January 14, 1882, February 5, 1884, February 26, 1884, carton 16, Atkinson Papers; Wells to Morrison, February 26, 1884, quoted in Barnes, *Carlisle*, 79–80.

[21] Beecher to Poultney Bigelow, October 4, 1883, Box 8, Poultney Bigelow Papers, NYPL.

exhaustively examined the relationship of the two subjects. He left to the abolitionist free traders to argue the "theme of slavery's likeness to protection," and focused his attention instead upon the plight of the black cotton grower dependent upon the bane of American protectionists: foreign manufacturers. Philpott concluded that none of the imaginary blessings of protectionism were "bestowed upon the Negro. His cotton is not taxed, but the shirt that was made of it is," as are the steel rails upon which his cotton travels seaboard for foreign purchase. Not coincidentally, in the June 1884 issue of the *Million*, Philpott made special note of the subscription of a "colored free trader," Charles Nelson of Springfield, Illinois, whose "fearlessness" regarding the "fight for revenue reform ought to put a good many white democrats to blush." Philpott also reprinted articles from black newspapers like the *Philadelphia Sentinel* on why blacks, as fellow American consumers, should support free trade and cheap products, and that because trade and labor unions did not allow black membership, American blacks should have "no interest in maintaining a tariff on commodities."[22]

Nor were Philpott and Nelson the only ones making themselves heard concerning African Americans and the tariff. Much like the rest of the country, African Americans found themselves on both sides of the polarizing debate. Some felt increasingly disaffected from the Republican party following the effective abandonment of Reconstruction in 1877 and the nearly unanimous 1883 Republican-controlled Supreme Court ruling that overturned the Civil Rights Act of 1875, and so turned against Republican protectionism. Philadelphia's African American newspaper the *Christian Recorder* felt unsympathetic to the supposed plight of protected US industries, sardonically calling the country's high tariff policy "American Industry Civil Rights." Although with reluctance the *Recorder* had once again thrown its support behind the 1884 Republican ticket, it also pointed out that tariff protection and civil rights protection were "largely similar. In their competition with white men, colored men, by reason of their immaturity, ask Congress to throw around them the arms of protection in the shape of a Civil Rights law .... In their competition with foreign industries, American industry, just like the colored man, by

---

[22] *Petition of the Manufacturers' Tariff Reform League*, May 8, 1884; Benjamin F. Dunlap [Organizing Secretary, Philadelphia Tariff Reform Club] to Bowker, June 25, 1884, Box 89, Bowker Papers, NYPL; Philpott to Bowker, November 29, 1883, December 11, 1883 Box 89, Bowker Papers, NYPL; Henry J. Philpott, "A Plea for the Negro," *Belford's Magazine* (July 1888), 220; *Million*, June 21, 1884, 128; "Negro Laborers and Tariff Laws," *Philadelphia Sentinel*, reprinted in *Million*, September 26, 1885, 235. According to the *Chicago Tribune*, Nelson was much sought after for garnering Democratic votes from western black communities. His son would afterward be handpicked for a position within the first Cleveland administration. *Chicago Tribune*, July 23, 1888, 2.

reason of immaturity, asks Congress to throw around it the arm of its protection in the shape of strong Tariff laws." However, if the former has been deemed unconstitutional, then so should the latter. "If the nation must protect its weak industries it surely ought to protect its weak men. The principle that abolishes Civil Rights," the paper concluded, "will bring Free Trade."[23] The *Recorder* had given its endorsement for free trade.

The *Christian Recorder* also noted how African Americans were split on the tariff issue. The *Recorder* found it "really amusing to see the zeal with which the majority of our colored exchanges come to the rescue of the Tariff. The very idea of Free Trade makes some of them wince as though under the lash of some Southern Bulldozer. In so far as we as a distinct class of the American people are concerned, the man who does not see that Free Trade would be a positive blessing to us is simply blind." And yet, the *Recorder* observed, Louisiana blacks were siding with the Sugar Trust on the issue of protectionism. While sympathizing with the black Louisiana laborer's difficult position, the paper's editor argued that the complete abolition of the tariff would help all the country's laborers, whereas "to keep up this protection forever is simply to make the rich richer and the poor poorer."[24] The tariff debate was beginning to cut across both racial and party lines.

Bolstered by the twin legacies of abolitionism and the ACLL, William R. Morrison summoned up the will to propose a bill to reduce tariffs by 20 percent across the board in 1884. Yet massive wage cuts and strikes owing to another economic downturn alongside the intractability of economic nationalists in Congress like Ohio Republican William McKinley and Democratic protectionists like Pennsylvania's Samuel J. Randall (forty-one Democrats voted against Morrison's proposal) made certain that the bill would not become law.[25] The predominance of economic nationalist ideology within the Gilded Age halls of Congress was pronounced.

---

[23] August Meier, "The Negro and the Democratic Party, 1875–1915," *Phylon* 17 (2nd Qtr. 1956): 175–176; "American Industry Civil Rights," *Christian Recorder*, December 13, 1883; July 10, 1884.

[24] *Christian Recorder*, January 10, January 31, 1884. Black supporters of the high tariff even found themselves the objects of mockery from minstrel composers. See J. W. Wheeler, *High Tariff Darkies on Parade* (Boston, MA: M. A. Blair, 1891), held in William L. Clements Library, University of Michigan, Ann Arbor, MI.

[25] On the Randallite protectionist Democrats, see Poulshock, "Pennsylvania and the Tariff"; Tom E. Terrill, *The Tariff, Politics, and American Foreign Policy, 1874–1901* (Westport, CT: Greenwood Press, 1973), chap. 4. On the 1886 bill, see Ida M. Tarbell, *The Tariff in Our Times* (New York: Macmillan, 1911), 143; Sidney Fine, *Laissez Faire and the General-Welfare State: A Study of Conflict in American Thought, 1865–1901* (Ann Arbor: The University of Michigan Press, 1956) 50; Terrill, *Tariff, Politics, and American Foreign Policy*, 102–103.

Foreseeing this unfavorable legislative outcome, Edward Atkinson ultimately advised against the final drafts of the proposed tariff bill of 1884
(and again in 1886). He instead encouraged Morrison and Wells to reach
out to "the [manufacturing] men who control the members of Congress"
through "a compact, moderate and well-organized system of clubs
throughout the country" where, as Horace White put it, "the ground
swell is beginning." Atkinson suggested to both Wells and R. R. Bowker
that the free traders focus instead on consolidating their clubs, while
keeping their actuall numbers a secret, so as to better use their relatively
small membership to political advantage, much as Cobden Club founder
Thomas Bayley Potter had effectively used the Union and Emancipation
Society's secret membership roles to deter British intervention during the
Civil War. If Atkinson's "mugwump, independent" club idea were to be
implemented, he predicted that the free traders would "hold the balance
of power between these two bitterly contending parties . . .. We can do
this. It was what Peel did in 1842 and 1846." Atkinson's Peelite recom-
mendations for Cobdenite principles, however, went largely ignored, and
Morrison's failed tariff bills had the effect of further alienating the
Democratic party's protectionist wing.[26]

Atkinson, once again proven right and ignored, threw up his pragmatic
hands. "The Democrats are a mob" and the American free-trade clubs'
current methods were accomplishing little except antagonizing and consolidating the protectionist opposition. "Reason will not prevail," he
dejectedly concluded to Bowker. "I am out of it and shall do nothing
more except to write my own articles . . .. With the pending struggle I will
have nothing to do."[27]

Amid Morrison's failed congressional tariff bills and such internal
dissent within free-trade ranks, economic nationalists once again showed
that they were better at using economic panics to their political advantage
than their cosmopolitan counterparts. Cobdenite Harvard Professor
Frank Taussig, in his *Tariff History of the United States*, was the first to
observe that the origins to "this common assertion" that free trade bred
economic panics were to be found in the writings of Listian Henry
C. Carey, "who has been guilty of many curious perversions of economic
history, but of none more remarkable than this."[28] The panic of 1883 was
no exception, and helped to further undermine popular support for freer

---

[26] Atkinson to Wells, February 2, 1886, June 29, 1886; Atkinson to Bowker, September 2,
1886, carton 17, Atkinson Papers.
[27] Atkinson to Bowker, December 22, 1886, carton 17, Atkinson Papers.
[28] John Edwards Russell, *The Panics of 1837 and 1857. An Address Delivered Before the New
England Free Trade League May 21, 1896*, 1–2; F. W. Taussig, *The Tariff History of the
United States* (New York and London: G. P. Putnam's Sons, 1888), 118.

trade in 1884. "The Carey school," Atkinson wrote wearily the following year, has "inoculated the people of this country so completely with the idea that Great Britain desires free trade in order to break us down that this is one of the chief obstructions to building ourselves up."[29] Grover Cleveland's presidency at least offered Atkinson and the American free-trade movement a glimmer of hope.

Cleveland's free-trade cabinet

Upon receiving the 1884 Republican presidential nomination, James G. Blaine utilized the Listian arguments of maintaining high wages through high tariffs and of harming British exports through a western-hemispheric customs union. These anti-British policies had the added bonus of drumming up support among Anglophobic German and Irish immigrants. In his forward-looking fashion, Blaine also sought government subsidization for American steamships in order to increase US economic integration in the Western Hemisphere. But more important still was his progressive Listian desire for maintaining a strong internal home market while opening up the markets of North and South America through reciprocal trade agreements, much as he had attempted in 1881 while briefly US secretary of state.

Blaine warned of the consequences of presumptuously globalizing the American economy through free trade. In doing so, he sought protectionist support from fence-sitting American farmers, men and women who, he warned, might otherwise be forced to compete with "the grain fields of Russia and from the distant plains of India" if free trade with the world were immediately established. For the industrial worker, he similarly offered up the frightening picture of American labor in "unfair competition" with Chinese contract and European pauper labor. Blaine's Pan-Americanism was a localized global vision, one that did not seek free trade with "all the world," but restrictive US-dominated trade within the Western Hemisphere. His was the progressive regional integrative vision of a Gilded Age Listian nationalist.[30]

[29] Morrison to Wells, March 2, May 28, 1884, reel 7, Wells Papers; Williamson, *Atkinson*, 146–147; *New York Tribune*, October 29, 1884, 8; Atkinson to Moreton Frewen, December 21, 1885, quoted in Williamson, *Atkinson*, 149. "Sunset" Cox, author of *Free Land and Free Trade: The Lessons of the English Corn Laws Applied to the United States* (New York: G. P. Putnam's Sons, 1880), considered Wells his "teacher" in the free-trade "cause." See Cox to Wells, April 23, 1880, reel 6, Wells Papers; William Van Zandt Cox and Milton Harlow Northrup, *Life of Samuel Sullivan Cox* (Syracuse, NY: M. H. Northrup, 1899), 59, 71.

[30] Draft copy, nomination acceptance speech, July 1884, reel 10, James Gillespie Blaine Family Papers, LOC. Cleveland's 1884 presidential campaign had generally "avoided

Cleveland's election offered transatlantic Cobdenites a potential end to the Republican party's protectionist "emasculation" of the US economy. American and British Cobdenites saw the promise of bringing an eventual end to the protective system which had been "taking from our people their sense of manly rivalry, of robust desire to compete on fair fields of contest, of self-reliance," as one Cleveland State Department official wrote to John Bright in England. J. Sterling Morton similarly believed that with the establishment of free trade under Cleveland, "we shall so assert American manhood and American inventive genius that we shall not be afraid to compete in the markets of the world."[31] In the eyes of the Gilded Age free trader, protectionism not only enslaved American commerce, but also threatened American manliness.[32]

In contrast to Blaine's progressive stance in favor of the American System and the imperialism of economic nationalism, Grover Cleveland himself admitted that he knew relatively little about the tariff issue when he entered office, and turned to his coterie of Cobdenites to educate him on the subject. Carl Schurz recalled how Cleveland confided to him upon his election: "I am ashamed to say it, but the truth is I know nothing about the tariff .... Will you tell me how to learn?" Cleveland reiterated his ignorance to the pro-free-trade *New York World*.[33]

American Cobdenites gladly worked to shape Cleveland's economic views. According to Cleveland biographer Allan Nevins, "from the moment of his election the tariff reformers had exerted every possible ounce of pressure upon Cleveland, talking with him, writing him letters, and sending him books." Wells, Beecher, and Bowker sent Cleveland a petition just before his inauguration concerning the obscene growth of surplus revenue brought about by the continued maintenance of the

---

the issue as well as they could," according to John Bright's American friend Edward L. Pierce. Pierce to Bright, November 19, 1884, Add. 43390, Vol. VIII, John Bright Papers, British Library, London, England. See, also, G. Patrick Lynch, "U.S. Presidential Elections in the Nineteenth Century: Why Culture and Economics Both Mattered," *Polity* 35 (Autumn 2002): 41–49.

[31] New York Free Trade Club, *National Conference of Free Traders*, 2–3.

[32] US State Department Official [Bayard?] to Bright, August 26, 1886, Add. 43391, Vol. IX, Bright Papers. For the interaction of late-nineteenth-century gender and imperialism, see Kristin L. Hoganson, *Fighting for American Manhood: How Gender Politics Provoked the Spanish-American and Philippine-American Wars* (New Haven, CT: Yale University Press, 1998).

[33] Henry L. Stoddard, *As I Knew Them: Presidents and Politics from Grant to Coolidge* (New York and London: Harper, 1927), 152. Moore himself had been greatly influenced by Cobden and Bright during his time in Manchester, England, in the late 1830s. "James Solomon Moore," *Appletons' Annual Cyclopedia and Register of Important Events of the Year 1892* (New York: D. Appleton and Company, 1893), 561; Wells on J. S. Moore at the 1873 Cobden Club annual dinner, *Free Trade and Free Enterprise*, 47; J. S. Moore, *The Parsee Letters* (New York: American Free Trade League, 1869).

excessive "war" tariff, and Cleveland gave their opinions special attention. Secretary of State Thomas Bayard wrote Wells that Cleveland "fully respects and values the 'Independents' and I do not think Horace White and his friends and associates will feel themselves without weight or just influence." The Democratic leadership correspondingly asked for White's advice concerning cabinet appointments and policies. Upon Cleveland's election, Wells himself was invited to a meeting with the president and his cabinet. They "talked tariff and silver," Wells recounted. Already an advisor to Congressmen "Sunset" Cox, William Morrison, John G. Carlisle, and Roger Q. Mills, as well as cabinet members like Treasury Secretary Daniel Manning and Secretary of State Bayard, Wells realized that he and President Cleveland would be very close: that Wells would essentially be a cabinet member regarding economic issues.[34]

US Cobdenites thus wielded great influence within Cleveland's administrations. Along with White and Wells, Edward Atkinson, Manton Marble, R. R. Bowker, Professor Arthur Latham Perry, Worthington C. Ford, and Jacob Schoenhof became unofficial economic advisors for various members of Cleveland's administration. Marble made a large amount of Manning's final decisions and wrote many of his reports; Bowker helped craft Cleveland's subsequent 1887 annual message calling for tariff reductions; Perry was offered (but declined) the position of treasury secretary upon the death of Manning in 1887; Ford headed the State Department's Bureau of Statistics; and Schoenhof was made Cleveland's consul to Tunstall, England, where, upon his arrival, he jokingly searched "for the barrels of British gold which he had heard the Cobden Club was sending over to this country to corrupt American politics, and break down the American tariff." Noticeable political and ideological battle lines over free trade had been drawn, and President Cleveland turned, not to the Democratic party's Jeffersonians, but to the

[34] Allan Nevins, *Grover Cleveland: A Study in Courage* (New York: Dodd, Mead & Co., 1933), 280–281; Fred Bunyan Joyner, *David Ames Wells, Champion of Free Trade* (Cedar Rapids, IA: The Torch Press, 1939), 168; Shearman to Cleveland, January 31,1885, microfilm, reel 5, Grover Cleveland Papers, LOC; Bayard to White, December 10, 1884, quoted in Joseph Logsdon, *Horace White, Nineteenth Century Liberal* (Westport, CT: Greenwood, 1971), 320; Cox to Wells, April 23, 1880, December 17, 1882, reel 6; Morrison to Wells, April 5, 1877, reel 5; January 14, 1882, reel 6; September 7, December 14, 1884, reel 7; Carlisle to Wells, March 20, 1883, reel 6; Mills to Wells, February 29, 1876, reel 4; Manning to Wells, September 8, 1886, reel 7; Bayard to Wells, May 27, 1880, reel 6; February 15, 1884, reel 7, Wells Papers; David Earl Robbins, Jr., "The Congressional Career of William Ralls Morrison" (PhD diss., University of Illinois, 1963), 53, 56, 146–150; James A. Barnes, *John G. Carlisle, Financial Statesman* (New York: Dodd, Mead & Co., 1931), 45, 79, 80.

Cobdenite leadership among the Bourbons and Mugwumps for economic advice.[35]

Most conspicuous of all to Cleveland's protectionist opponents during his two administrations was the Cobden Club membership of many of his cabinet members and close advisors: Secretary of State Bayard; Secretary of War William C. Endicott; Speaker of the House of Representatives John G. Carlisle during Cleveland's first administration, and treasury secretary in Cleveland's second; Secretary of the Interior L. Q. C. Lamar; Secretary of Agriculture in Cleveland's second administration J. Sterling Morton; along with the Chairman of the House Ways and Means Committee William R. Morrison, and the aforementioned unofficial cabinet advisors Bowker, Atkinson, Marble, White, Perry, and Wells.[36] Unlike in Congress where protectionists far outnumbered free traders, America's most prominent Cobdenites dominated Cleveland's administrations.[37] With so many Cobdenites so close to Cleveland, a thunderous economic nationalist response was rather predictably in the forecast.

In the years surrounding Cleveland's 1884 election, protectionists regrouped. The Industrial League of America, created in Chicago in 1880, found common cause with the Protective Tariff League (formed in 1885), and they strengthened their mutual ties throughout the country. Industrial League publications included the widely disseminated *Tariff League Bulletin* and its weekly *The Defender*. By the turn of the century, the league developed connections with over 5,000 newspapers and

[35] George T. McJimsey, *Genteel Partisan: Manton Marble, 1834–1917* (Ames: Iowa State University Press, 1971), 237–252; Perry to Francis Lynde Stetson, October 28, 1885; Perry to Daniel S. Lamont, October 27, 1885, reel 22, Cleveland Papers; Arthur Latham Perry, *Williamstown and Williams College* (New York: Charles Scribner's Sons, 1899), 697; Fine, *Laissez Faire and the General-Welfare State*, 49; Everett P. Wheeler, *Sixty Years of American Life: Taylor to Roosevelt, 1850 to 1910* (New York: E. P. Dutton & Company, 1917), 177. See, also, Tom E. Terrill, "David A. Wells, the Democracy, and Tariff Reduction, 1877-1894," *Journal of American History* 56 (December 1969): 550, 552; David A. Lake, "International Economic Structures and American Foreign Economic Policy, 1887–1934," *World Politics* 35 (July 1983): 528; Terrill, *Tariff, Politics, and American Foreign Policy*, 110–111.

[36] *Chicago Inter Ocean*, October 15, 1888, 8; July 11, 1877; *The Cobden Club. Report and List of Members for the Year 1903*; Potter to Bayard, April 13, 1883, Box 63, Bayard Papers, LOC. William Endicott was the son-in-law of Cobdenite merchant George Peabody. Endicott's daughter married Joseph Chamberlain, and his son, William C. Endicott, Jr. was active in the subsequent Anti-Imperialist League. Charles Fairchild, Cleveland's treasury secretary from 1887–1889, became a member of the Cobden Club in 1891.

[37] During Cleveland's first administration, congressional Cobden Club members in the House of Representatives included Clifton Rodes Breckenridge (D-AR), a member of the Committee on Ways and Means; John G. Carlisle (D-KY), Speaker of the House; W. C. P. Breckenridge (D-KY); Samuel S. Cox (D-OH); John Randall Tucker (D-VA); and in the Senate, Randall Lee Gibson (D-LA); and Joseph R. Hawley (R-CT). For a rare defense of American Cobdenism and its influence, see *New York Times*, January 12, 1885, 3.

distributed well over 14 million pages of literature. The Industrial League was rebranded as the Iron and Steel Association in 1888, and for many years to come would flex substantial political muscle in the Congressional Ways and Means Committee. The Southern Protective League would be formed in 1889; home market clubs sprung up in areas like Chicago and Boston; and more specialized groups like the Arkwright Club for Boston textile manufacturers, the Irish-American Protection Union of New York, and the New York Association for the Protection of American Industry (founded in 1883) were set up to offset the influence of their local free-trade counterparts.[38] America's economic nationalists had arrayed themselves across the nation to take on Cleveland's Cobdenite administration.

Cleveland's anti-imperialism of free trade

Enhancing the ideological divide, Grover Cleveland and his Cobdenite cabinet tended toward more amicable Anglo-American relations amid a time of pronounced Anglophobia, as well as a propensity for laissez-faire approaches to domestic and foreign relations. Cleveland's hands-off anti-imperial policies sparked conspiratorial speculation from Anglophobic economic nationalists. Charges of a British free-trade conspiracy were first leveled against Cleveland during the 1884 presidential campaign, and continued following his first message to Congress in 1885. In the latter, Cleveland, along with Secretary of State Bayard, "showed plainly" to their political adversaries that his incoming administration was amenable to British imperial interests when it came out in opposition to the construction of the Nicaraguan canal and the annexation of territory that came with it. Cleveland and Bayard viewed this canal attempt – under the previous administration's proposed 1884 Frelinghuysen–Zavala Treaty – as a violation of the 1850 Clayton–Bulwer Treaty, which guaranteed shared control of any future canal ventures between the United States and Britain. The 1884 Republican proposal was a clear challenge to England, and led to renewed speculation of armed Anglo-American conflict. It also promised to create a virtual American protectorate in Central America. On this point, Bayard feared intervention would inevitably lead to an overseas empire, signaling the end of the Republic.[39]

[38] *New York Tribune*, July 22, 1885, 4; January 20, 1899, 5; Tarbell, *Tariff in Our Times*, 173–174; Nelson W. Aldrich, *The Trap for New England* (Boston, MA: The Home Market Club, 1892), 2; *New York Tribune*, June 1, 1890, 1; November 19, 1896, 3; January 17, 1883, 8.
[39] Harlen Eugene Makemson, "Images of Scandal: Political Cartooning in the 1884 Presidential Campaign" (PhD diss., University of North Carolina at Chapel Hill, 2002), 145–146; Patrick Cudmore, *Cleveland's Maladministration: Free Trade, Protection*

Listian nationalists instead sought informal imperial control of Nicaragua. James Blaine supported American control over any canal attempts in Central America. Amid conspiratorial jabs at American Cobdenites, Patrick Cudmore outlined his own Listian desire for a canal and Republican-style restrictive reciprocity with Latin America, and supported it with detailed statistics highlighting the potential resources to be exploited from Latin American markets. Another Republican pamphleteer even coined the proposed canal zone "America's Egypt," meaning that any isthmian canal needed to be under the control of the United States and thereby bring the same military and trade benefits that the Suez brought the British – and that only Blaine's antagonistic Anglophobic defense of the Monroe Doctrine would properly see this isthmian venture through to the end.[40]

Cleveland's Cobdenites proved their critics partly correct with their early anti-imperial advocacy. In contrast to Blaine's imperial proposal, the incoming administration preferred to keep clear of any military dispute with England and to eschew imperial expansion. In Cleveland's first address, according to Cudmore, he had therefore also "openly avowed that he favored free trade and hostility to American manufacturers." England, Cudmore concluded, was fortunate to have "found such willing and ready friends" in the president and his cabinet.[41] Cleveland's opponents were quick to pick on his administration's early Cobdenite anti-imperial leanings, its desire for a laissez-faire foreign policy, and its cooperative spirit toward Britain.

Cleveland continued his Cobdenite opposition to American foreign interventionism when he disentangled himself from the Arthur administration's designs in the Congo. US commercial interest in Africa had been growing since the Europeans began scrambling for the continent in the early 1870s. As the European powers ratcheted up their African colonial expansion for the sake of prestige, economic exploitation, national security, or some mixture of the three, American interest in the "Dark Continent" also reached the national stage when Republican President Chester Arthur

---

and Reciprocity (New York, P. J. Kenedy, 1896), 3; Terrill, *Tariff, Politics, and American Foreign Policy*, 91.

[40] Patrick Cudmore, *Buchanan's Conspiracy, the Nicaragua Canal and Reciprocity* (New York: P. J. Kenedy, 1892); James Morris Morgan, *America's Egypt: Mr. Blaine's Foreign Policy* (New York: Hermann Bartsch, 1884). For Blaine's and Frelinghuysen's attempts to overturn the Clayton-Bulwer Treaty, see David M. Pletcher, *The Awkward Years: American Foreign Relations under Garfield and Arthur* (Columbia, University of Missouri Press, 1962), 28–33, 63–67; Pletcher, *The Diplomacy of Trade and Investment: American Economic Expansion in the Hemisphere, 1865–1900* (Columbia: University of Missouri Press, 1998), 136–138.

[41] Cudmore, *Cleveland's Maladministration*, 3.

redrew American attention to Africa in his 1883 annual message. Aggressive expansionists in Congress followed up on Arthur's message, some asking that the United States offer protection to its African missionaries, others believing that the Congo would make a good dumping-ground for the South's "excess" cotton produce and freed black population.[42]

From among the possible tools of globalization at their disposal, these American expansionists decided upon first establishing a steamship line between New Orleans, Charleston, and the Congo River. The African Trade Society at this time similarly sought a steamship and mail service between Liberia and New Orleans. The International African Association, under the auspices of Belgium's Leopold II, sought US recognition, which Arthur gave in April 1884. Germany's Bismarck, fearing imperial rivalry and possible German commercial exclusion in the Congo, thereafter called for a conference in Berlin in the fall of 1884. Arthur's Secretary of State Frelinghuysen sent Listian nationalist John A. Kasson to attend. The conferees agreed upon outlawing the slave trade, rules for colonizing the African interior, and establishing international freedom of commerce and navigation. Kasson himself wanted a US military installation along the Congolese coast.[43]

While some newspapers, businessmen, politicians, and missionaries favored the Berlin Conference resolutions, free-trade opponents looked askance upon its connotations for possible US territorial aggrandizements and political entanglements in Africa. The popular Mugwump organ the *Nation* questioned why Americans would want to have a helping hand in the European carving up of the mythical Dark Continent. It also noted with tongue in cheek how odd it was that a Republican administration could give its support to turning the Congo region into a free-trade paradise. Should it not have encouraged instead "a good tariff" to stimulate local industries as prescribed by Henry Carey, rather than covering the region "with the deadly upas tree of British free trade"? Dripping with still more irony, the *Nation* warned that now the Congo will "be speedily flooded with the products of the pauper labor of Europe," factories will close, and "the Cobden Club, too, will distribute its poisonous literature far and wide."[44]

---

[42] American interests were also drawn to the creation of a railway from the Persian Gulf to Tehran in 1886, but were foiled by the British. See John S. Galbraith, "Britain and American Railway Promoters in Late Nineteenth Century Persia," *Albion* 21 (Summer 1989): 248–262.

[43] Joseph A. Fry, *Dixie Looks Abroad: The South and U.S. Foreign Relations, 1789–1973* (Baton Rouge: Louisiana State University Press, 2002), 113; Milton Plesur, *America's Outward Thrust: Approaches to Foreign Affairs, 1865–1890* (De Kalb: University of Illinois Press, 1971), 144–156; Pletcher, *Awkward Years*, 309–324.

[44] Plesur, *America's Outward Thrust*, 144–156; Walter LaFeber, *The Cambridge History of American Foreign Relations Volume: America's Search for Opportunity, 1865–1913*

The Cleveland administration's non-interventionist approach to foreign affairs once again came to the fore. Like the proposed Nicaraguan canal plan, the Berlin treaty's ratification was timed to come up for a vote in 1885. Perhaps with the hope of making it more enticing to Cleveland's free traders, the International African Association had even couched its manifesto in Cobdenite language, claiming that its rule of governance and commerce coincided with the doctrine of John Bright and Richard Cobden. Such free-trade wordplay was nevertheless insufficient to procure support from Cleveland and his cabinet, as they feared the treaty's possible political and colonial entanglements. They promptly revoked recognition and refused to submit the treaty for Senate approval.[45]

Samoa was another area where Cleveland's Cobdenite anti-imperial approach contrasted with his Republican counterparts. After sending naval vessels to protect "American citizens and property" along with Samoan neutrality from German imperial encroachment, Cleveland announced in a special January 1887 message to Congress: "I have insisted that autonomy and independence of Samoa should be scrupulously preserved." At the subsequent 1887 Washington Conference, Secretary of State Bayard fought for Samoan independence, insisting that "the independence and autonomy" of Samoa "be preserved free from the control or preponderating influence of any foreign government." He suggested instead that the islands be "maintained for the common use of all nations" rather than a closed imperial port of call. The conference also allowed for a rotating prime ministerial position appointed by the treaty powers to help with Samoan administration, which, if implemented, would certainly have borne informal imperial trappings. The conference, however, ended up accomplishing little aside from temporarily thwarting Germany's attempt to annex Samoa. Following continued German interventionism in Samoan affairs, Cleveland turned the messy affair over to Congress, and would thereafter attempt to withdraw American informal influence entirely from Samoa during his second administration. These were hardly the acts of an imperial presidency.

(Cambridge: Cambridge University Press, 1995), 86; LaFeber, *The New Empire: An Interpretation of American Expansion, 1860-1898* (Ithaca, NY: Cornell University Press, 1963), 53; *Nation* 40 (January 1, 1885): 8–9; Murray Lee Carroll, "Open Door Imperialism in Africa: The United States and the Congo, 1876 to 1892" (PhD diss., The University of Connecticut, 1971).

[45] United States Department of State, *Index to the Executive Documents of the House of Representatives for the First Session of the 49th Congress* (Washington, DC: US Government Printing Office, 1885–1886), 259. Listian Blaine would afterward take renewed interest in the Congo in 1890, with one expansionist promising Blaine that Central Africa would be "the greatest market for our domestic cotton goods outside our own domains." Lysle E. Meyer, "Henry S. Sanford and the Congo: A Reassessment," *African Historical Studies* 4 (1971): 36.

Rather, Cleveland and his Cobdenite cabinet broadly practiced what British historian Oliver MacDonagh coined "the anti-imperialism of free trade."[46]

Goldbugs and greenbacks: morality and conspiracy

With the failed Republican imperial schemes fading to the background of the national political landscape, conspiratorial rumors would soon spread surrounding the Cleveland administration's continued support for the gold standard. National bimetallists sought the free coinage of both gold and silver regardless of international agreement, believing that the addition of silver reserves would counter the gold standard's deflationary tendencies and thus offer relief to indebted Americans. The US bimetallic policy had come to an end in 1873 with the *de facto* American turn toward the gold standard, but had been partially revitalized by the compromise Bland–Allison Act of 1878.[47]

For a vast majority of American Cobdenites, inflationary policies like national bimetallism and printing greenbacks were anathema. Cleveland's advisors Treasury Secretary Daniel Manning, Wells, White, Atkinson, and Bayard, along with a host of Cobdenite reformers, remained inveterate supporters of the gold standard, and favored the suspension of silver coinage. Like Cobden and Bright, they believed that inflationary policies – from greenbacks to national bimetallism – were uncivilized, and led to moral and economic decay.[48] Cobdenite

[46] Grover Cleveland, *The Public Papers of Grover Cleveland Twenty-Second President of the United States March 4, 1885 to March 4, 1889* (Washington, DC: Government Printing Office, 1889), 471; "Protocol of First Samoan Conference," June 25, 1887, *FRUS* (Washington, DC: Government Printing Office, 1890), 204–205; Henry C. Ide, "Our Interest in Samoa," *North American Review* 165 (August 1897): 155–158; Stuart Anderson, "'Pacific Destiny' and American Policy in Samoa, 1872–1899," *Hawaiian Journal of History* 12 (1978): 53–54; Oliver MacDonagh, "The Anti-Imperialism of Free Trade," *Economic History Review* 14 (April 1962): 489–501.

[47] On the monetary issue, see Francis A. Walker, *International Bimetallism* (New York: H. Holt and Company, 1896); Gretchen Ritter, *Goldbugs and Greenbacks: The Antimonopoly Tradition and the Politics of Finance in America, 1865–1896* (Cambridge: Cambridge University Press, 1997); Ted Wilson, *Battles for the Standard: Bimetallism and the Spread of the Gold Standard in the Nineteenth Century* (Aldershot: Ashgate, 2000).

[48] Hamer Stansfeld, *Money and the Money Market Explained, and the Future Rate of Discount Considered, an Appeal to Richard Cobden and John Bright* (London: Simpkin, Marshall, & Co., 1860); William Graham Sumner, *The History of American Currency* (New York: John F. Trow & Sons, 1878); David Ames Wells, *Robinson Crusoe's Money* (New York: Harper and Brothers, 1876); David M. Tucker, *Mugwumps: Public Moralists of the Gilded Age* (Columbia: University of Missouri Press, 1998), 59–72. The 1873 depression was closely tied to the monetary debate. See Nicolas Barreyre, "The Politics of Economic Crises: The Panic of 1873, the End of Reconstruction, and the Realignment of American Politics," *Journal of the Gilded Age and Progressive Era* 10 (October 2011): 403–423.

economist and Massachusetts politician Amasa Walker had been one of the earliest adversaries of the silver agitation, and called the greenback a "fictitious currency" that exhibited a particularly "false and pernicious" character; Atkinson believed that it was beyond the purview of the US government to issue paper money, and considered the currency question "the great *moral* question of today"; and Wells once recommended that the treasury department should begin burning greenbacks until they attained parity with gold, but even this process would have been "too slow" for Walker. Since the late 1860s, Horace White had similarly taken special aim at silverite interference in government, and Frank Taussig castigated silver "inflationists" for ignorantly tinkering with the currency as a remedy for "real or fancied evils."[49] American Cobdenites had little sympathy for inflationary bimetallic demands.

Silverites – particularly Greenbackers, silver mining interests, and indebted farmers – began characterizing the Cleveland administration as pro-British owing to its inveterate support for gold monometallism. Agrarians and other silverites perceived the "goldbugs" in office to be in partnership with England. Listian Henry Carey had been enunciating just such a theory since the mid-1860s, suggesting that an increase in the money supply would help end the postwar economic downturn; diminish the influence of the Bank of England upon the US financial system; encourage exports; and strengthen American protectionism by discouraging imports. He was particularly keen about "establishing for ourselves a standard different from that maintained by Britain."[50]

Silverites also highlighted how unfortunate it was that the price of silver had decreased sharply throughout the world at this time, while gold prices continued to appreciate owing in large part to the Anglo-American infatuation with the gold standard. Cheap silver, silverites charged, allowed British merchants to purchase more silver with their

---

[49] Walker to McCulloch, February 4, 1867, vol. 3, Hugh McCulloch Papers, LOC; Amasa Walker, *The Science of Wealth: A Manual of Political Economy. Embracing the Laws of Trade, Currency, and Finance* (Boston, MA: Little, Brown, and Company, 1866), 223, 360; Hamer Stansfeld, *Correspondence on Monetary Panics, with the Honorable Amasa Walker, Late Secretary of States for Massachusetts* (London: Simpkin, Marshall, & Co., 1860); Atkinson to McCulloch, November 17, 1867, vol. 3, McCulloch Papers; Atkinson to Henry Ward Beecher, October 1, 1867, carton 14, Edward Atkinson Letterbook, Atkinson Papers; David Ames Wells, *The Cremation Theory of Specie Resumption* (New York: G. P. Putnam's Sons, 1875); Logsdon, *White*, 330–336; Horace White, *Coin's Financial Fool; or the Artful Dodger Exposed, a Complete Reply to "Coin's Financial School"* (New York: J. S. Ogilvie, 1895); Frank W. Taussig, *The Silver Situation in the United States* (Baltimore: Guggenheimer, Weil & Co., 1892), 113.

[50] Rodney J. Morrison, *Henry C. Carey and American Economic Development* (Philadelphia, PA: American Philosophical Society, 1986), 69–70; Carey, quoted in ibid., 70.

gold. After all, the Indian rupee was silver-backed, which – when combined with the British merchants' vast amounts of silver bullion – then allowed them to purchase enormous quantities of Indian wheat and cotton. Missouri Democratic Congressman Richard Bland thought that America's "gold policy is driving the products of our silver mines to India, there to be used as money to employ Hindoos [sic] to raise wheat, corn, and cotton in direct competition with the farmers of America." Republican Senator Thomas M. Bowen of Colorado argued that Cleveland's monometallic policy provided England "the cudgel, or the bludgeon rather, with which to gradually drive us from the world's markets."[51] Thus, lower silver prices, compounded by the ease and lower costs of Indian wheat transports to Europe via the recently constructed Suez Canal, effectively subsidized Indian exports, forcing American farm products from European markets. As a counter move, many silverites instead sought silver coinage in the United States, with or without an international bimetallic agreement.

In a half-hearted attempt to appease the country's bimetallists and gauge western European sentiment regarding international bimetallism, Cleveland sent Manton Marble as a special envoy to a monetary conference in Europe in 1885. Marble was as yet a staunch gold monometallist, as well as a long-time free trader, Cobden Club member, former editor of the *New York World*, and close friend of David Wells and Horace White. With the British intractable on the gold issue, Cleveland's professed interest in international bimetallism turned into a sham. The conference came to naught. A Republican congressman wryly commented afterward that the silverites were "doubtless indebted" to Cleveland for appointing "a man to such a position when he was a notorious member of a foreign institution every British member of which is hostile to the coinage of the white metal."[52] While the monetary controversy did not go away, it would soon be eclipsed by the tariff question.

---

[51] Edward P. Crapol, *America for Americans: Economic Nationalism and Anglophobia in the Late Nineteenth Century* (Westport, CT: Greenwood Press, 1973), 148–150; Terrill, *Tariff, Politics, and American Foreign Policy*, 73–74; *Congressional Record* [hereafter *CR*], 48 Cong., 2 Sess., April 7, 1886, 3207, March 8, 1886, 2180; Minutes of February 9, 1872, CC MSS; Terrill, "David Ames Wells," 554.

[52] McJimsey, *Genteel Partisan*, 153–154, 218, 228; Marble to Bayard, July 7, 1885, Box 217, Bayard Papers; *CR*, 50 Cong., 1 Sess., May 5, 1888, 3757–3758. Marble, "a confirmed advocate of the gold standard," drafted Cleveland's letter against bimetallism in 1885, but returned from his European mission a confirmed international bimetallist and grew to loathe the political independence and strict gold adherence of White, Wells, Atkinson, and Perry. George T. McJimsey, *Genteel Partisan: Manton Marble, 1834-1917* (Ames: Iowa State University Press, 1971), 223–225, 231–237, 250–251.

The "Great Debate" of 1888 and free-trade culture

The tariff question – the "Great Debate" – overshadowed the ongoing threat of economic depression and the lingering silver issue following Cleveland's 1887 annual message.[53] Heavily influenced by Wells and Bowker, and following pressure from low-tariff midwestern and southern Democrats, Cleveland's annual message was devoted to requesting a tariff for revenue only and increases to the free list. The message also further marginalized the Democratic party's protectionist Randall wing, and created political waves both at home and across the Atlantic.[54]

American free traders felt that their faith in Cleveland had been vindicated. The *Chicago Tribune* – derisively called "the Cobden Club's *Chicago Tribune*" by its protectionist counterpart *Inter Ocean* – came to Cleveland's defense. *Belford's* declared that "the free-trade fight is on." And the New York Reform Club, created "under the auspices" of the New York Free Trade Club, distributed 926,000 copies of the message.[55]

[53] Cleveland did send Atkinson as his commissioner to Europe to ascertain sentiment (or the lack thereof, as it turned out) concerning the bimetallic issue that same year. Bayard to Atkinson, April 28, 1887; Atkinson to C. S. Fairchild, May 16, 1887; Atkinson to Fairchild, May 23, 1887; Atkinson to Fairchild, October 24, 1887, carton 3; Bayard to Atkinson, March 11, March 31, May 6, 1887, folder 6; August 27, 1887, folder 7, carton 12, Atkinson Papers; Edward Atkinson, *Bi-metallism in Europe. Report Made by Edward Atkinson to the President of the United States, October 1887* (Washington, DC: Government Printing Office, 1887); Williamson, *Atkinson*, 142, 148–149; *Belford's Magazine* 2 (December 1888): 92; Henry B. Russell, *International Monetary Conferences* (New York: Harper & Brothers, 1898), 346–350.

[54] Poulshock, "Pennsylvania and the Tariff," 303–304. The term "Great Debate" was coined in 1888, stemming from the length of debate in Congress, at the time the longest in US legislative history. The term first appears in William G. Terrell, ed., *An Appeal to the American People as a Jury: Speeches on the Tariff in the United States House of Representatives in the Great Debate, April 17–May 19, 1888* (Chicago, IL: Belford and Clark, 1888). On the "Great Debate," see Joanne Reitano, *The Tariff Question in the Gilded Age: The Great Debate of 1888* (University Park: Pennsylvania State University Press, 1994); Charles W. Calhoun, *Minority Victory: Gilded Age Politics and the Front Porch Campaign of 1888* (Lawrence: University Press of Kansas, 2008); J. Laurence Laughlin and H. Parker Willis, *Reciprocity* (New York: The Baker & Taylor Co., 1903), 127–133; Douglas A. Irwin, "Higher Tariffs, Lower Revenues? Analyzing the Fiscal Aspects of 'The Great Tariff Debate of 1888,'" *Journal of Economic History* 58 (March 1998): 59–72.

[55] Joyner, *Wells*, 172; E. McClung Fleming, *R. R. Bowker: Militant Liberal* (Norman: University of Oklahoma Press, 1952), 217; Terrill, "David Ames Wells," 553; *Chicago Tribune*, December 11, December 12, 1887; *Chicago Inter Ocean*, May 3, 1888, 4; *Chicago Inter Ocean*, May 4, 1890; New York Reform Club, *Officers and Committees, Members, Constitution, by-Laws, Rules, Reports, etc., 1889* (New York: Reform Club, 1889), 101–105; Reform Club to Worthington Chauncey Ford, December 1887, folder 1887, box 2, Ford Papers. See, also, New England Tariff Reform League. "James Russell Lowell's Speech at the Dinner of the Tariff Reform League, Boston, December 24," in *Our Day: A Record and Review of Current Reform*, 2 vols. (Boston, MA: Our Day Publishing Company, 1888), I, 110. The Massachusetts Tariff Reform League was founded in April 1884. Charles Francis Adams, Jr. was the first president, Wells, Sumner, and William Endicott were among its vice presidents, and William Lloyd Garrison, II its secretary. As it grew it

Outspoken author, single-tax proponent, and labor advocate Henry George described the message in masculine language as "a manly, vigorous, and most effective free-trade speech," and stumped for Cleveland's reelection in 1888.[56]

Unsurprisingly, Cleveland's message also sparked renewed protectionist speculation of a transatlantic free-trade conspiracy. Republican Senator William Frye of Maine (Blaine's congressional replacement) declared that Cleveland had thrown down the free-trade gauntlet, and as proof provided a litany of British praise for his message. According to the Republican National Committee, "they had already let the Democratic Free-Trade cat out of the Cleveland bag, and all the Free-Trade efforts in Great Britain and America cannot get it in again."[57] Although Cleveland denied that his message was a free-trade tract, *Inter Ocean* called the message a "Cobden Club homily." A former governor of Ohio thought that "that big boy in the White House" sounded in his speech "like an ardent youth fresh from the Cobden Club." Another critic noted that his message "was only a reiteration" from the club's pamphlets, showing that Cleveland "had read them closely and with a good memory. The President was evidently an easy convert to Cobdenism." If Cleveland and his Cobdenites wanted the upcoming presidential election to center around the tariff

changed its name to the New England Tariff Reform League in 1888, followed by the New England Free Trade League in 1894. By 1895, it had around 1,300 members in twenty states. *New York Tribune*, November 21, 1894, 3; May 1, 1896, 8; New England Free Trade League, *Constitution of the New England Free Trade League with a List of the Officers and Members, April 1, 1895* (Boston, MA: New England Free Trade League, 1895). David A. Lake has classified Cleveland's 1887 address as the moment in which the American tariff was effectively internationalized for the purposes of export promotion. David A. Lake, *Power, Protection, and Free Trade: International Sources of U.S. Commercial Strategy, 1887–1939* (Ithaca, NY: Cornell University Press, 1988), 6.

[56] Henry George, *Protection or Free Trade* (New York: Henry George, 1886), 324; Henry George, quoted in Thomas Hudson McKee, ed., *Protection Echoes from the Capitol* (Washington, DC: McKee &Co., 1888), 155; Elwood P. Lawrence, *Henry George in the British Isles* (East Lansing: Michigan State University Press, 1957), 83, 84; Louis F. Post, *The Prophet of San Francisco: Personal Memories & Interpretations of Henry George* (New York: Vanguard Press, 1930), 114–124; Thomas, *Alternative America*, 320. As a reporter and Republican in California in the 1860s and 1870s and a one-time subscriber to economic nationalism, George became a proponent of Cobdenism, coming to a belief "in the international law of God as Cobden called free trade." Charles Albro Barker, *Henry George* (New York: Oxford University Press, 1955), 72–78, 142. Like Cobden, George closely tied land reform to tariff reform.

[57] William P. Frye, *Protection against Free Trade* (Washington, DC: Gray & Clarkson, 1888), 1–2; James G. Blaine, "Views upon the Recommendation of the President," in *What Shall We Do with It?* (New York: Harper & Brothers, 1888), 15–24; Dawson, *The Republican Campaign Text-Book for 1888*, 87. See, also, *Tariff League Bulletin*, November 2, 1888, 205; Terrill, *Tariff, Politics, and American Foreign Policy*, chap. 5.

debate, the protectionists were more than willing to comply, while simultaneously twisting the lion's tail.[58]

James G. Blaine countered Cleveland's message with an enunciation of the imperialism of economic nationalism in a widely circulated interview for the *New York Tribune*. He labeled Cleveland's speech a free-trade measure because it called for a tariff for revenue only. Blaine warned that such a free-trade policy would drastically lower the treasury surplus, deluge US markets with the dumping of foreign imported goods, and force the country's manufacturing economy back into barbaric agricultural subsistence. Blaine suggested that the treasury surplus could instead be lowered through increased military spending and lower excise taxes. The New South needed industrial protection more than any other section, Blaine added, and, while the United States needed foreign markets, free trade was not the way to gain them. He called instead for a "new political economy," one that protected the home market and developed southern industry through protective tariffs, increased defense spending, and raised foreign trade "in all practical and advantageous ways, but not on the principle of the Free Traders." Blaine's militaristic call for a "new political economy" was a clear articulation of the imperialism of economic nationalism.[59]

The Democrats' subsequent proposed Mills Bill of 1888 attempted to enact some of the tariff reforms mentioned in Cleveland's 1887 message, lowering tariff rates by a modest 7 percent. The bill's enlarged free list included many South American raw materials, and would have allowed for freer trade with Latin America without the signing of restrictive reciprocity treaties, in contrast to the subsequent 1890 McKinley Tariff. Thereafter, under the direction of Manton Marble, John G. Carlisle, and Henry Watterson, the Democratic party platform of 1888 explicitly supported both Cleveland's tariff message and the Mills bill.[60]

Unlike the bill itself, reaction to it was anything but moderate. Outraged Republicans declared that the Mills Bill would further reduce

[58] *Inter Ocean*, December 7, 1887, 4; *CR*, 50 Cong., 1 Sess., May 5, 1888, 3757; *Washington Post*, December 26, 1887, 4; George B. Curtiss, *Protection and Prosperity: An Account of Tariff Legislation and its Effect in Europe and America* (New York: Pan-American Publishing, 1896), 626.

[59] *New York Tribune*, December 8, 1887. Blaine had started to woo Southern voters with protectionism during the 1884 campaign trail. See Terrill, *Tariff, Politics, and American Foreign Policy*, 138.

[60] Tarbell, *Tariff in Our Times*, 155; *CR*, 50 Cong., 1 Sess., May 5, 1888, 3761, 3757–3759, May 12, 1888, 4062–4063; *New York Times*, May 7, 1888, 5; Tarbell, *Tariff in Our Times*, 159; *Washington Post*, May 9, 1888, 2; McJimsey, *Genteel Partisan*, 248–249. Atkinson corresponded frequently with the Democratic Chairman of the Ways and Means Committee, William L. Wilson, as well as Democratic committee member C. R. Breckenridge.

Figure 5.2 "Cleveland Will Have a Walk-Over." Republican magazine *Judge* depicts Grover Cleveland balancing precariously on a fraying rope, holding a balancing pole labeled "Free Trade Policy" and carrying the Democratic Party donkey and John Bull on his back. John Bull's back pocket is stuffed with "Cobden Club Free Trade Tracts." *Judge*, August 25, 1888, centerfold

UNDER WHICH EMBLEM?

THE CITIZENS OF THE UNITED STATES on November 6th
will decide for a generation, between Free Foreign Trade which
has cursed every nation ever blessed (?) with it; and Protection
with its benedictions to all nations.

Here are the battle shields of the two parties. The British Cobden Club
seal with its "Free-Trade," and the American Protective Tariff League
seal with its emblems of Protection to home industries. Will you choose
the Cobden Club with its Free Trade strap and buckle, to bind you in
perpetual poverty, or the Protection emblem with its plow, anchor, loom
and anvil—emblems of agriculture, manufacture and commerce—the emblems of a nation's strength.

Figure 5.3 "Under which Emblem?" Above, the *Tariff League Bulletin*
explains to its readers a month before the 1888 presidential elections
that they must choose between the "battle shields of the two parties" –
either the shield of the Cobden Club [left], which will "bind you in
perpetual poverty," or the American Protective League [right],
representing American manufactures, commerce, and agriculture alike.
Tariff League Bulletin, October 8, 1888, 166

the wages of Irish-American laborers. One pamphleteer considered it a
resurrection of "the insidious craftiness of the Cobdenites and their
American allies," and that the Cobden Club, with its hundreds of members within British Parliament, had infiltrated Congress and was behind
the Mills Bill. And who were the American supporters of the bill? "A few
men anxious to surrender our markets ... to foreign possession ...
American pets of the British free-trade aristocracy." Fueling such
charges, some of the bill's most vocal proponents included Cobden
Club members such as Congressman Samuel "Sunset" Cox – a free
trader since "corn-law times" – and Democratic Speaker of the House
John Carlisle. In his minority dissent, Listian nationalist William

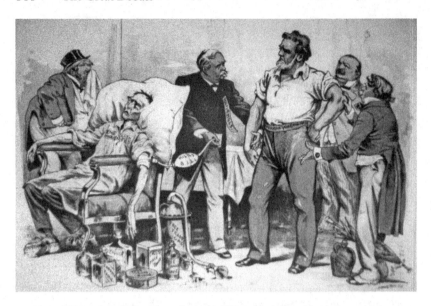

Figure 5.4 "The Transfusion of Blood – A Proposed Dangerous Experiment." *Judge* portrays "Dr. Mills" [middle] talking a healthy "American Workingman" into giving sustenance to the ailing "English Industries" intravenously through the "Mills Bill." Among the other attempted remedies [bottom left] is "Cobden Tonic." *Judge*, July 7, 1888, back cover

McKinley regarded the bill to be "a direct attempt to fasten upon this country the British policy of free foreign trade ... to diminish our trade and increase their own." With the presidential election fast approaching and with an intractable Congress, such opposition proved successful – the Mills Bill came to naught.[61]

Amid a neck-and-neck 1888 presidential contest between Cleveland and Benjamin Harrison, both sides of the Great Debate would attempt to garner potential African American swing votes. That year, Cleveland appointed the son of a prominent black free trader from Illinois, Charles Nelson, to a position in his administration, along with a handful

---

[61] Robbins, "William Ralls Morrison," 56; Curtis, *Protection and Prosperity*, 623; Tarbell, *Tariff in Our Times*, 155, 159; letter of S. S. Cox, *Free-Trader* (March 1870): 171; *CR*, 50 Cong., 1 Sess., May 5, 1888, 3761, May 12, 1888, 4062; *New York Times*, May 7, 1888, 5; *CR*, 50 Cong., 1 Sess., May 5, 1888, 3757–3759, May 12, 1888, 4063; *Washington Post*, May 9, 1888, 2; McKinley, excerpt from minority report, April 2, 1888; McKinley in the House of Representatives, May 18, 1888, microfilm reel 8, William McKinley Papers, LOC.

of other African Americans, a move that gained Cleveland some favor with the black community. These same appointees were then sent to the Democratic convention in Indianapolis with the ostensible goal of forming a "National Association of colored Democrats," although skeptics suggested that the true purpose was "to divide the colored vote in Indiana." But neither Republican economic nationalists nor American free traders could claim much success in making a compelling case to black voters, for whom the door to so many labor opportunities yet remained closed. Although the Great Debate certainly made its way into African American newspaper columns, issues surrounding suffrage and southern racial violence would retain center editorial stage. Indeed, as the 1888 tariff debate continued to dominate the national political scene, American blacks became dismayed at how little either candidate spent on civil rights issues. The Republican party's fiscal focus would thereafter continue to disaffect black Republicans during the Harrison administration.[62]

Cleveland's tossing of the free-trade gauntlet also inspired some of the era's literary giants to pick up the pen as the ideological debate spilled over into American culture. American poet Walt Whitman thanked Cleveland "heartily . . . for his Free-trade message." This was the same poet who had cried out "Great is . . . free-trade!" in *Leaves of Grass*, and who subscribed to the Cobdenite argument that free trade would bring world peace. In the late 1880s, he became even more outspoken against protectionism, saying to a friend: "We ought to invite the world through an open door . . . . My God! are men always to go on clawing each other – always to go on taxing, stealing, warring . . . . That is what the tariff – the spirit of the tariff – means."[63]

Edward Bellamy, author of the popular socialist novel *Looking Backward* (1888), was already looking forward to influencing the next four years of political upheavals. The Great Debate of 1888 doubtless

[62] Meier, "Negro and Democratic Party," 175; *Chicago Tribune*, July 23, 1888, 2; R. C. Ransom, "A National Shame. Closing the Doors of Various Trades against Colored People," *Christian Recorder* (Philadelphia), June 28, 1888; Leslie H. Fishel, Jr., "The Negro in Northern Politics, 1870–1900," *Mississippi Valley Historical Review* 42 (December 1955): 473–474; Vincent P. De Santis, "The Republican Party and the Southern Negro, 1877–1897," *Journal of Negro History* 45 (April 1960): 74.

[63] "Walt Whitman Backing the President," January 26, 1888, in Walt Whitman, *Daybooks and Notebooks*, ed. by William White, 3 vols. (New York: New York University Press, 1977), II, 446; Whitman, *Leaves of Grass* (New York: Fowler & Wells, 1856), 164, 41; Roger Asselineau, *The Evolution of Walt Whitman* (Iowa City: University of Iowa Press, 1999), 173; Andrew Lawson, *Walt Whitman and the Class Struggle* (Iowa City: University of Iowa Press, 2006), 15–17; Whitman, quoted in Martin T. Buinicki, *Negotiating Copyright: Authorship and the Discourse of Literary Property Rights in Nineteenth-Century America* (New York: Routledge, 2006), 119.

helped fuel the sales of Bellamy's socialist response to an improperly regulated market run rampant. In *Looking Backward*, Bellamy condemned both commercialism and industrial slavery. He also rather disdainfully skirted around the era's monetary and tariff debates when envisioning his socialist utopia. His was instead a future where money no longer exists, where the global economy is handled by only a "dozen or so merchants in the world," supervised by an international council and national bureaus of foreign exchange, and where "customs duties of every sort are of course superfluous." Bellamy thereafter attacked both sides of the ongoing Gilded Age free trade-protectionist conflict in the early 1890s, writing to a "Tariff Reformer" that "the tariff issue is mainly a quarrel between the manufacturers and traders as to which shall have the privilege of fleecing the people." He would once again come out in opposition to what he considered a spurious and distracting ideological conflict in *Equality* (1897), his less successful sequel to *Looking Backward*.[64] From Bellamy's socialist perspective, the Great Debate over American trade expansion was little more than innocuous infighting among American capitalists.

The culture of free trade also manifested itself violently in the writing of Mark Twain. He had been a supporter of the Republican protectionist policy up until Cleveland's 1887 tariff message, at which point he became a Mugwump. In *A Connecticut Yankee in King Arthur's Court* (1889), Twain's protagonist, Hank Morgan of Hartford, Connecticut, awakens to find himself transported to sixth-century England. As Hank traipses across the land, he comes across a smith by the name of Dowley. Hank and Dowley immediately begin discussing "matters of business and wages" over dinner. The sixth-century tributary kingdom in which Dowley abides appears at first glance quite prosperous in comparison to Hank's Hartford. "They had the 'protection' system in full force here," Hank explains, "whereas we were working along down toward free-trade, by easy stages," a veiled reference to Cleveland's speech and the proposed Mills Bill of 1888. The others at the Dark Age dinner table listened "hungrily" as Dowley began to question Hank on the rate of wages in Gilded Age America. "In your country, brother," asked Dowley, "what is the wage of a master bailiff, master hind, carter, shepherd, swineherd?" Upon hearing Hank's reply of a quarter cent, "the smith's face beamed with joy .... 'With us they are allowed the double of it! .... 'Rah for protection – to Sheol with free-trade!'" To which Hank, unmoved,

---

[64] Edward Bellamy, *Looking Backward, 2000–1887* (New York: Ticknor and Company, 1888), 88–90; Thomas, *Alternative America*, 265; Bellamy, *Talks on Nationalism* (Freeport, NY: Books for Libraries Press, 1938 [1969]), 73; Bellamy, *Equality* (New York: D. Appleton and Company, 1897), chap. 26.

"rigged up" his "pile-driver" to drive the smith "into the earth – drive him all in – drive him in till not even the curve of his skull should show above ground." Hank replies to Dowley that, while the wages in the smith's land were indeed double those of Connecticut, late-nineteenth-century Americans could buy goods at prices well less than half what Dowley and his countrymen paid, making the high wage argument superfluous. Hank thought he had scored a point against the blacksmith and had "tied him hand and foot." But Dowley "didn't grasp the situation at all, didn't know he had walked into a trap ... I could have shot him, from sheer vexation. With cloudy eye and a struggling intellect," Dowley admitted he did not understand Hank's argument. At which point their dinnertime discussion only deteriorated further.[65]

Twain's Hank was a literary representation of America's Cobdenite free traders, who prided themselves on their superior intellect and the economic soundness of their arguments, but who were frustrated time and again by what they perceived as pernicious protectionist propaganda that nevertheless struck a chord in the heart of the ignorant American laborer. Twain's extreme language hints as well at how fierce the Gilded Age tariff debate had become. Whether it was the pervasive rhetoric of antislavery, the culture of masculinity, Bellamy's fictionalized socialist alternative, or Twain's vexed Connecticut Yankee, Gilded Age free-trade culture pushed its way into the "Great Debate" over American prosperity and economic globalization.

Conclusion

The twin antebellum legacies of antislavery and the ACLL provided much-needed inspiration to the struggling American free-trade movement of the 1880s, as charges of a British conspiracy swirled around Cleveland's opposition to both the Republican party's imperialism of economic nationalism and the country's resurgent silverite agitation. Cleveland himself deserves much of the credit for turning the 1888 presidential contest into the "Great Debate" over how the United States should proceed on the path of economic development and global economic integration, whether through free trade or protectionism. And the debate manifested itself in Victorian-American free-trade culture, whether in the socialistic utopian vision of Edward Bellamy or the violence-tinged Dark Age dinner table of Mark Twain's Connecticut Yankee.

[65] Paul Fatout, ed., *Mark Twain Speaking* (Iowa City: Iowa University Press, 1976), 138–145; Mark Twain, *Connecticut Yankee in King Arthur's Court* (New York: C. L. Webster, 1889), 341–348.

The economic nationalist onslaught also was beginning to wear on Cleveland's 1888 presidential campaign, just as he signed off on a bipartisan bill calling for an inter-American peace conference. The Cleveland administration's fight for freer trade, its Cobdenite handling of Nicaragua, Samoa, and the Congo, a virulent fisheries dispute with Canada (see Chapter 6), and various charges of a transatlantic goldbug and free-trade conspiracy led up to what would become the final nail in Cleveland's 1888 campaign coffin. A die-hard Republican in California named George Osgoodby concocted a clever scheme in order to steal as many Irish votes as possible for the Republican presidential nominee, Benjamin Harrison. Osgoodby decided to write to the British minister to the United States, Lionel Sackville-West, as one "Murchison," claiming to be an Englishborn naturalized American. Osgoodby tricked the British minister into insinuating that the Democrats – and the Cleveland administration in particular – were pro-British regarding free trade.[66] Sackville-West fell into the trap, and Osgoodby passed Sackville-West's pro-Cleveland reply among his friends. It soon ended up in the hands of the rabidly Republican *Los Angeles Times*. By October, the "Murchison Letter" controversy spread throughout the country's protectionist press.

At the same time, Cleveland precipitously notified reporters that another campaign trick was about to be launched against him days before the election. He was to receive a series of complimentary resolutions "purporting to come from some English club of the Cobden order" for his administration's actions regarding "the tariff question," and that the press should "not give much credence to the rumour." Such a rumor never materialized, but the Murchison incident, along with the amiable settlement of a fisheries dispute and the administration's fallout with Tammany Hall, left a political scar leading up to the elections. Cleveland, although winning a slim margin of the popular vote, lost the electoral vote and the 1888 election to Harrison. The *New York Times* directly connected Cleveland's loss to his administration's friendly relationship with England. The newspaper "pardoned" the "poor Irishmen" who voted against Cleveland "for their credulity" in believing Cleveland would "surrender to British influence" owing to his administration's close ties to the Cobden Club.[67]

---

[66] George Osgoodby to Sackville-West, September 4, 1888, in *History of American Presidential Elections, 1789–1968*, 4 vols., ed. by Arthur M. Schlesinger, Jr. (New York: Chelsea House, 1971), II, 1680–1681.

[67] Sackville-West to Osgoodby, September 13, 1888, in *Presidential Elections*, ed. by Schlesinger, II, 1682; *London Times*, October 30, 1888, 5; Robert F. Wesser, "Election of 1888," in *Presidential Elections*, ed. by Schlesinger, II, 1644–1645; *New York Times*, November 14, 1888, 4. See, also, Nevins, *Cleveland*, 428–431; Charles S. Campbell,

With Blaine ready to assume control of Harrison's State Department, the protectionist *New York Tribune*'s Whitelaw Reid as minister to France, John Kasson a cabinet advisor, and William McKinley holding the fiscal reins in Congress, Republican Listian nationalists were ready to strike back, and strike hard. Cleveland's Cobdenite path toward closer Anglo-American relations, the gold standard, anti-imperialism, and freer trade was about to take an abrupt *volte-face* under the Listian administration of Benjamin Harrison. Yet American and Canadian Listians would first have to overcome the renewed demand for North American commercial union.

"The Dismissal of Lord Sackville," *Mississippi Valley Historical Review* 44 (March 1958): 635–648; T. C. Hickley, "George Osgoodby and the Murchison Letter," *Pacific Historical Review* 27 (November 1958): 359–370.

6   The cosmopolitan demand for North American commercial union, 1885–1889

> Between the United States and Canada ... the barriers should be completely obliterated that hitherto had prevented the freest intercourse between the two countries. The proposition, while so exceedingly simple in its statement, [is] freighted with consequences the most tremendous in its possible effects.   Erastus Wiman, 1887.[1]

> The Commercial Union Club seems disposed to play the part of a Canadian Cobden Club .... lay[ing] themselves open to the suspicion of intending to use Commercial Union as a means of bringing about political union with the States.   *The Week* (Toronto), December 1, 1887.

The political and economic "special relationship" between the United States and Canada is taken for granted in the twenty-first century, much as Canadian–American conflict was taken for granted in the long nineteenth. Canada's position as a contiguous British colony amid a time of strong Anglophobic sentiment in the United States meant that relations were often strained. Quarrels over boundary lines, fisheries rights, and tariff walls were frequent. Two possible solutions arose to circumvent future conflict. Choosing between the two options would force Canadians to decide as well on their long-term political economic future: whether to integrate more closely with the United States or with the British Empire. North American Cobdenites favored the former, Canadian Listian nationalists the latter. Much as American Listians increasingly preferred regionalized economic integration through hemispheric-wide protectionism mixed with coercive reciprocity, Canadian Listians like John Macdonald sought a similar system of infant industrial protectionism combined with imperial trade preference among the colonies of the British Empire.

Cobdenite policies had grown in popularity in Canada from the 1840s onward, and the idea of freer US–Canadian commerce was often on

---

[1] Erastus Wiman, *Commercial Union between the United States and Canada* (Toronto: Toronto News Company, 1887), 4.

Canadian minds.[2] The North American neighbors had even attempted limited trade reciprocity from 1855 to 1866.[3] But such trade liberalization dissolved as Canada and the United States respectively turned to protectionism in 1858 and 1861, a situation that worsened as American Anglophobia skyrocketed during and after the US Civil War.[4] Following the 1866 termination of reciprocity and the federation of Canada in 1867, Canadian governments, Conservative and Liberal alike, broached the United States on reinstating reciprocity to no avail. Amid the late-nineteenth-century Great Depression and a Republican-dominated era of economic nationalism, many Conservative Canadian nationalists would increasingly turn to the writings of Friedrich List and to the idea of Greater Britain – a strengthened and interconnected federation of the empire's white settler colonies – for spurring Canadian economic development.[5]

The politico-ideological fight between Canada's Listians and Canadian–American Cobdenites over the future of North American economic globalization would become frenzied by the late 1880s.[6] Canada's conflicting late-nineteenth-century global visions correspondingly spilled over into local American politics, just as American tariff politics came to dominate the Canadian political scene. Canadian Listians, at once retaliating against American economic nationalism and drawing inspiration from the seeming success of US protectionist policies, worked to nurse the Canadian infant industrial system to adulthood and to further integrate itself within the British Empire through a system of imperial trade preference. This, they believed, could best be accomplished through a combination of implementing protectionism; tying Canada's economic future ever more closely to Great Britain and the empire's white settler

---

[2] Craufurd D. W. Goodwin, *Canadian Economic Thought: The Political Economy of a Developing Nation 1814–1914* (Durham: Duke University Press, 1961), 59–70. On Canadian commercial policy, see O. J. McDiarmid, *Commercial Policy in the Canadian Economy* (Cambridge, MA: Harvard University Press, 1946); Stephen Scheinberg, "Invitation to Empire: Tariffs and American Economic Expansion in Canada," *Business History Review* 47 (Summer 1973): 218–238; Simon J. McLean, *The Tariff History of Canada* (Toronto: Warwick Bros. & Rutter, 1895); J. H. Perry, *Taxes, Tariffs, and Subsidies: A History of Canadian Fiscal Development* (Toronto: University of Toronto Press, 1955).

[3] See Chapter 1; J. Laurence Laughlin and H. Parker Willis, *Reciprocity* (New York: The Baker & Taylor Co., 1903), chap. 2.

[4] On the 1859 Canadian tariff, see A. A. Den Otter, "Alexander Galt, the 1859 Tariff, and Canadian Economic Nationalism," *Canadian Historical Review* 63 (1982): 151–178; J. H. Dales, *The Protective Tariff in Canada's Development* (Toronto: University of Toronto Press, 1966); D. F. Barnett, "The Galt Tariff: Incidental or Effective Protection?," *Canadian Journal of Economics* 9 (1976): 389–407.

[5] K. Henley, "The International Roots of Economic Nationalist Ideology in Canada, 1846–1885," *Journal of Canadian Studies* 24 (1989–1990): 107–121.

[6] Coincidentally, this chapter provides a remarkable historical reflection of the debates over NAFTA that would occur a century later.

colonies in Australasia and South Africa; and subsidizing the construction of Canadian railroads, telegraphs, and steamship lines to facilitate intra-imperial trade, defense, and communications. Canadian-American Cobdenites instead viewed North American commercial union as the most effective way toward ending the continent's ongoing economic depressions and hostilities. For them, Canadian–American economic integration appeared both natural and inevitable.

The Canadian–American political economic chessboard was set. The winner would determine the future of North American economic globalization. The onset of a new Canadian–American fisheries dispute in the 1880s spurred the Cobdenites to make their opening move: a demand for North American free-trade union. Canadian Listians countered with calls for retaliatory tariffs, British imperial trade preference, and imperial federation. From this Listian–Cobdenite ideological perspective, what followed would become a critical moment for the economic development of Canadian globalization and North American integration.[7] The dispute also exacerbated the growing tension between North America's Cobdenite cosmopolitans and Listian nationalists. The debate took on global proportions as Canadian Liberals and Conservatives respectively wielded the arguments of Cobden and List – sharpened by new instruments of transportation and communication, the modern tools of global integration – in order to determine the country's political economic orientation for decades to come.

The Canadian fisheries dispute and the demand for commercial union

The Democratic Cleveland administration's Cobdenite desire to avoid foreign entanglements contrasted with those who thought that the British

[7] Previous work on this episode is largely bereft of ideological analysis. See Carl Berger, *The Sense of Power: Studies in the Ideas of Canadian Imperialism 1867–1914* (Toronto: University of Toronto Press, 1970); Ian Grant, "Erastus Wiman: A Continentalist Replies to Canadian Imperialism," *Canadian Historical Review* 53 (1972): 1–20; Robert Craig Brown, *Canada's National Policy 1883–1900: A Study in Canadian-American Relations* (Princeton, NJ: Princeton University Press, 1964), 161–169; Peter B. Waite, *Canada 1874–1896: Arduous Destiny* (Toronto and Montreal: McClelland and Stewart, 1971), 205–208; John Herd Thompson and Stephen J. Randall, *Canada and the United States: Ambivalent Allies* (Athens: University of Georgia Press, 2002 [1994]), 54–62; Gary Pennanen, "American Interest in Commercial Union with Canada, 1854–1898," *Mid-America* 47 (January 1965): 24–39; Charles Callan Tansill, *Canadian-American Relations, 1875–1911* (New Haven, CT: Yale University Press, 1943), 372–411; Tansill, *The Foreign Policy of Thomas F. Bayard, 1885–1897* (New York: Fordham University Press, 1940), 521–561; Donald F. Warner, *The Idea of Continental Union: Agitation for the Annexation of Canada to the United States, 1849–1893* (Lexington: University of Kentucky Press, 1960); David M. Pletcher, *The Diplomacy of Trade and Investment: American Economic Expansion in the Hemisphere, 1865–1900* (Columbia: University of Missouri Press, 1998), 219–236.

Empire ought to be stripped of its remaining western-hemispheric strong-holds. These conflicting approaches to Anglo-American relations had previously been put on display when Grover Cleveland reversed his Republican predecessor's imperial policies toward Nicaragua and the Congo. Soon thereafter Anglophobic conspiracy theories were leveled against Cleveland over a northeastern fisheries dispute with Canada (its foreign policy yet under British imperial control), which broke out when several American ships were seized by Canadian authorities between 1885 and 1886. In March 1887, the US Congress authorized Cleveland to deny Canadian fishermen access to American waters. Cleveland, how-ever, refused to use this aggressive response. He preferred instead to negotiate – a diplomatic approach that gained the support of Canadian-American Cobdenites, but also brought Anglophobic fury down upon his administration.[8]

The fisheries dispute became ever more politically delicate when the English appointed as their delegate in the issue Joseph Chamberlain, a man hated by American Irish men and women for his vocal opposition to Irish home rule.[9] Senator Harrison Holt Riddleberger of Virginia insinu-ated that Cleveland's non-aggressive diplomacy was further proof that his administration was "a pro-English organization." A Republican con-gressman afterward pointed out in the House of Representatives that Secretary of State Thomas Bayard's "cringing apology to the British foreign office" eminently qualified his Cobden Club membership. The 1888 majority report of the Republican-controlled Foreign Relations Committee even concluded that "the President of the United States may be under influence of foreign and adverse interests."[10] Once again,

---

[8] Edward P. Crapol, *America for Americans: Economic Nationalism and Anglophobia in the Late Nineteenth Century* (Westport, CT: Greenwood Press, 1973), 146; Pletcher, *Diplomacy of Trade and Investment*, 221–223; Charles S. Campbell, Jr., "American Tariff Interests and Northeastern Fisheries, 1883–1888," *Canadian Historical Review* 45 (September 1964): 212–228; James Morton Callahan, *American Foreign Policy in Canadian Relations* (New York: The Macmillan Company, 1937), 363–382. James G. Blaine also covered the long-standing fisheries controversy in great detail in *Twenty Years of Congress: From Lincoln to Garfield with a Review of the Events which Led to the Political Revolution of 1860*, 2 vols. (Norwich, CT: The Henry Bill Publishing Company, 1886), II, 615–637.

[9] On the broader effects of Irish nationalism and foreign policy, see David Sim, *A Union Forever: The Irish Question and U.S. Foreign Relations in the Victorian Age* (Ithaca, NY: Cornell University Press, 2014); M. J. Sewell, "Rebels or Revolutionaries? Irish-American Nationalism and American Diplomacy, 1865–1885," *Historical Journal* 29 (September 1986): 723–733. For Chamberlain's early flirtation with free trade, see Roland Quinalt, "John Bright and Joseph Chamberlain," *Historical Journal* 28 (September 1985): 623–646.

[10] *Congressional Record* [hereafter cited as *CR*], 50 Cong., 1 Sess., August 2, 1888, 7155–7157; *CR*, 50 Cong., 1 Sess., May, 5, 1888, 3757; *Majority Report of the Committee on*

Cleveland's ameliorative approach to Anglo-American relations had opened him up to partisan attack and charges of a transatlantic free-trade conspiracy.

Cleveland therefore attempted an outwardly tough retaliatory response in order to sidestep the jingo charge. But his facade of Anglophobic ferocity was apparently transparent enough to those closely following the issue in Canada and the United States. The Toronto-based journal the *Week* observed how, "according to Mr. Blaine and the Republican press, he [Cleveland] has been 'euchred' ... stroking the lion's mane and giving it sugar sticks." The newspaper agreed, suggesting that "there is no occasion for Canadians to lose either head or heart over President Cleveland's so-called retaliation message to Congress," as it was "intended exclusively for home consumption, and, after the Presidential election, will cease to have the slightest interest."[11] The Republican magazine *Judge* in turn depicted John Bull and "free trade" hiding transparently behind the retaliation message [figure 6.1].

Matters were further exacerbated when Bayard and Chamberlain thereafter came to an unofficial *modus vivendi* preventing further seizures. According to Listian pamphleteer Patrick Cudmore, Bayard had requested nothing more than "a feeble note for an explanation" in the face of England and Canada's "insults to the American flag and the injuries to American rights." Outraged by the issue's peaceful settlement, San Francisco's Republican newspaper the *Evening Bulletin* colorfully wrote that Cleveland "is just as much an Anglo-maniac as the dude who turned up his trousers and spread his umbrella on a fine day in New York, because they had just had a dispatch at his club that it was raining in London."[12] Cleveland's figurative umbrella, however, would prove rather ineffective against such political mudslinging. Cleveland's Cobdenites were once again reminded that maintaining peaceful Anglo-American relations in the Gilded Age was indeed a dangerous – and dirty – political practice.

Foreign Relations on the Fisheries Treaty, Senate Misc. Doc. No. 109, 50 Cong., 1 Sess., 1888, 17; Crapol, *America for Americans*, 161.

[11] *Week*, August 30, 1888, 633–634.

[12] Charles W. Calhoun, *Minority Victory: Gilded Age Politics and the Front Porch Campaign of 1888* (Lawrence: University Press of Kansas, 2008), 143; Patrick Cudmore, *Cleveland's Maladministration: Free Trade, Protection and Reciprocity* (New York: P.J. Kennedy, 1896), 3; *San Francisco Evening Bulletin*, August 15, 1888, 2; *Washington Post*, August 17, 1888, 4. Listian Cudmore was a strong silverite advocate of Blaine's protectionism-cum-reciprocity for gaining US access to Latin American markets, dedicating over forty pages to the subject in *Buchanan's Conspiracy, the Nicaragua Canal and Reciprocity* (New York: P. J. Kenedy, 1892), 18–59.

Figure 6.1 "Too Thin!" *Judge* insinuates that John Bull, holding a free-trade bill behind his back, hides behind Cleveland's transparent message of retaliation over the fisheries dispute. *Judge*, September 15, 1888

The "Manchester Colonial Theory" vs. Canadian economic nationalism, 1867–1887

The fisheries dispute also sparked another important development in the history of North American economic integration: the resurgence of the movement for Canadian–American commercial union. Goldwin Smith led the charge. He numbered among the most cosmopolitan of Cobdenites. Born in England, educated in the classics, a journalist, intellectual radical, Cobden Club member, and Regius Professor of Modern History at Oxford, Smith had immigrated to North America in 1868, taking up an unpaid professorship at Cornell University in upstate New York. While a great admirer of the United States, he nevertheless soon found the nation's rampant Anglophobia suffocating. Three years after his arrival in Ithaca, Smith moved to Toronto, where he remained.[13]

Smith also numbered among the first mid-Victorian proponents of Canadian independence. In *The Empire* (1863), he advocated for the demilitarization and devolution of the settlement colonies, Canada included. One contemporary critic rather aptly described Smith's anti-imperial scheme the "Manchester Colonial Theory."[14] Following Canadian confederation in 1867, Smith thereafter became the lead advocate for commercial – and eventual political – union between Canada and its growing trading partner to the south. For Smith, it was the natural integrative course, considering that the two countries were already tied so closely through trade, Anglo-Saxon heritage, and geographical nearness.

The "Manchester Colonial Theory" had grown in popularity in Canada from the 1840s onward, and freer commerce between the two neighbors was by no means a novel idea.[15] Canada and the United States had previously tried liberalizing trade from 1855 to 1866, the existence of which American Cobdenite Edward Atkinson believed had kept the two

[13] Christopher A. Kent, "Smith, Goldwin (1823–1910)," in *Oxford Dictionary of National Biography*, ed. by H. C. G. Matthew and Brian Harrison (Oxford, 2004); online ed., ed. by Lawrence Goldman, January 2008, www.oxforddnb.com.ezproxy.lib.utexas.edu/view/article/36142; Paul T. Phillips, *The Controversialist: An Intellectual Life of Goldwin Smith* (London: Praeger, 2002), 45–53.

[14] "A Canadian" [Egerton Ryerson], *Remarks on the Historical Mis-Statements and Fallacies of Mr. Goldwin Smith in his Lecture "On the Foundation of the American Colonies," and his Letters on the Emancipation of the Colonies"* (Toronto: Leader Steam Press Establishment, 1866 [1863]), 14; Goldwin Smith, *A Series of Letters, Published in "The Daily News," 1862, 1863* (Oxford and London: John Henry and James Parker, 1863). See, also, Smith, *England and America: A Lecture, Delivered by Goldwin Smith, Before the Boston Fraternity During his Recent Visit to the United States* (Manchester: A. Ireland and Co., 1865), vii–x, 30.

[15] Goodwin, *Canadian Economic Thought*, 59–70.

countries from armed conflict during the Civil War, and which the AFTL had unsuccessfully fought to maintain in 1866.[16] Such reciprocity, however, came to an end as Canada and the United States respectively turned to protectionism in 1858 and 1861, and as American Anglophobia reached new heights during and after the Civil War.[17] Canadian governments, Conservative and Liberal alike, unsuccessfully broached the United States on reinstating reciprocity for many years following the treaty's 1866 termination.

US Cobdenites also came to the classical liberal defense of Canadian–American trade. The AFTL lobbied on behalf of renewed reciprocity following its abrogation, and David Ames Wells, William Cullen Bryant, Arthur Latham Perry, and Cyrus Field lent their support to the American Commercial Reciprocity League, with the objective of informing the North American public of "the advantages of freedom of commercial intercourse between Canada and this country." Yale Professor William Graham Sumner also frequently called for commercial union between Mexico, Canada, and the United States in the pages of New York City's IFTA publication *New Century*. Henry George, in his popular *Protection or Free Trade* (1886), in like fashion advocated for free trade and its corresponding spirit of "fraternity and peace" to fight against that "spirit of protectionism ... national enmity and strife." He proposed as a first step the elimination of trade barriers between the United States and Canada, thereby making "the two countries practically one."[18] In 1883, New York Cobdenite R. R. Bowker similarly took aim at the formal imperialism of economic nationalism as exemplified by former President Grant's desire "to annex San Domingo ... that we could then trade freely with her. Why not without the cost of annexation," Bowker suggested, and why limit our trade expansion to San Domingo, when the United States might also trade with South America, Canada, and the world? "Let us have at least 'reciprocity' with our neighbors as the first step toward free trade," he concluded in clear Cobdenite verbiage, and

[16] Edward Atkinson, *Taxation and Work: A Series of Treatises on the Tariff and the Currency* (New York and London: G. P. Putnam's Sons, 1892), 105; American Free Trade League, *Memorial of the American Free Trade League to the Senate and House of Representatives* (February 1866).

[17] See Otter, "Alexander Galt, the 1859 Tariff, and Canadian Economic Nationalism," 151–178.

[18] American Free Trade League, *Memorial of the American Free Trade League to the Senate and House of Representatives*; Melville Egleston to David Wells, January 11, 1876, reel 4, microfilm 15, 662–9P, Wells Papers; *New Century* (December 1875): 3–6; (February 1876): 53–54; Henry George, *Protection or Free Trade: An Examination of the Tariff Question with Especial Regard to the Interests of Labor* (New York: Henry George, 1886), 352–353.

thereby let "America be the apostle among nations of the gospel of 'peace on earth, good-will among men.'"[19]

Edward Atkinson took a prominent role in the fight for North American commercial unity. He was in frequent communication on the subject with Canadian commercial unionist Erastus Wiman. Atkinson also lobbied the New York Chamber of Commerce, which in late 1887 appointed a special commission to look further into this growing demand for unrestricted reciprocity with Canada. Atkinson's off-handed suggestion that the United States might buy New Brunswick and Nova Scotia in order to end the fisheries dispute and alleviate Canada's debt – to his surprise – also gained remarkable traction, and was thereafter touted by the *Boston Herald*. Wiman accordingly made sure to reinforce to Atkinson that the "vast majority of the Canadian people is unalterably opposed to annexation," except perhaps after half a century of commercial union. "At present," however, "the tariff is a barrier that completely separates them, and as long as it exists it will have that effect," and "the fishery question . . . is of the same family as the tariff question."[20]

While Canadian and American Cobdenites joined forces in their attempt to integrate the North American economy, Friedrich List's progressive protectionist ideas were also finding a welcome economic nationalist audience in late-nineteenth-century Canada.[21] Beginning in the 1850s, protectionist defenders of Canadian infant industries turned to List's writings, including J. B. Hurlbert, Toronto economist and Canadian civil servant; Toronto businessman Isaac Buchanan, founder of the Association for the Promotion of Canadian Industry in 1858; Cléopas Beausoleil, editor of *Noveau-Monde* in Quebec; and John MacLean,   founding   member   of   the   Ontario   Association   of

---

[19] R. R. Bowker, proof copy, *Free Trade the Best Protection to American Industry* (New York: New York Free Trade Club, 1883), Box 89, Bowker Papers, NYPL.

[20] Wiman to Atkinson, November 17, 1887; November 22, 1887; December 2, 1887; December 6, 1887; *Commercial Union with Canada. Preamble and Resolution Adopted by the New-York Chamber of Commerce, at its Regular Meeting, November 3, 1887*; F. H. Thurber [Chairman, Special Committee of the Chamber of Commerce of the State of New York] to Atkinson, November 7, 1887, carton 3; Atkinson to Butterworth, September 28, 1887; Atkinson to Taussig, October 31, 1887; Atkinson to Wiman, August 3, 1888, carton 18; Wiman to Atkinson, August 4, 1888, carton 4, Atkinson Papers.

[21] Goodwin, *Canadian Economic Thought*, 46–59. For some of the era's Canadian protectionists' arguments, see A. Baumgarten, *Industrial Canada: The Duty of Development and How to Accomplish It* (Montreal: Gazette Printing House, 1876); "A Freeholder," *To the Freeholders of Canada: Political Facts for Consideration with a Short Treatise on Free Trade and Protection* (1877); R. W. Phipps, *Free Trade and Protection, Considered with Relation to Canadian Interests* (Toronto: s.n., 1878); J. R. Lithgow, *Tariff Literature, Letters to the People* (Halifax: s.n., 1878).

Manufacturers in 1867.[22] Not coincidentally, at about the same time that North American Cobdenites were coming to the conclusion that eventual continental commercial and political union were a necessity for peace and prosperity between the two neighbors, Canada's Conservative party coalesced around a strong platform of infant industrial protectionism, after their attempts at Canadian–American reciprocity had been stymied by the likes of Anglophobe James G. Blaine, who feared extending any olive branch to the British Empire.[23]

Canada's Conservative "National Policy" came into being in March 1879. Tariff rates on manufactured goods were raised from about 17 percent to between 30 and 40 percent, alongside specific *ad valorem* duties to protect Nova Scotia's iron, steel, and coal industries, as well as Ontario and Quebec's manufactures. This economic nationalist policy also emphasized government-subsidized internal improvements, particularly the speedy completion of the transcontinental Canadian railway (completed in 1885), which promised to expand Canadian imperial trade ties with the Australian colonies and with England. Philadelphia's protectionist paper the *North American* astutely observed that this Canadian protectionist upswing "is the bitterest pill that the followers of Cobden have had to swallow for some time."[24]

By 1880, Conservative spokesmen and news outlets like the *Toronto Globe* also began to label the so-called Continentalists as unpatriotic conspirators. Lead "conspirator" Goldwin Smith was quick to respond, countering that there was "no conspiracy except the mutual interest of the two nations gave it birth." His own desires, Smith noted, only followed the precepts of the Cobden Club, and its twin aims of world peace and free trade could only be accomplished through continental union. He also pointed out that the Continentalist movement was predominantly economic in motivation, though it admittedly "brings political feelings into play." Much like the Liberal Republican and Mugwump organizations in the United States, the Canadian commercial union movement was largely a nongovernmental one, led by businessmen and journalists rather than

---

[22] Goodwin, *Canadian Economic Thought*, 46–52; Robin Neill, *A History of Canadian Economic Thought* (New York: Routledge, 1991), 48.

[23] James G. Blaine to S. D. Lindsey, July 3, 1874, reel 7, James Gillespie Blaine Family Papers, LOC. For other late-nineteenth-century attempts at reciprocity with Canada, see A. H. U. Colquhoun, "The Reciprocity Negotiation with the United States in 1869," *Canadian Historical Review* 8 (1927): 233–242; Ronald D. Tallman, "Reciprocity, 1874: The Failure of Liberal Diplomacy," *Ontario History* 65 (1973): 87–105; Rodney J. Morrison, "The Canadian-American Reciprocal Trade Agreement of 1874: A Pennsylvanian's View," *Pennsylvania Magazine of History and Biography* 102 (October 1978): 457–468; Allen P. Stouffer, "Avoiding a 'Great Calamity': Canada's Pursuit of Reciprocity, 1864–1870," *Upper Midwest History* 4 (1984): 39–55.

[24] Goodwin, *Canadian Economic Thought*, 55–59; *North American*, September 20, 1878.

politicians. Smith also predicted that another conflict over fisheries rights might "be kindled again," and "bring this question to a head."[25]

The outbreak of just such a fisheries dispute occurred in 1887. That same year, in response, the Canadian Liberal party officially came out in support of unrestricted reciprocity with the United States. Canada's Conservative party leaders countered by emphasizing instead the long-standing and politically palatable fear associated with the scheme: the dual loss of Canadian independence and British imperial ties stemming from American annexation. Economic nationalist Alexander T. Galt (1817–1893) – Canadian businessman, Conservative politician, and author of Canada's protectionist 1858 tariff – expressed his own fears of American annexation following the coming to power in England of the Cobdenite Gladstone government in 1868. Galt had been unable to shut his eyes "to the fact that" Gladstone's administration wanted to rid itself of Canada, as the Cobdenite leadership in London had "a servile fear of the United States and would rather give us up than defend us."[26]

Canadian Conservative fears of American filibustering were grounded in historical precedent. Americans had forcibly tried to take Canada during the American Revolution and the War of 1812. Another more peaceful attempt arose following the repeal of the Corn Laws in 1846, when Britain began ending tariff preferences that had previously maintained a protected imperial market for various Canadian products (see Chapter 1). In response to the adverse effects of the English metropole's newfound free-trade policies, some merchants in Montreal had founded the Free Trade Association, while others turned to the United States for more direct intervention. In 1849, the latter drew up the unsuccessful Annexation Manifesto, which sought "friendly and peaceable separation from British connexion, and a union upon equitable terms" with the United States that included reciprocal free trade. After the 1855 reciprocity treaty between the United States and Canada fell apart at the end of the US Civil War, American demands for Canadian annexation frequently garnered public attention, whether owing to Civil War Anglophobia, as subsequent payment over the *Alabama* claims, or to obtain support for the Republican party by promising to satiate both America's land-hungry expansionists and the growing number of Irish nationalist immigrants who enjoyed any twisting of the British lion's tail.[27]

---

[25] Goldwin Smith, "Canada and the United States," *North American Review* 131 (July 1880), 14, 15, 17–18, 19, 24–25.

[26] Galt, January 14, 1867; Galt to Cartier, September 14, 1869; Granville to Galt, March 15, 1870, MG 27 ID 8 Vol. 3, Alexander Tilloch Galt Papers, LAC.

[27] Annexation Association of Montreal, *Annexation Manifesto of 1849* (Montreal, 1881); Goodwin, *Canadian Economic Thought*, 61–62; Robin W. Winks, *The Civil War Years:*

Three other events also weighed heavily on the looming Canadian choice over how to approach global economic integration: the confederation of Canada's provinces in 1867; Republican Secretary of State William Seward's expansionist designs in the late 1860s; and, following the 1871 Treaty of Washington, the withdrawal of most of Britain's military forces from Canada. The combination of these geopolitical actions would contribute both to the Liberal desire for North American commercial union and to the Conservative imperial vision of a consolidated "Greater Britain."[28]

After 1870, the idea of Greater Britain began picking up adherents throughout the British Empire. This was particularly the case following the influential 1883 publication of *The Expansion of England* by J. R. Seeley, who was coincidentally Cobdenite Goldwin Smith's Regius professorial counterpart at Cambridge University. Seeley expounded that, while the British Empire may have come about in "a fit of absence of mind," for "Greater Britain" to come into existence England and the white settler colonies must mindfully be brought closer together.[29] Seeley's publication received a great deal of transatlantic attention for decades to come and provided much of the intellectual framework for the burgeoning imperial federation movement. A letter from Seeley was accordingly read aloud at the first meeting of the Imperial Federation League (IFL, 1884–1893) in England.[30]

Such demands for imperial federation were by no means solely coming from Seeley and the English metropole. Aggressive US expansionist designs and growing Canadian nationalism had spawned as well the Canada First party, formed by George T. Denison and W. A. Foster in 1868, the same year that Gladstone's Cobdenite government came to power and the same year that the term "Greater Britain" was first coined.[31] Denison and Foster's nationalism was tied intimately to love of

---

Canada and the United States (Montreal and Kingston: Harvest House, 1998), 166–167; Sim, *A Union Forever*. See, also, James Morton Callahan, *American-Canadian Relations Concerning Annexation, 1846–1871* (Bloomington: Indiana University Studies, 1925); Paul-Andre Dube, "Crise annexionniste a Quebec, 1848–1850" (MA thesis, Université Laval, 1978); Lester B. Shippee, *Canadian-American Relations, 1849–1874* (New Haven, CT: Yale University Press, 1939).

[28] See, for instance, David M. L. Farr, "Sir John Rose and Imperial Relations: An Episode in Gladstone's First Administration," *Canadian Historical Review* 33 (January 1952): 19–38.

[29] J. R. Seeley, *Expansion of England* (London: Macmillan, 1883), 8, 63.

[30] Ernest R. May, *American Imperialism: A Speculative Essay* (Chicago, IL: Imprint Publications, 1991 [1967]), 129–130, 155, 171, 184, 205; A. L. Burt, *Imperial Architects* (Oxford: B. H. Blackwell, 1918), 217.

[31] George T. Denison, *The Struggle for Imperial Unity* (London: MacMillan, 1909), 10–11, 50–55; Charles Dilke, *Greater Britain* (London: MacMillan, 1868).

the Mother Country. Denison himself hoped for a future confederation of the British Empire. Foster in turn guided the Canada First movement into political action, beginning with the creation of the Canadian National Association in 1874. Notably, the first goal of its platform was the desire for "connection" and "consolidation" of the British Empire. A decade later, Canada's leading economic nationalists numbered among the leaders of imperial federation and trade preference: Galt himself was a founding member of the IFL, as were Charles Tupper, high commissioner for Canada, and Oliver Mowatt, premier of Ontario.[32]

Cobdenite Goldwin Smith was prone to taking swipes at the imperial unionists. In 1878, for example, he diminutively described their proposed imperial federative connection between England and her colonies as but a "slender filament." While the distance, "shortened by steam and telegraph," worked well to strengthen a despot's rule, it did little to further representative government. He warned that geography was against the scheme and "few have fought against geography and prevailed."[33] Smith derisively called the idea a "Jingo fallacy" that "Canada is to be divorced economically from the Continent ... incorporated by an Imperial Zollverein" with Australia, South Africa, and Great Britain. "This scheme is a chimera," he scoffed, "and must fail."[34] In response to such Cobdenite opposition, Galt and other Canadians wrote prolifically on behalf of imperial unity in the years after Canada's 1867 confederation.[35]

The Canadian Conservative demand for imperial unity was crucial to the growth in popularity of the Listian vision of regionalized economic integration within a protectionist British Empire. The initial Canadian chapter of the IFL was established in Montreal in May 1885. Representatives from all the self-governing colonies then met in London in April 1887 for the first Colonial Conference, the idea for which had been proposed by Montreal businessman Peter Redpath the year before. Canadian delegates kept much of the discussion focused on the future of British imperialism and globalization: imperial defense; the development

---

[32] Burt, *Imperial Architects*, 218; David M. L. Farr, "The Imperial Federation League in Canada, 1885–1894" (MA thesis, University of Toronto, 1946), 59.

[33] Goldwin Smith, *The Political Destiny of Canada* (Toronto: Willing & Williamson, 1878), 9, 20–21.

[34] Burt, *Imperial Architects*, 218; Farr, "Imperial Federation League," 59.

[35] See for instance, Alexander Galt, *The Relations of the Colonies to the Empire: Present and Future* (London: M'Corquodale and Company, 1883); Jehu Mathews, *A Colonist on the Colonial Question* (Toronto: Adam, Stevenson, and Co., 1872); Thomas Macfarlane, *A United Empire* (Montreal: s.n., 1885); George Hague, *Imperial Federation: The Position of Canada* (Montreal: Imperial Federation League in Canada, 1886). Canadian Listians devised some of the most innovative ideas concerning imperial federation. See Seymour Ching-Yuan Cheng, *Schemes for the Federation of the British Empire* (New York: Columbia University Press, 1931), 89–92.

of telegraphic communications connecting London to all the colonies; the Canadian Pacific Railway; a uniform imperial postage; a steamship line between Vancouver and Hong Kong; postal services with Australia, India, and China via Canada; and the laying of an undersea Pacific cable from Vancouver to Australia. All were seen to be necessary developments as "the intercommunication between the various parts of the British Empire is growing with amazing rapidity."[36] It was in late 1887 as well that the IFL in Canada, with Denison as a vice president, became more active. It also decided to move its branch headquarters from Montreal to Toronto "specifically to oppose the local agitation for closer economic relations with the United States."[37]

Canada for Canadians: The debate over North American economic union

Alongside these growing Listian demands for imperial federation, agitation for North American union also increased sharply. The idea's most recent incarnation arose after repeal of reciprocity in 1866, Canada's 1867 confederation, and the 1873 onset of the late-nineteenth-century Great Depression. In 1876, for instance, US Congressman Elijah Ward had called for commercial union in the House of Representatives, and continental union generally appeared more feasible alongside increases in Canadian–American trade, railroad connections, travel, tourism, and immigration.[38] Goldwin Smith, foreseeing an "impending fiscal war," in 1880 once again asserted that Canada's destiny lay in American commercial union. His continental Cobdenite dream of freer trade became ever more popular among export-reliant farmers following the onset of another economic downturn in the mid-1880s.[39]

Commercial union became the centerpiece of serious North American debate by the end of the decade. Proponents of a North American Zollverein were a motley mixture: Erastus Wiman, Canadian citizen, president of the Great North-Western Telegraph Company, and resident

---

[36] Imperial Federation League, *The Imperial Conference of 1887* (London: Imperial Federation League, 1887), 9, 17, 19, 27–28; *Proceedings of the Colonial Conference, 1887* (London: Colonial Office, 1887), 5–7; *Proceedings of the Colonial Conference of 1887 in Relation to Imperial Postal and Telegraphic Communications through Canada* (Ottawa: Brown Chamberlin, 1888), 4, 8–9, 11, 83–86, 90–118, 132–155; Richard Jebb, *The Imperial Conference: A History and Study* (London: Longmans, Green and CO., 1911), 1: 9; Paul Knaplund, "Intra-Imperial Aspects of Britain's Defence Question, 1870–1900," *Canadian Historical Review* 3 (1922): 136.
[37] Farr, "Imperial Federation League," 100.
[38] Smith, *Political Destiny of Canada*, 71–72.
[39] *Congressional Record*, 44, 1 Sess., 3158–3164; Smith, "Canada and the United States," 14–25.

of New York City; Samuel Ritchie, Ohio businessman and president of the Central Ontario Railway; Benjamin Butterworth and Robert Hitt, Republican representatives in the US Congress; American Cobdenites R. R. Bowker, Edward Atkinson, Henry George, and David Wells; Edward Farrer, editor of the *Toronto Mail*; and of course Goldwin Smith. Calls for North American union rose in pitch after the outbreak of the virulent fisheries dispute in 1885–1887, which reached new levels following the Canadian seizure of US shipping vessels and as the United States increasingly sought greater access to restricted Canadian waters.

Cobdenite calls for Canadian–American commercial union soon began receiving modest support from more progressive protectionists within the Republican party, demonstrating the ambiguous resonance of "reciprocity" by this time. Republican Congressman Benjamin Butterworth submitted a bill to the US House of Representatives in February 1887, for example, calling for full reciprocity between the United States and Canada. In contrast to the Cobdenite rationale behind North American commercial union, however, Butterworth did so because he believed that with Canada's economic inclusion, the US market would become *more* insulated from foreign competition. He also submitted it as a response to the "controversies . . . growing out of the construction of treaties affecting fishing interests." Commercial union would "remove all existing controversies and causes of controversy in the future." Wiman, happy to see any legislation in favor of commercial union regardless of motivation, told a reporter from the *Toronto Globe* that while the Butterworth bill might pass the House, the Senate seemed obstinate. Wiman nevertheless held out hope that obdurate protectionist senators might realize that commercial union was "the best settlement of the Fishery question." Edward Atkinson also approved "most heartily" of Butterworth's desire for commercial union, although Atkinson admitted to Butterworth that, "looking at it from a free-trade standpoint," he would have liked to see such a union with Mexico as well.[40] In April, with progressive Listian motivations similar to those of Butterworth, Republican Congressman Robert R. Hitt of Illinois proposed another bill, which called for commercial union in order to end permanently "our troubles with Canada." Hitt explained that, "in one sense, there would be a business annexation of each nation by the other." Although the Butterworth and Hitt bills failed, this small group of Republican congressmen, which also included Republican Senator John Sherman of Ohio, would continue to express

---

[40] "Butterworth Bill," in Erastus Wiman, ed., *Commercial Union in North America. Some Letters, Papers, and Speeches* (Toronto: Toronto News Company, 1887), 5; *Toronto Globe*, October 15, 1887; Atkinson to Butterworth, September 28, 1887, carton 18, Atkinson Papers.

their desire for "Canada to be part of the United States": a key component of their protectionist, regionalized vision for American economic globalization.[41]

These Republican congressmen also received some support from the economic nationalist heartland of Pennsylvania. The protectionist paper *Philadelphia American* (which had recently asked Goldwin Smith for his views on the subject) came out in favor of commercial union: "In language, in faith, in culture, in governmental methods the two countries more closely resemble each other than either resembles any other in either the old or the new world. Why, then, not establish absolute freedom of commercial intercourse between them?" Countering the free-trade dimensions of commercial union (as had Butterworth, Hitt, and Sherman), the newspaper instead saw this as a way of further protecting the already protected economic interests of the two countries, "in that it would impart a permanence to the protective polity in both which it does not now possess. For the sake of this freedom of national intercourse the people of both would stand by Protection."[42]

Such pro-reciprocity sentiments had been expressed as early as 1880 by the protectionist president of the Philadelphia Board of Trade and former minister to Britain, John Welsh, in response to comments by Cobden Club secretary T. B. Potter before the New York Free Trade Club. Philadelphia's Listian nationalist Wharton Barker had responded similarly that same year when the subject of Canadian reciprocity came before the House Ways and Means Committee.[43] The adverse effects of Canadian tariff walls on American goods were therefore also turning some progressive protectionists toward trade reciprocity. A few US economic nationalists now favored North American commercial union, albeit with a protectionist regional vision for American economic integration in mind.

In Canada, Goldwin Smith helped organize local Commercial Union Leagues throughout Ontario, and worked closely with the pro-free-trade Farmers' Institutes in reaction to the fisheries controversy and

[41] "Hitt Bill," in Wiman, *Commercial Union*, 6–7; *CR*, 50 Cong., 1 Sess., 7286, August 7, 1888.

[42] "The Way Out of the Canadian Difficulty," *Philadelphia American*, in Wiman, *Commercial Union*, 10.

[43] John Welsh, *Protection under the Guise of Free-Trade as Practiced by Great Britain and Ireland Compared with Protection as Practiced by the United States of America* (Philadelphia, PA: J. B. Lippincott & Co., 1880), 14–15; Welsh, *Tariff Tract No. 1. 1880: Free Trade and Protection* (Philadelphia, PA: The American Iron and Steel Association, 1880), 6; Wharton Barker, *Our Canadian Relations. A Letter to Hon. James A. Garfield, Philadelphia, April 27th, 1880* (Philadelphia, PA: Press of Edward Stern & Co. 1880), folder 1884, box 1, Worthington Chauncey Ford Papers, NYPL; Pennanen, "American Commercial Union with Canada," 28–31.

Butterworth's and Hitt's proposals. With Smith as Commercial Union League president, the organization became the nucleus of the Canadian free-trade movement, and, anticipating Conservative attacks, Smith made sure to downplay the annexationist angle. Smith and Wiman thereafter set out on a speaking tour of Canada beginning in 1887.[44]

Owing to the efforts of Smith, Wiman, and the Commercial Union League, the prospect for Canadian–American reciprocity grew in Canadian popularity. At Lake Dufferin, Ontario, Wiman pointed out that on the issue of unrestricted reciprocity, "no other subject occupied so large a space in the private talk among members [in Ottawa]. To the exclusion of almost every other subject, it had been discussed day in and day out." He suggested a proposal for the lifting of all tariffs. If fulfilled, Canada's "would be the destiny to teach the ages hereafter . . . side by side with a republic speaking the English language, governed by English laws, and influenced by English literature." The United States already practiced free trade among its various states, he pointed out. But "the complete and unrestricted interchange of commodities between the great commonwealths on this continent had contributed more than anything else to the building up of a great interior means of communication, and these arteries of commerce had served, in a greater degree than any other, to bind the people together."[45] For Wiman and Smith, continental free trade was but the next logical step for integrating the Anglo-Saxon neighbors.

Wiman also felt that the new developments in transportation would enhance the commercial union cause. The building of the Canadian Pacific Railway was "one of the greatest achievements of modern times," Wiman noted, offering Canada "a means of communication within itself and a connection with the United States." Alongside Canada's interconnected and "wonderful system of waterways . . . a complete interchange of products" between the North American nations would follow, while canals, railways, telegraphs, "and every other avenue of communication and transportation would be benefited by the activity which would result."[46] These new tools of transportation and communication would thus pave the way toward greater North American economic integration.

Canadian immigration to the United States was a further problem that commercial union would easily fix, Wiman argued. The census of 1860

---

[44] J. S. Willison, *Sir Wilfrid Laurier: A Political History*, 2 vols. (Toronto: George N. Morang and Company, 1903), II, 123–124. For a descriptive overview of Wiman's "economic" continentalism, see Grant, "Erastus Wiman."

[45] Wiman, *Commercial Union*, 4, 5.

[46] Smith, "Canada and the United States," 22, 16–17; Wiman, *Commercial Union*, 6–7.

reported about 250,000 Canadians in the United States; the census of 1885 reported 950,000. Here, instead of pulling on the purse strings of Canadian businessmen, Wiman pulled upon the heartstrings of Canadian mothers: "If commercial union could accomplish nothing else than keep our young men at home, it would be a boon of the greatest magnitude ... if the clear blue eyes of the little baby girl look inquiringly into the mother's anxious face, what fate does she read there? Why, if her brothers and half the boys of the neighborhood are leaving the country, how hopeless is her life likely to be," Wiman dramatically concluded. The girl's "budding womanhood" would thus vainly "wait in vain for the sturdy farmer boy who should win her ...... Mothers must think of these things, and with a far-seeing vision which a mother's love will prompt, should take an interest in this great movement ... and thus secure the happiness and the future of the sweet girls of this fair land" by keeping Canada's young men from immigrating to the United States.[47]

This internal Canadian conflict over commercial union reflected the growing ideological debate occurring between Listians and Cobdenites throughout the globe. Wiman also observed that Canada's infant industries were hostile to the idea of North American commercial union. But why? Canadian manufacturers could already compete with their American counterparts, and free fishing privileges would only further spur growth. "As to the opposition's cheap talk about patriotism ... it was impossible to conceive a higher patriotism than that which would develop in the largest degree the resources now latent" in Canada. Furthermore, while some have said that "commercial union was but a step to annexation" and would lead to discrimination of English goods, both considerations formed "the strongest argument" for North American free trade. In 1888, another continental unionist observed how Canada "has striven to make Liverpool as near as Boston, London as New York, and it has failed"; for too long North America had ignored "Nature's unity ... from Southern Gulf to the white line of northern snow, making in itself a prairie empire that would feed half the world."[48] Imperial federation, Canadian free traders argued, was a pipedream, whereas Canadian–American commercial union was inevitable.

Canadian Listian nationalists remained unconvinced. Canadian–American calls for reciprocity were met with opposition from Canadian imperial federationists. Listian Conservative politician John Macdonald (1815–1891) wrote to his friend Charles Tupper in 1884 that Canadians

---

[47] Wiman, *Commercial Union*, 18.
[48] Ibid., 8, 16; W. H. H. Murray, *Continental Unity* (Boston, MA: C. W. Calkins, 1888), 7, 19.

could not support a North American Zollverein: "Our manufactures are too young and weak yet ... they would be crushed out just now."[49] John Hague, an outspoken proponent of "Canada for Canadians," was prominent among those who worried that commercial union was but another term for annexation. He gave a powerful speech before the Toronto branch of the IFL in January 1889, in reply to the "promoters of the Annexation of Canada" to the United States. "I lift up a protest against the sacrifice of Canada on the altar of American ambition," he roared. North American union was "a barbarous conception." These anti-imperial disciples of Goldwin Smith sought "to tie the red arteries between the heart of England and the hands of Canada, so as to stop the circulation of trade life flowing freely across the deep which Britannia rules." Smith and Wiman were thus "seeking to seduce Canada into what in Free Trade language is an 'act of war' against Great Britain ... preaching 'a gospel based upon the logic of dynamite and assassination,' – the assassination of a nascent nationality."[50]

The timbre and temper of the debate grew respectively more shrill and heated as Canadian Cobdenites sprung into action. In *Canada and the Canadian Question* Goldwin Smith argued that closer political union would guarantee hemispheric peace and that Canadians and Americans shared "geography, commerce, identity of race, language and institutions." The only barriers remaining were along economic and political lines. Edward Farrer's *Toronto Mail* likewise supported a customs union, vowing that reciprocity would bring an end to the fisheries dispute: "the only objection to it from this side of the line is that it might endanger British connection." On October 13, 1887, Sir Richard Cartwright – the former Dominion Finance Minister, staunch enemy of protectionism, one of Canada's leading Cobden Club members, and now a prominent member of the Canadian Liberal party – stated that "the advantages of commercial union to both countries ... are so great that scarcely any sacrifice is too severe to secure them." He argued rather presciently (see Chapter 8) that "refusal or failure to secure free trade with the United States is much more likely to bring about just such a political crisis as these parties affect to dread than even the very closest commercial connection that can be conceived."[51]

---

[49] Tansill, *Canadian-American Relations*, 381–382; Harold Francis Williamson, *Edward Atkinson: The Biography of an American Liberal, 1827-1905* (Boston, MA: Old Corner Book Store, 1934, 163; Macdonald to Tupper, July 28, 1884, John Macdonald Papers, LAC.

[50] John Hague, *Canada for Canadians* (Toronto: Hart, 1889), 5, 10, 13, 16, 19.

[51] Smith, *Canada and the Canadian Question* (London: MacMillan, 1891), 268, 278–279; *Toronto Mail*, March 1, September 2, 1887; Cartwright quoted in Prosper Bender,

To the joy of Cobdenites and the dismay of Canada's Listians, the policy of commercial union was fast becoming entrenched in the Canadian Liberal party platform. With the added support of J. D. Edgar and Wilfrid Laurier, the new head of the Liberal party, the Liberals adopted a resolution of unrestricted reciprocity in November 1887, with a stipulation that both countries would retain ultimate control of their own tariff policies. A few months later, and with US State Secretary Bayard's backing, Cartwright introduced a bill in the Canadian House of Commons asking for "full and unrestricted reciprocity." Upon the bill's defeat, Goldwin Smith consoled Bayard, writing him that it was not the "decision of the Canadian people, but simply that of Parliament elected before Commercial Union had come into the field." The next elections would tell "a very different tale," Smith promised. He was further encouraged by the friendly disposition of the Cleveland administration, and he held out hope that commercial and even political union could yet be achieved. The Canadian-American commercial union movement, after all, was spreading quickly.[52]

Conclusion

A politico-ideological approach to the fight over North American commercial union illuminates how the growing conflict between Listians and Cobdenites was reaching ever more international proportions. The stakes were high. The future of Canadian global economic integration hung in the balance. Much like in the United States, however, the Cobdenite battle for continental free trade was an uphill one. Remarkably, Cobdenites began receiving some American Listian aid within the US Congress on the issue of Canadian–American reciprocity, although the latter were approaching the issue from a decidedly protectionist viewpoint, envisioning instead a regionalized and insulated American-controlled economic zone throughout the Western Hemisphere that included Canada. In contrast to this temporary American alliance, Canadian Cobdenites like Goldwin Smith and their Liberal party allies were encountering sizeable Listian nationalist opposition from within the Conservative party, whose leaders sought infant industrial protectionism and a Greater British imperial federation bolstered by intra-imperial trade

"Canada: Reciprocity, or Commercial Union," *Magazine of American History* 19 (1888): 24.

[52] Willison, *Laurier*, II, 141; Robert M. Stamp, "J. D. Edgar and the Liberal Party: 1867–1896," *Canadian Historical Review* 45 (1964): 108–112; Tansill, *Canadian-American Relations*, 400–401, 404, 408–409; Waite, *Arduous Destiny*, 191–193.

preference. Theirs was an alternative regionalized vision of Canadian economic integration – one with a decidedly imperial bent.

The late-Victorian battle between Listian nationalists and Cobdenite cosmopolitans over the future of North American economic integration was becoming ever more tempestuous even as the fisheries dispute itself reached a peaceable settlement. In January 1888, a "travelling Commissioner" of London's *Pall Mall Gazette* noted that "Commercial Union is the coming question for Canada .... My own experience is that outside of Ottawa ... three out of five of the most intelligent men I have met are enthusiastic Commercial Unionists." Over the next three years, Goldwin Smith, Erastus Wiman, the Liberal newspapers, and the Liberal leadership would work to persuade their fellow Canadians of the viability of North American free trade. Comparing the free-trade movement to that of the earlier one in England, Smith felt quite certain of the North American movement's ultimate success. Whereas the ACLL had taken seven years to fulfill its goals, he noted, "in less than a year the Commercial Union Club has seen the policy which it advocates adopted by one of the great political parties as the principal plank of the party platform."[53]

Canadian Conservatives and various manufacturing interests attacked the Liberal platform centered upon North American commercial union. Economic nationalist Conservatives in Canada made sure to include an amendment to Cartwright's bill that protected Canada's infant industries, in order that free trade with the United States "may not conflict with the policy of fostering the various industries and interests of the Dominion." The Toronto branch of the IFL passed a resolution in favor of imperial preference at its 1888 annual meeting. Imperial federationist George Denison called upon fellow imperial loyalists in Canada "to rally round the old flag and frustrate the evil designs of traitors." Canadians, Denison warned, needed to be especially wary in their dealings with their hostile southern neighbor. "I believe they will endeavour to destroy our national life by force or fraud whenever they can, with the object of absorbing us." While Goldwin Smith and Erastus Wiman crisscrossing Canada's countryside, the IFL sent their Canadian spokesmen George Parkin and Principal Grant to Australasia to garner enthusiasm

---

[53] "Travelling Commissioner" quoted in W. R. Graham, "Sir Richard Cartwright, Wilfrid Laurier, and Liberal Party Trade Policy, 1887," *Canadian Historical Review* 33 (1952): 12–13; Willison, *Laurier*, II, 150; *Handbook of Commercial Union: A Collection of Papers Read before the Commercial Union Club, Toronto, with Speeches, Letters and Other Documents in Favour of Unrestricted Reciprocity with the United States*, ed. by Mercer Adam, Introduction by Goldwin Smith (Toronto: Commercial Union Club of Toronto, 1888), xxx–xxxi, xxxiii.

for the IFL and to help foment "the spirit of Imperialism" among the British colonies of Australia and New Zealand, giving the movement a further impetus.[54] The Listian–Cobdenite ideological conflict over Canada's position within the global economy was reaching a head – although its conclusion would await the passage of the 1890 McKinley Tariff under the Listian Republican administration of Benjamin Harrison.

[54] *Toronto Globe*, December 31, 1887; *Canada, Debates of the House of Commons* (March 15, 1888), 194; Denison, *Struggle for Imperial Unity*, 92, 124–127.

7 "A sea of fire"

The McKinley Tariff and the imperialism of economic nationalism, 1889–1893

Protection is spreading the world over, and the mission of the Cobden Club will, before many years, be over, when they see they can in no country or colony obtain a foothold.

Tariff League Bulletin (New York), 1888.[1]

The British have been waiting with an abiding faith in their Cobden theories for the world to acknowledge their supremacy in manufacturing and to tear down their tariff walls .... John Bull laughed sneeringly at their lack of faith in the creed of Cobden and waited for time to teach the American, the German and the Frenchman the error of their ways. But time has done just the opposite .... Verily, Cobden's theory was unsound. *Lowell Daily Courier* (Massachusetts), August 17, 1891.

Despite his promise to David Ames Wells that he would "keep clear of the Philadelphians altogether," from the mid-1880s to the mid-1890s, Edward Atkinson kept up a brutally candid correspondence with Philadelphia's Henry Carey Baird (1825–1912) on their opposing visions of the past, present, and future of the American political economy. Not surprisingly, Atkinson differed "fundamentally" with Baird on the issues of the day. Atkinson was a prominent Cobdenite free trader who considered protectionism a "perversion of the taxing power of the United States," and "among the worst of the sequels of slavery." He was also an outspoken critic of "the wretched silver business" and of Republican imperialism, as well as an unabashed Anglophile. Baird instead was a disciple of his uncle, Listian nationalist Henry Charles Carey. Baird had inherited his uncle's Anglophobic, protectionist worldview and his monetary predilections for national silver coinage. To Baird, Atkinson's persistent attacks against protectionism showed him to be a "lunatic" for single-mindedly seeking his free-trade system of cheapness. Cheap foreign commodities only resulted in an idle labor force that might otherwise have been employed in the home market, Baird asserted, and "the philosophy which aims at these things should be denounced, and the philosophers themselves put

---

[1] "Protection in New Zealand," *Tariff League Bulletin*, November 9, 1888, 213.

down."[2] Baird sought to educate Atkinson on Pennsylvania's rich Listian nationalist tradition – a realist, progressive, protectionist doctrine that sought regionalized foreign market expansion by way of high tariff walls, coercive retaliatory trade reciprocity, and, when necessary, formal imperialism. Atkinson in turn hoped that Baird might at least grudgingly come to accept some of the basic tenets of Cobdenism, the anti-imperial belief that international free trade and a non-interventionist foreign policy would bring about American prosperity and world peace.

Recalcitrance was met with recalcitrance. Their conflicting global visions for American economic integration were irreconcilable. Baird proved particularly intransigent, ideologically proud of the material fruits procured from Gilded Age protectionist productivity. Atkinson, in an attempt to match Baird's "dogmatic effusion," expressed his own incomprehension regarding the mid-century ideological shift from free trade to protectionism of Baird's uncle. Baird returned the favor, questioning whether American Cobdenite leader David Ames Wells had ever truly been a disciple of Carey: that Wells was instead duplicitously posing "before the world ... as a man who once sat at the feet of Carey, but who finally saw the truth." Baird suggested that unless Atkinson, Wells, and Grover Cleveland could do a better job of "convincing the American people of the truth of the British free trade ideas," they "had better retire from the field," because Baird's protectionist philosophy would continue to enlist "in its behalf strong and earnest men, who in former days were British free traders."[3] Baird's progressive brand of Anglophobic protectionism was rising in prominence among an influential cohort of Republican politicians, among them William "Pig Iron" Kelley (R-PA); Congressman William McKinley (R-OH); New York Tribune editor Whitelaw Reid, Benjamin Harrison's ambassador to France (1889–1892) and vice-presidential running mate in 1892; Republican advisor John Kasson; and the "Plumed Knight" of Maine, James G. Blaine, the incoming Republican secretary of state. Friedrich List's American System had found formidable late-nineteenth-century defenders, and they found themselves in powerful positions for expanding American markets through the imperialism of economic nationalism.

These Listian Republican leaders of economic nationalism in turn would receive ideological reinforcement from multiple new and enterprising sources. One came from the neo-mercantilist work of Alfred Thayer

---

[2] Atkinson to Wells, April 5, 1890, carton 20; Atkinson to Baird, July 29, 1885, carton 17; Baird to Atkinson, January 7, 1885, carton 3; Baird to Atkinson, April 20, 1892; April 22, 1892, carton 5, Edward Atkinson Papers, MHS.

[3] Atkinson to Baird, January 22, 1891, carton 20; Baird to Atkinson, January 23, 1891; Baird to Atkinson, March 3, 1893, carton 6, Atkinson Papers.

Mahan, the influential proponent of American colonial expansion and "navalism." Another came from the Gilded Age Christian advocates of the Social Gospel, who combined their missionary zeal with a desire for economic nationalist legislation in order to bring about social justice at home. They themselves received strong intellectual support from the late-nineteenth-century American leaders of the German Historical School. With Friedrich List as the school's foremost forerunner, this new economic nationalist school had arisen in Germany as a challenge to *Manchestertum* (the German term for the "Manchester School" or "Cobdenism") in the 1870s and 1880s, coinciding with the establishment of List's long-sought German Zollverein.[4] Many young Americans undertook an "Atlantic crossing" to study at German universities from the 1870s onward. They brought the teachings of the German Historical School back to the United States, reinforcing the economic nationalist opposition to the Cobdenite teachings commonplace within American universities. The transatlantic rise of the German Historical School consolidated into the "German-American school of economics."[5]

Alongside such newfound economic nationalist support, Listian legislation was of course high on the Harrison administration's imperial

[4] Yuichi Shionoya, ed., *The German Historical School: The Historical and Ethical Approach to Economics* (London: Routledge, 2001), 7, 189; Shionoya, *The Soul of the German Historical School: Methodological Essays on Schmoller, Weber and Schumpeter* (New York: Springer, 2005), 1, 14; Andrew Zimmerman, *Alabama in Africa: Booker T. Washington, the German Empire, and the Globalization of the New South* (Princeton, NJ: Princeton University Press, 2012), 74–75; Peter Koslowski, ed., *The Theory of Ethical Economy in the Historical School: Wilhelm Roscher, Lorenz von Stein, Gustav Schmoller, Wilhelm Dilthey and Contemporary Theory* (Berlin: Springer, 1997), 59; Daniele Archibugi and Jonathan Michie, eds., *Technology, Globalisation and Economic Performance* (Cambridge: Cambridge University Press, 1997), 6; Erik Grimmer-Solem, *The Rise of Historical Economics and Social Reform in Germany, 1864–1894* (New York: Oxford University Press, 2003), 32–33; Daniel T. Rodgers, *Atlantic Crossings: Social Politics in a Progressive Age* (Cambridge, MA: Harvard University Press, 1998), 82–83; Geoffrey Hodgson, *How Economics Forgot History: The Problem of Historical Specificity in Social Science* (London and New York: Routledge, 2001), 58.

[5] See Rodgers, *Atlantic Crossings*, chap. 3; Jurgen Herbst, *The German Historical School in American Scholarship: A Study in the Transfer of Culture* (Ithaca, NY: Cornell University Press, 1965), chap. 6; Brian Balogh, *A Government Out of Sight: The Mystery of National Authority in Nineteenth-Century America* (New York: Cambridge University Press, 2009), chap. 9; Axel R. Schafer, *American Progressives and German Social Reform, 1875–1920* (Stuttgart: F. Steiner, 2000), 37–40; Sidney Fine, "Richard T. Ely, Forerunner of Progressivism, 1880–1901," *Mississippi Valley Historical Review* 37 (March 1951): 599–624; Jack C. Myles, "German Historicism and American Economics: A Study of the Influence of the German Historical School on Economic Thought" (PhD Diss., Princeton University, 1956); Carl Diehl, *Americans and German Scholarship, 1770–1870* (New Haven, CT: Yale University Press, 1978); James T. Kloppenberg, *Uncertain Victory: Social Democracy and Progressivism in European and American Thought, 1870–1920* (New York: Oxford University Press, 1986); Keith Tribe, *Strategies of Economic Order: German Economic Discourse, 1750–1950* (Cambridge: Cambridge University Press, 1995).

agenda. Yet revisionist histories have instead portrayed these imperial policies as "mechanisms of free trade imperialism" on behalf of an American "Open Door Empire."[6] On the contrary, in marked contrast to the Cobdenite policies of the previous Cleveland administration, Harrison embraced a combination of imperial expansion, retaliatory reciprocity, and high tariff walls in order to increase foreign market access. These Listian policies sought the establishment of an expansive closed-door empire by way of the imperialism of economic nationalism: an imperial policy enacted largely in *response to* British free-trade imperialism in South America and the Pacific, and fears of British free-trade imperialism in the United States. This Listian implementation of the imperialism of economic nationalism was made possible upon the passage of the revolutionary 1890 McKinley Tariff, and put into practice through the Harrison administration's subsequent coercive expansionist designs toward the "uncivilized" markets of Latin America and the Pacific.

Protectionism's second wave: the social gospel, Mahan, and the rise of the German-American school of economics

Cleveland's 1888 presidential loss, the Republican rise to power of a Listian nationalist administration, and the mounting attacks against free trade once again disheartened American Cobdenites while putting protectionists, orthodox and progressive alike, on the offensive. Anti-free-trade ideological ranks swelled with the addition of Protestant adherents to the Social Gospel, women and men who found themselves at odds with the growing Social Darwinian laissez-faire belief that the biological "survival of the fittest" theory might also apply to the capitalist marketplace. Proselytizers of the Social Gospel instead viewed the inevitable societal conflict and economic inequalities associated with Social Darwinism as immoral and unchristian, even as their own missionary zeal began taking on imperial manifestations in the Asia-Pacific at the turn of the century.[7]

---

[6] Steven Topik, *Trade and Gunboats: The United States in the Age of Empire* (Stanford: Stanford University Press, 1996), 4. W. A. Williams, Walter LaFeber, and other revisionists have placed the Harrison administration's policies firmly within their influential "Open Door Empire," what Williams first defined as "America's version of the liberal policy of informal empire or free trade imperialism." W. A. Williams, *The Tragedy of American Diplomacy* (New York, 1972 [1959]), 97, 55–56. Elizabeth Cobbs Hoffman, in turn, suggests President McKinley merely copied the British "with respect to free trade," in her provocative *American Umpire* (Cambridge, MA: Harvard University Press, 2013), 194.

[7] Sidney Fine, *Laissez Faire and the General-Welfare State: A Study of Conflict in American Thought, 1865-1901* (Ann Arbor: The University of Michigan Press, 1956), 169–197; Barbara Reeves-Ellington, Kathryn Sklar, and Connie Shemo, eds., *Competing Kingdoms: Women, Mission, Nation, and the American Protestant Empire, 1812-1960* (Durham: Duke University Press, 2010); Ian Tyrrell, *Reforming the World: The Creation of America's Moral*

Proponents of the Social Gospel found strong intellectual leadership following the late-nineteenth-century American establishment of the List-inspired German Historical School. The latter arose as a late-nineteenth-century challenge to Cobdenism, just as the German Zollverein was coming to fruition.[8] As a counter to the classical laissez-faire doctrines that dominated nineteenth-century American and British political economy classrooms, these German political economists and sociologists openly attacked the Manchester School and instead laid out a progressive Listian vision of economic nationalism before an eager transatlantic audience.

This German doctrine of anti-*Manchestertum* soon made its way to US shores, ushering in a second wave of American Listian nationalism. The 1870s and 1880s witnessed a demonstrable increase in US students traveling to Germany to study under these deans of the German Historical School. Their teachings provided US students with a Listian critique of Cobdenism alongside an inductive approach to economics that relied upon historical observation rather than upon the deductive "laws" of British classical economics. American students returned from their studies at German universities instilled with the positive notions of an activist government – and a negative view of Cobdenism.[9]

Among the hundreds of Americans who studied in Germany from the 1870s onward, a handful stood out for finding academic sanctuary in the United States from which they could spread the Listian nationalist gospel.[10] The University of Wisconsin welcomed sociologist Albion Small, who habitually lectured his students on the "abomination of

---

Empire (Princeton, NJ: Princeton University Press, 2010); Tyrrell, *Woman's World/ Woman's Empire: The Woman's Christian Temperance Union in International Perspective* (Chapel: University of North Carolina Press, 1991); Carol C. Chin, "Beneficent Imperialists: American Women Missionaries in China at the Turn of the Twentieth Century," *Diplomatic History* 27 (June 2003): 327–352.

[8] The late-nineteenth-century inheritors of List's economic nationalist doctrine notably included German professors Gustav Schmoller, Willhelm Roscher, Johannes Conrad, and Adolph Wagner.

[9] Rodgers, *Atlantic Crossings*, 77.

[10] Harvard was similarly inculcated with the teachings of the historical school following the arrival of English economists William J. Ashley and William J. Cunningham in the 1890s. Ashley and Cunningham were associated with the so-called English Historical School – a variant of the German Historical School – and they would go on to support Joseph Chamberlain's Edwardian Tariff Reform Movement. See Katherine Clark Harris, "The Rise and Fall of the Practical Man: Debates Over the Teaching of Economics at Harvard, 1871–1908" (BA honors thesis, Harvard University, 2010); Edward S. Mason and Thomas S. Lamont, "The Harvard Department of Economics from the Beginning to World War II," *Quarterly Journal of Economics* 97 (August 1982): 383–433; Robert L. Church, "Sociology at Harvard 1891–1900," in *Social Sciences at Harvard, 1860–1920: From Inculcation to the Open Mind*, ed. by Paul Herman Buck (Cambridge: Harvard University Press, 1965).

laissez-faire," and W. F. Allen, strong opponent of "the extreme laissez faire of the dominant economics." James Riley Weaver was determined to put in his "best *licks* to destroy the pernicious influence of that old Manchester school" from his classroom pulpit at Indiana's DePauw University. Black intellectual W. E. B. Du Bois, a student of Gustav Schmoller at the University of Berlin in the early 1890s, similarly developed a predilection for economic nationalism, seeing in it a way to help the plight of African Americans. He thereafter spent time at Wilberforce University in Ohio, the University of Pennsylvania, and Atlanta University. Economists Richard T. Ely, Edmund James, and Simon Patten all studied at the University of Halle in Berlin under the direction of Johannes Conrad. Upon returning to the United States, Ely first joined the Johns Hopkins University (1881–1892), followed by the University of Wisconsin (1892–1925).[11] James and Patten found a welcome home at the University of Pennsylvania's new Wharton School in the early 1880s, where Robert Ellis Thompson, "much influenced by Friedrich List's nationalism in political economy," had already set up shop to teach students in the tradition of "the German-American school of economists founded by List and represented by H. C. Carey." Ely, James, and Patten would go on to found the American Economic Association (initially named the Society for the Study of National Economy) in 1885, which was to act as an American counterpart to the German Historical School's *Verein für Sozialpolitik* in their concerted transatlantic attack upon *Manchestertum*.[12] As historian Daniel Rodgers has described it, these young Americans set about to undermine "the intellectual edifice of laissez-faire." The arguments of Henry Carey and Friedrich List, the latter of whom Richard T. Ely considered "the ablest of the protectionists," aided these intellectual sappers and miners in their economic nationalist siege work.[13]

---

[11] Rodgers, *Atlantic Crossings*, 98, 102; Weaver quoted in John Braeman, "Charles A. Beard: The English Experience," *Journal of American Studies* 15 (August 1981): 172; Joseph Dorfman, "The Role of the German Historical School in American Economic Thought," *American Economic Review* 45 (1955): 20; Zimmerman, *Alabama in Africa*, 104–109, 209–212; Axel R. Schafer, "W. E. B. Du Bois, German Social Thought, and the Racial Divide in American Progressivism, 1892–1909," *Journal of American History* 88 (December 2001): 935–939.

[12] Robert Ellis Thompson, *Social Science and National Economy* (Philadelphia, PA: Porter and Coates, 1875), 28–29, 132; "Robert Ellis Thompson," *Home Market Bulletin* 11 (October 1899): 316; Rodgers, *Atlantic Crossings*, 98, 102; Zimmerman, *Alabama in Africa*, 104–109, 209–212; Schafer, *American Progressives and German Social Reform*, 52.

[13] Rodgers, *Atlantic Crossings*, 97; Richard T. Ely, *Problems of To-Day: Discussion of Protective Tariffs, Taxation, and Monopolies* (New York: Thomas Y. Crowell & Co., 1888), 56, 215; Ely, *An Introduction to Political Economy* (New York: Hunt & Eaton, 1889), 53–54, 210;

The Wharton School at the University of Pennsylvania, centered as it was within the protectionist heartland of Philadelphia, would provide one of the more attractive stations for American disciples of the German Historical School. Indeed, Pennsylvania industrialist Joseph Wharton had founded the Wharton School in 1881 in order to counteract the Cobdenite doctrines so prevalent within American universities. Wharton had been a longtime attendee of Henry Carey's weekly "Vespers," and a close friend of another local Philadelphia Listian, Stephen Colwell, who had solicited the first American translation of List's *National System* in the 1850s.[14]

Wharton quickly became a leader of the American protectionist movement. He helped to form the Industrial League of America in 1880, and was thereafter appointed vice president of the league's successor organization, the American Iron and Steel Association. Most notably, by founding the Wharton School, Germanophile Wharton ended up playing a pivotal role in expanding the Listian nationalist doctrine throughout the United States by providing an academic forum for returning young German-American political economists. As Axel Schafer has noted, it was here where Listians like Edmund James and Simon Patten were able "to help in the transformation of American civilization from an English to a German basis."[15]

American Listians found further intellectual support in 1890 with the publication of Alfred Thayer Mahan's popular study, *The Influence of Sea Power upon History*. In it, Mahan lavished praise upon that "man of great practical genius," the seventeenth-century French mercantilist Jean-Baptiste Colbert. According to Mahan, Colbert had managed to implement "the whole theory of sea power" through his expansion of naval power and central state authority in order to increase production, shipping, and the monopolistic exploitation of colonial economies for the benefit of the home market. Mahan subscribed to the realist proverb "in time of peace prepare for war," a maxim with which Listian nationalists like James G. Blaine wholeheartedly agreed. Neo-mercantilist Mahan believed that government policies ought to aid in the growth of industry and market expansion, and that peaceful commerce of necessity rested upon a strong navy. He extolled the Anglo-Saxon national character and

Ely, *The Story of Economics in the United States*, ed. by Warren J. Samuels (Oxford: JAI, 2002 [unpublished, 1931]), 101–104.

[14] Frederick List, *National System of Political Economy*, translated by G. A. Matile, preliminary essay by Stephen Colwell (Philadelphia, PA: J. B. Lippincott & Co., 1856).

[15] Steven A. Sass, *The Pragmatic Imagination: A History of the Wharton School 1881–1981* (Philadelphia: University of Pennsylvania Press, 1982), 15, 16, 28, 79, 84; Schafer, *American Progressives and German Social Reform*, 95.

the corresponding "unique and wonderful success" of the British-style settler colonial system, which he believed Americans were quite capable of replicating within "any fields calling for colonization." While American geographical isolation was "in one way a protection," it was one that would soon disappear with the development of an isthmian canal in Central America. In contrast to the southern and Cobdenite desire for a small and inexpensive naval force (believing that a large navy did not guarantee greater trade), Mahan advocated for a strong American navy to protect "one of the great highways of the world." He thus argued that the growth of protectionism, imperialism, global connectivity, and navalism were entwined. Harrison's secretary of the navy, Benjamin Tracy, would correspondingly oversee the creation of a new fleet of battleships, which added a further justification for a high tariff and contributed to the material benefit of American steel producers.[16] Such were the insurgent progressive protectionist forces that took the ideological fight to the American college classroom, to Cleveland's Cobdenites, and to the halls of Congress.

The protectionist evolution of William McKinley

Throughout the 1888 campaign trail, Harrison supporters had accentuated the supposed ties between Grover Cleveland and England. In political posters and cartoons, Cleveland had been depicted bowing before John Bull or standing under the British flag, in contrast to Harrison under the stars and stripes. Republican slogans included "Cleveland runs well in England" and "America for Americans – no Free Trade."[17] Cobdenites like David Ames Wells, Henry Ward Beecher, and MIT Professor Francis Amasa Walker may have deemed the farmers of the West as "the most fertile field ... for the dissemination of the virus of free trade," but the American Protective League reported triumphantly in the *Tariff League Bulletin* that Des Moines, Iowa's local "Cobden Club and American Free Trade organ" – Henry Philpott's *The Million* – had been suspended now

---

[16] A. T. Mahan, *The Influence of Sea Power Upon History, 1660–1783* (Boston, MA: Little, Brown, and Company, 1894 [1890]), 70–71, 27–28, 331, 82–83, 56–58, 33–34, 88; Peter Trubowitz, *Defining the National Interest: Conflict and Change in American Foreign Policy* (Chicago, IL: University of Chicago Press, 1998), 37–52. For the era's American Cobdenite critique of navalism, see, for instance, "The Uses of a Navy," *Nation* (April 18, 1889): 319–320; "Commerce and Big Guns," *Nation* (December 16, 1897): 470; Edward Atkinson, "A Forecast of the Future Commercial Union of the English-Speaking People," *American Association for the Advancement of Science for the Forty-Third Meeting Held at Brooklyn, N.Y. August, 1894* (Salem: Permanent Secretary, 1895), 416.

[17] Harry J. Sievers, *Benjamin Harrison Hoosier Statesman, 1865–1888* (Chicago, IL: H. Regnery Co., 1959), 408; Alfred E. Eckes, *Opening America's Market: U.S. Foreign Trade Policy since 1776* (Chapel Hill: University of North Carolina Press, 1995), 38–41.

that Iowa's farmers had seen through the paper's "thin guise of duplicity and anti-American interest." Republicans also worked to obtain the Irish vote by quoting the *London Times,* which had effectively stated that the "only time England can use an Irishman is when he emigrates to America and votes for free trade."[18]

American opposition to the Cobden Club swelled. Membership in the Anti-Cobden Club of Philadelphia had grown to over 1500, and Benjamin Harrison would end up appointing the club's president, David Martin, to the high federal position of Collector of Internal Revenue. Republican campaign tracts explicitly tied Cleveland to the Cobden Club. These pro-Harrison protectionists argued that voters had to choose between a Republican leader of "American Workingmen" on the one hand, and the "Cobden Club, British Manufacturers, and the Calhoun Autocracy of the South with Cleveland at their head" on the other. Voters were to "assume that there is a private understanding between the Cobden Club of England and the President of the United States," considering that Cleveland was "indebted" to the Cobden Club "for his political promotion" and was now surrounded by a cabinet made up of its members.[19]

With their anti-Cobdenite onslaught, the protectionists temporarily gained the political upper hand. Although it is difficult to measure their influence with precision, Cleveland's 1887 tariff message, his cabinet's connections to the Cobden Club, the failed 1888 Mills Bill, the amicable settlement of the Canadian fisheries dispute, and Sackville-West's political blunder in the Murchison affair all helped garner charges of a British conspiracy against Cleveland and win Anglophobic votes for Harrison. While Cleveland narrowly won the popular vote, he lost the electoral. The Listians entered the White House.

The new Republican administration found its spokesmen from among the party's leading Listian intellectuals. Fifty-nine-year-old James G. Blaine took control of the State Department and immediately went to work developing his longtime protectionist vision of a western-hemispheric Zollverein. Republican congressmen in turn looked to middleaged Ohio Representative William McKinley, the "Napoleon of Protection," for intellectual leadership.

McKinley's rise to Republican prominence had occurred nearly as rapidly as had Blaine's a couple decades earlier. McKinley first entered

---

[18] *Tariff League Bulletin* 1: 4 (October 1887): 25; John Devoy, "Irish Comments on an English Text," *North American Review* 147 (September 1888): 289.

[19] *Civil Service Record* 10 (June 1891): 120–122; Home and Country Protection Brotherhood Club, *England against America!* (Brooklyn, NY: Standard-Union Print, 1888), 1, 5, 11–12.

Congress's doors in 1876 at the age of thirty-four. A cigar-smoking, clean-shaven, good-natured congressman and respected orator, he almost single-mindedly tied his political fortunes to the Republican party's majority adherence to tariff protection. Pennsylvania's William "Pig Iron" Kelley, Henry Carey's longtime congressional protégé, helped direct McKinley's progressive economic nationalist development. In the late 1870s, Kelley took young McKinley under his protectionist wing, and McKinley was often referred to as "Pig-Iron Kelley's lieutenant." Under Kelley's tutelage, McKinley came to see high protective tariffs as essential to maintaining high wages for American labor and industrial development. Like many Midwesterners, McKinley was also sympathetic to the inflationary argument of the silverites. He had even voted for the 1878 Bland–Allison Act, which promised limited silver coinage, although in doing so he had ignored his own party's majority opposition to it. As he moved up the Republican political ranks, he would become quite adept at avoiding the subject of silver. Despite this, his earlier pro-silver position would come back to haunt him in the 1890s.

Yet monetary issues were always a distant second to that of the tariff for McKinley, and he entered national politics just as the tariff issue began to dominate the national scene. He established himself as the congressional expert when it came to defending the Republican party's majority protectionist position. In the early 1880s, McKinley also found himself in one of the most enviable and powerful positions as a member of the House Ways and Means Committee. He thereafter played an instrumental part in insuring that the Arthur administration's 1883 "Mongrel Tariff" – initially meant to lower tariffs and decrease the federal surplus – retained a strong protectionist bent. McKinley was likewise a pivotal force in blocking William Morrison's tariff reduction bills of 1884 and 1886; he endorsed both James G. Blaine and the 1884 Republican platform of high tariffs and international bimetallism; and he railed thunderously against Cleveland's 1887 annual message calling for liberal tariff reform.[20]

In McKinley's political economic worldview, protectionism epitomized American nationalism – and became akin to a religious conviction for him. He believed that "free trade, or a revenue tariff . . . has no respect

---

[20] David Ames Wells, "Tariff Reform: Retrospective and Prospective," *Forum* (February 1893): 703; Ida Tarbell, *The Tariff in Our Times* (New York: Macmillan and Co., 1911), 185–186; H. Wayne Morgan, *McKinley and His America* (Syracuse: Syracuse University Press, 1963), 54–66, 69, 74–78, 106–108; Edward Stanwood, *American Tariff Controversies in the Nineteenth Century*, 2 vols. (Boston, MA and New York: Houghton, Mifflin, 1903), II, 259–297; J. Laurence Laughlin and H. Parker Willis, *Reciprocity* (New York: The Baker & Taylor Co., 1903), 177–226; Tom E. Terrill, *The Tariff, Politics, and American Foreign Policy, 1874–1901* (Westport, CT: Greenwood Press, 1973), 53–55. Wells helped craft the Democratic minority report to the Mongrel Tariff.

for labor." Despite what the free traders would have the country believe, tariff-protected American manufacturers did not "bring cholera – they bring coin." In 1885, he proclaimed himself "a high protectionist." He juxtaposed the Republican protectionist doctrine with the Democratic "fallacies of Cobden and Bright and Calhoun, and the leaders of the Southern Confederacy," and he frequently denounced the "hypocritical cant" and "false and alluring appeal" of Cobdenism. He characterized US tariff reformers as "blind followers of Cobden," and suggested that their appeal to cheap products would degrade "American manhood." He further distinguished himself by crafting the dissenting minority report and gathered together some of his most invective orations against the proposed 1888 Mills bill, which he claimed drew its inspiration from the "Cobden school of political science" in its aim of "free-trade or a revenue tariff," and which "all Europe is watching the progress ... with the deepest concern and anticipating the rich harvest which awaits them when our gates shall be opened" and "our industrial defenses torn down." These Anglophobic protectionist attacks thrust him further into the national spotlight.[21] McKinley's general sentiments regarding the protective tariff – that it was essential for not only raising revenue but also for protecting infant industries and American laborers – persisted until his death.

McKinley's Listian outlook regarding foreign markets during the last two decades of the century would take quite a progressive turn, especially following the Panic of 1893. But from the mid-1880s to the early 1890s, he yet viewed global affairs in stark terms: "America as against the world," he once put it. During this period, he described the Democrats as "the pro-British party," allied "with the manufacturers and the traders of England, who want the American market." A closed home market sustained American industries and thus American labor, he believed, until the market eventually became fully prepared for international competition. The "markets of the world" were as yet "a snare and a delusion. We will reach them whenever we can undersell competing nations, and no sooner." In 1890, McKinley therefore initially expressed some doubt concerning Secretary of State Blaine's possible addition of a reciprocity provision to the McKinley Tariff.[22]

---

[21] Robert M. La Follette, *Robert La Follette's Autobiography: A Personal Narrative of Political Experiences* (Madison, WS: The Robert M. La Follette Co., 1913); William McKinley, *Speeches and Addresses of William McKinley from his Election to Congress to the Present Time* (New York: D. Appleton and Company, 1893), 190, 351, 290–335, 528, 489, 117–118, 340, 593; McKinley, *Mills Bill* (Washington, DC: Government Printing Office, 1888), 5, 28–29; Morgan, *McKinley and His America*, 108–114.

[22] McKinley, *Speeches*, 350.

But by the time McKinley entered the White House in early 1897 in the immediate wake of the 1890s economic depression, he would be a full-fledged Listian fan of foreign markets. He requested that "especial attention should be given to the reenactment and extension of the reciprocity principle of the law of 1890, under which so great a stimulus was given to our foreign trade in new and advantageous markets for our surplus agricultural and manufactured goods." He also called for making commercial treaties with "the end in view always to be the opening up of new markets for the products of our country." In 1899, he suggested that the tariff debate had all but disappeared, as the whole country turned its attention to "seeking our share of the world's markets." McKinley's economic nationalist ideology has frequently been construed as one of free trade.[23] Rather, McKinley's evolving protectionist vision from congressman to president epitomized the progressive expansionist worldview of a late-nineteenth-century Listian nationalist.

Protectionist politics and the passage of the 1890 McKinley Tariff

When Benjamin Harrison took office in early 1889, the Republicans controlled all three federal branches of government for the first time in many years, and so they went quickly to work on instituting protectionist legislation. They did so under the congressional guidance of Congressman William McKinley (R-OH), now chairman of the House Ways and Means. At this point, McKinley was still suspicious of the promised benefits of Listian trade reciprocity and foreign markets, and so he began work on a more orthodox protectionist bill.

While McKinley prepared his bill between 1889 and 1890, Secretary of State Blaine and William E. Gladstone, a mid-century Cobdenite convert and on-again-off-again British prime minister (1868–1874, 1880–1885, mid-1886, 1892–1894), publicly exchanged their views on the US economy. Gladstone predicted that the United States, to the benefit of both countries, would "outstrip" England in "the race" once the United States adopted a policy of free trade. Blaine responded by arguing that Britain had maintained a policy of protectionism so long as it was to its advantage, and only then shifted to free trade; Gladstone "speaks only for the free trade party of Great Britain and their followers on this side of the ocean." Blaine feared that a move away from protection in 1890 would result in economic recolonization by Britain, wherein the United States

---

[23] William McKinley, *Speeches and Addresses of William McKinley* (New York: Doubleday and McClure Co., 1900), 6–7, 198–199.

would essentially become a British dependency like Canada or Australia. According to Blaine, British Cobdenite encouragement of free trade was anything but altruistic; it was little more than British free-trade imperialism in disguise, recollecting how Cleveland's 1887 free-trade message exactly "adopts the line of argument used by the English Free-Trader."[24]

Blaine and Gladstone's public give and take received substantial transatlantic coverage. Edward Atkinson of course sided with Gladstone, having "never seen such an exhibition of conscious ignorance" as in Blaine's replies. Most egregious to Atkinson were Blaine's "misstatements ... so glaring" about England in the 1840s under Peel's reforms, as well as Blaine's "attempts to connect commercial crises with changes in the American Tariff." Atkinson also recognized that Blaine now had his hand on the executive and legislative "tiller." After all, he had been able to obtain Republican votes from every part of the country for the McKinley bill, and the administration had yet to fully use its trump card. "What is their trump card? Reciprocity," Atkinson noted with some prescience, just months before the successful insertion of the reciprocity provision and the bill's ultimate passage.[25]

Atkinson did attempt to rid William McKinley's new tariff bill of its more objectionable aspects. He did so by maintaining correspondence with the bill's most outspoken opponents, men like Democratic Congressmen John Carlisle, William L. Wilson, and Roger Q. Mills. When their opposition appeared futile, Atkinson, ever the pragmatist, thereafter encouraged Mills to switch tactics altogether by adding as much as he could to the new tariff's dutiable list in order to "load it down," with the aim of turning more than a few manufacturing interests against it. McKinley's rising influence within the Republican party also suggested to Atkinson "that the old party which I esteemed so much in former days has committed political suicide by making McKinley its leader."[26]

Atkinson also urged the various tariff reform leagues to set up a coordinated petition campaign in order to help sway the debate in the Republican-controlled Ways and Means Committee and to offset the protectionist propaganda. Yet he expressed his own private doubts to T. B. Potter, British founder of the Cobden Club, about bringing freer

[24] William Gladstone and James G. Blaine, in William Ewart Gladstone, et al., *Both Sides the Tariff Question by the World's Leading Men* (New York: Alonzo Peniston, 1890), 20, 57, 64, 61.

[25] Atkinson to Dawes, February 5, 1890, carton 19; "Memorandum," June 6, 1890, carton 20, Atkinson Papers.

[26] Atkinson to Mills, May 7, 1890, carton 20; Atkinson to Dawes, February 5, 1890, carton 19, Atkinson Papers.

trade to the United States in the near future. Atkinson feared that the country's prosperity would not force "people's attention ... to the excess of taxation." He also fully expected to "be charged with being a member of the Cobden Club and subject to the subtile [sic] influence of British gold" for his efforts. The ultimate passage of the 1890 McKinley Tariff – of which the dissenting report was devised by John G. Carlisle and David A. Wells – only confirmed Atkinson's doubts.[27]

Following great internal Republican debate, the McKinley Tariff also came to contain a retaliatory reciprocity provision that signified a demonstrable Listian shift in US protectionism for decades to come.[28] Secretary of State James G. Blaine was the mastermind behind this development, inspired by the Pan-American Congress being held in Washington at the same time as the tariff was being crafted, backed with the blessing and support of Harrison himself, and developed with the advisory aid of John A. Kasson. This revolutionary reciprocity provision had sturdy protectionist strings attached. While it provided the admittance of some agricultural goods from South American countries on an individual basis in return for their own duty-free acceptance of US goods, it also allowed for the president to raise rates in retaliation if a country offered unequal reciprocal rates, thereby granting a substantial increase in executive power regarding US foreign trade policy. Furthermore, in contrast to the inclusive most-favored-nation version of reciprocity favored by Anglo-American free traders so as to encourage an expansion of international trade liberalization, Blaine's exclusive reciprocity policies had the ability to instead encourage international retaliatory increases in tariff rates. As Blaine saw it, such coercive tariff measures would have the added benefit of inducing Latin American signatories – whose revenues came almost entirely from tariffs – to trade solely with the United States, thereby undermining the economic influence of the European powers in the Western Hemisphere, especially Britain's.

McKinley himself found the reciprocity idea intriguing, but was not enticed enough to help sway the Ways and Means Committee's more reluctant congressional Republicans, home-market protectionists who were yet distrustful of Blaine's regionalized economic nationalist vision for foreign market expansion. The proposed provision therefore did not

[27] Atkinson to Wells, January 2, 1890; Atkinson to Potter, December 31, 1889, carton 19, Atkinson Papers; Edward Atkinson, *Taxation and Work: A Series of Treatises on the Tariff and the Currency* (New York and London: G. P. Putnam's Sons, 1892), 266; Terrill, "David Ames Wells," 550; James A. Barnes, *John G. Carlisle, Financial Statesman* (New York, Dodd Mead & Co., 1931), 189–192.

[28] Carolyn Rhodes, *Reciprocity, U.S. Trade Policy, and the GATT Regime* (Ithaca, NY: Cornell University Press, 1993), chap. 2.

initially make it into the first draft put before the House of Representatives. Robert La Follette, a Republican committee member, afterwards recalled being most surprised by the initial misunderstanding surrounding Blaine's reciprocity doctrine: "It was astonishingly confused with what might be called the Democratic doctrine. The Republican doctrine, as expounded by Blaine ... is a kind of double protection for American industries – protection of the home market against foreigners, and extension of the foreign market for Americans." Blaine's proposed provision was, La Follette acknowledged, the opposite of the Democratic version of reciprocity.[29]

Even though Republicans controlled both houses of Congress and the executive, passage of the tariff bill was not a foregone conclusion. McKinley led the protectionist charge in the House debate, claiming that the tariff bill – still bereft of its reciprocal punch – was but fulfilling the Republican mandate of the 1888 elections. McKinley's economic nationalist convictions showed throughout; he advocated for protectionism "because enveloped in it are my country's highest development, and greatest prosperity ... out of it come the greatest gains to the people ... the widest encouragement for manly aspirations," and "elevating our citizenship, upon which the safety and purity and permanency of our political system depend."[30] McKinley sympathized with his fellow Republicans' fears of Blaine's proposed retaliatory reciprocity policy and the extra power Congress would be ceding to the executive. McKinley did not, however, exclude the possibility of its future addition. Thus, without the inclusion of Blaine's provision, the House bill passed upon party lines: 164 Republicans in favor to 142 Democrats in opposition.

Now it was the Republican-controlled Senate Finance Committee's turn with the bill. The committee was headed by none other than elderly Vermont Senator Justin Morrill – author of the Republican party's first protectionist legislation back in 1861 (see Chapter 2) – who designated a younger protectionist senator, Nelson Aldrich, to take the legislative lead. When the bill finally reached the Senate floor, it contained over 400 new amendments. The embryonic US tin plate industry gained strong

---

[29] William McKinley, *The Tariff in the Days of Henry Clay and Since. An Exhaustive Review of Our Tariff Legislation from 1812 to 1896* (New York: Henry Clay Publishing Co., 1896), 139; Morgan, *McKinley and His America*, 129–130; Kasson to Blaine, December 26, 1888, reel 11, Blaine Papers; La Follett, *Autobiography*, 111–114; *Washington Post*, July 26, 1890, 1. The bill was also tied up with Blaine's retaliatory measures against an ongoing European boycott of American pork. See Tyler, *Foreign Policy of Blaine*, 292–301; John L. Gignilliat, "Pigs, Politics, and Protection: The European Boycott of American Pork, 1879–1891," *Agricultural History* 35 (January 1961): 11–12.

[30] *CR*, 51 Cong., 1 sess., 6256–6259; McKinley, *Speeches* (1893): 397–430; Laughlin and Willis, *Reciprocity*, chaps. 6–7.

protectionist support. Duties were also placed upon farm goods for the purpose of blocking Canadian and European importations of various foodstuffs, both as a way to entice western agrarians and to demonstrate that the new tariff was more than just an eastern manufacturer's bill.[31]

Yet Senate Republicans still remained disunited behind the legislation. A small but pivotal group of Silver Republican senators representing the western states realized that their bloc vote could potentially determine the McKinley bill's success or failure, and decided to use their position to obtain silver concessions from their fellow Republicans. The sound-money Republican majority therefore reluctantly conceded a modest silver bill in order to maintain tariff cohesion. Alongside Republican machinations regarding wool and federal military pensions, the resulting 1890 Sherman Silver Purchase Act thus temporarily united the Republican party's free silver, international bimetallic, and gold wings, garnering the votes needed to push McKinley's high tariff bill through the Senate.[32]

Blaine also used this senatorial confusion to his advantage. He once again sought to put in place his Listian reciprocity provision, coupled with an extended free list on non-competitive goods in order to provide certain American manufacturers with cheaper access to raw materials. He went to great lengths to gain support, promising that increased US exports to Latin America would follow reciprocity, complemented by US-subsidized pan-American railroad and steamship lines. He gave impassioned pleas before McKinley's House Ways and Means Committee. And he garnered agrarian support for reciprocity by arguing that the bill as it stood would not open up any new markets for agricultural products, whereas with reciprocity the bill would at once spread American influence throughout Latin America, maintain the Republican policy of protection, and increase foreign exports. On this account, he wrote an open letter to a member of the Senate Finance Committee warning that Great Britain was securing wheat from India, and that Russia was arising as another competitor in the European wheat market. Blaine argued that the United

---

[31] Douglas A. Irwin, "Did Late-Nineteenth-Century U.S. Tariffs Promote Infant Industries? Evidence from the Tinplate Industry," *Journal of Economic History* 60 (June 2000): 335–360; Morgan, *McKinley and His America*, 130–151.

[32] Led by Senator Henry Teller of Colorado, the small contingent of Silver Republicans would bolt upon the 1896 Republican National Convention's endorsement of gold. Fred Wellborn, "The Influence of the Silver Republican Senators, 1889–1891," *Mississippi Valley Historical Review* 14 (March 1928): 467–471; H. Wayne Morgan, "Western Silver and the Tariff of 1890," *New Mexico Historical Review* 35 (1960): 118–128; Jeannette P. Nichols, "Silver Diplomacy," *Political Science Quarterly* 48 (December 1933): 579–580; Richard Franklin Bensel, *The Political Economy of American Industrialization, 1877–1900* (Cambridge: Cambridge University Press, 2000), 488–506.

States needed "to use every opportunity for the extension of our market on both of the American continents." In part owing to Blaine's persistence, McKinley was beginning to come around to the reciprocity idea, and he also saw the extended free list and reciprocity provision as a way to sugarcoat the bill for mid- and northwestern agrarian consumption by offering farmers new export markets in Latin America and Europe.[33]

With McKinley's newfound support in the House, Blaine's hard-fought retaliatory reciprocity provision was finally incorporated, and Harrison signed the bill into law on October 1, 1890. McKinley afterwards described the tariff as "protective in every paragraph, and American in every line and word. It recognized and fully enforced the economic principle of protection, which the Republican party from its birth had steadfastly advocated." It was as Blaine and Harrison had wanted: a system of reciprocity that did not "attack the protective system," but complemented it.[34]

Blaine, with the backing of Harrison, had begun to align the Republican party behind his Listian nationalist vision. Yet this protectionist shift did not come about because Blaine was appealing to the Republican party's "free trade sentiment," to establish a "free trade zone," or out of some desire for an informal free-trade empire, as various revisionist imperial historians have suggested.[35] It was quite the opposite. The Republican party was by now effectively bereft of any free-trade sentiment. Rather, Blaine had to persuade the party's various powerful orthodox protectionists who still stubbornly favored the home market over potential foreign ones that his reciprocity scheme upheld the American System. So where American Cobdenites could claim some small measure of success stemming from Cleveland's 1887 annual message, the reciprocity provision of the McKinley bill can be viewed as an indelible mark of progress for American Listian nationalism. Enough

---

[33] Douglas A. Irwin, "Explaining America's Surge in Manufactured Exports, 1880–1913," *Review of Economics and Statistics* 85 (May 2003): 374; Morgan, *McKinley and His America*, 130–151, 143; David S. Muzzey, *James G. Blaine: A Political Idol of Other Days* (New York: Dodd, Mead Co., 1934), 437–450; Joseph Smith, *Illusions of Conflict: Anglo-American Diplomacy Toward Latin America, 1865–1896* (Pittsburgh, PA: University of Pittsburgh Press, 1979), 144; Blaine letter, in Gail Hamilton, *Biography of James G. Blaine* (Norwich, CT: The Henry Bill Publishing Company, 1895), 686; Hilary A. Herbert, "Reciprocity and the Farmer," *North American Review* 154 (April 1892): 414–423; Trubowitz, *Defining the National Interest*, 75–91.

[34] McKinley, *The Tariff in the Days of Henry Clay and Since*, 141; Harrison to Blaine, October 1, 1891, in Albert T. Volwiler, ed., *The Correspondence between Benjamin Harrison and James G. Blaine, 1882–1893* (Philadelphia, PA: American Philosophical Society, 1940), 202.

[35] Topik, *Trade and Gunboats*, 2, 4; Walter LaFeber, *The Cambridge History of American Foreign Relations Vol. 2: The American Search for Opportunity, 1865–1913* (Cambridge: Cambridge University Press, 1993), 109.

Republican protectionists had finally begun to recognize the maturation of American farming and manufacturing so as to overrule the anti-reciprocity opposition, those men who were still unwilling or unable to admit that some of America's once-infant industries and products now needed foreign markets alongside domestic ones. Over the coming years, the US would accordingly transform itself from a large net importer to net exporter of manufactured goods. Dubbed by European critics as the "American commercial invasion," manufacturing exports would surge from 20 percent in 1890 to 35 percent in 1900 to almost 50 percent in 1913.[36] Following the passage of the McKinley Tariff, retaliatory reciprocity would become a common theme in US protectionist legislation. In 1890, the decades-long Listian era of Republican tariff policy – protectionism mixed with reciprocity – had begun.

Soon after the bill's enactment, other protectionists fell under Blaine's reciprocity spell. With retaliatory reciprocity, the act was, according to the protectionist *New York Tribune*, "not in conflict with a protective tariff, but supplementary thereto." Other Republican journals similarly fell into line. The *New York Times* reported on this change of view by the protectionist press. Within a year after the bill's passage, the Tariff Protection League's news organ had come to understand Blaine's "largeness of view," after initially condemning his reciprocity scheme as a traitorous assassination of protectionist principles. Nor was the league alone in its conversion. The *Times* noted that "now the same high-tariff journals . . . strive to soften the ire of dissatisfied Republicans by pointing out the beauties of 'reciprocity.'"[37] Reciprocity would thereafter become the lynchpin of Harrison's 1892 presidential run.

The free-trade press rather predictably waxed disconsolate. The *Chicago Tribune* argued that the McKinley Tariff was "economic stupidity," its reciprocity provision "the safeguard of protection." The New York Reform Club publication *Tariff Reform*, in its edition dedicated to the subject, labeled reciprocity "A Bungling Attempt to Patch up Protection," and "a sad commentary upon the home market theory."[38]

In contrast, American economic nationalists celebrated. The *New York Times* covered what it described as the "Tax Eater's Banquet," held in honor of William McKinley, the "hero of the hour," in the newly remodeled and massive Madison Square Garden. The lavish affair was a veritable nationalistic mockery of the era's cosmopolitan London and

---

[36] Irwin, "Explaining America's Surge in Manufactured Exports, 1880–1913," 364–365. See, also, Gavin Wright, "The Origins of American Industrial Success, 1879–1940," *American Economic Review* 80 (September 1990): 651–668.

[37] *New York Tribune*, August 31, 1890, 6; *New York Times*, August 29, 1891.

[38] *Chicago Tribune*, July 3, 1890, 4; *Tariff Reform*, March 30, 1892, 19.

Figure 7.1 **"All She Has to Hang on to."** Pro-Democratic *Puck Magazine* mockingly illustrates the new role of reciprocity within the Republican platform, with a weeping Republican party wrapping its arms around Blaine's "reciprocity" neck. *Puck Magazine*, February 11, 1891, front cover

New York free-trade club dinners. The enormous dinner hall was swathed in red, white, and blue, the walls lined with American palms and creeping vines. The mottos of the various states covered the gallery's front, each motto set in a rosette made of American flags. The food was served on crockery from Trenton, New Jersey. The 500 attendees, with smoke from domestic cigars encircling their heads, sipped on American wines from California, New York, and Ohio, and made toasts with four varieties of American-crafted champagne. The menu offered "Chicago Sausages," "chicken, Maryland style," "Washington tenderloin," and "Long Island asparagus." The less-than-objective *Times* reporter could not help but notice that among the finely tailored suits of the attendees, however, not one contained even "a vestige of homespun." The *Times* reporter predicted that the same probably went for the "underwear warming the sleek bodies of those who sat at the table." Near the end of the festivities, McKinley rose to speak amid great applause. He praised his protectionist legislation, while making sure to give a respectful nod to "that great statesman, James G. Blaine" and his retaliatory reciprocity provision.[39]

Republican festivities rallied the free-trade opposition. Taking aim at such protectionist celebrations, the 1892 Democratic party plank denounced the tariff's reciprocity element as antithetical to Democratic doctrine. With his eye on the 1892 presidential prize, Grover Cleveland described the measure as a counterproductive limp "in the direction of freer commercial exchanges. If 'hypocrisy is the homage vice pays to virtue,' reciprocity may be called the homage prohibitory protection pays to genuine tariff reform." American Cobden Club member Thomas G. Shearman wrote in the *London Times* that the McKinley Tariff had been "framed, advocated, and carried out in a spirit of hatred towards England, and in the hope of destroying many of her industries and ruining many of her people," as the Republicans themselves had argued on the 1888 campaign trail. The Harrison administration knew well how to twist the lion's tail – and tie it in a knot, too.[40] With the newfound support of William McKinley, the Listian "Plumed Knight" had also proven himself adept once again at counteracting the Cobdenite opposition. And the McKinley Tariff's granting to the executive branch the power to impose retaliatory duties further eased the way for the Listian application of the imperialism of economic nationalism.

Harrison's imperialism of economic nationalism

The new Republican tariff policy aligned neatly with Anglophobic expansionist designs. The revolutionary Listian tariff of 1890 followed on the heels of the publication and dissemination of an inflammatory map that suggested how Canada might be divided and incorporated through American annexation [figure 7.2]. An Anglo-American controversy arose surrounding fur-seal hunting by British vessels in the Bering Sea. Upon taking office, Harrison declared the British practice illegal. Arrests followed. The controversy reached a critical point between 1890 and 1891, as American newspapers warned of a possible outbreak of war,

[39] *New York Times*, April 30, 1891.
[40] McKinley, *The Tariff in the Days of Henry Clay and Since*, 159–160; *London Times*, October 6, 1890, 5; Grover Cleveland, *Addresses, State Papers and Letters*, ed. by Albert Ellery Bergh (New York: The Sun Dial Classics Co., 1908), 337; *London Times*, September 14, 1891, 11. For the global British reaction to the tariff, see Chap. 8.

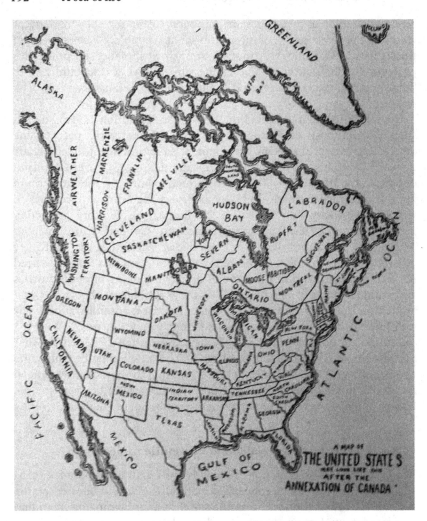

Figure 7.2 "A Map of the United States May Look Like This After the Annexation of Canada." Above is an alleged *New York World* map reprinted in a pamphlet distributed to the Toronto Branch of the Imperial Federation League. John Hague, *Canada for Canadians* (Toronto: Hart & Company, 1889)

Anglophobic sentiment swelled. Blaine himself fell ill amid the diplomatic conflict, whereby a satisfactory solution was settled upon that appeased both the British and American governments, but left Canadians outraged when they did not receive any payment for damages suffered at the hands of the United States. The issue made Canadian–American relations all the more acerbic for years to come, and deteriorated further when Anglophobic Republican opposition barred reciprocity with Canada under the McKinley Tariff.[41]

Canada and the British West Indies were effectively excluded from Blaine's Pan-American protectionist vision. The Pan-American Conference convened in Washington, DC, from 1889 to mid-1890, and the exclusion of the two British colonies indicated that the conference was a decidedly anti-British affair. The conference had been a pet project of Blaine's for some time now, desirous as he was to see US influence supplant that of the British Empire in Latin America. He had supported federal subsidization of steamship lines between the United States and Brazil as early as 1878, and he had nearly succeeded in bringing the Latin American states to the conference table as secretary of state under James Garfield, until Garfield's 1881 assassination halted the proposed conference. Blaine's Pan-American vision sought to bring perpetual peace to North and South America by ousting Britain from its dominant trading position in Latin America, and by cultivating commerce within the Western Hemisphere so as to "lead to a large increase in the export trade of the United States." His Anglophobic Latin American obsession also helps explain Blaine's support for the Chilean government when a revolt broke out in 1891, especially after the US minister to Chile reported his suspicions that the rebels were working for the British.[42]

The Pan-American Conference of 1889–1890 was a decidedly Listian enterprise. Blaine desired protectionist regional economic integration would minimize commercial competition from Europe and Asia through

[41] Charles S. Campbell, Jr., "The Anglo-American Crisis in the Bering Sea, 1890–1891," *Mississippi Valley Historical Review* 48 (December 1961): 393–414; Campbell, *The Transformation of American Foreign Relations, 1865–1900* (New York: Harper & Row, 1976), 122–125; Paul Gibb, "Selling out Canada? The Role of Sir Julian Pauncefote in the Bering Sea Dispute, 1889–1902," *International History Review* 24 (December 2002): 817–844. For a general overview of Harrison's "aggressive" foreign policy, see Homer E. Socolofsky and Allan B. Spetter, *The Presidency of Benjamin Harrison* (Lawrence: University Press of Kansas, 1987), 125–156.

[42] Smith, *Illusions of Conflict*, 130–154; A. Curtis Wilgus, "James G. Blaine and the Pan American Movement," *Hispanic American Historical Review* 5 (November 1922): 662–708; Russell H. Bastert, "A New Approach to the Origins of Blaine's Pan American Policy," *Hispanic Historical Review* 39 (August 1959): 375–412; James G. Blaine, *Political Discussions: Legislative, Diplomatic, and Popular 1856–1886* (Norwich, CT: The Henry Bill Publishing Company, 1887), 411; LaFeber, *American Search for Opportunity*, 80.

the adoption of hemispheric high-tariff walls, while allowing American exports privileged access to Latin American markets through the establishment of reciprocal trade, targeting tropical nations containing non-competitive exports. First and foremost, the Pan-American Conference promised a closed western-hemispheric trading bloc, a customs union that "would have meant practically that we had succeeded in forcing our tariff system upon the smaller countries associated with us, and that we had secured the territory of these smaller states as a field for the sale of our manufactures," according to Laughlin and Willis's detailed contemporary study.[43] Through reciprocal agreements, the Latin American signatories' excess raw materials would in turn receive privileged access to US markets.

Representatives from eighteen Latin American nations met in Washington from 1889 to 1891. They were greeted upon their 1889 arrival by "a palid figure with penetrating eyes, hair down on his forehead, an imperial smile and a smooth hand," as Cuban delegate José Martí described Secretary of State Blaine.[44] The conferees initially sought hemispheric unification not only through a customs union, but also through common silver coinage, a pan-American railroad system, increased port communications, an international bank, a uniform system of weights and measures, and international arbitration of disputes. The Argentine delegates found themselves in disagreement with the American proposals, however, and viewed Blaine's plan as little more than a ploy to dominate the markets of Latin America, where most countries relied almost entirely upon tariffs for their national revenue. The other Latin American delegates then chose one side or the other. Stalemated, Blaine's Pan-American Conference fell into disarray, although he would procure some of his desired reciprocal trade agreements with Brazil, Spain (on behalf of Cuba and Puerto Rico), the Dominican Republic, the British West Indies, El Salvador, Guatemala, Honduras, and Nicaragua between 1891 and 1892 owing to the McKinley Tariff's reciprocity provision, with drastic consequences for their tariff-dependent economies. These Listian shifts in US tariff policy in the early 1890s would not only destabilize the economies of Hawaii and Cuba – they would also spark revolutions.[45]

---

[43] Laughlin and Parker, *Reciprocity*, 134, 131–138.
[44] Bill J. Karras, "Jose Marti and the Pan American Conference, 1889–1891," *Revista de Historia de America* 77/78 (January–December 1974): 84.
[45] Smith, *Illusions of Conflict*, 130–154; David M. Pletcher, "Reciprocity and Latin America in the Early 1890s: A Foretaste of Dollar Diplomacy," *Pacific Historical Review* 47 (February 1978): 53–89; Pletcher, *The Diplomacy of Trade and Investment: American Economic Expansion in the Hemisphere, 1865–1900* (Columbia: University of Missouri Press, 1998), 237–279; David Healy, *James G. Blaine and Latin America* (Columbia: University of Missouri Press, 2001), chap. 9; Edward P. Crapol, *James G. Blaine: Architect of Empire* (Wilmington, DE: Scholarly Resources, 2000), 65–66, 111–136;

The Harrison administration's imperial impulse was put on further display when Harrison, Blaine, and Mahanite Secretary of the Navy Benjamin Franklin Tracy began actively seeking naval bases and coaling stations in the Caribbean and the Pacific. In the Caribbean, the administration looked to Mole St Nicholas in Haiti in 1891 as a future American coaling station and naval base to protect any future isthmian canal. The US government had never recognized the provisional government of Haiti that had been in power since 1888. Military aid was then funneled to Haitian insurgents after Harrison sent naval vessels to intimidate the unrecognized Haitian government. These US actions sped up the provisional government's overthrow. Frederick Douglass was then sent as the US minister to meet with Haiti's new leader, Hyppolite. Part of Douglass's mission was to secure a coaling station at Mole, and he was given further support for the undertaking with the arrival of US Admiral Gherardi. But Hyppolite refused both men's entreaties. With no other option than to seize the port by military force, Blaine, Harrison, and Tracy preferred instead to try to bloodlessly acquire Samaná Bay in the Dominican Republic. Rumors of the proposal were enough to outrage the Dominican people, who exiled their state secretary. Caribbean pride and Yankeephobia had foiled the Caribbean designs of Harrison, Tracy, and Blaine, much as the Pan-American Conference had similarly been undone.[46]

The Harrison administration's imperial efforts in the Pacific bore more fruit, or at least more sugar. At the Berlin Conference of 1889, Listians Blaine and John Kasson, with the support of a Republican-controlled Senate, made sure that American interests in Samoa were maintained, particularly US control over Pago Pago, which had become an important naval and coaling station along the US trade route to Asia over the years. At the conference Samoa was once again divvied up between the United States, Germany, and Britain. A decade later, under William McKinley's presidential watch, American Samoa would formally be added to the new US empire.[47]

Terrill, *Tariff, Politics, and American Foreign Policy*, 162–163; John D. Martz, "Economic Relationships and the Early Debate over Free Trade," *Annals of the American Academy of Political and Social Science* 526 (March 1993): 25–35.

[46] Healy, *Blaine*, 180–204; Crapol, *Architect of Empire*, 129–130; Alice Felt Tyler, *The Foreign Policy of James G. Blaine* (Hamden, CT: Archon Books, 1965 [1927]), 91–96; Ludwell Lee Montague, *Haiti and the United States, 1714–1938* (Durham, NC: Duke University Press, 1940), 94–109; Allan Spetter, "Harrison and Blaine: Foreign Policy, 1889–1893," *Indiana Magazine of History* 65 (September 1969): 214–227.

[47] Henry C. Ide, "Our Interest in Samoa," *North American Review* 165 (August 1897): 155–173; Ide, "The Imbroglio in Samoa," *North American Review* 168 (June 1899): 679–693; Sylvia Masterman, *The Origins of International Rivalry in Samoa, 1845–1884* (Stanford: Stanford University Press, 1934); G. H. Ryden, *The Foreign Policy of the United States in*

Lastly, the McKinley Tariff transformed the international sugar trade by placing raw sugar on the free list, while also offering a substantial bounty to the American beet sugar industry. The bounty artificially stimulated US sugar growing, which threatened the protected beet sugar interests in Europe and cane sugar exporters in Hawaii and Latin America. This subsidized boost to the US sugar industry in turn led to the substantial American growth of the so-called Sugar Trust.[48]

The sudden shift in sugar policy also had the effect of a "body blow on the Hawaiian sugar economy," as historian Robert Ferrell described it, thereby triggering the Hawaiian revolution that began in January 1893.[49] Simply put, since 1876 the United States had established reciprocal trade relations with Hawaii, and, since 1884, the US had extended its right to a coaling station at Pearl Harbor so as to take advantage of Hawaii's possible strategic and commercial role in accessing the long-sought China Market. However, the McKinley Tariff ended this earlier reciprocal agreement, displacing Hawaiian sugar from its favored position of unfettered access to the protected US market.

The change in policy precipitated an economic depression in Hawaii. Sugar made up 93 percent of the country's exports, and the 1890 tariff suddenly forced Hawaiian sugar growers into direct competition with the rest of the world's sugar producers, particularly those of Latin America and the heavily subsidized beet sugar industry in Europe. The new bill allowed raw sugar to enter the United States duty free, in part so that the Europeans would lift their embargo on American pork. The new bounty offered to US sugar producers therefore suggested to Hawaii's revolutionary leaders – predominantly US businessmen – that only American annexation could solve the myriad problems surrounding the islands' newly depressed sugar trade and Queen Liliuokalani's power grab. Those in favor of annexation also believed the Hawaiians were unfit for self-government, and hoped Hawaiian sugar producers might thereafter

Relation to Samoa (New Haven, CT: Yale University Press, 1933); Paul M. Kennedy, *The Samoan Tangle: A Study in Anglo-German-American Relations, 1878–1900* (Dublin: Irish University Press, 1974); Tyler, *Foreign Policy of Blaine*, 227–253; Milton Plesur, *America's Outward Thrust: Approaches to Foreign Affairs, 1865–1900* (Dekalb: Northern Illinois University Press, 1971), 198–204.

[48] Laughlin and Willis, *Reciprocity*, 139–176. For the confluence of the sugar lobby, the McKinley Tariff, and the 1890s depression, see, also, Leonard J. Arrington, "Science, Government, and Enterprise in Economic Development: The Western Beet Sugar Industry," *Agricultural History* 41 (January 1967): 1–18; Scott Reynolds Nelson, *A Nation of Deadbeats: An Uncommon History of America's Financial Disasters* (New York: Knopf, 2012), chap. 10.

[49] Robert Ferrell, *American Diplomacy* (New York: W. W. Norton, 1969), 329.

receive the same bounty US domestic producers had procured and thus bring an end to the Hawaiian economic depression.[50]

Blaine, his June 1892 State Department successor John Foster, and Harrison himself were more than happy to oblige the Hawaiian annexationists. They became all the more eager when the US minister to Hawaii and Blaine's close friend, John Stevens, intimated that Britain would annex the islands if the United States did not. Anglophobic sentiment was put on further display when it was reported that the Hawaiian attorney general, a Canadian, was leaning toward establishing an oceanic cable and steamship line with Vancouver and a reciprocity treaty with Canada. With this added Anglophobic bolstering, Alfred Thayer Mahan also threw his neo-mercantilist support behind the annexationist scheme.[51] Coinciding with Mahan's added intellectual backing, the Harrison administration seconded its support for the annexationists with naval power. US sailors landed on Hawaiian shores to protect American property and to intimidate the royalists in mid-January 1893. The queen was deposed the next day.

With anti-imperialist Cleveland's presidential win in late 1892 weighing heavily upon his mind, Harrison's new Republican Secretary of State John Foster desired speedy annexation. He therefore crafted a treaty that the US Senate might ratify before Harrison stepped down from office in early March. To hurry ratification, Foster turned down the annexationists' controversial requests for funding improvements at Pearl Harbor, as well as a clause allowing for the laying of an oceanic cable between Honolulu and the United States and a provision that would have allowed the Hawaiians to preserve their contract labor system. The treaty of annexation was signed on February 14, 1893, but was stalled in the Senate and stymied by the incoming Cobdenite administration of

---

[50] More than a few Hawaiian sugar producers, with scarce labor forces, initially opposed the revolution and annexation, fearing that US prohibition of Chinese labor would also apply to Hawaii. See LaFeber, *American Search for Opportunity*, 94; Merze Tate, "British Opposition to the Cession of Pearl Harbor," *Pacific Historical Review* 29 (November 1960): 381–394; Eric T. Love, *Race over Empire: Racism and U.S. Imperialism, 1865–1900* (Chapel Hill: University of North Carolina Press, 2004), 74–78; Julius W. Pratt, *Expansionists of 1898: The Acquisition of Hawaii and the Spanish Islands* (Chicago, IL: Quadrangle Books, 1964 [1936]); Richard D. Weigle, "Sugar and the Hawaiian Revolution," *Pacific Historical Review* 16 (February 1947): 41–58; William A. Russ, Jr., "The Role of Sugar in Hawaiian Annexation," *Pacific Historical Review* 12 (December 1943): 339–350; George W. Baker, "Benjamin Harrison and Hawaiian Annexation: A Reinterpretation," *Pacific Historical Review* 33 (August 1964): 295–309; Gignilliat, "Pigs, Politics, and Protection," 3–12; David M. Pletcher, *The Diplomacy of Involvement: American Economic Expansion across the Pacific, 1784–1900* (Columbia: University of Missouri Press, 2001), 234–242.

[51] Tyler, *Foreign Policy of Blaine*, 205; Alfred T. Mahan, "Hawaii and Our Future Sea Power," *Forum* 15 (March 1893): 1–11.

Grover Cleveland (see Chapter 9). The Listian implementation of the imperialism of economic nationalism in the Pacific would have to wait.[52]

Free trade strikes back

Imperial Republicans believed their progressive tariff policies had broad popular support, but between the November 1890 congressional elections and the 1892 presidential elections, American voters suggested otherwise. The promised benefits of the McKinley Tariff and its reciprocity provision did not materialize in time to maintain the Republican majority in Congress in November 1890. That month's congressional elections returned control of the House to the Democrats in a landslide: 236 Democrats to 88 Republicans. Edward Atkinson and his free-trade friends viewed with encouragement the Democratic congressional sweep just a month after the McKinley bill's passage, as it seemed to them that the American people were signaling their condemnation of the current state of high protectionism. West Virginia's William L. Wilson, a leading Democratic tariff reformer in the House, correspondingly vowed to Atkinson that "the organization of the next House will be aggressively Tariff reform," albeit with a "cautious and conservative" temper.[53]

Losing congressional ground to Cleveland's Cobdenites, Harrison's Listian administration lashed out. In February 1891, McKinley, still stinging from the 1890 Republican congressional losses, conspiratorially singled out US Cobden Club Secretary David Wells and his transatlantic ties, and noted that the Democratic sweep "established beyond dispute or controversy the existence of a partnership between Democratic free trade leaders in the United States and the statesmen and ruling classes of Great Britain."[54] In a press release, McKinley asserted that there had also been a successful "conspiracy between importers and free trade" to inflate prices and then "charge it upon the McKinley Bill." Johnstown, New York's partisan *Daily Republican* instead expressed skepticism about the apparent upswing in national support for freer trade: "Mugwumps and other theorists may construe the victory as an indorsement of Cobdenism," but the "Protectionist Democrats of the Randall School" were now growing restless. The Cobdenites might currently have

---

[52] Spetter, "Harrison and Blaine," 227; LaFeber, *Cambridge History*, 94; Love, *Race over Empire*, 73–78.

[53] Cobden Club, *The Annual General Meeting of the Cobden Club, 1893*, 3–4, 7; Atkinson to Fowler, June 14, 1890, carton 20; Wilson to Atkinson, December 2, 1890, carton 4, Atkinson Papers.

[54] McKinley, reported in *London Times*, February 14, 1891, 7; *London Times*, November 14, 1891; Gerald W. McFarland, *Mugwumps, Morals & Politics, 1884–1920* (Amherst: The University of Massachusetts Press, 1975), 65–67.

"command of the Democratic hosts," but "when the battle is on," the protectionist Democrats will be welcomed within the protectionist congressional ranks, and "as Protectionists, not as Republicans, we will teach politicians that no party can win by fighting under the banner of the Cobden Club."[55] The newspaper envisaged a new national political realignment based solely around the tariff rather than party allegiance.

In his 1892 letter of acceptance of the Republican presidential nomination, Harrison highlighted his four years of Anglophobic tariff legislation, hoping it might resonate with the American public. He made sure to note the adverse impact of the reciprocity treaties and the McKinley Tariff upon British trade. He also noted that British exports to Latin America had dropped significantly owing "directly to the reciprocity policy of the United States." The Republican national platform supported international bimetallism and resolutely defended its policy of protection mixed with reciprocity, noting that it had "enlarged markets" and would "eventually give us control of the trade of the world." A common Harrison campaign slogan, "Protection and Reciprocity," was illustrated in print in 1892 by a new pro-Harrison news organ entitled *Protection and Reciprocity*. The Harrison administration's Listian cry for foreign markets nevertheless fell flat amid a rising tide of Populism and silver agitation across the nation. Agrarian hardship was not only fueling the Populist movement, it was also turning some farmers away from protectionism and toward free trade. Furthermore, neither Harrison nor Blaine were able to campaign as they had in 1888, owing to a variety of personal issues, all of which took away a sizeable chunk of Republican votes.[56]

Nor had American Cobdenites given up on their hope for freer trade during the last four years of Harrison and Blaine, although the Listian administration had certainly tried their patience. During this period, free-trade clubs sprouted up in Maryland, Illinois, Massachusetts, Pennsylvania, and Missouri, and agitation grew in South Dakota and New Jersey. The absolute free trader Henry George observed: "Radical free trade is rapidly gaining ground." The Free Trade Club of Cleveland, Ohio, in turn sought to "drain" America's "dooryards of the foul stagnant miasmatic pool of protection" at their commemoration of Richard

[55] McKinley, quoted in Quentin R. Skrabec, Jr., *William McKinley: Apostle of Protectionism* (New York: Algora Publishing, 2008), 99; and Edward Thornton Heald, *The William McKinley Story* (Canton, OH: Stark County Historical Society, 1964), 61; *Daily Republican*, May 28, 1891.

[56] Republican National Convention, *Proceedings of the Tenth Republican National Convention, 1892* (Minneapolis, MN: Harrison and Smith, 1892), 167, 86; Donald Marquand Dozer, "Benjamin Harrison and the Presidential Campaign of 1892," *American Historical Review* 54 (October 1948): 49–77.

Cobden's birthday in June 1889. Presaging Cleveland's reelection, they noted that free trade was "a potent, living factor of progress and power for this country," and would "at no distant time ... become an adopted system of our people."[57] Alongside their usual propaganda campaigns, ever since the Great Debate of 1888 free-trade elements had taken to debating their protectionist counterparts as both sides vied for public support. For its part, the New York Reform Club – referred to by Rome, New York's *Roman Citizen* as the "twin sister of the Cobden Club" – debated the Protective Tariff League throughout the country in the lead-up to the 1890 elections. With over 500 attendees at its massive 1890 annual banquet in celebration of "the triumph of Tariff Reform" in the November congressional elections, the Reform Club's president proudly announced that their club had spent upwards of $55,000 during the 1890 elections, emphasizing as well for their Republican detractors that none of it was "British gold." The Reform Club furnished free-trade literature for "salting Protectionist meetings," as well as agrarian centers in Iowa and Ohio. Hundreds of newspapers also received and printed the club's free-trade literature on a weekly basis. And the Cobdenite American journal *Tariff Reform* was replete with depictions of Anti-Corn Law agitation alongside articles denouncing the McKinley Tariff and decrying the supposedly harmful effects of protectionism upon the laborer and the farmer, particularly the latter group as southern and western Populist agitation picked up momentum.[58]

More Americans were also looking toward Mexico as a potential trading partner. This had been a topic of some discussion ever since the proposal of a reciprocity treaty back in 1859. The prospect gained traction following the southern neighbor's reaction to US import duties on lead: duties put in place in the late 1880s and continued under the McKinley Tariff. In retaliation, the Mexican government had implemented its own duties on American meats and ship tonnage. This time, such retaliatory tariffs had their desired effect; aside from Colorado's miners,

[57] Wells to Charles Francis Adams, Jr., May 12, 1892, Folder 3, Box 2, Charles Francis Adams, Jr. Papers, MHS. *New York Tribune*, June 14, 1889, 6; March 28, 1892, 3; Ralph Russell Tingley, "American Cobden Clubs" (MA thesis, University of Chicago, 1947), 55–56, 59; Harold Francis Williamson, *Edward Atkinson: The Biography of an American Liberal, 1827-1905* (Boston, MA: Old Corner Book Store, 1934), 149–150; George to T. F. Walker, October 17, 1890, reel 5, Henry George Papers, NYPL; Ohio Free Trade Club, *Richard Cobden's Birthday* (Cleveland: Ohio Free Trade Club, 1889), 18, 19.

[58] *Roman Citizen*, November 22, 1890; Reform Club, *Report for 1890, with Summary Financial Statement* (New York: Reform Club, 1890), 10; *New York Tribune*, September 8, 1890, 6; September 29, 1890, 6; *Tariff Reform*, December 30, 1890, 2, 4; Reform Club, *Reform Club, Officers and Committees, Members, Constitution, By-Laws, Rules, Reports, &c* (New York: Albert B. King, 1890), 118–119, 122–128.

THE BELOW, COPIES OF WHICH THE AMERICAN PRO-
TECTIONISTS HAVE BEEN CIRCULATING, IS THE IDENTICAL
POSTER USED IN 1844 BY THE BRITISH MONOPOLISTS
AGAINST DANIEL O'CONNELL IN HIS FIGHT FOR FREE
BREAD AND CHEAPER FOOD FOR IRISH LABORERS.

O'CONNELL SUCCEEDED, AND GOT FOR IRISH LABORERS
CHEAPER FOOD AND TWICE THE DAILY WAGES THEY HAD
BEFORE. THE TARIFF REFORMERS ARE NOW FIGHTING
HERE FOR FREE WOOL, CHEAPER CLOTHES, AND HIGHER
WAGES FOR AMERICAN WORKMEN.

Figure 7.3 "Daniel O'Connell." The New York Reform Club
publication *Tariff Reform* republished the above poster, copies of which
"the American Protectionists have been circulating." In order to
connect their movement to the Anti-Corn Law League as well as gain
Irish-American support, *Tariff Reform* noted that the cartoon was
identical to the "poster used in 1844 by the British monopolists" against
Irish nationalist and abolitionist Daniel O'Connell "in his fight for free
bread and cheaper food for Irish laborers." *Tariff Reform*, June 15,
1889, 113[59]

[59] On the transatlantic influence of Daniel O'Connell, see David Sim, *A Union Forever: The
Irish Question and U.S. Foreign Relations in the Victorian Age* (Ithaca, NY: Cornell
University Press, 2014).

who gained most from the lead duties, US interest in reciprocal trade with Mexico was renewed.[60]

Mexico was of course not the only country that some Americans gazed upon with freer trade in mind. Edward Atkinson observed to Canadian businessman and commercial union advocate Erastus Wiman that "that there is a point in which the protectionist and the free-trader can come together," and that issue was Canadian reciprocity (see, also, Chapter 6). The industrial and agricultural areas bordering the two countries along New Hampshire and Maine were increasingly coming to understand that freer trade in a variety of raw materials was mutually beneficial. American duties on Nova Scotian coal, for instance, had been an area of complaint from New England manufacturers since the abrogation of Canadian–American reciprocity in 1866. This complaint resurfaced even more heatedly following the passage of the McKinley Tariff, which precluded the possibility of reciprocity with Canada.[61] Republican Anglophobia would nevertheless continue to effectively counter the ameliorating promise of Canadian–American reciprocity.

Condemnation of the Sherman Silver Purchase Act of July 1890 was also finding bipartisan support, with both silverites and goldbugs dissatisfied with the end result. The Cobdenite supporters of Cleveland remained staunch enemies of the free silver agitation. The group's handful of international bimetallists – seeking silver coinage solely on an

---

[60] Laughlin and Willis, *Reciprocity*, 10–11; Edward McPherson, ed., *The Tribune Almanac for 1893* (New York: The Tribune Association, 1893), 43–44; El Paso Board of Trade, *A Compilation of Resolutions, Statistics, and Useful Information Pertinent to the Mexican Silver-Lead Ore Question* (El Paso, TX: Times Publishing Company, 1889); Posey S. Wilson [Denver], "Reciprocity," *Million*, July 24, 1886; Pletcher, "Reciprocity and Latin America," 75–76; George E. Paulsen, "Fraud, Honor, and Trade: The United States-Mexico Dispute over the Claim of La Abra Company, 1875–1902," *Pacific Historical Review* 52 (May 1983): 187–188; Tyler, *Foreign Policy of Blaine*, 173–190; Walter LaFeber, *The New Empire: An Interpretation of American Expansion 1860–1898* (Ithaca, NY: Cornell University Press, 1998 [1963]), 28, 46–52; David M. Pletcher, *The Awkward Years: American Foreign Relations under Garfield and Arthur* (Columbia: University of Missouri Press, 1961), 180–190, 338–339.

[61] "How the Eastern States may Secure Cheap and Abundant Supplies of Bituminous Coal from Nova Scotia," *Free-Trader* 3 (February 1870): 147–148; "Reciprocity," *Million*, November 20, 1886, 297; "Reciprocity with Canada," *Million*, February 26, 1887, 406; Peleg McFarlin, *New England's Lost Supremacy. Shall it be Regained?* (Boston, MA: New England Tariff Reform League, 1891); Atkinson to Wiman, April 2, May 27, 1889, carton 19, Atkinson Papers.

international basis – was also strongly against the national bimetallic movement, and feared Democratic support for a free silver platform. Atkinson wrote Grover Cleveland that, "the free coinage of silver ... is condemned alike by every intelligent student of the currency ... whether bi-metallist or mono-metallist. I think it will promote a disaster or a panic such as we have never seen." Presaging the 1896 elections, Atkinson recognized that if the Democrats "are going wrong on the Money question, I, and plenty more of my kind, will join any other set of men, what ever party they belong to, and help them to break the Democrats and crush them into powder; as they ought to be crushed if they behave like fools."[62]

Cleveland responded as Atkinson hoped. The presidential hopeful wrote to the chairman of the Reform Club that unlimited coinage of silver was "a dangerous reckless experiment." Atkinson remarked to Wells in his usual prophetic manner that had Cleveland "not spoken on the silver question, he might have been nominated, but would have been defeated. Having spoken, he will be nominated and will be elected." Atkinson also felt that "the people are sick and tired of McKinleyism ... they will quietly support Cleveland in the reform of the Tariff," which he predicted would supersede the silver issue in due course.[63]

Atkinson therefore encouraged the Democrats to focus on the tariff question rather than monetary policy. He suggested that Wells use his ongoing debates with rogue Cobdenite Henry George over the Single Tax to focus attention on tariff reform. If George would thus "make the Single Tax secondary" to the tariff, "the alliance would be a very powerful one." Henry George was in apparent agreement. More than one million copies of his *Protection or Free Trade* were reprinted and distributed in support of Cleveland. Although George was fast becoming disillusioned with what he considered the Cobden Club's halfway solutions to revenue reform, he believed that Cleveland should get the nomination "because the tariffits [sic] of all degrees fear him, and well justified their fear. We should not permit any question to come up that will divert attention from the tariff fight. When men are attacked by wolves, they have no time to kill rats or

---

[62] Atkinson to Edmund Hudson, January 3, 1891; Atkinson to Cleveland, January 9, 1891, carton 20, Atkinson Papers; Williamson, *Atkinson*, 154–157.

[63] Cleveland to E. Ellery Anderson, February 10, 1891, in *Writings and Speeches of Grover Cleveland*, ed. by George F. Parker (New York: Cassell Publishing Company, 1892), 374; Atkinson to Wells, February 13, 1891, carton 20; Atkinson to Nordhoff, October 10, 1892, carton 22, Atkinson Papers.

fight gold-bugs." In proper Cobdenite verbiage, George then predicted that a united world "in the bonds of commerce and its guarantee of peace among the nations" was close at hand. Democratic Congressman William L. Wilson wrote to Atkinson that "the Mugwumps can do much" by "keeping the Tariff issue to the front to the exclusion of all others."[64] Cleveland accordingly won reelection on a tariff reform platform.

Conclusion

Cleveland's 1892 upset victory signaled yet another temporary halt to the Listian Republican implementation of the imperialism of economic nationalism. The Democratic political resurgence that followed the passage of the 1890 McKinley Tariff also revitalized the transatlantic Cobdenite prospect of an anti-imperial Free Trade America. But their laissez-faire approach to government belied the difficulties they yet faced. Fittingly, in a final letter to Atkinson following Cleveland's return to the White House in March 1893, an embittered Henry Carey Baird warned of the country's feigned desire for free trade: "What you see is a mere mirage, no more; all your propositions being false, society would not tolerate you or your societary nostrums, in practice in this country even for three months."[65]

Baird's prediction was not entirely off the mark. Although Benjamin Harrison may have lost his run for reelection, his presidency had shown growing Republican support for an aggressive policy of restrictive reciprocity coupled with high tariff walls and imperial expansion. The Listian nationalist vision of a more progressive, regionalized, imperial approach to American global economic integration was gaining ground among Republicans, and the disciples of the Social Gospel, Alfred Thayer Mahan, and the List-inspired German Historical School all gave their invaluable support to this protectionist ideological revolution.

Nor was this economic nationalist metamorphosis being felt only in the United States. From the McKinley Tariff to imperial designs in the Caribbean and the Pacific, the Harrison administration's imperialism of

---

[64] Atkinson to Wells, July 18, 1890, carton 20, Atkinson Papers; "A Rare Opportunity: Henry George's Great Work, 'Protection or Free Trade,'" *Free Trade Broadside* 4 (April 1912): 1; Henry George, *Protection or Free Trade: An Examination of the Tariff Question with Especial Regard to the Interests of Labor* (New York: Henry George, 1886), 247; George to Louis Post, March 31, April 2, 1891, reel 5, George Papers; Wilson to Atkinson, December 26, 1891, January 11, 1892, carton 5, Atkinson Papers.

[65] Baird to Atkinson, March 7, 1893, carton 6, Atkinson Papers.

economic nationalism had laid the progressive protectionist groundwork for the American empire building of 1898 and beyond. This Listian revolution would send shockwaves throughout the globe – and its strongest tremors would shake the very Cobdenite foundations of the British Empire.

8   Free trade in retreat
The global impact of the McKinley Tariff upon
the British Empire, 1890–1894

And the bacilli of Cobden we
Will scatter to the gale,
... Till the hopeful British Lion drops
His elevated tail!
For the Major [McKinley] leads the column,
And so conquer sure we must;
On our banner is Protection,
Let Free Traders bite the dust.

Blackburn Standard (Scotland), August 1891.[1]

The manufacturers of Great Britain don't like the McKinley tariff bill. The manufacturers of Germany don't like the McKinley tariff bill. The manufacturers of France don't like the McKinley tariff bill. The Anglomaniac Free Traders of the United States don't like the McKinley tariff bill. This furnishes four excellent reasons why the bill should become a law.   *Fair Trade* (London), 1890.[2]

Ironic sentiments like those of Scotland's *Blackburn Standard* and the Fair Trade League (1881–1891) in England toward the passage of an extreme American protective tariff – the McKinley Tariff of 1890 – exemplified the burgeoning crisis within Britain's imperial system. The system's free-trade proponents had doubtless begun to wonder what was causing the global economic crises and militarism of the late nineteenth century. While they might not have been alone in their speculations, among the nations of the world they alone stood by their Cobdenite ideals. Britain's industrial superiority and free-trade advocacy had helped inspire a rival economic nationalist policy of infant industrial protectionism among its competitors. Free Trade England's Cobdenite hands-off approach to imperial management also had incidentally allowed for its white settler colonies to implement protectionist policies of their own. Such policies were often in imitation of (or in retaliation to) protectionist policies in Europe and North America, particularly the United States,

---

[1] "M'Kinley Leads the Column," *Blackburn Standard*, August 29, 1891, 5.
[2] *Fair Trade* (England), June 6, 1890, 413.

which topped the list of countries engaging in government-subsidized internal improvements and in the construction of high tariff walls. Such protectionist competitors were also increasingly overtaking Britain in the production of basic commodities like steel and pig iron.

Britain's real and perceived economic decline relative to these rising powers, and the wide-ranging effects of the late-nineteenth-century "Great Depression" (*c.* 1873–1896) more generally, sounded the alarm to Conservatives and economic nationalists throughout the British Empire who desired closer political, military, and economic ties between England and its colonies. Drawing ideological inspiration from the writings of Friedrich List and the German Historical School, they increasingly wanted an interconnected, interdependent Greater Britain: a regionalized, protectionist, imperial federative cure-all to the economic ills that had arisen alongside economic globalization.[3] Their Listian vision for a protectionist Greater Britain was fast becoming an enticing alternative to what they diminutively termed "Little England," the Cobdenite vision of a devolutionary British Empire.

Free traders throughout the empire correspondingly found themselves in retreat. Listian demands for Greater Britain increased dramatically after 1890 in response to the American passage of the McKinley Tariff, with an *ad valorem* rate of nearly 50 percent. In 1890, the Republican-controlled US Congress passed the McKinley Tariff owing to domestic political pressures alongside a Listian desire to both protect American infant industries from the perceived onslaught of British manufactures, and to open up new markets so as to insulate the country from the era's unpredictable boom-and-bust economic cycle. The tariff, devised by Republican Congressman William McKinley (OH) and Secretary of State James G. Blaine, combined the Republican party's long-standing adherence to the protective tariff with a retaliatory reciprocity policy that offered Latin American nations concessions on materials such as sugar and wool following concessions of their own – and threatened them with punitive tariffs if they deviated from the agreement (see Chapter 7). The Listian reciprocity provision's retaliatory inducements also discouraged

---

[3] Gary B. Magee and Andrew S. Thompson, *Empire and Globalisation: Networks of People, Goods and Capital in the British World, c. 1850–1914* (Cambridge: Cambridge University Press, 2010), 63, 235. On the influence of the German Historical School in England, see Gerard M. Koot, *English Historical Economics, 1870–1926: The Rise of Economic History and Neomercantilism* (Cambridge: Cambridge University Press, 1987); Ellen Frankel Paul, *Moral Revolution and Economic Science: The Demise of Laissez-Faire in Nineteenth-Century British Political Economy* (Westport, CT: Greenwood Press, 1979); Charles McClelland, *The German Historians and England: A Study in Nineteenth-Century Views* (Cambridge: Cambridge University Press, 1971).

signatories from trading with other nations, doubtless with the British Empire in mind.

British imperial historians have examined multiple influential factors contributing to demands for imperial federation and protectionism, but have largely overlooked the McKinley Tariff's particular imperial impact.[4] American historians have likewise offered a predominantly national focus on the tariff's origins and effects.[5] Yet the bill's passage sent economic and political shockwaves across the globe.[6] The McKinley bill's combination of highly protectionist tariff rates and discriminatory reciprocity policies threatened the British Empire's markets in North and Latin America. The US tariff thus affected not only Free Trade England itself, but also the British West Indies, South Africa, Australasia, and Canada. The McKinley Tariff might then be viewed in part as a nationalistic response to the Cobdenite cosmopolitanism of Free Trade England.[7] But the geographically and politically far-reaching British Listian reaction to American economic nationalism and competition can also fruitfully be analyzed beyond the national level. The Harrison administration's imperialism of economic nationalism had global reverberations across the British Empire.

This chapter therefore takes a global historical approach to subjects previously viewed within the confines of national boundaries. In doing so, it offers a new politico-ideological perspective to the British movement

---

[4] An exception to the rule is Edmund Rogers, "The United States and the Fiscal Debate in Britain, 1873–1913," *Historical Journal* 50 (2007): 593–622.

[5] See Edward P. Crapol, *America for Americans: Economic Nationalism and Anglophobia in the Late Nineteenth Century* (Westport, CT and London: Greenwood Press, 1973), 173–179, 184–185; Howard Wayne Morgan, *William McKinley and His America* (Syracuse: Syracuse University Press, 1963), chap. 8; Joanne Reitano, *The Tariff Question in the Gilded Age: The Great Debate of 1888* (University Park, PA: Penn State Press, 1994), 129–131; Clarence A. Stern, *Protectionist Republicanism: Republican Tariff Policy in the McKinley Period* (Oshkosh, WI: Self-published, 1971), 21–42; Tom E. Terrill, *The Tariff, Politics, and American Foreign Policy, 1874–1901* (Westport, CT and London: Greenwood Press, 1973), chap. 7.

[6] For case studies on the economic influence of American manufacturers upon Britain during this period, see R. A. Church, "The Effect of the American Export Invasion on the British Boot and Shoe Industry 1885–1914," *The Journal of Economic History* 28 (June 1968): 223–254; S. J. Nicholas, "The American Export Invasion of Britain: The Case of the Engineering Industry, 1870–1914," *Technology and Culture* 21 (October 1980): 570–588; Mathew Simon and David E. Novack, "Some Dimensions of the American Commercial Invasion of Europe, 1871–1914: An Introductory Essay," *Journal of Economic History* 24 (December 1964): 591–605.

[7] Martin Daunton, "Britain and Globalization since 1850: I. Creating a Global Order, 1850–1914," *Transactions of the Royal Historical Society* 16 (2006): 3–4; Harold James, *The End of Globalization: Lessons from the Great Depression* (Cambridge, MA: Harvard University Press, 2001), 4–5; Kevin H. O'Rourke and Jeffrey G. Williamson, *Globalization and History: The Evolution of a Nineteenth-Century Atlantic Economy* (Cambridge, MA: Harvard University Press, 1999), 93–94, 286–287.

toward imperial federation by incorporating American economic policies with those of the British Empire on a global scale. The McKinley Tariff's Listian imperial policies helped call into question Britain's own liberal ideological attachment to Cobdenism by drumming up support for an imperial, protectionist, preferential Greater Britain. Such British Listian demands for imperial union and protectionism in turn increased demands in the colonies for national sovereignty and federation. As a result, international NGOs like the Cobden Club and their protectionist counterparts extended their networks across the British Empire, and ratcheted up their oppositional struggle over the empire's economic course.[8] Many throughout the empire would even come to believe that the McKinley Tariff was part of a Republican-designed conspiracy to annex Canada. The American tariff also sped up the demand for, and development of, more efficient transportation and communications – technological developments that made imperial federation all the more viable – within the British Empire. This is thus a global history of the McKinley Tariff's impact upon the British Empire, as well as a study of the tariff's effect upon the history of late-nineteenth-century global economic integration.

The McKinley Tariff and the demand for imperial unity

The abolition of the Corn Laws in 1846 had marked the beginning of over two decades of British free trade, hegemonic preeminence, and relative hemispheric peace. The Cobdenite worldview of a *Pax Britannica* had never appeared stronger. British hopes for international free trade and peace appeared within reach as the United States and much of Western Europe had begun to adopt less protective policies alongside the gold standard, to the respective benefit of British trade and finance. A series of events thereafter jeopardized the promised *Pax Britannica*: in 1873, a global economic depression struck; the European "Scramble for Africa" in the early 1880s demonstrated that atavistic empire-building and imperial rivalry were still alive and well; the powerful House of Baring collapsed in 1890; and, aside from Britain, Denmark, and the Netherlands, economic nationalism became the system of choice throughout Europe and the Americas. A tariff war was waged between France and Italy from 1887 to 1892, for instance, and from the late 1870s higher tariffs were instituted in Belgium, Switzerland, Germany, Austria-

---

[8] Duncan Bell, *The Idea of Greater Britain: Empire and the Future of World Order, 1860–1900* (Princeton, NJ: Princeton University Press, 2007); Magee and Thompson, *Empire and Globalisation*.

Hungary, Sweden, Italy, Spain, Portugal, Russia, Canada, and the United States.[9]

The most drastic measures were taken in the United States. The McKinley Tariff had a global impact. The instability that followed the tariff's restrictive reciprocity provisions would destabilize various Latin American signatories, including increased Cuban anti-colonial agitation. Revolution broke out in Hawaii. Indian calls for protectionism mounted. Thousands were left jobless in Austria and Germany, even driving one owner of a wool mill in Lichtenberg to suicide. And although former French ministers of commerce urged France to "hold entirely aloof from an economic struggle with America," France eventually sought the McKinley Tariff's repeal, as well.[10] Gazing with trepidation at the high tariff walls of its international commercial competitors and its own colonies, some within Free Trade England and its colonies began to look askance at the efficacy of Cobdenism. A Listian nationalist vision of British imperial politico-economic unity and retaliatory protectionism arose as a viable alternative.

Scattered protectionist rumblings had begun much earlier – indeed, as early as 1868. At the apex of the *Pax Britannica*, Britain's Cobdenite Prime Minister, William Gladstone, had sought to decrease government expenditures on colonial defense, provoking oppositional cries for stronger imperial ties first from within the colonies themselves and, more slowly, from the Conservative party in England. British intellectuals and politicians in the colonies and at home, fearing the growing economic competition, protectionism, and potential of the United States, began to question the utility of Britain's unilateral policy of free trade. Skeptics of Britain's Cobdenite policy desired instead an imperial, federated, protectionist Greater Britain.

Whereas in the time of Adam Smith imperial federation had seemed an impossibility owing to the temporal and geographical distance separating

---

[9] Scott C. James and David A. Lake, "The Second Face of Hegemony: Britain's Repeal of the Corn Laws and the American Walker Tariff of 1846," *International Organization* 43 (Winter 1989): 1–29; Michael Tracy, *Government and Agriculture in Western Europe 1880–1988* (New York: New York University Press, 1989 [1964]), 20–32.

[10] *London Times*, November 1, 1890, 5; October 27, 1890, 5; August 10, 1891, 5; August 13, 1891, 3; *Moonshine* (London), July 22, 1893, 39; Walter LaFeber, *The New Empire, an Interpretation of American Expansion 1860–1898* (Ithaca, NY: Cornell University Press, 1963), 120; Manu Goswami, *Producing India: From Colonial Economy to National Space* (Chicago, IL: University of Chicago Press, 2004), 216; *Fair Trade*, January 9, 1891, 158; *Blackburn Standard*, March 5, 1892, 2; August 29, 1891, 8; *Huddersfield Chronicle*, October 20, 1890, 3; French Committee for the Repeal of the McKinley Bill, *France and the United States* (Paris: Comité Francais, 1894). The Sugar Trust was instrumental in taking sugar off the free list in 1894. See Steven Topik, *Trade and Gunboats: The United States in the Age of Empire* (Stanford: Stanford University Press, 1996), 117–118.

the various areas of the British Empire, developments in modern transportation and communications – particularly the railroad, the steamship, and the telegraph – allowed for renewed and realistic speculation.[11] Disraeli himself had argued that the white colonies' increased self-government should also have been tied to "a great policy of imperial consolidation, it ought to have been accompanied by an imperial tariff, by securities for the people of England."[12]

British Liberals, however, especially of the Cobdenite wing, continued to fight for the informal laissez-faire system currently in place, and eyed those calling for imperial federation with great distrust.[13] Imperial protectionists in Britain increasingly gained the ear, and later became the mouthpiece, of the Conservative party. While the "cheap loaf" remained popular throughout the 1860s and 1870s, Conservative policymakers like Salisbury hesitantly began to question the liberal economic system, becoming "scornfully critical of the lofty claims of Cobdenite orthodoxy." Lord Randolph Churchill wanted to overthrow the Cobdenite system, which, he argued, was "the certain cause of the long continued depression in this country." The oyster of foreign markets needed to be opened with a "strong clasp knife, instead of being tickled with a feather."[14]

---

[11] Marc-William Palen, "Adam Smith as Advocate of Empire, c. 1870–1932," *Historical Journal* 57 (March 2014): 179–198. On the connection between imperialism, globalization, and technological advancements, see Roland Wenzlhuemer, *Connecting the Nineteenth-Century World: The Telegraph and Globalization* (Cambridge: Cambridge University Press, 2012); Emily S. Rosenberg, ed., *A World Connecting 1870–1945* (Cambridge, MA: Belknap Press, 2012); Robert W. D. Boyce, "Imperial Dreams and National Realities: Britain, Canada, and the Struggle for a Pacific Telegraph Cable, 1879–1902," *English Historical Review* 115 (February 2000): 39–70; Lewis Pyenson, "Science and Imperialism," in *Companion to the History of Modern Science*, ed. by Robert Cecil Olby and Geoffrey N. Cantor (London and New York: Routledge, 1990); Daniel Headrick, *The Tools of Empire* (New Oxford: Oxford University Press, 1981); Headrick, *The Tentacles of Progress: Technology Transfer in the Age of Imperialism, 1850–1940* (Oxford: Oxford University Press, 1988); Headrick, *The Invisible Weapon: Telecommunications and International Politics, 1851–1945* (Oxford: Oxford University Press, 1991); Bell, *Idea of Greater Britain*, 63–119.

[12] T. E. Kebbel, ed., *Selected Speeches of the late Rt. Hon. The Earl of Beaconsfield*, 2 vols. (London: Longmans, 1882), II, 530. See, also, P. J. Cain and A. G. Hopkins, *British Imperialism, 1688–2000* (London: Pearson Education, 2002 [1993]), 185–191.

[13] Roger Mason, "Robert Giffen and the Tariff Reform Campaign, 1865–1910," *Journal of European Economic History* 25 (1996): 171–188. Free traders had not developed a consensus regarding opposition to imperial federation. Adam Smith himself had concocted a free-trade system of imperial federation, and some free traders sought its implementation in the 1890s.

[14] Lady Gwendolen Cecil, *Life of Robert, Marquis of Salisbury*, 2 vols. (London: Hodder and Stoughton, 1915), I, 1921–1935, 337; *Bradford Observer*, September 19, 1881, quoted in Benjamin H. Brown, *The Tariff Reform Movement in Great Britain, 1881–1895* (New York: Columbia University Press, 1943), 61. See, also, Luke Trainor, "The British Government and Imperial Economic Unity, 1890–1895," *Historical Journal* 13 (March 1970): 68–84; and Trainor, "The Imperial Federation League in Britain and Australia, c.

The continued global depression, a series of bad English harvests and livestock epidemics in the late 1870s, alongside increased protectionism from Britain's competitors and colonies, all inspired Listian mobilization. British protectionists found inspiration in the national economic philosophy of Germany's Friedrich List. British Listian nationalists W. Farrer Ecroyd and Birmingham manufacturer Sampson Samuel Lloyd (who produced the first British translation of List's *National System of Political Economy* in 1885) led the vanguard against the liberal economic order in England. Protectionist imperial leagues were formed in Birmingham, Sheffield, Wolverhampton, and various other manufacturing areas in England. Continued consolidation and cooperation led to the founding of the National Fair Trade League in 1881. Ecroyd, the league's founder, saw England's free-trade system as a failing enterprise. The fair traders sought minimal duties on manufactured imports, as well as stronger ties with the "white" empire, including a system of preferential tariffs. The IFL was founded a few years later in order to bring further aid to the Listian cause. While the "cheap loaf" continued to maintain mass popularity and political support throughout the 1860s and 1870s, these protectionists had not yet been able to speak above a whisper without risking political suicide. However, according to historian Benjamin Brown, by the late 1880s "the whispering became a tumult."[15]

The political pariah status of imperial protectionists began to reverse significantly after the 1890 passage of the McKinley Tariff in the United States and the subsequent 1891 economic depression that struck in England. As Benjamin Brown noted: "It is not too much to say that the shock caused by the McKinley Tariff did more than ten years of Fair Trade agitation to bring discredit to the Cobdenite school. While protectionists were striking hammer blows for retaliation, Cobdenites seemed to be clouting phantoms." The *Cheshire Observer* noted the same: "The Fair Trade movement will probably be strengthened by the operation of the new American tariff," and will be "a terribly bitter pill for the out-and-out Cobdenites who have been hoping against hope that the leading politicians of the United States might show some sign, however slight, of a possible conversion to Free Trade principles." The Fair Traders also considered the McKinley Tariff the primary cause of the English depression that struck in 1891, an economic downturn that only worsened

1884–1900," in *The Round Table: The Empire/Commonwealth and British Foreign Policy*, ed. by Andrea Bosco and Alex May (London: Lothian Foundation Press, 1997), 161–176.

[15] Friedrich List, *The National System of Political Economy*, trans. by Sampson S. Lloyd (London: Longmans, Green, and Co., 1885); Brown, *Tariff Reform Movement*, 16–18, 58; Tracy, *Government and Agriculture*, 41; Cain and Hopkins, *British Imperialism*, 191.

following the Panic of 1893: an American financial crisis that contributed to another global economic shockwave.[16] Listian Ecroyd predicted that the McKinley Tariff, because of its injurious effects upon British industries, "will probably hasten the decline of the Cobden Club."[17]

Some English Cobdenites admitted to finding wry satisfaction in the continued American adherence to what they considered outmoded mercantilism. Most British free traders, however, were outraged. The Cobden Club, its members apoplectic, called the McKinley Tariff an "outrage on civilization" that promised "to destroy British trade" and "to lead to the [American] annexation of Canada."[18] The *London Times* considered the McKinley Tariff an unprovoked virtual "war on the British Empire" designed to appeal to Irish-Americans and to acquire Canada. Within a year, however, the same *London Times*, previously a supporter of the British free-trade system, appeared more ambivalent. Its editors now suggested that imperial federation "is the great task which lies before the British statesmanship of the future. With the colonies massed around us we can hold our own in the ranks of the world Powers .... Without them we must sink to the position of a merely European kingdom – a position which for England infallibly entails slow but sure decay."[19]

The ambivalence of the *London Times* hinted at the widespread effects of the McKinley Tariff upon the prevailing British Cobdenite disposition, as well as the tariff's impact upon the pocketbook of British merchants and manufacturers. Cecil Spring-Rice, secretary to the British legation in the United States, wrote to his brother: "We must reconcile ourselves to it [the McKinley Tariff] and look for new markets. A serious aspect of it is the reciprocity clause, which drives us out of the West Indies and South America." Charles Tupper, Canadian Prime Minister in 1896, remarked

---

[16] Joseph Smith, *Illusions of Conflict: Anglo-American Diplomacy toward Latin America, 1865–1896* (Pittsburgh, PA: University of Pittsburgh Press, 1979), 143–145; Brown, *Tariff Reform Movement*, 76; *Cheshire Observer*, October 11, 1890, 5; Sydney H. Zebel, "Fair Trade: An English Reaction to the Breakdown of the Cobden Treaty System," *Journal of Modern History* 12 (June 1940): 183. See, also, Zebel, "Joseph Chamberlain and the Genesis of Tariff Reform," *Journal of British Studies* 7 (November 1967): 131–157; Trainor, "British Government and Imperial Economic Unity," 68–69. Cases involving illegal child labor in Ireland even found the American tariff to blame. *Huddersfield Chronicle and West Yorkshire Advertiser*, October 21, 1890, 3.

[17] *London Times*, October 20, 1890, 3.

[18] Anthony Howe, *Free Trade and Liberal England, 1846–1946* (Oxford: Clarendon Press, 1997), 196–197; *Annual General Meeting of the Cobden Club, 1893*, 7. See, also, Lyon Playfair, *The Tariffs of the United States in Relation to Free Trade* (London: Cassell & Co., 1890); Robert Giffen, "The Relative Growth of Free Trade and Protection," May 25, 1892, Cabinet Memo, May 25, 1892, in *Battles over Free Trade*, 3 vols., ed. by Anthony Howe and Mark Duckenfield (London: Pickering & Chatto, 2008), III, 88.

[19] *London Times*, October 6, 1890, 5; June 18, 1891, 9.

that the primary objective of the McKinley Tariff had been to paralyze British trade, ruin its industries, and strike "a severe blow at England's great dependency, the Dominion of Canada." British leaders of the Fair Trade League claimed with some accuracy that export-oriented manufactures in such areas as Sheffield would be "almost annihilated."[20] In Sheffield itself, even as passage of the McKinley Tariff Act was pending, various manufacturers and workers met to demand retaliation, with the town's mayor sending a letter to every other mayor in the United Kingdom calling for action. A few months after the McKinley Act's new rates were implemented, the *Cheshire Observer* wrote that Sheffield firms had been forced to reduce wages, and that the tariff had sent thousands of "workers into the streets at a blow . . .. England is suffering frightfully . . . from her inability to offer the slightest resistance to hostile tariffs, even to one so unjust and so injurious as the M'Kinley Tariff." The newspaper, giving its endorsement to the Fair Trade League, also warned that "the great danger" was English job flight: "English manufacturers will transfer their machinery and foremen to the States, and set up factories."[21] Howard Vincent, a leader of the IFL and an MP from Sheffield, also complained of increased economic emigration: "Four well-known English textile firms have moved a whole or a portion of their plant across the Atlantic . . .. A remedy is ready when the people awake," a double dose of protectionism and imperial federation. Vincent continued to attack the Cobdenite policy of the British Liberal government, warning that such continued one-sided free trade invited the United States to "strike us yet again." From atop their high protectionist walls, Republican economic nationalists were hurling "the doctrines of the Cobden Club in our faces."[22]

Coinciding with the rise of modern consumer culture, women were also taking an increasing interest in the British debate over the McKinley Tariff. The *Women's Herald* of London came to the Cobden Club's

[20] Spring-Rice to Ferguson, November 6, 1891, in Cecil Spring-Rice, *The Letters and Friendships of Sir Cecil Spring-Rice*, ed. by Stephen Gwynn, 2 vols. (Boston, MA: Houghton Mifflin Co., 1929), I, 116; Charles Tupper, *Preferential Trade Relations between Great Britain and her Colonies: An Address Delivered before the Montreal Board of Trade, January 20, 1896*, 23; Lister, quoted in Brown, *Tariff Reform Movement*, 56. Many periodicals expressed outrage at the McKinley Tariff's impact on England. See, for instance, *Women's Signal* (London), February 1, 1894, 74; *Sporting Times* (London), September 17, 1892, 5; *Journal of the Manchester Geographical Society*, April 1, 1892, 82; *Blackburn Standard*, September 17, 1892, 3.
[21] *London Times*, October 6, 1890, 13; October 13, 1890, 14; January 15, 1891, 8; *Sheffield Independent*, May 5, 1892, 7; *Cheshire Observer*, October 25, 1890, 7.
[22] *London Times*, November 1, 1892, 12; April 26, 1892, 10; October 15, 1890, 7. For industries moving from England to the United States, see, for instance, *London Times*, October 29, 1890, 5.

defense. Finding their purchases "for their households ... dearer than before the McKinley law," the women's news organ promised the support of all those "women who indulge in that feminine mania, shopping." The *Herald* also warned "if protection were really tried" in England, "women would resent it bitterly, and they would undoubtedly so influence public opinion as to abolish any tariff that might be imposed."[23]

The imperial federationists also turned to women for support. At a well-attended meeting of the IFL's Toronto branch the previous year, the following resolution was unanimously passed: "The time has arrived when it is in the best interests of the League to invite the cooperation of women as active members of the organization." Following the resolution's endorsement by the league's national executive committee, its members were "earnestly requested to enlighten women of all classes" and to engage them because "the men being at their business all day, have very little time to devote to this very important work." By 1891, the Toronto branch alone laid claim to approximately one hundred female members.[24] This added feminine bolstering only heightened the importance of the imperial ideological conflict. Throughout the British Empire, imperial federation and trade preference appeared to be on the ascendency, while Cobdenism floundered in the face of American Listian legislation.

The McKinley Tariff and the British Empire

The 1890 McKinley Tariff's political economic reverberations were being felt throughout the British Empire, particularly within the British World, the white settler colonies of the empire. An American traveling among the British colonies observed in late 1891 that the perceived success of the US system of protectionism had greatly shaken many colonists' faith in the British system of free trade. Increased American economic interests in South America also caused a stir. British businessmen in Lancashire became excited over the Blaine–Mendonca Accord between Brazil and the United States, derived from the reciprocity provisions of the McKinley Tariff. The *London Times* observed how Brazilian–American reciprocity was "menacing Great Britain's $31,000,000 of yearly exports to Brazil ... but unfortunately Great Britain can do nothing, as British free trade has deprived the Government of advantages which it might have by trading with Brazil." The *Lancaster Gazette*

---

[23] *Women's Herald*, August 20, 1892, 3.
[24] Imperial Federation League, *Principles of the Imperial Federation League and Rules and List of Members of the Toronto Branch, April, 1891* (Toronto: Johnston & Watson, 1891), 23.

similarly noted that Englishmen needed to open their eyes "to the fact that this Blaine treaty is a blow to the success of our free-trade system."[25]

The British Foreign Office immediately began to reexamine whether it was in possession of a most-favored-nation agreement with potential signatories of reciprocity agreements in Latin America. There was apprehension that Brazil would sign a reciprocity treaty with the United States, and so the Foreign Office proposed its own unsuccessful treaty. British fears became reality in March 1891 when Brazil signed just such a treaty with the United States. The signing of the reciprocity treaty, along with the creation of a Brazilian republic, brought about renewed attention from European governments. American ministers in Rio de Janeiro began to suspect, albeit inconclusively, that British businessmen and officials were seeking the restoration of the Brazilian monarchy so as to abrogate the reciprocal agreement. Such reactions, historian Joseph Smith notes, showed that "the United States had indeed a club with which to beat much of the rest of the world": especially the British Empire.[26]

The British West Indies also felt the effects of the McKinley Tariff, where more and more the protectionist "cry is raised about England's Free Trade crushing out their life and retarding development," and where the prospect of American annexation was becoming ever more popular. The subsidized growth of European sugar-beet production by the late 1880s had already begun to displace British West Indian sugar, leading to a declining British refinery industry and unsuccessful calls for protectionist retaliation. Following the passage of the McKinley Tariff, Cecil Spring-Rice observed that the United States was either seeking to gain preferential duties in the West Indies, putting Great Britain and Canada "at a disadvantage, or else to force us to refuse an offer of that nature and by the ruin of our colonies to drive them into discontent and possibly annexation." The West Indies found it "difficult to refuse the inducement held out" by the McKinley Tariff, and they had already shown a proclivity toward commercial union with the United States throughout the mid-1880s. In 1891, James G. Blaine was even claiming that the British West Indies had already been successfully brought within the commercial network of the United States. Yet London adopted a Cobdenite hands-off

[25] "British Problems, as Viewed by an American Observer," *Anti-Jacobin*, December 19, 1891, 1182, Goldwin Smith Papers, microfilm reel 4, Cornell University Library, Cornell, New York; *London Times*, May 20, 1891, 5; Smith, *Illusion of Conflict*, 147; Topik, *Trade and Gunboats*, 109; *Lancaster Gazette*, May 23, 1891. For more on the significance of the Blaine–Mendonca Accord on US foreign policy, see Topik, *Trade and Gunboats*.

[26] Smith, *Illusion of Conflict*, 147–149, 156; Topik, *Trade and Gunboats*, 142–144.

approach, perhaps in response to growing demands for local management of West Indian economic policy as was happening elsewhere in the empire, thereby allowing the West Indians to take control of the US negotiations. The West Indians thereafter concluded an agreement with the United States in February 1892.[27]

Unlike Her Majesty's Government, the Canadian government decided upon a more hands-on approach to its threatened trade relations with the British West Indies. From 1885 to 1911, Canadians came to view the British West Indies much like the United States saw China, as a potential area of "unrivaled trade opportunities." Canadian trade commissions had previously been sent to the West Indies between 1888 and 1889. The Canadians now sent their finance minister, George E. Foster, to establish a trade agreement with the West Indies in 1890, particularly to reduce duties on sugar exports to Canada, spurring speculation among some in Trinidad that such offers stemmed from Canadian reaction to the McKinley Tariff.[28] From Antigua, supporting this Trinidadian speculation, Foster wrote to Sir Mackenzie Bowell: "the steamer on which I am a passenger is filled with just the products which Canada can & should send to these islands. I find too a very warm & friendly feeling towards Canada – not lessened by the McKinley Bill." Canada, desirous of its own "China market" and in response to the McKinley Tariff, nearly doubled its trade with the West Indies between 1887 and 1892.[29]

Similar concerns over growing global protectionism were expressed in British South Africa. During this period, the movement toward South African federation peaked. The South African Customs Union had been created in 1889, providing a uniform tariff on foreign imports coupled with a promise of free trade within the various Customs Union colonies

[27] "British Problems, as Viewed by an American Observer," *Anti-Jacobin*, December 19, 1891, 1182, microfilm, reel 4, Smith Papers; Howe, *Free Trade and Liberal England*, 204–205; *London Times*, May 20, 1891, 5; Charles Dilke, *Problems of Greater Britain* (London and New York: Macmillan and Co., 1890), 99–100; Terrill, *Tariff, Politics, and American Foreign Policy*, 180, 147–148; Spring-Rice to Lowther, October 26, 1891, quoted in Smith, *Illusions of Conflict*, 148.

[28] Robin W. Winks, *Canadian-West Indian Union: A Forty-Year Minuet* (London: Athlone Press, 1968), 21, 22. As late as 1919, Canadian desire arose for annexing areas of the West Indies. See, for instance, Paula Hastings, "Dreams of a Tropical Canada: Race, Nation, and Canadian Aspirations in the Caribbean Basin, 1883–1919" (PhD diss., Duke University, 2010); Andrew Smith, "Thomas Bassett Macaulay and the Bahamas: Racism, Business and Canadian Sub-imperialism," *Journal of Imperial and Commonwealth History* 37 (March 2009): 29–50.

[29] Foster to Bowell, November 17, 1890, quoted in Robert Craig Brown, *Canada's National Policy 1883–1900: A Study in Canadian-American Relations* (Princeton, NJ: Princeton University Press, 1964), 223. For an anti-imperial federation view of West Indian economic issues, see John William Root, *The British West Indies and the Sugar Industry* (London: Hazell, Watson & Viney, 1899).

and states themselves. The Cape Colony and Orange Free State were the first to join in 1889, followed by British Bechuanaland, Basutoland, and Bechuanaland Protectorate in 1890, 1891, and 1893, respectively. Cecil Rhodes – who, along with his predecessor Sir John Gordon Sprigg, was one of the biggest proponents of South African federation – gave a speech on July 6, 1890, two months before becoming prime minister of the Cape Colony, and just months before the McKinley Tariff was signed into law. In his speech, Rhodes called for "a South African Union ... that we may attain to perfect free trade as to our own commodities, perfect and complete internal railway communication, and a general customs union."[30]

The McKinley Tariff acted as a further impetus to Rhodes's federative schemes. In 1891, Rhodes, now premier of Cape Colony, wrote to Sir John Macdonald, the Canadian prime minister, of his worries over the McKinley Tariff and of his corresponding desire to expand federation throughout the empire. Rhodes followed this up with a similar letter to Sir Henry Parkes, premier of New South Wales. To Macdonald, Rhodes asked: "Can we invent some tie with our mother-country that will prevent separation? It must be a practical one, for future generations will not be born in England. The curse is that English politicians cannot see the future. They think they will always be the manufacturing mart of the world, but do not understand what protection coupled with reciprocal relations means." Rhodes went further, even asking Parkes to rename the future federation of Australia "Dominion of Australia," rather than the proposed "Commonwealth of Australia," as the latter "indicates a desire for separation" from the British Empire. Such a name change, Rhodes thought, "would enormously strengthen our demands for preferential consideration as to our products."[31] Rhodes's imperial federative vision was seconded by Jan Hofmeyer, an influential South African politician. He too called for a protectionist response to the McKinley Tariff. He proposed an imperial preferential reprisal scheme that effectively called for import tariffs upon all foreign countries, "without disturbing

[30] A. J. Bruwer, "Protection in South Africa" (PhD diss., University of Pennsylvania, 1923), 98, 99, 101. On Sprigg's desire for imperial federation and a customs union, see Howard Vincent, *Commercial Union of the Empire* (London: United Empire Trade League, 1891), in Howe and Duckenfield, ed., *Battles over Free Trade*, III, 69.

[31] Rhodes to Macdonald, May 8, 1891, reprinted in *London Times*, September 1, 1903, 6; Rhodes to Parkes, May 1891, ibid., September 1, 1903, 6. The Cape Colony's exports to the United States fell drastically during this period. During the quarter ending on December 31, 1890, its exports to the United States totaled $85,400; for the quarter ending on June 30, 1891, its exports totaled $13,475. *Commercial Relations of the United States with Foreign Countries during the Years 1890 and 1891. Annual Reports of the Consuls of the United States on the Commerce, Manufactures, Industries, etc., of their Several Districts for the Above Years* (Washington, DC: Government Printing Office, 1892), 391.

the Free-trade attitude of the United Kingdom, or interfering with the diverse tariffs of the colonies."[32] Imperial federation, preference, and protectionism in South Africa thus became ever more viable after 1890, much as they were in the Australian colonies.

Global ideological conflict in Australian microcosm

"There was a time when, in my earlier years, I was half caught by the fascinations of some of the Cobdenic theories," reflected Benjamin Hoare in 1904, writing from Victoria, Australia. "Fortunately for me the pro-founder reasonings of the German school of economics came as a corrective." Hoare's Edwardian reminiscences illuminate how the ideological battle between List and Cobden had reached global proportions by the late nineteenth century, as had the effects of American Listian legislation.[33]

Various Australian colonies once again called for reform regarding imperial tariffs stemming in part from the McKinley Tariff, which had indirectly affected the Australasian wool industry once British exports to the United States plummeted upon the bill's passage. As Perth's *Western Mail* reported in January 1891, "there is probably no country in the world with anything to export that is not affected by the McKinley tariff … Australia is no exception to the rule. Her chief staple, wool, is as severely treated as can well be imagined." The tariff was, however, apparently good news for Australian imperial federationists. Within a couple years, the *Adelaide Advertiser* observed that substantive growth in Canadian–Australian trade loomed on the horizon thanks to the McKinley Tariff. Such intercolonial reciprocal relations would have the added bonus of tending "still further injury" to the United States.[34]

---

[32] Edmund E. Sheppard, "The McKinley Bill and Imperial Federation," in *Belford's Monthly* (New York: Belford's Magazine Co., 1891), VI, 36–61.

[33] Benjamin Hoare, *Preferential Trade* (London: Kegan Paul, Trench, Trubner & Co., 1904), v. For more on Australian imperial federation, see Trainor, "IFL in Britain and Australia"; Leonie Foster, "The Victorian Imperial Federation League and the Genesis of the Australian Round Table," in *Round Table*, ed. by Bosco and May, 177–190.

[34] Ernst Arthur Boehm, *Prosperity and Depression in Australia 1887–1897* (Oxford: Clarendon Press, 1971), 79; "Australian Wool and the McKinley Tariff," *Western Mail* (Perth), January 17, 1891, 16; "Canada and Australia. The Reciprocity Negotiations," *Advertiser*, October 30, 1893, 5. See, also, "The McKinley Act," *West Australian* (Perth), November 17, 1890, 2. For earlier demands for imperial tariff reform, see Cephas Daniel Allin, *Australasian Preferential Tariffs and Imperial Free Trade: A Chapter in the Fiscal Emancipation of the Colonies* (Minneapolis: University of Minnesota Press, 1929); John A. La Nauze, "Australian Tariffs and Imperial Control," *Economic Record* 24 (1948): 218–234. More generally, see Alexander J. Reitsma, *Trade Protection in Australia* (Leiden: H.E. Stenfert Kroese, 1960), 5–11. Victoria, for instance, saw its direct exports to the

As historian Edmund Rogers has elucidated, the tariff battle within the British Empire was playing out in microcosm between free-trade New South Wales and protectionist Victoria. The two colonies provided an ideal local testing ground for the global Cobdenite–Listian ideological fight. "In no other part of the world were two communities to be found peopled by the same race and so nearly alike in the character and extent of the resources under their control, and in their government and laws, which were, in fact, practically identical except in their methods of taxation," observed the free-trade editor of the *British-Australasian*, Charles Henry Chomley. The pro-free-trade Cobden Club maintained close ties with New South Wales's leading free trader, Henry Parkes, and British Cobdenite Louis Mallet believed that colony to be "the centre and hope of the Free Trade policy in Australia."[35] New South Wales had been Australia's central hub of Cobdenite ideology since the mid-century arrival from England of Robert Lowe, who passed along the laissez-faire messages of Cobden, Peel, Adam Smith, and Jean-Baptiste Say within the pages of his newspaper *Atlas*. By the 1860s, Henry Parkes had established himself as the most profound prognosticator of the Manchester School in Australia after being converted "one cold winter's night" by Richard Cobden himself.[36]

American Cobdenite publications also proved to be of use in New South Wales's free-trade fight. Parkes and other Australian Cobdenites began reprinting extracts from the AFTL organ *The League* and cited the writings of American Cobden Club members like David Ames Wells, Henry George, and Amasa Walker to try to show that the US economy thrived *in spite* of its protectionist policies. In similar fashion, Bernhard Ringrose Wise – Cobdenite politician, social reformer, Australian Federation advocate, and president of New South Wales's Free Trade Association – utilized the work of American Cobden Club members William Graham Sumner and Frank Taussig in his defense of free trade. Wise also used them to denounce the disciples of the "morbid and diseased mind" of Friedrich List, a man who had seen "wickedness

---

United States drop between the quarter ending on December 31, 1890, and the quarter ending on June 30, 1891, from $1,778,498 to $26,798. *Commercial Relations of the United States, 1890–1891*, 408.

[35] Edmund Rogers, "Free Trade versus Protectionism: New South Wales, Victoria, and the Tariff Debate in Britain, 1881–1900," *Australian Studies* 1 (2009): 5; Chomley, quoted in ibid., 6. See, also, Craufurd D. W. Goodwin, *Economic Enquiry in Australia* (Durham, NC: Duke University Press, 1966), 3–59; G. D. Patterson, *The Tariff in the Australian Colonies 1856–1900* (Melbourne: F. W. Cheshire, 1968).

[36] Goodwin, *Economic Enquiry in Australia*, 42; J. A. La Nauze, "'That Fatal, That Mischievous Passage,' Henry Parkes and Protection, 1859–1866," *Australian Quarterly* 19 (June 1947): 59–60; Howe, *Free Trade and Liberal England*, 120, 127, 140.

in every action of Great Britain . . . just as the average American voter is instructed to beware of 'British gold' and the 'Cobden Club.'"[37] Both the alleged conspiracy of free trade in the United States and the progressive economic nationalist influence of Friedrich List were gaining global notoriety.

Protectionist defenders in Victoria responded in kind, turning to the economic nationalist writings of American System defenders Friedrich List, Henry Clay, Henry Carey, and Alexander Hamilton to support their imperial economic nationalist vision.[38] From the 1860s to 1870s, Melbourne merchant and politician George Ward Cole published portions of List's *National System of Political Economy* and the speeches of Henry Clay to explain the failings of "the cosmopolitan or free trade system" in contrast to the prosperity wrought from the "national or protective system." Beginning in 1860, the popular *Melbourne Age* became the leading Australian mouthpiece for the protectionist doctrine. The legislature of Victoria soon thereafter passed the McCulloch Tariff in 1865, the first proclaimed protectionist tariff in the Australian colonies, and which shared much in common with Listian Alexander Galt's tariff that had passed a handful of years earlier in Canada (see Chapters 2 and 6).[39]

[37] *The League*, reprinted in the Melbourne *Argus*, July 13, 1868, 6; Henry Parkes, *Speeches on Various Occasions Connected with the Public Affairs of New South Wales 1848–1874* (Melbourne: George Robertson, 1876), 393–398; George H. Reid, *Five Free Trade Essays: Inscribed to the Electors of Victoria* (Melbourne: Gordon & Gotch, 1875); "Mr. Henry George on Protection," *Bathurst Free Press and Mining Journal* [NSW], March 13, 1890, 2; Sumner, quoted in *Sydney Morning Herald*, March 4, 1890, 3; B. R. Wise, *Industrial Freedom: A Study in Politics* (Melbourne: Cassell & Company, Ltd., 1892), 48ff., 138. At the turn of the century, Wise turned away from Cobdenism and instead became a supporter of Joseph Chamberlain's Tariff Reform campaign. See B. R. Wise, "Preferential Trade," November 21, 1903, ML MSS 6107, Vol. 6, Box 2, folio. 12, B. R. Wise Papers, State Library of New South Wales, Sydney, Australia; B. R. Wise, "Cobden's Imperial Policy," *London Times*, December 28, 1905; *Pall Mall Gazette*, October 23, 1905, 3; and Howe, *Free Trade and Liberal England*, 241.

[38] See, for instance, George Ward Cole, *Protection as a National System Suited for Victoria: Being Extracts from List's National System of Political Economy* (Melbourne: George Robertson, 1860); David Syme, *Outlines of an Industrial Science* (Philadelphia, PA: Henry Carey Baird, 1876); Francis Gould Smith, *The Australian Protectionist* (Melbourne: Self-published, 1877), 26, 29–30; Smith, *Danger Ahead! Anti Imperial Federation of Australasia* (Melbourne: Australasian-American Trading Company, 1889); Hoare, *Preferential Trade*; E. W. O'Sullivan, "The Policy of Protection," *Quanbeyan Age* [NSW], July 4, 1894, 4. They also frequently cited J. S. Mill's oft-quoted and misused defense of infant industries. Goodwin, *Economic Enquiry in Australia*, 24–25.

[39] Goodwin, *Economic Enquiry in Australia*, 13–17; G. W. Cole, *How a Protective Tariff Worked in America: To the Editor of the Age* (Melbourne: s.n., 1861); Cole, *A Policy of Action, in Employment for the People* (Melbourne: Samuel Mullen, 1871); Cole, *Tracts for the Times. Facts for Free Traders* (Melbourne: Wm. Goodhugh & Co., 1861), Box 4328/9, MS 9275, George Ward Cole Papers, State Library of Victoria, Melbourne, Australia. See, also, John Lucas, "Protection v. Free Trade," *Empire* [Sydney], May 1, 1858, 3; G. W. Cole, "How a Protective Tariff Worked in America," *Cornwall Chronicle*

But not all Victorian colonists came down on the side of protectionism and imperial federation. Melbourne Cobdenite Frederick Haddon, editor of the *Argus* from 1867 to 1898, had tried to counter the growing influence of the "unscrupulous" American System-inspired economic nationalism of the Australian Listians by promoting freer trade in the Australian colonies. To aid in this cause, Haddon was given encouragement from John Bright to take on protectionism in Victoria. Haddon was also introduced to the "Cobden of America" David A. Wells through letters of introduction from the Cobden Club's London secretary, Richard Gowing, and its founder, Thomas Bayley Potter. By the end of the 1870s, Haddon was requesting articles from Wells, whose "Creed of Free Trade" pamphlet had already made him "so well known in all the Australian colonies as a writer on free trade." Wells's contributions to the *Argus*, Haddon suggested, "would have great weight with both free traders and protectionists."[40]

Wells's dense writing was apparently not weighty enough. Following the McKinley Tariff's passage and as the 1890s global depression approached, economic nationalism held sway in Australasia, even within the former free-trade colonial stronghold of New South Wales. None would now "tolerate the policy of the Manchester school," the protectionist *Melbourne Age* happily noted in 1895. Tasmanian legislatures also turned to Victorian protectionists for economic advice, and New Zealand would soon "go further down the road towards McKinleyism" as a retaliatory response to the protective tariff policies of the Australian colonies. A common protective tariff would thereafter be established following Australian federation in 1901.[41] Australian protectionists

[Tasmania], February 6, 1861, 2; "Protection to Native Industry," *South Australian Advertiser* [Adelaide], January 3, 1861, 3; Alfred K. Holden, "Free Trade v. Protection," *Maitland Mercury* [NSW], September 7, 1889, 6; William Robinson, *Protection to Native Industry* (Melbourne: W. H. Williams, 1861); Archibald Forsyth, *Free, Fair, and Protected Trade: Which is the Best for England, New South Wales and Australia?* (Sydney: William Dymock, 1885); Forsyth, *Freetrade or Protection* (Sydney: C.E. Fuller, n.d.); Forsyth, *The Lines on Which a Federal Tariff Should be Based* (Sydney: Southern Cross Printing Works, n.d.); Forsyth, "Relations between Capital and Labour Examined," *Australian Economist* 1 (1888–1890): 99–103.

40   Bright to Haddon, March 26, May 26, 1879, MS6952-53, Box 377/1(b); Gowing to Haddon, June 6, June 8, 1879, MS 6961–62, Box 377/1(d); Potter to Haddon, MS 6994 Box 377/2(d), May 29, May 31, 1879, MS 6994–95, Frederick William Haddon Papers, State Library of Victoria, Melbourne, Australia; Haddon to Wells, March 4, 1876, microfilm reel 4, David Ames Wells Papers, LOC.

41   *The Protectionist's Handbook* (Melbourne: The *Age* Office, 1895), 28; Goodwin, *Economic Enquiry in Australia*, 30; Matthew Macfie, "Australia under Protection," *Economic Journal* 3 (June 1893): 297–307; and W. P. Reeves, "Protective Tariffs in Australia and New Zealand," *Economic Journal* 9 (March 1899): 36–44; Guy H. Scholefield, *New Zealand in Evolution* (London: T. Fisher Unwin, 1909), 321–323; Douglas A. Irwin,

would continue to use the McKinley Tariff and the writings of Henry Carey and Friedrich List to defend the maintenance of protectionism to increase domestic wages. In 1891, an older gentleman in Australia summed up the Australasian politico-ideological crisis over dinner with an American acquaintance: "These wise chaps back in England ... don't seem to realize that steam and electricity and the spread of education have introduced new elements into political economy. They keep on telling us that Free Trade makes everybody rich, and Protection makes everybody poor; yet as far as I can see the countries with Protection are getting about all the prosperity that's floating around."[42] This late-nineteenth-century Australasian fiscal debate therefore arose in large part owing to the growing popularity of Cobdenite and Listian political ideologies alongside coverage of the North American tariff debates in the latter half of the nineteenth century.

Coupled with the economic impact of American Listian legislation, corresponding Australasian calls for imperial union would grow even louder in 1893, amplified by the development of new tools of global economic integration.[43] The eventual opening of a Panama canal, some argued, would offer Australia and New Zealand a connection by way of the West Indies to Great Britain; through Canada, another route was potentially available. Major General Sir Bevan Edwardes noted "how mutually dependent the scattered parts of the Empire must necessarily be," and how the Canada Pacific Railway would aid in intra-imperial communications and defense.[44] In 1894, Defense Minister of Victoria Robert Reid and Chief Secretary of Queensland Thomas M'ilwraith journeyed to Britain. They were similarly worried about Australian defenses, especially the perceived threat of potential Asian, French, or German militancy, as well as of continued American protectionism.

"The Impact of Federation on Australia's Trade Flows," *Economic Record* 82 (September 2006): 315–324.

[42] A. Duckworth, "Notes on Tariff Restrictions," *Australian Economist* 2 (1890–93): 229–233; E. W. O'Sullivan, *Protection or Stagnation; Which?* (Sydney: Beatty, Richardson & Co., 1897); Free Trade League of Victoria, *Wages under the McKinley Tariff* (Melbourne: T. G. Ramsay & Co., 1894); *Protectionist's Handbook*, 23, 52; *Anti-Jacobin*, "British Problems, as Viewed by an American Observer," December 19, 1891, 1182, Smith Manuscripts, microfilm, reel 4.

[43] Such calls were also preceded by the outbreak of a financial crisis. See Boehm, *Prosperity and Depression in Australia*, chap. 10; Charles R. Hickson and John D. Turner, "Free Banking Gone Awry: The Australian Banking Crisis of 1893," *Financial History Review* 9 (October 2002): 147–167; and Mark Hearn, "A Wild Awakening: The 1893 Banking Crisis and the Theatrical Narratives of the Castlereagh Street Radicals," *Labour History* 85 (November 2003): 153–171.

[44] George Robert Parkin, *Imperial Federation, the Problem of National Unity* (London and New York: Macmillan and Co., 1892), 211; Edwardes, quoted in Parkin, *Imperial Federation*, 201.

These fears acted as a further impetus for the speedy establishment of a Canadian–Australian telegraph line as well as enhanced imperial postal routes in order to create "swifter" and "safer" communications with Britain. Reid and M'ilwraith also focused their discussions around Australia's need for an expanded wool market stemming from the McKinley Tariff's impact on British exports. Offering a preview of the upcoming Inter-Colonial Conference in Ottawa, Reid attempted to persuade the Imperial Government in London to accept the Australian Constitution Act Amendment, which would have allowed the Australian colonies to expand preferential trade advantages throughout the Empire, especially with Canada, as well as repeal foreign treaties, such as those with Belgium and Germany. Reid told his British audience: "We in Australia want to trade as freely with Canada and South Africa as Kent trades with Surrey, or Surrey with Yorkshire. With the introduction of restrictive tariffs and with foreign countries taking away our trade in all directions, our cry must be 'Britain for the British.'"[45] The McKinley Tariff thus precipitated not only imperial unity, but also a Listian demand for increased global transportation and communications in order to integrate the British Empire as never before.

The McKinley Tariff and Canada's "conspiracy" of annexation

British anxiety over both the close geographical proximity of Canada to the United States and the corresponding threat of American annexation could be traced back throughout the long nineteenth century (see Chapter 6). By 1890, the potential for continental union between the United States and Canada – either through political or economic means – had become a consistent and contentious theme within British–American relations. Owing to continued material and psychological distancing from the metropole, intellectuals in England and Canada at times had very divergent views on the Canadian Question. For instance, J. R. Seeley, Regius Professor of Modern History at the University of Cambridge, in *Expansion of England* (1883), thought that for "Greater Britain" to exist, "Canada and Australia would be to us as Kent and Cornwall."[46] Goldwin Smith, Cobden Club member, former Regius Professor of Modern History at Oxford, Cornell professor, and Canadian resident, preferred

---

[45] *London Times*, March 26, 1894, 5; March 20, 1894, 5; Brown, *Tariff Reform Movement*, 122–123.

[46] J. R. Seeley, *Expansion of England* (London: Macmillan and Co., 1883), 63. For a critical analysis of imperial union, see, for instance, Alfred Caldecott, *English Colonization and Empire* (New York: Charles Scribner's Sons, 1891).

to unite Canada and the United States in order to strengthen ties of trade and friendship and to prevent any future conflicts between the continental neighbors.[47] Seeley and Smith's contradictory proposals exemplified larger political rifts throughout the British Empire.

When attempts at reciprocity with its southern neighbor failed in the years following the American Civil War and Canadian confederation, Canada turned to American economic nationalist imitation. It sought to pay the United States "in their own coin" through a policy of high tariffs in order to promote its manufactures in steel, textiles, and coal, as well as to strengthen internal trade through the 1880s construction of the Canadian Pacific Railway. Responding to critics of Canadian protectionism, the *Canadian Monthly and National Review* pointed out that "those who talk idly of a 'Chinese Wall' seem to forget that it has been already erected by our neighbors."[48]

When the McKinley Tariff was passed in 1890, unsurprisingly, the decrease of Canadian agricultural exports to the United States – falling from $9 million in 1889 to $4.5 million in 1892 – further ratcheted up Liberal Canadian support for unrestricted reciprocity with its neighbor to the south. Although many Canadians desired to maintain a liberal commercial policy with the United States, the continued American refusal to make reciprocal treaties with Canada caused some once again to threaten retaliatory protectionism, which, according to Sir Alexander Galt – the first Canadian High Commissioner in London and strong proponent of imperial federation – "is the only argument applicable in the present case."[49] The incorporation of Canada within a Greater Britain quickly became a driving issue for Conservative proponents of imperial federation.[50]

Apparently unaware or unworried about such growing Canadian agitation, James G. Blaine, Listian secretary of state in the Republican

---

[47] John Herd Thompson and Stephen J. Randall, *Canada and the United States: Ambivalent Allies* (Athens: University of Georgia Press, 2002 [1994]), 56; Goldwin Smith, *The Empire* (Oxford and London: John Henry and James Parker, 1863); "List of Members," March 1866, CC MSS.

[48] Thompson and Randall, *Canada and the United States*, 56–57; Brown, *Canada's National Policy*, 193.

[49] Brown, *Canada's National Policy*, 220; Skelton, *Galt*, 275. Total Canadian exports to the United States continued to fall, for instance, from $37,280,572 in 1891 to $33,830,696 in 1892, while its exports to Great Britain during that period rose by more than $20,000,000. *Commercial Relations of the United States with Foreign Countries during the Years 1891 and 1892* (Washington, DC: Government Printing Office, 1893), 274–275. See, also, Robert H. Lawder, *Commerce between the United States & Canada, Observations on Reciprocity and the McKinley Tariff* (Toronto: Monetary Times Printing Co., 1892), 17.

[50] Rogers, "United States and Fiscal Debate in Britain," 602–603.

Harrison administration, preferred Canadian annexation rather than continued Canadian–American competition over fish and timber. Blaine publicly stated that he hoped for "a grander and nobler brotherly love, that may unite in the end" the United States and Canada "in one perfect union." Lower tariffs were off the table for Blaine, who was "teetotally opposed to giving the Canadians the sentimental satisfaction of waving the British Flag ... and enjoying the actual remuneration of American markets." In private, he told President Harrison that by denying reciprocity, Canada would "seek admission to the Union."[51]

Various English and Canadian politicians gave public voice to Blaine's private annexationist musings. British Cobdenite Lyon Playfair warned that the 1890 tariff made it appear as though the United States were "making a covert attack on Canada" in order that it might become part of a North American Zollverein or an additional American state. If the tariff act's objective "really be (as the Canadian Prime Minister, Sir John Macdonald, thinks) to force the United States lion and the Canadian lamb to lie down together, this can only be accomplished by the lamb being inside the lion," he warned. Earl Grey of England, a longtime and vocal proponent for colonial self-government, free trade, and personally disgusted by the "absurdity of the McKinley Tariff," agreed with Professor Goldwin Smith that, owing to their "many common interests," the United States and Canada needed "free intercourse with each other, that to impede such intercourse between them by artificial and needless obstacles is to commit a folly" injurious to both. Grey had severe reservations, however, concerning Smith's radical "conclusion that the incorporation of British America in the American Republic is therefore desirable."[52]

But Goldwin Smith would find stronger support in North America. Canadian Liberals such as Erastus Wiman, a Canadian financier living in New York City, and Edward Farrer, an editorialist for the *Toronto Globe* openly worked with Smith toward a continental, free-trade union, an idea which at first gained strong support among Canadian farmers. Canadian politician Mackenzie Bowell, himself an opponent of the idea of continental or commercial union, noted in Ontario: "There is no hiding the fact that the free-trade idea with the United States, has a much stronger

---

[51] *London Times*, February 17, 1891, 5; Blaine, quoted in Thompson and Randall, *Canada and the United States*, 60. For Blaine's unwillingness to include Canadian reciprocity see Allan B. Spetter, "Harrison and Blaine: No Reciprocity for Canada," *Canadian Review of American Studies* 12 (1981): 143–156. McKinley himself was at this time against commercial union. Brown, *Canada's National Policy*, 191–192.

[52] Playfair, *Tariffs of the United States*, 18; Henry George Grey, *Commercial Policy of the British Colonies and the McKinley Tariff* (London: Richard Clay and Sons, 1892), 66–68.

hold upon the farmer's mind than I could have believed, particularly along the frontier countries."[53]

But owing to an outpouring of patriotic protectionist propaganda emphasizing an alleged US plot to annex Canada, more and more Canadians began to subscribe to the imperial protectionist perception of the McKinley Tariff: that the bill was "a heavy blow struck alike at our home industries and at the prosperity and independence of the Dominion of Canada – an unprovoked aggression, an attempt at conquest by fiscal war." Such a reaction stirred "love for Queen, flag, and country," according to economic nationalist George T. Denison, president of the British Empire League in Canada. This patriotic outpouring had been caused by "the belief that a conspiracy has been on foot to betray this country into annexation. The McKinley Bill was part of the scheme."[54] Unrestricted reciprocity was little more than "veiled treason," John Macdonald similarly argued, intended "to starve Canada into annexation." He noted that the McKinley Tariff "so strongly hits our agricultural classes that the disloyal opposition is working on them in concert with Wiman and other American filibusters to promote unrestricted reciprocity with the United States." Such charges of a conspiracy, though false, proved effective.[55]

Denison and Goldwin Smith began a war of words that Canadians followed with great interest. Denison, who had once considered Goldwin Smith a close friend, by 1891 found his speeches and writings to be of "a deliberate and treasonable design … to undermine the loyal sentiment that held Canada to the Empire." Cobdenite Smith, Denison charged, had been attempting to undermine Canadian pride and patriotism for several years, sneering especially "at 'loyalty,' at 'aristocracy,' at

---

[53] Brown, *Canada's National Policy*, 208–209; Bowell to Macdonald, February 17, 1891, vol. 190, MG26-A, Sir John A. Macdonald Papers, LAC. For Wiman's desire for US–Canadian commercial unity, see Erastus Wiman, *The Greater Half of the Continent* (Toronto: Hunter, Rose & Co., 1889). Congressman Robert R. Hitt and Smith maintained close correspondence during the drafting of the McKinley Bill, as Hitt unsuccessfully attempted to include a Canadian reciprocity provision. See Hitt to Smith, June 30, 1890; and Hitt to Smith, September 5, 1890, reel 4, Smith Papers.

[54] *London Times*, October 20, 1890, 3; George T. Denison, *The Struggle for Imperial Unity: Recollections & Experiences* (London and New York: MacMillan and Co., 1909), 160. For more on the "Wiman conspiracy," which Smith thoroughly debunked, see *New York Independent*, "The *London Times* on Canadian Elections," February 11, 1892, Smith Manuscripts, microfilm, reel 4; *New York Times*, "The Wiman 'Conspiracy,'" April 30, 1891, 9; and *Sheffield Independent*, February 19, 1891, 5.

[55] Macdonald, February 18, 1891, quoted in Thompson and Randall, *Canada and the United States*, 61; Donald G. Creighton, *John A. Macdonald, The Old Chieftain* (Toronto: Macmillan, 1952–1955), 546; Macdonald to Tupper, September 26, 1890, Vol. 285, MG26-A, Macdonald Papers; Aaron William Boyes, "Canada's Undecided Future: The Discourse of Unrestricted Reciprocity and Annexation in Quebec, 1887–1893" (MA thesis, University of Ottawa, 2010), 56–76.

'jingoism'; by 'perverting history.'" Smith's acceptance of the presidency of the Continental Union Association, which sought US–Canadian union, was the last straw for Denison. "Smith's conduct is treason of the worst kind." In any other country, Denison asserted, Smith would have been lynched or imprisoned. By playing up loyalist sentiment and ratcheting up the fear of "national suicide" through annexation, Denison and other Imperial Federationists were able to force many Liberals away from the issues of commercial and continental union in the 1891 elections.[56]

Denison and Macdonald's efforts at labeling the continental and commercial unionists as traitors paid off politically. Macdonald, owing in large part to such attacks upon the opposition's involvement in "a deliberate conspiracy, by force, by fraud, or by both, to force Canada into the American union," as well as the growing unpopularity of the program of commercial union among Liberals, incrementally increased public support for his National Policy. Macdonald and his allies were thus able to force the elections of 1891 largely into a national referendum concerning Canadian–American relations, pulling off a narrow victory over those favoring unrestricted reciprocity by working "the 'Loyalty' cry for all it was worth and it carried the country . . . . But," Macdonald cautioned, "we are not safe yet."[57]

Macdonald felt that Canada had reached precarious crossroads regarding the future course of Canadian economic globalization. He told a close friend that "the great contest that is now going on ... will determine whether Canada is to remain British or become part of the United States. I can assure you, we are in great danger." Emotionalism for the Mother Country appeared to be the best solution to the problems wrought by the McKinley Tariff. In a speech at Morrisburg in September 1890, Macdonald had remarked soon before the McKinley Tariff's passage that the Canadians "are not going to cry like children" but respond with "manly spirit." The markets of New York could just as easily become the markets of London, he assured them. Macdonald also called for the globalizing of Canadian trade and communications. He urged Canadians to seek new and open markets not only in Great Britain, but in the West Indies, Australia, China, and Japan as well – markets all

[56] Denison, *Struggle for Imperial Unity*, 169, 171–177, 184, 191.
[57] Brown, *Canada's National Policy*, 208, 211; W. J. Ashley, "Review: Canada and the Canadian Question," *Economic Review* 1 (London: Percival & Co., 1891): 606; Macdonald to W. H. Smith, April 8, 1891, Vol. 534, MG26-A, Macdonald Papers. For the effects of the conspiracy charges on the 1891 elections, see Donald F. Warner, *Idea of Continental Union: Agitation for the Annexation of Canada to the United States, 1849–1893* (Lexington: University of Kentucky Press, 1960), 218–230.

the more available following the recent completion of the Canadian Pacific Railway. Their "Australian fellow colonists" had also met the Canadians with "the most perfect spirit of reciprocity," and were desirous of greater trade relations. Macdonald therefore encouraged the laying of a cable – "the precursor to trade" – between Australia and British Columbia, and the creation of a steamship line.[58] The *London Times* suggested that England could occupy "the vacated place" of the United States with respect to Canadian goods. Canada needed only to gradually "unloose all the commercial fetters" from American bonds, and instead bind "more closely the unsevered link between the daughter and the mother country."[59] The McKinley Tariff thus created the backdrop for Canadian–American commercial union's climactic nineteenth-century rise and ultimate demise. Canadian eyes instead increasingly gazed west to Australasia, south to the West Indies, and east to England.

By January 1893, the commercial bonds of empire sought by Macdonald and the *London Times* had begun to be established. Canadian Minister of Trade and Commerce Mackenzie Bowell informed his colleagues with delight that "the McKinley Bill, instead of destroying the trade of this country, has only diverted it from the United States to England . . .. Our neighbours are cutting off their own noses to spite us." Agricultural products to England increased from \$3.5 million in 1889 to \$15 million in 1892; during that time, animal and produce exports also increased from \$16 million to \$24 million.[60] Such growing commercial ties only fed the flame of imperial federation.

The chimera of imperial federation

For too long imperial federation "has been scoffed at by the uninformed as a chimera, the idle vision of patriotic dreamers and impractical imperialists," remarked the editor of Toronto's *Saturday Night*, Edmund E. Sheppard. Yet the movement, he noted, was quickly gaining adherents in Australasia, South Africa, and Canada. "All that was needed was an occasion to bring the question into practical politics, and that opportunity has been afforded by the McKinley Bill." If the British Empire were to

[58] Macdonald to Kirby, July 8, 1889, quoted in Brown, *Canada's National Policy*, 206; Macdonald, reported in the *London Times*, October 6, 1890, 13. See, also, *London Times*, November 22, 1890, 7; and his speech in Halifax reported in *Huddersfield Chronicle*, October 4, 1890, 2. For a US protectionist response to his speech, see Joseph Nimmo, Jr., *Canadian Protection Compared with the Provisions of the McKinley Tariff Act, A Reply to Sir John Macdonald's Speech at Halifax* (October 1890).

[59] *London Times*, October 18, 1890, 9.

[60] Canada, Parliament, *Debates of the Senate of the Dominion of Canada*, January 31, 1893, 29.

form an imperial federation, he continued, and a preferential imperial tariff established, "the United States will suffer, and will receive no sympathy." Sheppard realized the implications and opportunities for imperial federation offered by the McKinley Tariff. "All parts of the British Empire have been moved together" by the bill's "selfish and unstatesmanlike provisions . . . born in the brain of a village politician." All the nations of the world, he concluded felt its sting and its contempt for international commerce.[61]

Following the observations of imperialists like Sheppard, the IFL in Canada acted quickly to use the American tariff to its advantage. The Canadian IFL desired that all Canadians, across party lines, join together on behalf of imperial federation: "to open up new channels of trade with the scattered colonies of the Empire and with the mother country" to avoid being "subjected to sudden and uncontrollable interferences by foreign legislation." Included within the idea of federation was the understanding that Canadians would share in all the privileges and responsibilities that full citizenship within the British Empire entailed.[62] Henceforth, both Canadian Liberal and Conservative commercial policies contained an imperial proclivity. The 1891 election and the McKinley Tariff shifted the idea of commercial unity between Canada and Britain from a private one of the Canadian IFL to an overt national policy.[63]

In London, Sir Alexander Galt hoped to further undermine the Cobdenite orthodoxy of Free Trade England by raising alarming questions about the McKinley Tariff and by organizing imperial federative forces under the umbrella of the United Empire Trade League (UETL, 1891–1903). He first warned Gladstone that the purpose of the McKinley Tariff was "to create a state of feeling in Canada hostile to the maintenance of the Colonial question," and to threaten British trade in South

---

[61] Sheppard, "McKinley Bill and Imperial Federation," 360, 364, 365–366.

[62] *Imperial Federation*, November 1890, quoted in Tyler, *Struggle for Imperial Unity*, 190; George Monro Grant, *Imperial Federation* (Winnipeg: Manitoba Free Press, 1890), 1. See, also, Arthur H. Loring and R. J. Beadon, eds. *Papers and Addresses by Lord Brassey, Imperial Federation and Colonisation from 1880 to 1894* (London: Longmans, 1895); F. P. de Labilliere, *Federal Britain, or, Unity and Federation of the Empire* (London: Sampson Low, Marston & Co., 1894); Denison, *Struggle for Imperial Unity*; and Frederick Young, *A Pioneer of Imperial Federation in Canada* (London: George Allen, 1902).

[63] Tyler, *Struggle for Imperial Unity*, 190. See, also, James Douglas, *Canadian Independence, Annexation and British Imperial Federation* (New York and London: G. P. Putnam's Sons, 1894). In response, proponents of continental union such as Goldwin Smith, Andrew Carnegie, and various other business and political figures in New York and Toronto founded the Continental Union League in 1892, albeit prematurely, with the League dismantled two years later. See David Orchard, *The Fight for Canada: Four Centuries of Resistance to American Expansion* (Toronto: Stoddart, 1993), 78; Denison, *Struggle for Imperial Unity*, 109.

America through its reciprocity provision. Following the American tariff's passage, Galt, along with members from the Canadian branch of the IFL, backed Howard Vincent, head of the IFL in England, and James Lowther – both protectionist Conservative members of British Parliament – in the creation of the UETL as the successor to the Fair Trade League. The new league's purpose was to extend British trade and strengthen commercial ties between Britain and its colonies throughout the empire. With Spain, Russia, and France following the American example of high protection, Vincent called for British commercial union to strengthen Greater Britain, rather than "for the benefit of the Universe," as the Cobdenites espoused. Imperial federationists on both sides of the Atlantic effectively used the McKinley Tariff, "the chief helper in the cause," to steer Canadian and West Indian trade from the United States to England and to increase demand for imperial unity.[64]

The year 1894 saw the climax of the colonial tariff reform and federation movement of the late nineteenth century at the Intercolonial Conference at Ottawa. The new Canadian Conservative government called the conference "3000 miles from the shrine of the Free Trade fetish" in part "to advertise the Imperial policy which they had been strenuously advocating as the great alternative to commercial union with the United States" in the wake of the McKinley Tariff. With many of its Australasian attendees for the first time traveling across the Pacific by way of a new line of British steamers followed by a ride along the Canadian–Pacific Railway, it was a purely colonial affair from inception to end, called for by Mackenzie Bowell, Canadian Minister of Trade and Commerce.[65]

Delegates arrived from throughout the British World, with interimperial security and trade uppermost in mind. Presaging the later imperial protectionism of the Ottawa Conference of 1932, delegates in attendance came from Canada, South Australia, New Zealand, Victoria, Tasmania, Queensland, New South Wales, and the Cape of Good Hope. The Australian delegates were particularly excited to attend, hoping to speed up the laying of a Pacific Cable and an imperial steamship line. More generally, the conference attendees desired British commercial unity, "cable connection ... with all Colonies which form part of this tariff

---

[64] Oscar Douglas Skelton, *Life and Times of Sir A. T. Galt* (Carleton: McClelland and Stewart, 1966), 275; *London Times*, March 3, 1891, 14; Vincent, *Commercial Union of the Empire* (1891), in Howe and Duckenfield, ed., *Battles over Free Trade*, III, 67; Marquis Lorne, "Latest Aspects of Imperial Federation," *North American Review* 156 (October 1893): 490.

[65] Richard Jebb, *The Imperial Conference: A History and Study*, 2 vols. (London: Longmans, Green and Co., 1911), I, 163, 167, 159.

union," and resolved to ask for the ability to establish imperial commercial reciprocity and trade preference.[66] The Inter-Colonial Conference represented a significant new shift in the history of British tariff reform, and its creation owed much to the McKinley Tariff's passage. The conference was nevertheless a largely unsuccessful enterprise. So too was the Fair Trade League, dissolved in 1891, and the IFL, which came to an anticlimactic end in 1893.

Why did the late-nineteenth-century imperial protectionists fail? After all, from 1895 to 1902 imperial unity and Listian nationalism ought to have had their greatest influence with a Conservative government holding the imperial reins in London, with Joseph Chamberlain, future champion of imperial Tariff Reform, as Colonial Secretary, and with the City of London increasingly willing to sacrifice free trade for indirect taxation in the colonies. The rise of protectionism among Britain's trading partners – particularly the Listian nationalist policies enacted in Germany and the United States – and Britain's loss of a competitive edge in the race for industrial preeminence also ought to have strengthened the imperial coalition's support for economic nationalism. Furthermore, with the onset of a "second fiscal revolution" marked by the McKinley Tariff's passage and the increasing popularity of discriminatory reciprocity policies in Europe, the British business community had become increasingly discouraged by the Cobdenite system.[67] Added to this crisis surrounding the international economic order, British advocates of bimetallism had also become closely tied to the imperial federation movement. There were a growing number of farmers, manufacturers, and Conservatives – the "producers' alliance" – in Britain who began to question the efficacy of the gold standard that, alongside the rapid rise of international protectionism, was blamed for the ongoing "Great Depression" of the late nineteenth century. Such questions over continued maintenance of the gold standard arose owing to its deflationary tendencies as well as growing trade difficulties with silver standard areas. British farmers and

---

[66] *Proceedings of the Royal Colonial Institute*, XXVI, 38; Jebb, *Imperial Conference*, I, 168; II, 376. For the Ottawa Conference, see, also, J. E. Kendle, *The Colonial and Imperial Conferences, 1887-1911* (London: Longmans, 1967), 17–18. For Gladstone's anti-imperialism, see C. A. Bodelsen, *Studies in Mid-Victorian Imperialism* (London: Heinemann), 87–114; P. Knaplund, *Gladstone and Britain's Imperial Policy* (London: G. Allen & Unwin, 1927), chap. 4.

[67] Cain and Hopkins, *British Imperialism*, 185; Steven E. Lobell, "Second Image Reversed Politics: Britain's Choice of Freer Trade or Imperial Preferences, 1903–1906, 1917–1923, 1930–1932," *International Studies Quarterly* 43 (December 1999): 672–677; Rogers, "United States and Fiscal Debate in Britain," 602; Frank Trentmann, "The Transformation of Fiscal Reform: Reciprocity, Modernization, and the Fiscal Debate within the Business Community in Early Twentieth-Century Britain," *Historical Journal* 39 (1996): 1011–1012.

manufacturers, suffering most from the economic depression, in particular began to call for both imperial bimetallism and protectionism, and none other than Listian nationalist Sampson Samuel Lloyd led the bimetallic charge.[68] With this added monetary impetus, at first glance imperial federation's late Victorian failure might seem all the more perplexing.

Yet the Listian imperial federation movement was overly precipitous in three ways. First, it underestimated the power of the City of London. Put simply, while London's financial elites were willing to allow for some protectionism among the colonies and silver usage (India), the general dismantling of both English free trade and the gold standard were out of the question. British Listian nationalists met their match in the City's "goldbug" Cobdenite cosmopolitans. Pro-gold-standard Cobdenites were further successful through resurrecting the mid-century spectre of the "dear loaf." They did so by linking bimetallism's inflationary prescriptions to potential skyrocketing food prices; as Gladstone portrayed it, bimetallism was little more than "protection in disguise."[69]

Second, British bimetallic federationists found little support beyond English shores. Australia and Canada, otherwise key ideological bastions of imperial federation, failed to get on board. One reason for this is that the City of London, through heavy investment, maintained informal financial influence at the structural level within the Canadian and Australasian markets.[70] Another reason for the lack of support was that,

---

[68] E. H. H. Green, "Rentiers versus Producers? The Political Economy of the Bimetallic Controversy c. 1880–1898," *English Historical Review* 103 (July 1988): 588–612; Anthony Howe, "Bimetallism, c. 1880–1898: A Controversy Re-Opened?," *English Historical Review* 105 (April 1990): 378; Jeannette P. Nichols, "Silver Diplomacy," *Political Science Quarterly* 48 (December 1933): 580–584. See, also, Green, "The Bimetallic Controversy: Empiricism Belimed or the Case for the Issues," *English Historical Review* 105 (July 1990): 673–683; and Green, "Gentlemanly Capitalism and British Economic Policy, 1880–1914: The Debate over Bimetallism and Protectionism," in *Gentlemanly Capitalism and British Imperialism: The New Debate on Empire*, ed. by R. E. Dumett (London: Longman, 1999), 44–67.

[69] Green, "Rentiers versus Producers?," 595.

[70] Andrew Dilley, "'Rules of the Game': London Finance, Australia, and Canada, c. 1900–14," *Economic History Review* 63 (November 2010): 1003–1031; Dilley, "Empire and Risk: Edwardian Financiers, Australia, and Canada, c. 1899–1914," *Business and Economic History Online* 7 (2009): 1–12. The extent of the City of London's financial imperial power has since been called into question. See Robert V. Kubicek, "Economic Power at the Periphery: Canada, Australia, and South Africa, 1850–1914," in *Gentlemanly Capitalism and British Imperialism*, ed. by Dumett, 113–127; Jim McAloon, "Gentlemanly Capitalism and Settler Capitalists: Imperialism, Dependent Development and Colonial Wealth in the South Island of New Zealand," *Australian Economic History Review* 43 (July 2002): 204–223. In response, see A. G. Hopkins, "Gentlemanly Capitalism in New Zealand," *Australian Economic History Review* 43 (November 2003): 287–297; Bernard Attard, "From Free-Trade Imperialism to Structural Power: New Zealand and the Capital Market, 1856–1868," *Journal of Imperial and Commonwealth History* 35 (December 2007): 505–527.

in contrast to Canada's southern neighbor, "suspicion and distrust" of the banking system was nearly absent. This also helps explain why, unlike in the United States, the 1896 Canadian elections were also notable for the near absence of monetary issues.[71] Thus, a lack of support from Australia or Canada, both of which otherwise played an economically and geographically pivotal role regarding the idea of Greater Britain, further impeded the bimetallic wing of the federative movement in England.

Third, the protectionist movement toward imperial federation was overly hasty in its attempt to overthrow the Cobdenite orthodoxy. England as a whole was not ready for its displacement, nor was the protectionist movement ever able to gain the emotional or political momentum akin to the ACLL. As Frank Trentmann has described it: "Free Trade ... was the closest modern Britain ever came to a national ideology ... a genuine national and democratic culture, reaching all classes and regions, mobilizing men, women, and children, and cutting across party political divides."[72] The "cheap loaf," the City's adherence to fiscal orthodoxy, the lack of any serious monetary controversy in Canada, Gladstone's intransigence, and prolific propaganda spread by free-trade proponents like the Cobden Club weathered – and withered – the oppositional onslaught of the imperial protectionists.

As much as free-trade orthodoxy largely nullified moves toward imperial protection and federation in the era of the McKinley Tariff – and again a decade later during Chamberlain's Tariff Reform movement – internal disunity among the imperial unionists played its part, as well. Those preferring preference often canceled out those wanting an imperial Zollverein or those just seeking retaliatory tariffs; imperial unionists who believed that increased commercial ties were the key to a successful Greater Britain found themselves at odds with others who put political unity or Salisbury's Kriegsverein – imperial defense – at the ideological vanguard. While the McKinley Tariff helped the imperial federation movement reach its late-nineteenth-century zenith, such dissimilar

---

[71] James Baker, *International Bimetallism Speech before the Legislative Assembly of British Columbia* (January 24, 1894), held in the LAC; B. E. Walker, *Why Canada is Against Bimetallism* (London: Gold Standard Defence Association, 1897), 4, 8; Goldwin Smith, *Essays on Questions of the Day Political and Social* (New York and London: MacMillan and Co., 1893), 26–35; John Davidson, "Canada and the Silver Question," *Quarterly Journal of Economics* 12 (1898): 152, 143, 142. The silver issue also received little attention in Australia, to the chagrin of some Australian farmers' unions. See William Alison, *Bimetallism* (Sydney: The Australasian Pastoralists' Review, 1893).

[72] Howe, "Bimetallism, *c.* 1880–1898," 389; Frank Trentmann, *Free Trade Nation: Commerce, Consumption, and Civil Society in Modern Britain* (Oxford and New York: Oxford University Press, 2008), 2.

means to the movement's desired ends, along with the continued pre-dominance of free-trade and monetary orthodoxy in England, brought about the demise of late-nineteenth-century imperial fair trade, federa-tion, and unity. Nevertheless, American protectionism and the gold standard would continue to be issues of division between imperial protec-tionists and Cobdenites through the Edwardian period – and the McKinley Tariff would also prove instrumental in turning Joseph Chamberlain from Cobdenism to imperial preference, an ideological conversion that would lay the intellectual groundwork for the subsequent Edwardian Tariff Reform movement.[73]

Conclusion

The 1890 McKinley Tariff's mixture of high protective tariffs and dis-criminatory reciprocity treaties created both real and perceived threats to the British Empire's manufacturing and agricultural interests, harmed exports, and increased unemployment. It coincided with, and sped up demand for, national economic programs and localized federation throughout the British Empire, especially in Canada, where the McKinley Tariff was viewed by many as an attempt at annexation, bring-ing about a contentious national election that forced Canadians to con-sider seriously whether to unite more closely with the British Empire or become commercially – and perhaps politically – enjoined with the United States. The McKinley Tariff also supported and enhanced global calls for a Greater Britain tied economically between England and its white colonies – the British World – and led to closer intercolonial unity, exemplified by the 1894 Ottawa Conference. Such efforts served as the foundations for the more famous Tariff Reform movement begun in the early years of the twentieth century by Cobdenite-turned-Listian Joseph Chamberlain, and served as an oft-overlooked precursor to the 1932 Ottawa Conference, wherein an empire-wide system of trade preference would finally be developed.

The McKinley Tariff also acted as an impetus for better global com-munications and transportation in order to better connect the temporally

[73] Tyler, *Struggle for Imperial Unity*, 199–208, 45; Roland Quinalt, "John Bright and Joseph Chamberlain," *Historical Journal* 28 (September 1985): 635. On this period's connection to the subsequent Edwardian era's tariff reform and federation movement, see Rogers, "United States and Fiscal Debate in Britain"; Andrew Marrison, "Insular Free Trade, Retaliation, and the Most-Favoured-Nation Treaty, 1880–1914," in *Free Trade and its Reception, 1815–1960: Freedom and Trade*, 3 vols., ed. by Andrew Marrison (London and New York: Routledge, 1998), I, 224–242. On imperial defense, see Richard A. Preston, *Canada and "Imperial Defense": A Study of the Origins of the British Commonwealth's Defense Organization, 1867–1919* (Toronto: University of Toronto Press, 1967).

and spatially disparate British Empire. Following the passage of the US tariff, imperial demand increased rapidly for a trans-Pacific cable, the transcontinental Canadian railroad, steamship lines, a better imperial postal service, usage of the Suez Canal, and the possible benefits of one in Panama: all to augment the defensive and commercial advantages that imperial federation offered, developments which American protectionists ironically viewed as an aggressive British attempt to take possession of US trade in the Pacific.[74] The global impact of the McKinley Tariff of 1890 upon the British Empire exemplifies the global consequences of what has previously been viewed in terms of narrower domestic or national affairs.

A global historical approach to the subject offers a more complex and clear picture of economic globalization in the late nineteenth century. The McKinley Tariff was in part a Listian nationalist backlash against the Cobdenite cosmopolitanism of Great Britain. Ironically, the McKinley Tariff, in its response to the spread of British Cobdenite cosmopolitanism, enhanced the desire for a Listian Greater Britain, a protectionist white settler empire firmly knit together politically and commercially, made all the more viable owing to the technological tools of globalization. An examination of the global impact of the McKinley Tariff upon the British Empire thus demonstrates the close relationship between Listian nationalism and imperial expansionism, as well as debates over global economic integration and foreign relations. A global historical approach to economic nationalism thus helps to better grasp the ebb and flow of Anglo-American relations in the nineteenth century and beyond: especially with an American Cobdenite resurgence looming on the political horizon.

---

[74] Charles Heber Clark, "The Policy of Commercial War," in *A Tariff Symposium* (Boston, MA: Home Market Club, 1896), 12.

9   Republican rapprochement

Cleveland's free traders, Anglo-American relations,
and the 1896 presidential elections

> The Cobden Club has labored for forty years without making a single
> national convert . . . . Great Britain champions free trade and promotes it
> at the cannon's mouth.   Cyrus Hamlin.[1]

> The Democratic party . . . supposing that the Buffalo Cobden was the
> Moses who would lead it to the fair and happy land of revenue reform,
> elected him [Cleveland] President again.
> *American Protective Tariff League* (New York).[2]

> Every one of the Republican League clubs in the United States may be
> set down as an anti-Cobden club.
> *The Republican Magazine* 1 (October 1892): 382.

At the dawning of the "reckless decade" of the 1890s, the crisscrossing of
railroads, steamship lines, cables, and canals heralded a new global integrative system. Such modern technological developments now connected
markets, cultures, people, and policies at levels never before imagined.
The American titans of industry were reaping abundant rewards from
such rapid advances in global transport, communications, and industrialization. From behind high tariff walls, the capitalist colossus of the
United States arose triumphant. The unveiling of new steam engines,
the Bell telephone, and electric street lights at the 1893 World's Fair in
Chicago illuminated still further the modern marvels of turn-of-the-century American globalization.

But these innovations would also cast long shadows over globalization's
discontents. American democracy was in turmoil. Frederick Jackson
Turner – perturbed by the 1890 national census and inspired by the
writings of Henry George and Francis Amasa Walker – introduced to
the World's Fair's attendees his gloomy speculation about the end of the
"American Frontier." Indian resistance to US westward expansion continued to be squashed ruthlessly. Ongoing suppression of African

---

[1] Cyrus Hamlin, "The Morals of the Protective Tariff," in *A Tariff Symposium* (Boston,
MA: Home Market Club, 1896), 8.
[2] *American Economist* [American Protective Tariff League], March 10, 1899, 118.

American civil liberties made a mockery of the Fourteenth and Fifteenth Amendments. Growing global trade meant increased global competition. Prices on farm products fell to new lows. As corn and cotton prices plummeted, American farmers in the drought-stricken West and debt-ridden New South grew restless and agitated. Added to this, hundreds of thousands of immigrants continued to pour onto US shores, driving down the wages of the American laborer and exacerbating ethnic and racial tensions. The federal government, for its part, was noticeable only for its seeming absence, coming across as either uncaring or impotent in alleviating the suffering of so many struggling Americans.[3]

Widespread and desperate demands for a more active and interventionist federal government hinted at the obstacles facing the laissez-faire reform efforts of Grover Cleveland's second Cobdenite administration. The onset of yet another economic depression within weeks of Cleveland taking office – the Panic of 1893 – only heightened the political and ideological tension. Indebted Americans, critical of the deflationary effects of the present gold standard system, developed a potent local and national campaign for "free silver." By making the dollar cheaper, they surmised that such an inflationary national bimetallic system would allow them to pay off their debts more quickly. "Goldbug" defenders like Grover Cleveland, believing that the gold standard provided stability in an era of economic uncertainty, faced mounting countrywide opposition. Despite this troubling political economic backdrop, Cleveland retook the executive and the Democrats gained control of both houses of Congress in the elections of 1892, all with the strong support of free-trade organizations throughout the country.[4]

American Cobdenites once again wielded great influence within Cleveland's executive, either through formal appointments or as economic advisors: John G. Carlisle became Cleveland's treasury secretary; Nebraska politician J. Sterling Morton was appointed Secretary of Agriculture; Thomas Bayard was made American minister to Britain; A. B. Farquhar, cotton exporter and friend of Edward Atkinson, had the ear of Cleveland in the White House regarding fiscal matters; Professor Arthur Latham Perry found himself preparing a "short, sharp, logical, and popular demolition of the whole silver pretensions" for the new cabinet; and Atkinson speculated that, while neither he nor David Ames Wells would likely accept cabinet positions, they would be "in a better position as advisers," especially as both he and Wells already were

---

[3] H. W. Brands, *The Reckless Decade: America in the 1890s* (Chicago, IL and London: University of Chicago Press, 1995), 24, 90–253; Brands, *American Colossus: The Triumph of Capitalism, 1865–1900* (New York: Doubleday, 2010), 387–479.

[4] *New York Tribune*, January 5, 1892, 6; December 3, 1899, 1.

advising leading members in both houses of Congress on monetary and tariff reform issues.[5] America's leading Cobdenites had returned to Washington.

Amid growing political opposition and a renewed economic depression, the incoming Anglo-Saxonist Cleveland administration would stubbornly continue its defense of the gold standard as well as the Cobdenite anti-imperial principles of free trade and non-interventionism in Samoa, Hawaii, Nicaragua, and Venezuela. The contentious presidential campaign of 1896 in turn would see the Listian and Cobdenite ideological camps, despite their inherent antagonism, reluctantly arrive at one last political rapprochement. They would temporarily put aside their decades-long feud so as to defeat the radical Democratic free silver platform of Jeffersonian William Jennings Bryan – much as the opposing ideological camps had briefly come together under the Republican banner of antislavery forty years before. Bryan's silverite platform was one that both Listians and Cobdenites believed would undermine the very fabric of the global economy, and they were therefore willing to put aside their politico-ideological struggle over the future course of global economic integration to see him defeated. Because of this final rapprochement, however, Republican Listians would regain the executive in 1897. As a result, Republican advocates of the imperialism of economic nationalism would oversee the dawning of a new American century – and the acquisition of an American colonial empire.

The panic of 1893 and globalization's discontents

Transatlantic Cobdenites regarded the 1892 Democratic sweep as a referendum for freer trade. David Ames Wells, now in his sixties, believed that after more than thirty years of restricting foreign commerce, the American people had "abandoned" that policy for one that "would do much to promote peace and good-will between the United States and the rest of the world, in place of the fear, hatred, and distrust which all nations . . . now entertain toward this country." He speculated as well that this American about-face would aid in undermining continental Europe's protectionist system, which only fostered further international hostility, militarism, and poverty.[6] The seventy-five-year-old English founder of the Cobden Club, Thomas Bayley Potter, seconded Wells's pacific pronouncements. Potter stated at the club's 1893 London dinner that in

---

[5] Arthur Latham Perry, *Williamstown and Williams College* (New York: Charles Scribner's Sons, 1899), 697; Williamson, *Atkinson*, 178–179, 204–205.

[6] David Ames Wells, "Tariff Reform: Retrospective and Prospective," *Forum* (February 1893), 697, 714.

reelecting Cleveland the American people had sanctioned a change from protectionism to free trade, for which the club should congratulate itself on the progress of its nearly three-decade-long propaganda campaign.[7] Sixty-five-year-old Edward Atkinson wrote with similar optimism to journalist Charles Nordhoff that "the revolution has come." The country had condemned "McKinleyism" and "now demands to be governed ... by those who represent the principle of Free Trade." He also pragmatically recognized that the road to freer trade and maintaining the more stable system of the British-led gold standard would yet prove perilous. Atkinson compared the ensuing fight to the Civil War: the McKinley Tariff was "the first shot on Fort Sumter"; the "scare about silver is the first Bull Run."[8]

Comparing the oncoming political conflict to the bloodiest war in US history was not wholly hyperbolic – the dueling ideological camps had long been fighting for the political support of the population at large. Cobdenite cosmopolitans and Listian nationalists worked harder than ever to bring into their respective camps the poverty-stricken American laborer and farmer. To further this end, the incoming Cleveland administration charged that the McKinley Tariff had failed in its most strongly touted objective of keeping the workingman and woman's wages high. Listians in turn blamed an inadequately regulated global market and cheap international labor for plummeting US wages.

While the ideological camps exchanged blows, desperate industrial workers and indebted agrarians took matters into their own hands. They organized; they marched; they went on strike. Labor unions sought federal regulation of abusive industrial practices, and they largely subscribed to the protectionist argument that high tariffs led to high wages.[9] The Populist party grew in political prominence, gaining a number of seats in state and national government. In contrast to labor unions, many Populist politicians preferred an elimination of all tariffs, particularly protective ones, seeking direct rather than indirect taxation. They saw protectionism as just one more way the government took care of industry at the expense of agriculture. The new movement also gained tangible

[7] *London Times*, July 24, 1893, 7.
[8] Atkinson to Nordhoff, November 28, 1892, carton 22, Edward Atkinson Papers, MHS; Harold Francis Williamson, *Edward Atkinson: The Biography of an American Liberal, 1827–1905* (Boston, MA: Old Corner Book Store, 1934), 178–179, 204–205; *London Times*, July 24, 1893, 7; Edward Atkinson, *Taxation and Work: A Series of Treatises on the Tariff and the Currency* (New York and London: G. P. Putnam's Sons, 1892), 110; Atkinson to Nordhoff, July 13, 1893, carton 23, Atkinson Papers.
[9] Horace White and Amasa Walker, for instance, had long been laissez-faire opponents of a government-enforced eight-hour workday. See Nancy Cohen, *The Reconstruction of American Liberalism 1865–1914* (Chapel Hill: University of North Carolina Press, 2002).

support from the socialist efforts of Edward Bellamy, and even from a few disillusioned Cobdenites like Henry Demarest Lloyd, the former fanatical AFTL secretary turned independent muckraker and anti-monopolist – a wayward free trader who was fast becoming a socialist reformer following a fruitful visit with the leaders of Britain's Fabian Society.[10]

Despite a shared penchant for freer trade, the Populists were generally at odds with American Cobdenites. Even the Populist absolutist opposition to tariffs was too extreme for many Cobdenites, for whom the indirect British system of a tariff for revenue only was preferable to a complete elimination of duties and a sudden shift to direct taxation. The Populist condemnation of the gold standard further alienated them from the predominantly goldbug Cobdenites, as did the Populist call for the nationalization of American railways. In the early years of the 1890s, the laissez-faire radicalism of Cobdenism and the hands-off approach of Grover Cleveland were making few friends among those subscribing to the turn-of-the-century radicalism of labor and Populism.

Along with the election of an American "Free Trade President," the 1890s saw the revival of the free silver issue. According to its proponents, the free coinage of silver promised to inflate deflated prices and open up markets in silver-standard China and Latin America, thereby freeing the Anglophobic American farmer from the dictates of the gold-standard British market. The 1890 Sherman Silver Purchase Act and the temporary failure of the powerful financial firm Baring Brothers had led to the exportation of large amounts of American gold overseas. The Sherman Act had ended up adding surplus funds to northeastern financial coffers, funds that quickly made their way into the hands of European investors. The Baring failure in turn had undercut confidence in the international securities market, and the subsequent large-scale sale of US securities led to a further drain on American gold reserves. A large American wheat harvest and a coinciding European crop failure in 1891 had reversed this gold flight, but only temporarily. Even as Cobdenite John G. Carlisle took over the Treasury Department, the Treasury's gold reserves hit minimum levels.

When the 1893 financial panic struck, Cleveland's goldbugs attempted to use the renewed depression to their political advantage. They laid most of the fiscal blame on three issues: (1) America's depleted gold reserves; (2) the growing deficit, exacerbated by the McKinley Tariff's sizeable bounties to US sugar growers; and (3) the inflationary effects of

[10] John L. Thomas, *Alternative America: Henry George, Edward Bellamy, Henry Demarest Lloyd and the Adversary Tradition* (Cambridge, MA and London: Belknap Press, 1983), 80–81, 136, 149, 275–277, 279–280, 309; Thomas P. Jenkin, "The American Fabian Movement," *Western Political Quarterly* 1 (June 1948): 113–123.

Congress's overly sympathetic silver sentiment, illustrated by congressional passage of the 1890 Sherman Silver Purchase Act. American gold proponents instead viewed the long-term financial success of England as proof that the gold standard was superior to either free silver coinage or international bimetallism – and an essential ingredient for stability during an era dominated by unpredictable economic panics. American goldbugs even began insinuating a correlation between the cheap labor systems of China, Japan, Siam, and India with those countries' adherence to free silver coinage.[11]

Silverites instead interpreted the 1893 economic panic as but a further demonstration of American overreliance on gold. Agrarian free silver advocates perceived (correctly) that the shrinking supply of money in circulation and the falling price levels of the 1880s and 1890s resulted in part from the demonetization of silver in 1873. Remonetization would put more money into circulation, they argued, bringing about currency inflation and lower interest rates, thus relieving indebted American farmers from their economic plight. Furthermore, it seemed obvious to silverites that Great Britain, as the world's creditor, had been the ultimate victor in the demonetization of silver. Anglophobic silverites also assumed that the high ratio of silver to gold correlated with the collapse of the price of foodstuffs, thereby further aiding England, the largest importer of foodstuffs in the world, especially from silver-backed India. Both sides of the local American monetary debate thus utilized global trade and monetary policies to bolster their arguments.[12]

American farmers drew nefarious connections between Indian exports and bimetallism throughout the late nineteenth century, owing to India's continued silver backing of the rupee. Silverite Senator Thomas C. Power took it as "an accepted fact that an ounce of silver bullion will always purchase a bushel of wheat in India and pay its transportation to Liverpool." American farmers believed they needed similar export capabilities. Sir Robert N. Fowler – a banker, ex-mayor of London, member of British Parliament, friend of Edward Atkinson, and Cobden Club

---

[11] "The Experience of Eastern Asia, the Great Home of Silver, with that Metal – an Object Lesson to America," in confidential correspondence, Barrett [US Legation, Bangkok, Siam] to William McKinley, September 8, 1896, microfilm reel 1, William McKinley Papers, LOC. On the Panic of 1893, see Scott Reynolds Nelson, *A Nation of Deadbeats: An Uncommon History of America's Financial Disasters* (New York: Knopf, 2012), chap. 10; John Sperling, *Great Depressions: 1837–1844, 1893–1897, 1929–1939* (Chicago, IL: Scott, Foresman, 1966); Gerald T. White, *The United States and the Problem of Recovery after 1893* (University: The University of Alabama Press, 1982).

[12] Jeffry A. Frieden, "Invested Interests: The Politics of National Economic Policies in a World of Global Finance," *International Organization* 45 (Autumn 1991): 425–451; Frieden, "Monetary Populism in Nineteenth-Century America: An Open Economy Approach," *Journal of Economic History* 57 (June 1997): 367–395.

member – had even stated in 1886 that "the effect of the depreciation of silver must be the ruin of the wheat and cotton industries of America, and the development of India as the chief wheat and cotton exporter of the world," a quote frequently cited by silverites as alleged proof of a British monometallic conspiracy.[13]

Foreign market competition from India and other silver-using countries therefore helped bring together bimetallic and protectionist elements in the United States, as was similarly occurring in Britain (see Chapter 8). Joseph Wharton's nephew, Philadelphia's Listian nationalist Wharton Barker, argued in *Bimetallism and Protection Inseparable. Gold Mon-metallism means Free Trade* (1896) that so long as the United States remained on the gold standard its farmers would remain impoverished and unable to compete with silver-backed countries. A mixture of bimetallism and protectionism alternatively would raise the price of US farm exports by increasing the gold price of silver in the British-controlled global market. This could be accomplished, Barker put forth, through silver coinage in the United States. Such localized independent silver usage would increase the global demand for silver while concurrently lowering demand for gold, and thus bring up the global market price of silver. "Bimetallism and Protection are inseparable," he explained, whereas "Gold-monometallism and Protection" were "irreconcilably hostile." As it stood, however, silver-using markets were essentially closed to gold-backed British, American, and German manufactures, forcing the latter countries to glut European markets. This put them in direct competition with US exports to Europe, argued Barker, which further lowered US agricultural prices to the detriment of the American farmer. Such had been the pattern since the German and French demonetization of silver in 1873. The needs of US silver miners, manufacturers, and farmers therefore overlapped, Barker suggested. At the same time that protective tariffs were stimulating the home market, national bimetallism would lessen global market competition, raise the price of agricultural products, and thereby give farmers more money with which to buy US manufactures. The only proper US tonic, Barker hammered home, was protective tariffs mixed with national bimetallism.[14]

By this time, some American bimetallists even began envisioning a North American bimetallic union that included the United States,

---

[13] Thomas C. Power, *Silver, the Friend of the Farmer and the Miner* (Washington, DC: Government Printing Office, 1893), 8, 10; H. E. Taubeneck, *The Condition of the American Farmer* (Chicago, IL: Schulte Publishing Co., 1896), 51; Edward Atkinson to Wells, July 8, 1898, microfilm reel 8, David Ames Wells Papers, LOC.

[14] Wharton Barker, *Bimetallism and Protection Inseperable. Gold Mono-Metallism Means Free Trade. A Letter Addressed to the Members of the Manufacturers' Club of Philadelphia*, March 28, 1896, 5.

Mexico, South America, and Canada, an idea that had made an earlier appearance in Listian Secretary of State James G. Blaine's Pan-American scheme (see Chapter 7). One such proponent, under the pseudonym "Par," sought "the most advantageous means of promoting reciprocal trade exchanges between the descendants of Columbus": what he called the "Three Americas' Trade Movement." To the detriment of North American debtors, Par argued, the United States and Canada were in a position of "financial servility" to Britain, the great creditor. Rather, a "natural homogeneity of commercial interests ... should bind all American republics in one zolverein, a Pan-American customs union." Par used recent calls for commercial union to strengthen his argument. With Europe's earlier bimetallic Latin Monetary Union as a prototype, Par recommended this union could best be accomplished through a bimetallic agreement freed from British financial control.[15] Par thus offered another potential continental alliance, albeit one that was fiscal anathema to North America's goldbug Cobdenites.

Nor did such bimetallic arguments persuade British or American financial lenders, who largely sided with the pro-gold-standard Cleveland administration.[16] Both Wall Street and the City of London continued to prefer the deflationary system of gold monometallism to an inflationary bimetallic system. Their continued adherence to the gold standard stemmed in part from fears that debtors would quickly pay off their obligations in inflated money and thereby undermine England's – and to a lesser extent New York's – financial leadership, and in part because they believed that such a non-international bimetallic system was immoral and economically unstable.

The US government's presumed complicity in the goldbug "plot" through its continued backing of the gold standard increased silverite ire. Half measures such as the Sherman Silver Purchase Act of 1890 and the earlier 1878 Bland-Allison Act had done little to defuse the tension. Western Republicans and Populists insinuated that Wall Street bankers and Congress were nothing more than British puppets. The Panic of 1893 drove even more silver supporters into the Populist party, to the detriment of both major parties.[17]

---

[15] "Par," *The Three Americas* (Washington, DC, 1892), 5, 4, 127, 128, 130, 132.

[16] For the City of London's and Canadian opposition to bimetallism, see, respectively, Chapter 8 and Craufurd D. W. Goodwin, *Canadian Economic Thought: The Political Economy of a Developing Nation 1814–1914* (Durham: Duke University Press, 1961), 71–106.

[17] Bradley J. Young, "Silver, Discontent, and Conspiracy: The Ideology of the Western Republican Revolt of 1890–1901," *Pacific Historical Review* 64 (May 1995): 243–265; Edward P. Crapol, *America for Americans: Economic Nationalism and Anglophobia in the Late Nineteenth Century* (Westport, CT: Greenwood Press, 1973), 201.

Cleveland stubbornly maintained his unpopular support for the gold standard throughout his second administration. He did so with Wells and Atkinson once again as economic advisors, and with Horace White's and William Lloyd Garrison, II's respective editorial support at the *New York Evening Post* and the *Nation*. Against strong opposition from the country's silver mining interests, Cleveland quickly went to work to repeal the Sherman Silver Purchase Act. His efforts alienated powerful Republican and Democratic silverite congressmen and also brought corresponding indictments of a transatlantic conspiracy. The editor of the Populist *National Bulletin* stated that Cleveland was a tool of Britain. In the summer of 1893, Cleveland's opponents further asserted that the president appeared "to have an understanding with England, as he was copying everything British on tariff, free trade, and finance. He saw everything through British glasses." Thomas Bayard likewise was "more English than the English themselves . . . . He is a confirmed Anglomaniac" and "should be compelled to resign" from his position as minister to England. Following Republican calls for his impeachment, Bayard was even censured by Congress in 1895 for speeches he made in Great Britain condemning the US protectionist system.[18] A new fiscal war was brewing as the Cleveland administration's goldbugs stubbornly squared off against the potent silverite and protectionist fermentation.

The 1894 Wilson–Gorman Tariff and the ACLL's legacy

Repealing the Sherman Silver Purchase Act was a difficult affair, and one that only further alienated congressional silverites from the Cleveland administration. With repeal (and fewer congressional allies) behind them, Cleveland's cabinet members and advisors then turned their attention to overturning the 1890 McKinley Tariff. The result, the Wilson–Gorman bill of 1894, appeared to be a modicum of success for Anglo-American Cobdenites, although few on either side of the politico-ideological divide were thrilled with the end product, a hodge-podge of tariff revisions that did little to disrupt the American System. "Cobdenism is not suited to the United States," New York's *Oswego Daily Times* concluded in 1896. Such was the protectionist response to Cleveland's attempt to replace the

---

[18] Joseph Logsdon, *Horace White, Nineteenth Century Liberal* (Westport, CT: Greenwood, 1971), 335; Crapol, *America for Americans*, 201; Jeannette Paddock Nichols, "The Politics and Personalities of Silver Repeal in the United States Senate," *American Historical Review* 41 (October 1935): 26–53; Patrick Cudmore, *Cleveland's Maladministration: Free Trade, Protection and Reciprocity* (New York: P. J. Kennedy, 1896), 7; *Congressional Record*, 54 Cong., 1 Sess., December 10, 1895, 114–126.

McKinley Tariff with "the free or freer trade features of the Wilson bill."[19]

Making the political climate all the more acrimonious, the rhetoric of antislavery continued to permeate the ensuing tariff debate. "The denial to any individual, for the benefit of some private interest, of the right to exchange the product of his labor, involves the principle of slavery," Wells argued in the pages of the *Forum*. The secretary of Boston's Home Market Club, Albert Clarke, returned rhetorical fire by maintaining that precipitous free trade brought about industrial slavery and degraded labor. It also enabled a powerful country like Britain to destroy the more infant industries of the United States. "Is it in accordance with human freedom to give the strong this advantage over the weak?" he asked. "Yet this is the feast to which the Cobden school invites young men who are imbued with love of humanity and who are allured by the pleasant sound of freedom."[20]

Within this hyperbolic political environment, US tariff reformers began work upon the last congressional attempt toward freer trade in the nineteenth century; and they did so with the mid-century successes of Sir Robert Peel and the ACLL still in mind. The Wilson–Gorman Tariff Act of 1894 modestly sought to undo some of the work of the 1890 McKinley Tariff – including repeal of the latter's retaliatory reciprocity clause. Treasury Secretary Carlisle invited Wells and Atkinson to offer their advice in the crafting of the new legislation. They became advisors to the bill's author, Democratic Congressman William L. Wilson, chairman of the House Ways and Means Committee. Under Wells and Atkinson's guidance, Wilson – an avowed tariff reformer and goldbug – developed a bill that, in order to be palatable to the congressional majority, conservatively sought to lower tariffs and created a free list comparable to that of the 1888 Mills Bill. The new bill also condemned the McKinley Tariff's "erroneously" titled reciprocity provision. In contrast to the Anglophobic and anti-Canadian bent of the McKinley Tariff, an early version of the Wilson bill even would have allowed for free entry of Canadian agricultural products. Atkinson speculated that the Wilson bill would receive support from both parties because "McKinleyism has killed the Republican party." He also justified the new bill's moderate approach because the United States was in a similar position to that of England in the early 1840s, "and what I am trying to do is to follow and improve upon the methods of Sir Robert Peel and his successors." Cobdenite

---

[19] *Oswego Daily Times* (NY), August 29, 1896.
[20] Wells, "Tariff Reform," 702; Albert Clarke, "Free Trade is not Freedom," in *A Tariff Symposium* (Boston, MA: Home Market Club, 1896), 9.

Congressman Michael D. Harter (D-OH), although admitting the bill did not go far enough, similarly found hope for the country's political economic future after reading Trumbull's *History of the Free Trade Movement in England*.[21] The American free-trade legacy of the ACLL remained prominent.

Atkinson, ever the pragmatist, hoped to reach across the aisle in support of his moderate approach to obtaining free trade. Writing to Cobdenite-turned-Listian Senator Henry Cabot Lodge (R-MA), Atkinson hoped that they might both agree that the McKinley bill "is dead." To Atkinson, tariff reform winds seemed sure, especially with William Wilson at the congressional helm, "a Free Trader by conviction on the most solid ground who will use wise judgment as Sir Robert Peel did in leading the reform." Atkinson suggested that Lodge join him in removing the tariff issue from politics: "The true protection for American industry is gradually to remove every type and form of artificial obstruction by which we are now prevented from extending our home market all over the world."[22] His appeal, however, fell on deaf ears. For Lodge, the time had not yet come to turn from protectionism to free trade.

Atkinson was also as yet unaware that so much of Cleveland's political capital had already been spent on overturning the Sherman Act. As a result, the Wilson bill ended up being a far cry from even the moderate reforms that American Cobdenites desired. Thanks especially to the lobbying efforts of the Sugar Trust, retaliatory duties were placed on refined sugar and a 40 percent *ad valorem* duty was placed on raw sugar, with the side effect of disrupting the Cuban sugar economy, inciting further revolution within the Spanish colony. Furthermore, despite its various protectionist elements and modest tariff reductions, the Wilson bill's economic nationalist opponents rather predictably suggested it had

---

[21] Festus P. Summers, *William L. Wilson and Tariff Reform* (New Brunswick, NJ: Rutgers University Press, 1953), 73–74; Tom E. Terrill, "David A. Wells, the Democracy, and Tariff Reduction, 1877-1894," *Journal of American History* 56 (December 1969), 551; William McKinley, *The Tariff in the Days of Henry Clay and Since* (New York: Henry Clay Publishing Co., 1896), 201; J. Laurence Laughlin and H. Parker Willis, *Reciprocity* (New York: The Baker & Taylor Co., 1903), 68; William L. Wilson to Atkinson, March 25, December 8, 1892, carton 5; September 23, October 10, 1893; Carlisle to Atkinson, October 24, 1894, carton 6; Atkinson to Nordhoff, February 14, 1893, carton 22, Atkinson Papers; Harter to Everett P. Wheeler, August 21, 1894, in Everett P. Wheeler, *Sixty Years of American Life: Taylor to Roosevelt, 1850 to 1910* (New York: E. P. Dutton & Company, 1917), 215.

[22] Atkinson to Lodge, August 29, 1893, carton 23, Atkinson Papers. See, also, Edward Atkinson, "A Forecast of the Future Commercial Union of the English-Speaking People," in *American Association for the Advancement of Science for the Forty-Third Meeting held at Brooklyn, N.Y. August, 1894* (Salem: Permanent Secretary, 1895), 407–419, 417. Much of the "Atkinson Plan" was incorporated into the Wilson Bill. Williamson, *Atkinson*, 184–190.

been "passed in the interest of England," owing to the legislation's half steps toward freer trade. Maryland's conservative Democratic Senator Arthur Pue Gorman proved quite effective at neutralizing the House bill in the Senate. He charged that "Cleveland's whole energy has been directed to legislate for England and Canada," Anglophobic sentiments that were echoed by the protectionist press [figure 9.1].[23]

The House tariff bill sent to the Senate may have gone too far for protectionists in both parties, but the Senate's watered-down version did not go nearly far enough for free traders like William Wilson, Democratic Senator Roger Q. Mills, and President Grover Cleveland. Considering the choice between this new moderately protectionist Democratic bill and the current McKinley Tariff, Cleveland cynically preferred the latter so that Republicans might not shift the blame for the ongoing economic panic upon the Wilson–Gorman bill. Cleveland could not even bring himself to sign the final product when it crossed his desk. His inability to garner stronger Democratic loyalty for passing a lower tariff bill also upset Wells and William R. Morrison, the latter now a member of the Interstate Commerce Commission. Yet Atkinson, ever the optimist, saw even the bill's moderate reductions as a promising step, writing Wilson that protection was "intellectually dead." While the bill was not ideal, he wrote Charles Nordhoff, it "was as long a step as ought to have been made," as its reform measures "will bear a close resemblance to Sir Robert Peel's."[24] The legacy of the 1846 repeal of the Corn Laws continued to reverberate within the 1890s free-trade movement, despite the fact that congressional support for tariff reform appeared wanting.

Wilson's tepid tariff bill was apparently much more acceptable to free traders in England than those in the United States. In September 1894, about a month after the bill's passage, Wilson traveled to London where he was incessantly interviewed and affectionately termed "Tariff" Wilson – he was also kept under the watchful eye of the protectionist press back home. After toasting the Queen alongside his English hosts, Wilson noted that America's "protectionists have been building defenses to keep you out and other nations from competing with us in our home markets. The tariff reformers are breaking down these defenses." His words, in the view of the protectionist opposition, showed how grateful Britons were to Wilson for trying to wrest control of the American market for English

---

[23] Laughlin and Willis, *Reciprocity*, 235–242; David M. Pletcher, *The Diplomacy of Trade and Investment: American Economic Expansion in the Hemisphere, 1865–1900* (Columbia: University of Missouri Press, 1998), 230; Cudmore, *Cleveland's Maladministration*, 8.

[24] Mills to Atkinson, March 19, 1894, carton 6; Wells to Atkinson, June 22, 1894, folder 29, carton 13, Atkinson Papers; Edward Atkinson to Wilson, July 5, 1894, carton 23, Atkinson Papers; Summers, *William L. Wilson*, 172–208.

Figure 9.1 "Wilson Wears It." Above, the American Protective
League's weekly depicts William L. Wilson and his tariff bill in the
"livery" of "the J. Bull model of the Cobden Club." *American Economist*,
June 5, 1896, 273

interests. The Anglophobic *Washington Post* lashed out at Wilson for
"abusing the institutions of his own country for the delectation of foreigners." London's *Commerce*, on the other hand, called Wilson "the most
distinguished American statesman of the day, holding and representing as
he does opinions so heartily in accord with those of his British hearers."
Whether from American protectionist criticism or British free-trade

praise, Wilson's bill brought with it renewed conspiratorial charges against the Cleveland administration's policies.[25]

The protectionist press redoubled its attack. Economic nationalists saw their position strengthened in Congress following substantial gains in the November 1894 elections, owing in part from blaming the Wilson–Gorman Tariff for the continued depression, just as Cleveland had feared. For his part, Edward Atkinson blamed the "silver craze," and denied that the Republican gains were a referendum on free trade. Listian intellectual Henry Carey Baird, nephew of Henry C. Carey, instead warned free traders to "flee from the economic fallacies of Mr. Edward Atkinson, as it would from the plague, the black death, or from leprosy, for these fallacies are microbes that breed a social leprosy."[26] Clearly, neither side of the ideological battlefield could claim a monopoly on hyperbole.

The cosmopolitanism of Anglo-Saxonism

Cleveland's cabinet included multiple subscribers to Anglo-Saxonism, the belief in an English-speaking race, and often containing a desire to unify the Anglo-Saxon world for the betterment of mankind. Historians have since turned their attention to the rise of Anglo-Saxonism, particularly the movement's racist underpinnings, its role in the development of Anglo-American rapprochement, and its confluence with late-nineteenth-century expansionism, Canadian–American relations, and American anti-imperialism.[27] And the motivation for Anglo-Saxonism

---

[25] Summers, *William L. Wilson*, 211–212; *London Times*, September 28, 1894; *Washington Post*, September 29, 1894; Cudmore, *Cleveland's Maladministration*, 8–9; *London Commerce*, October 3, 1894. See, also, *Macon Telegraph*, October 8, 1894; *Portland Morning Oregonian*, September 28, 1894, 2.

[26] Atkinson to Swire Smith, November 10, 1894, carton 24, Atkinson Papers; Baird, quoted in Williamson, *Atkinson*, 209.

[27] Reginald Horsman, *Race and Manifest Destiny: The Origins of American Racial Anglo-Saxonism* (Cambridge, MA: Harvard University Press, 1981); Michael L. Krenn, ed., *Race and U.S. Foreign Policy in the Ages of Territorial and Market Expansion, 1840–1900* (New York: Garland Pub., 1998); Matthew Frye Jacobson, *Barbarian Virtues: The United States Encounters Foreign Peoples at Home and Abroad, 1876–1914* (New York: Hill and Wang, 2000); Stuart Anderson, *Race and Rapprochement: Anglo-Saxonism and Anglo-American Relations, 1895–1904* (Rutherford, NJ: Fairleigh Dickinson University Press, 1981); Edward P. Kohn, *This Kindred People: Canadian-American Relations and the Anglo-Saxon Idea, 1895–1903* (McGill: Queen's University Press, 2005); Eric T. L. Love, *Race over Empire: Racism and U.S. Imperialism, 1865–1900* (Chapel Hill: University of North Carolina Press, 2004); Charles DeBenedetti, *The Peace Reform in American History* (Bloomington: Indiana University Press, 1980), chap. 4; Duncan Bell, "The Project for a New Anglo Century: Race, Space, and Global Order," in *Anglo-America and its Discontents: Civilizational Identities beyond West and East*, ed. by Peter Katzenstein (London: Routledge, 2012): 33–56.

did indeed contain a sense of racial superiority. But, although racism and cosmopolitanism were by no means mutually exclusive, Anglo-Saxonism also contained within it an oft-overlooked cosmopolitan *esprit de corps*.

Many American Cobdenites subscribed to the belief that the Anglo-Saxon race was superior and more civilized than the rest, especially following the intermingling of Social Darwinian thought with Cobdenism in the latter decades of the nineteenth century. Various late-nineteenth-century North American commercial unionists, for example, were prone to utilizing Anglo-Saxonist arguments (see Chapter 6). David Ames Wells argued outright for Anglo-Saxonism in the 1890s. So too did Edward Atkinson call for bringing the disparate Anglo-Saxon race "into the closest commercial union." This was to be accomplished through a universally shared gold standard to ease commercial transactions, alongside demilitarization and unrestricted trade, especially between the United States, Canada, and Britain. In doing so, he dreamt of the day when the English-speaking people would have "the peaceful control of the commerce of the world."[28]

Atkinson even began dabbling in the Anglo-Saxonist philosophy of British imperialists like J. R. Seeley, author of the popular publication *Expansion of England* (1883). After a seeming Anglo-American crisis arose from an 1895 boundary dispute between Britain and Venezuela, and with American Anglophobes clamoring for war in order to defend the Monroe Doctrine, Atkinson wistfully began to wonder about how much South America might have benefited from British rather than Spanish rule. He wrote J. Sterling Morton that it had been "a pity England did not take over the whole of South America . . . what a blessing to that continent English rule would have been and *would be now* if it were possible." David Wells similarly recommended that Great Britain should receive control of the Orinoco River in Venezuela for the sake of Anglo-American relations and international free trade.[29] Anti-imperialists Atkinson and Wells were beginning to express some decidedly imperial sentiments, albeit in favor of the British Empire rather than an American one. Such British imperial apologetics among the cosmopolitan leadership of the Gilded Age anti-imperial movement further demonstrated the growing power of Anglo-Saxonism during the 1890s.

---

[28] David Ames Wells, "The United States and Great Britain. Their True Governmental and Commercial Relations," in *America and Europe: A Study of International Relations* (New York: G. P. Putnam's Sons, 1896), 3–72; Atkinson, "Forecast of the Future," 415, 419.

[29] Atkinson to Senator Hawley, January 2, 1896; Atkinson to D. C. Gilman, December 4, 1895; Atkinson to Morton, January 3, 1896, carton 56, Atkinson Papers; Wells, "United States and Great Britain."

But there was more to 1890s Anglo-Saxonism than a racial defense of British free-trade imperialism. North American Cobdenites were also highly critical of ethnic and racial groups that they viewed as incompatible with their vision of a united cosmopolitan world. Non-whites, Jews, and French-Canadians – either through exclusion or exclusivity – were seen as serious stumbling blocks toward the realization of the Cobdenite vision of continental, and eventual global, inclusivity.

Canadian Cobdenite Goldwin Smith had long numbered among the most vocal advocates of Anglo-Saxonism. He correspondingly landed himself in hot water in the late 1890s when he tried to give some justification for Jewish persecution in Europe and Russia. A critic took him to task for one such article that had appeared within "the cosmopolitan pages" of the *North American Review*. In the article, Smith had suggested that Jews were not being persecuted solely because of their religion. Rather, it was primarily "economical and social," "because they refuse everywhere to live the life of the country in which they dwell." Smith explained "the whole trouble": how Jews "insert themselves" into new countries "while they retain a marked and repellent nationality of their own." He took similar issue with Armenians, Gypsies, and the French-Catholic separatists of Canada. Such nationalistic "exclusiveness" was certainly compounded by Christian intolerance, Smith granted, but these groups' maintenance of "tribal isolation" inherently created much of their "unpopularity." In a similar 1893 article entitled "Anglo-Saxon Union," Smith suggested that the future of Canada and the United States was of great importance in the wake of the McKinley Tariff and the British imperial federation movement, both of which sought to sever Canada from the United States. Another obstacle was the "isolation" of French Canadians, an isolation that has left them "backward . . . in education, in intelligence, and in industrial activity." He nevertheless believed that the shared language and race of North America's Anglo-Saxon race would overcome these impediments.[30] Anglo-Saxonism certainly had a pronounced racist dimension, but for Cobdenite adherents, at least, it also contained a strong dose of cosmopolitanism. Their adherence to Anglo-Saxonism would find further outlets in the realm of foreign policy during the second Cleveland administration.

---

[30] Isaac Besht Bendavid, "Goldwin Smith and the Jews," *North American Review* 153 (September 1891): 257–258; Goldwin Smith, "New Light on the Jewish Question," *North American Review* 153 (August 1891): 133, 137; Goldwin Smith, "Anglo-Saxon Union: A Response to Mr. Carnegie," *North American Review* 157 (August 1893): 170–185, 177.

The anti-imperialism of free trade, 1893–1897

Revisionist open-door imperial scholarship has long struggled to fit the non-consecutive Democratic Cleveland administrations into its bipartisan imperial paradigm. In trying to force Cleveland into the "Open Door," for instance, W. A. Williams termed him and other critics of Republican imperialism "so-called anti-imperialists," and suggested that proponents of laissez-faire naturally sanctioned economic expansion, which for Williams and his school was indistinguishable from imperialism.[31] As a result, Thomas McCormick concluded that Cleveland advocated for "free-trade imperialism." Some of the most influential open-door histories have accordingly highlighted various innocuous foreign policy actions during the Cleveland eras in order to position the Cleveland administrations within a bipartisan free-trade imperial framework.[32]

Gallagher and Robinson's "imperialism of free trade" label, however, fits uncomfortably upon Cleveland's Cobdenite administrations. Both the state of the US political economy and the anti-imperial dimensions of Cleveland's foreign policy contradict the thesis. First, one cannot ignore that, despite Cleveland's various attempted classical liberal reforms, US fiscal policy remained protectionist throughout both his terms. For another, placing Cleveland within the open-door or free-trade imperial thesis downplays the sizeable anti-imperial dimensions of Cleveland's Cobdenite administrations.[33] While Anglo-Saxonism,

---

[31] William Appleman Williams, *The Tragedy of American Diplomacy* (Cleveland, OH: World Pub., 1959), 30–32, 33–34, 47.

[32] For example, from 1893 to 1895 the Cleveland administration provided naval protection to American merchant ships headed toward civil-war-torn Brazil, ultimately escorting the vessels through the rebel-backed blockade in Gaunabara Bay. For revisionists, this was a clear act of economic imperialism, despite an American adherence to neutrality and the absence of either US military occupation or economic exploitation. Only one shell was fired by a US naval vessel (without instruction from the Cleveland administration), and only after being fired upon. The only casualty was the US naval cruiser *Detroit*'s assistant paymaster, who shot himself in the leg. Brazil's civil war carried on for more than a year afterward. Williams nevertheless described Cleveland as intervening "boldly" in the Brazilian Revolution. Williams, *Tragedy*, 30. Steven Topik provides a more even-handed account in *Trade and Gunboats: The United States in the Age of Empire* (Stanford: Stanford University Press, 1996), 8, 120, 132–154. See, also, Walter LaFeber, *The Cambridge History of American Foreign Relations Volume II: The American Search for Opportunity, 1865-1913* (Cambridge: Cambridge University Press, 1993), 122; LaFeber, "United States Depression Diplomacy and the Brazilian Revolution, 1893–1894," *Hispanic American Historical Review* 40 (February 1960): 107–118; LaFeber, "The Background of Cleveland's Venezuelan Policy: A Reinterpretation," *American Historical Review* 66 (July 1961): 947–967; William Appleman Williams, *The Contours of American History* (Cleveland, OH: World Pub. Co., 1961), 340–341.

[33] McCormick's analysis adds that "Cleveland's 'free-trade imperialism' and McKinley's 'pragmatic expansionism' shared in common a great deal of intellectual real estate," including a preference for "commercial Open Doors over closed colonies or spheres of

upholding the Monroe Doctrine, and a desire for new markets certainly motivated Cleveland's cabinet, it remains problematic to paint either Cleveland administration in free-trade imperial colors.

Revisionist attempts to place Cleveland and his Cobdenite advisors alongside their imperial Republican predecessors and successors are eerily reminiscent of British historiographical disagreements surrounding the "imperialism of free trade" thesis. In 1962, Oliver MacDonagh countered Gallagher and Robinson's 1953 informal imperial argument with his own: what he called the "anti-imperialism of free trade." MacDonagh persuasively argued that the staunchest British adherents to Victorian free-trade ideology were inherently opposed to imperialism in all its guises. American Cobdenites by and large expressed similar anti-imperial free-trade sentiments. Cleveland and his Cobdenite cabinets time and again thwarted Republican formal annexationism, informal imperial designs, and militarism throughout the 1880s and 1890s, while also attempting to ameliorate the Republican protectionist system through attempting to institute freer trade. MacDonagh's "anti-imperialism of free trade" thesis therefore more closely encapsulates the Cobdenite foreign policies of the Cleveland administrations.[34]

While historians of the Open Door Empire may have overlooked the Cobdenite anti-imperial dimensions of Cleveland's foreign policy, Republican Listian nationalists, promulgating instead the imperialism of economic nationalism, did not. They would once again castigate Cleveland's second administration for its hands-off approach to potential territorial acquisitions from the Asia-Pacific to Central America.

In early 1893 Cleveland's second administration was quick to halt Blaine and Harrison's recent attempts to annex Hawaii. The Cleveland cabinet's anti-imperial move was reminiscent of Cleveland's first act of office during his first term in 1885 when he opposed the Republican-backed proposal to build a Nicaraguan canal. As to Hawaii, the 1890 McKinley Tariff itself had played a crucial role in precipitating the Hawaiian revolution of 1893 and the ouster of Queen Liliuokalani (see Chapter 7). Particularly, the tariff had eliminated Hawaiian sugar's preferential treatment in the US market, creating an economic crisis that was compounded further by the 1893 economic depression. The Listian

influence." Thomas J. McCormick, *China Market: America's Quest for Informal Empire, 1893–1901* (Chicago, IL: Ivan R. Dee, 1967), 35, 77, 184, 105. See, also, Marc-William Palen, "The Imperialism of Economic Nationalism, 1890–1913," *Diplomatic History* 39 (January 2015): 157–185; Hugh de Santis, "The Imperialist Impulse and American Innocence, 1865–1900," in *American Foreign Relations: A Historiographical Review*, ed. by Gerald K. Haines and J. Samuel Walker (Westport, CT: Greenwood Press, 1981), 71.
[34] Oliver MacDonagh, "The Anti-Imperialism of Free Trade," *Economic History Review* 14 (April 1962): 489–501; McCormick, *China Market*, 77, 105.

Harrison administration had been supportive of the annexationist movement then taking root both among Hawaiian planters and Listian nationalists in the United States. On the other hand, opponents utilized a variety
of arguments against annexation: that it was inconsistent with the principles of the founding fathers; it was contrary to the half-century precedent
recognizing Hawaiian independence; it was inimical to the racial principles of Anglo-Saxonism; or it would lead to yet more undesirable and
militant territorial acquisitions.[35]

When Cleveland entered office, he and Secretary of State Walter
Q. Gresham – in line with the new administration's Cobdenite views on
anti-imperialism and free trade – immediately scrapped the Harrison
administration's annexation treaty. Cleveland afterward explained this
decision, that from the beginning he had been "utterly and constantly
opposed to it." Although overlooking the ideological role of Cobdenism,
biographer Allan Nevins rightly noted that Cleveland's anti-imperial
approach "brought out in sharp relief the conflict between Cleveland's
foreign outlook and the expansionist tendencies fostered by Blaine."
Cleveland's consistent foreign policy was "radically different" from
those of Seward, Blaine, and John Hay, and "revealed the force of the
economic and nationalistic impulses that were pressing for expansion
overseas."[36]

The imperial designs that the Listian nationalists sought in the Pacific
were a far cry from Cleveland's minimalist approach to either Samoa or
American militarization, let alone his previous 1886 call for more intimate
relations with Hawaii in order to obtain "a stepping-stone" to the Asian
market while yet maintaining the islands' autonomy. This was far from
setting out to create an American informal empire. His anti-imperial
approach to the Pacific, which also included an attempt to end US
influence in Samoa, correspondingly upset Anglophobic congressmen

---

[35] Thomas J. Osborne, *Annexation Hawaii* (Waimanalo: Island Style Press, 1998), 1–49;
Osborne, *"Empire can Wait": American Opposition to Hawaiian Annexation, 1893–1898*
(Kent, OH: Kent State University Press, 1981), chaps. 4 and 5; Love, *Race over Empire*,
73–114; David M. Pletcher, *The Diplomacy of Involvement: American Economic Expansion
across the Pacific, 1784–1900* (Columbia, MO: University of Missouri Press, 2001),
242–246.

[36] Grover Cleveland, "Statement to Associated Press," January 24, 1898, in *Letters of Grover
Cleveland, 1850–1908*, edited by Allan Nevins (Boston, MA, and New York: Houghton
Mifflin Company, 1933), 491; Allan Nevins, *Grover Cleveland: A Study in Courage* (New
York: Dodd, Mead & Co., 1933), 549. For Gresham's views, see Gresham to
D. P. Baldwin, August 17, 1893; Gresham to John H. McMahan, August 28, 1893;
Gresham to Bayard, October 29, 1893; Gresham to Bayard, December 17, 1893;
Gresham to Charles E. Dyer, May 2, 1894, Walter Q. Gresham Papers, Letterbook,
March 9, 1893– April 12, 1895, Box 48, Library of Congress, Washington, DC.

who viewed it as yet another weak example of Cleveland's pro-British sympathies.[37]

American free traders proved instrumental in opposing Hawaiian annexation from 1893 to 1894, and played a sizeable role in the Cleveland administration's ultimate anti-imperial decision-making. Carl Schurz was particularly outspoken, and his argument carried some weight with Gresham. Roger Q. Mills in turn denounced annexation in the Senate. Free-trade news organs like the *New York World*, the *New York Times*, the *New York Evening Post*, and the *Nation* in turn blamed Hawaii's US-dominated "Sugar Trust" for the agitation, although the sugar planters themselves were not united in calling for annexation.[38]

Cleveland struggled to find a viable way out of this Hawaiian quandary. Edward Atkinson offered Cleveland one possible answer. Atkinson first described his proposed solution to the Hawaiian problem to Secretary of Agriculture J. Sterling Morton, US minister to Britain Thomas Bayard, David Ames Wells, and A. B. Farquhar, all of whom were close to Cleveland. Atkinson's proposal, inspired by the demilitarization of the Great Lakes following the War of 1812, suggested that Hawaii be turned into an open free-trade port of call for various European powers and Japan. His plan would have made Hawaii a safe zone, devoid of militarization by any of the powers. It was, he added, in "the interest of the people of the islands that their ports and harbors should be free to all," and would encourage the "great powers" to lessen their military expenditures. "May not," he asked, "the sanctuary of free commerce be established in this great Pacific sea, where men may serve each other's need without fear or 'commerce destroyers'?"[39]

Farquhar immediately took Atkinson's missive to the president, "where it received the most careful attention," Farquhar reported. In response Cleveland called a confidential meeting. Farquhar, Cleveland, and Morton read over Atkinson's proposal multiple times. Farquhar wrote that Atkinson's Hawaiian solution "pleased the President. He fully agreed with our view of the case," but also strongly suspected that Congress

---

[37] "Annual Message to Congress, December, 1886," in *The Public Papers of Grover Cleveland March 4, 1885, to March 4, 1889* (Washington, DC: Government Printing Office, 1889), 185; Peter Trubowitz, *Defining the National Interest: Conflict and Change in American Foreign Policy* (Chicago, IL: University of Chicago Press, 1998), 59. Cleveland even threatened to shut down the Naval War College.

[38] Osborne, *Annexation Hawaii*, 17–39; Nevins, *Cleveland*, 549–562. On the "Sugar Trust" and 1890s tariff legislation, see et al. Laughlin and Willis, *Reciprocity*, chap. 5, 242–251.

[39] Farquhar to Atkinson, February 2, 1895, carton 7; Atkinson to Bayard, February 13, 1895; Atkinson to Wells, March 13, 1895; Atkinson to Farquhar, February 11, 1895, carton 24, Atkinson Papers; Edward Atkinson, "The Hawaiian Problem," *New York Times*, March 12, 1895; "Advice to the Jingoists," *New York Times*, May 17, 1895.

would never go along. With Congress as an obstacle, Morton encouraged Atkinson instead to "start an outside movement in favor of making the Sandwich Islands a free-trading center for all the world." The United States could then enter into treaties with Britain, Japan, Germany, and France to bring about "a sort of inner sanctuary of commercial freedom," whereupon a republican government could be maintained in Hawaii.[40]

Atkinson took Morton's advice, sending out a barrage of letters to various free-trade and anti-imperialist news organs in order to drum up popular support for his plan. Horace White and E. L. Godkin promised to print Atkinson's proposal in the *New York Evening Post*. Godkin himself thought Atkinson's plan was "visionary," but believed obtaining it would involve a hard fight.[41] The *New York Times* printed Atkinson's plan on multiple occasions, and the president of the American Peace Society, Robert Treat Paine, Jr., also gave Atkinson's plan his blessing and reprinted it in the pages of the society's news organ, *Advocate for Peace*. The Peace Society's secretary, Benjamin Trueblood, then engaged the support of London's International Arbitration and Peace Association in order to start a transatlantic movement for the neutralization of Hawaii.[42] Reminiscent of former Secretary of State Bayard's unsuccessful proposal for solving the Samoan issue in 1887, Atkinson soon began advocating for an informal government made up of the United States and the European "great powers" that would make up an "Advisory Council ... to whom all questions relating to foreign affairs might be submitted" by the ostensibly independent Hawaiian government.[43] By seeking a diminution of Hawaiian sovereignty with respect to foreign policy, his proposal therefore did end up containing an element of free-trade imperialism, but was never put into practice.

Atkinson's Anglo-Saxonist temperament became more aggressive when the jingoist opposition began attempting "to create a prejudice against his [Cleveland's] administration of the Hawaiian question by alleging that England is waiting to seize these islands." Atkinson first denied the allegation. He then digressed into a defense of British imperialism: "Wherever England establishes her control or protectorate it is to

[40] Atkinson to Morton, February 9, 1895, carton 24; Morton to Atkinson, February 11, 1895, carton 7, Atkinson Papers.

[41] Atkinson to White, February 27, 1895, carton 24; Godkin to Atkinson, March 1, 1895, carton 7, Atkinson Papers.

[42] Edward Atkinson, "The Hawaiian Problem," *New York Times*, March 12, 1895; "Advice to the Jingoists," *New York Times*, May 17, 1895; Robert Treat Pain, Jr., to Atkinson, February 15, 1895; Trueblood to Atkinson, April 4, 1895; Trueblood to Atkinson, April 8, 1895; Trueblood to Atkinson, June 24, 1895, carton 7, Atkinson Papers. Paine would become an officer of the AFTL.

[43] Atkinson to Farquhar, February 15, 1895, carton 24, Atkinson Papers.

the benefit of the masses of the people of that land, even though they resist the somewhat rough and tactless methods by which they themselves are benefited."[44] While his plan for a peaceful Pacific never came to light, Anglo-Saxonist Atkinson's anti-imperial colors temporarily bled British imperial hues. Yet these various free-trade imperial proposals were never implemented.

Cleveland would ultimately deny the Listians their Hawaiian prize, and his Cobdenite touch in the Pacific drew corresponding Listian contempt. Henry Cabot Lodge took the Cleveland administration to task: "Under this Administration, governed as it is by free-trade influences," the great expansionist Jeffersonian legacy of the Democratic party "has been utterly abandoned." Cleveland has worked "to overthrow American interests and American control in Hawaii" and was "eager to abandon Samoa." The Democratic leadership has "been successfully Cobdenized, and that is the underlying reason for their policy of retreat .... We have had something too much of these disciples of the Manchester school." Cobdenite-turned-Listian Theodore Roosevelt privately expressed to Lodge similar outrage; the "antics" of the bankers and "Anglomaniacs generally are humiliating to a degree .... As you say, thank God I am not a free-trader. In this country pernicious indulgence in the doctrine of free trade seems inevitably to produce fatty degeneration of the moral fibre." He then suggested that the imprisonment of the free-trade "peace at any price" editors of the *New York Evening Post* and the *New York World* would give him "great pleasure." He made a similar complaint to Alfred Thayer Mahan as to how unfortunate it was that the United States now contained the transatlantic Cobdenite remnants "of the Little English movement."[45] These two ex-Cobdenites had moved far away indeed from the anti-imperial ideology of their former free-trade friends.

Cleveland's actions in Nicaragua redoubled such charges. Jose Zelaya had taken dictatorial control of Nicaragua in 1893. In early 1894, he acted less than amicably toward British and American citizens in the country, even arresting Britain's consul. In response, the British landed marines in

[44] Edward Atkinson, "Jingoes and Silverites," *North American Review* 468 (November 1895): 554–560. For Bayard's earlier Samoan plan, see Alice Felt Tyler, *The Foreign Policy of James G. Blaine* (Hamden, CT: Archon Books, 1965 [1927]), 231–232. The British had briefly seized the Hawaiian Islands in the Spring of 1843. David M. Pletcher, *The Diplomacy of Annexation: Texas, Oregon, and the Mexican War* (Columbia: University of Missouri Press, 1973), 208.

[45] Lodge, "Our Blundering Foreign Policy," 15; Roosevelt to Lodge, December 27, 1895, *Selections from the Correspondence of Theodore Roosevelt and Henry Cabot Lodge*, 2 vols. (New York: Charles Scribner's Sons, 1925), I, 203–205; Roosevelt to Mahan, December 13, 1897, in *Theodore Roosevelt Letters*, 8 vols., ed. by Elting E. Morison (Cambridge, MA: Harvard University Press, 1951–1954), I, 741. See, also, Cudmore, *Cleveland's Maladministration*, 3–5.

Nicaragua in April 1894. Cleveland and his secretary of state, Walter Gresham, took measures to make sure that the British would remain only temporarily. Cleveland's nonaggressive response, however, led to labels of spinelessness. Outraged jingoists cried out "for one day of Blaine." Atkinson suggested that the origin of this Anglophobic jingoism was to be found "in the extreme view of protection." The popular silverite publication *Coin's Financial School*'s support for war with England further cemented the prevailing Cobdenite view that protectionists and silver sympathizers had become sinisterly entwined with imperialism, as did Lodge's "ridiculous" 1895 attempt to coerce Great Britain into adopting a bimetallic treaty by threatening to put differential US duties upon British products. The American people were wiser, Atkinson asserted, than to accept the position of "such a false prophet" as Henry Carey, who once said "he would regard a ten years' war with England as the greatest material benefit that could happen to this country."[46]

When a boundary dispute between Great Britain and Venezuela arose a year later, Cleveland was ready to act more decisively, enforce the Monroe Doctrine, and squelch his critics' diatribes. Much like the fisheries dispute in the lead-up to the 1888 presidential campaign, the 1895 Orinoco River dispute between Venezuela and Britain allowed Cleveland to reposition himself outwardly as anti-British in the foreign policy realm. First, Cleveland renewed efforts to restore diplomatic relations between Venezuela and Britain in order to allow for arbitration.[47] Second, in a special message, Cleveland brazenly articulated his desire to uphold the Monroe Doctrine, and called for the United States itself to determine the correct boundary line and to resist any British efforts to the contrary, fully aware that his speech might suggest a looming Anglo-American crisis – which at first it appeared to do. His language was indeed inflammatory, as he outwardly out-jingoed the jingoes, belying his Cobdenite motivations.

Atkinson, not immediately privy to the president's underlying rationale, reacted with great dismay to Cleveland's seemingly militant message to Congress. Agriculture Secretary J. Sterling Morton, part of the president's inner circle, reported to Atkinson that the message was only

---

[46] Edward Atkinson, "Jingoism, or War upon Domestic Industry," *Engineering Magazine* 10 (February 1896): 801–810; Williamson, *Atkinson*, 213; Atkinson, "Jingoes and Silverites," 554, 558; Nevins, *Cleveland*, 608; Patrick J. McDonald, *The Invisible Hand of Peace: Capitalism, the War Machine, and International Relations Theory* (New York: Cambridge University Press, 2009), 168–176. Canadian free traders similarly tied imperial protectionists to the "silver craze." See, for instance, D. C. Marker [Montreal] to the editor of the *Weekly Chronicle*, "Canadian Jingoes and American Silverites," November 16, 1895, draft copy, carton 7, Atkinson Papers.

[47] Michel Chevalier, *Free Trade and the European Treaties of Commerce* (London and Paris: Cassell, Petter and Galpin, 1875), 36.

meant to undercut congressional jingoes. But Atkinson could not yet follow Morton's line of thinking. Atkinson sent off a flurry of telegrams to various congressmen, cabinet members, British officials, and President Cleveland himself to express his disagreement.[48] Farquhar talked him down a few days later, following Farquhar's own "long interview" with Cleveland on December 22. Farquhar assured Atkinson that Cleveland "wishes to have peace established between England and America upon so firm a foundation that it never can be interfered with," but Cleveland also had to listen to the advice of both the late Secretary of State Gresham and his successor Richard Olney, who believed "that England's action in Venezuela is a clear infraction of the Monroe Doctrine and certainly should be in a position to know." As reported by Farquhar after his meeting with the president, Cleveland also claimed domestic motivations for his aggressive stance. Cleveland "evidently hoped that he would stir up some patriotism among Congressmen by his message," and thereby "get on full through to relieve the Treasury" by halting the depletion of its gold deposits.[49] Thus, along with maintaining peaceful Anglo-American relations, quieting the jingoes, and upholding the Monroe Doctrine, Cleveland also hoped to garner congressional support for his flagging monometallic money agenda.

As Morton's and Farquhar's recounting of Cleveland's motives suggests, the situation was not as dire as contemporaries like Atkinson at first believed, or as historians have since tended to portray it. First, Cleveland was playing the domestic jingo card for political gain. Second, Anglo-Saxon unionists, especially among transatlantic Cobdenite Anglophiles, called for a peaceful settlement through arbitration and were instrumental in maintaining lines of communication between the two countries. Third, British attention was quickly becoming diverted owing to renewed agitation in South Africa in early 1896.[50] In line with the Cleveland

---

[48] Morton to Atkinson, December 18, 1895; Atkinson to George Hoar, December 20, 1895; Atkinson to William L. Wilson and Sec. of Treasury Carlisle, December 20, 1895; Atkinson to Morton, December 20, 1895; Atkinson to Lord Farrer, December 20, 1895; Atkinson to Cleveland, December 20, 1895, carton 7, Atkinson Papers. See, also, Atkinson, "The Cost of an Anglo-American War," *Forum* (March 1896): 74–88; Atkinson, "Jingoism, or War upon Domestic Industry."

[49] Farquhar to Atkinson, December 23, 1895, carton 7, Atkinson Papers. For more on Gresham and Olney in the dispute, see Charles W. Calhoun, *Gilded Age Cato: The Life of Walter Q. Gresham* (Lexington: The University Press of Kentucky, 1988), 214–220; McDonald, *Invisible Hand of Peace*, 155–180; George B. Young, "Intervention under the Monroe Doctrine: The Olney Corollary," *Political Science Quarterly* 57 (June 1942): 247–280.

[50] Jennie A. Sloan, "Anglo-American Relations and the Venezuelan Boundary Dispute," *Hispanic American Historical Review* 18 (November 1938): 486–506; T. Boyle, "The Venezuela Crisis and the Liberal Opposition, 1895–1896," *Journal of Modern History* 50 (September 1978): D1185–D1212; Joseph J. Mathews, "Informal Diplomacy in the

administrations' previous Cobdenite encounters with Britain, a peaceful solution to the crisis was found. Also, owing to his publicly aggressive stance on the issue amid the contentious 1896 presidential campaign, Cleveland had become an anti-British hero to American Anglophobes overnight. He had realized that the Venezuela issue could potentially galvanize much-needed support if he hoped to retain control of the Democratic party, and he had found a potential cause to cut off predictable Republican "pro-British" labels. William Wilson, now Cleveland's postmaster-general, noted that "the Venezuela matter has dwarfed or relegated to the background all other and lesser foreign questions on which the Republicans were getting ready to attack the administration for its 'weak and un-American' foreign policy, and to that extent has done us good politically."[51]

Some among the silverite Populists at the time were also skeptical of Cleveland's ulterior goldbug motives. They observed that the threat of war was being used "for the purpose of riveting the goldbug shackles," and that Cleveland's "jingo message is all rot." Instead, he merely "seeks by a show of Americanism, to recover some of the ground lost by his party by his culpable course, but it will fail."[52] These Populists were more perceptive than they realized; at the 1896 Democratic National Convention, Cleveland lost the leadership of the Democratic party to silverite William Jennings Bryan.

The 1896 elections: a temporary Republican rapprochement

Upon Bryan's presidential nomination at the 1896 Democratic National Convention in Chicago, Republican nominee William McKinley was told that now "the money issue is a vital thing." But McKinley disagreed: "I am a Tariff man, standing on a Tariff platform. This money matter is unduly prominent. In thirty days you won't hear anything about it." George B. Curtiss, a Republican lawyer from Binghamton, New York,

Venezuela Crisis of 1896," *Mississippi Valley Historical Review* 50 (September 1963): 195–212; T. W. Reid, *Memoirs and Correspondence of Lyon Playfair* (London: Cassell and Company, 1899), 402–426.

[51] William L. Wilson, January 3, 1896, in *The Cabinet Diary of William L. Wilson, 1896–1897*, ed. by Festus P. Summers (Chapel Hill: University of North Carolina Press, 1957), 5. Similarly, see John A. S. Grenville and George B. Young, *Politics, Strategy, and American Diplomacy: Studies in Foreign Policy, 1873–1917* (New Haven, CT: Yale University Press, 1966), 167.

[52] *People's Party Paper*, December 27, 1895; *Southern Mercury*, December 26, 1895, quoted in Crapol, *America for Americans*, 208. On the rampant Populist mistrust for the goldbugs, see Richard Hofstadter, *The Age of Reform: From Bryan to F.D.R.* (New York: Vintage Books, 1955), 70–81.

similarly believed the tariff controversy of paramount importance, publishing his international history of protectionism, *Protection and Prosperity* (1896), with Friedrich List, Henry Carey, and the German Historical School as his intellectual guides.[53] American Cobdenite Thomas G. Shearman, amid his 1896 castigation of "McKinleyism" before the Cobden Club in England, also found himself in reluctant agreement with McKinley's sentiment. Trying to find a bright side, Shearman also held out hope that McKinley's likely election might once again galvanize the American free-trade movement as his 1890 tariff previously had done. Cobdenite efforts were unsuccessful, however, in overturning either the Populist tide, the Republican party from protectionism, or free silver's continued bipartisan popularity. Nor did it stem continued protectionist attacks [figure 9.2]. Bryan's surprise Democratic nomination alienated many of that party's free-trade and gold standard supporters, especially New York City's financiers and most members of the Cobden Club on both sides of the Atlantic.[54] To the chagrin of both McKinley and the Cobdenites, the "silver mania" would indeed overshadow the tariff issue over the forthcoming campaign.

Cleveland's Cobdenites had at first sought to steer the 1896 Democratic party and the political debates back to tariff reform, but proved unable to control the "silver craze." The Democratic party thereafter found itself split into two wings, Gold and Silver, with the latter controlling a majority. With silverite Bryan's Democratic nomination and Listian McKinley topping the Republican ticket, US Cobdenites hoped to run an independent free-trade and monometallic ticket, much as they had when they created the Liberal Republican party in the early 1870s. Horace White, J. Sterling Morton, John Bigelow, Henry Watterson, George Foster Peabody, and Charles Francis Adams, Jr. gave their backing to the new independent Gold

[53] William T. Horner, *Ohio's Kingmaker: Mark Hanna, Man & Myth* (Athens: Ohio University Press, 2010), 179; George B. Curtiss, *Protection and Prosperity: An Account of Tariff Legislation and Its Effect on Europe and America* (New York: Pan-American Publishing, 1896). List's influence becomes even more pronounced in Curtiss's *The Industrial Development of Nations*, 2 vols. (Binghamton, NY: George B. Curtiss, 1912). See, also, Edgar Jay Dwyer, "Protection Insures Domestic Production," *Protectionist* 30 (March 1919): 633.
[54] Charles Pelham Villiers, *The Fiftieth Anniversary of the Repeal of the Corn Laws, June 27, 1896* (London: Cassell and Co., Ltd., 1896), 54–55; Crapol, *America for Americans*, 208; Richard Franklin Bensel, *The Political Economy of American Industrialization, 1877–1900* (New York: Cambridge University Press, 2000), 77–81, 242–243; Sven Beckert, *Monied Metropolis: New York City and the Consolidation of the American Bourgeoisie, 1850–1896* (New York: Cambridge University Press, 2003). For the gold issue in the campaign, see Horner, *Ohio's Kingmaker*, 118–212; Richard Franklin Bensel, *Passion and Preferences: William Jennings Bryan and the 1896 Democratic National Convention* (New York: Cambridge University Press, 2008), esp. chap. 4; Stanley L. Jones, *The Presidential Election of 1896* (Madison: University of Wisconsin Press, 1964), 191–203.

Figure 9.2 "The Old 'Cobden' Boat Must Keep Off Shore." Signifying
the importance of McKinley's presidential victory, the American
Protective Tariff League's *American Economist* depicts John Bull,
standing at the stern of the "Cobden" boat filled with British goods,
being kept from US shores. *American Economist*, December 11,
1896, 285

Democratic wing. Even Atkinson, having pointedly avoided meddling
directly in national party politics since the Liberal Republican debacle of
1872, became a driving force behind the "Gold" or "True" Democratic
convention in Indianapolis. Sound Money Clubs in turn raised large
amounts of money to bring the monetary fight to the silverites. Atkinson
wrote to Wells that the Gold Democratic organization reminded him of
"the old Free-Soil Party in its origins and motive. It will as surely rule the
country in four or eight years as that party did when it had gained its

position under the name of 'Republican,' since so misused." Carlisle and
Morton were considered for the party's presidential nomination, as was
William Wilson. All three declined, and seventy-nine-year-old Senator
John C. Palmer of Illinois, a former Free Soil Democrat and Liberal
Republican, was nominated instead. Grover Cleveland gave his blessing
to the convention's choice, raising the delegates' spirits higher. The party
platform touted both the gold standard and a tariff for revenue only.[55]

Illustrating the primacy of the silver issue during the 1896 elections,
Cobdenites overlooked Democratic nominee William Jennings Bryan's
free-trade tendencies owing to his free silver advocacy. He was labeled a
radical, an anarchist, a socialist. Aside from reluctant support from a
handful of moderate silver supporters and disillusioned Cobdenites like
Henry George, Bryan received little but ridicule from the Cobdenite wing
of the Democratic party.[56] Their anxiety stemmed both from Bryan's
Jeffersonian Anglophobia and his support for national bimetallism. In
sympathy with the Populists, Bryan wanted to reorient American power
through the national establishment of the silver standard: "A silver standard ... would make us the trading center of all the silver-using countries
of the world ... more than one-half of the world's population." Why, he
wondered, is the American farmer forced to rely upon Free Trade
England and the goldbug City of London? "Why not reverse the proposi-
tion and say that Europe must resume the use of silver in order to trade
with us? ... Are we an English colony," he asked, "or an independent
people?" Such statements, and Bryan's free silver advocacy generally,
were more than enough to overshadow his free-trade propensity and to
frighten transatlantic Anglophiles and goldbugs. His stance proved too
radical even for international bimetallists like the president of MIT,
Francis Amasa Walker, and France's famous international bimetallic
spokesman, Henri Cernuschi.[57]

---

[55] Farquhar to Atkinson, May 4, 1894, carton 6; Farquhar to Atkinson, May 3, 1895;
Morton to Atkinson, August 22, 1895; Goldwin Smith to Atkinson, August 14, 1896,
carton 7; Atkinson to W. E. Russell, July 10, 1896, carton 25, Atkinson Papers; Logsdon,
White, 346; Atkinson to Wells, September 4, 1896, carton 25, Atkinson Papers; *National
Democratic Party Campaign Text-Book* (Chicago, IL: National Democratic Committee,
1896); David T. Beito and Linda Royster Beito, "Gold Democrats and the Decline of
Classical Liberalism, 1896–1900," *Independent Review* 4 (Spring 2000): 555–575; James
A. Barnes, "The Gold-Standard Democrats and the Party Conflict," *Mississippi Valley
Historical Review* 17 (December 1930): 422–450.

[56] Louis F. Post, *The Prophet of San Francisco: Personal Memories & Interpretations of Henry
George* (New York: Vanguard Press, 1930), 127–129; John L. Thomas, *Alternative
America: Henry George, Edward Bellamy, Henry Demarest Lloyd and the Adversary
Tradition* (Cambridge, MA, and London: Belknap Press, 1983), 190, 334–335, 338–339.

[57] James Phinney Munroe, *A Life of Francis Amasa Walker* (New York: H. Holt and
Company, 1923), 355–356; Atkinson to Cernuschi, May 2, 1894, carton 23, Atkinson

With the Republican platform officially unwilling to adopt silver coinage except through an international agreement, the Gold Democrats and the GOP agreed upon an unofficial sound money alliance to defeat Bryan. Amid the hard-fought race, the Gold Democratic vote may indeed have helped McKinley carry Kentucky. That is not to suggest that the Cobdenites were at all happy with the Republican nomination of Listian nationalist William McKinley. But they were relieved when he finally endorsed a sound money platform, the most decisive issue in the 1896 campaign. Thomas Shearman accurately predicted to the Cobden Club that "the currency question" would likely cause "many thousand inflexible Free Traders to vote for him [McKinley]," although Shearman himself threw his unbending support behind the Gold Democratic nominee, Palmer, who in the end only attracted a lackluster 200,000 votes. Charles Francis Adams, Jr., after thirty years of political agitation, had found himself "'rounded up' into McKinleyism as infinitely the less of two evils." In despair of the elections and his family's financial troubles following the 1893 panic, he melodramatically added that he had come to the conclusion that "life is a failure."[58] With more optimism and certainly less melodrama, Atkinson tried to justify himself to Goldwin Smith: "McKinley is a respectable mediocrity, without mental capacity or comprehension either of the tariff question or of the money question." He granted that his own eventual vote for McKinley was a difficult one, arising purely over McKinley's monetary stance. He also hoped he had discovered a silver lining, in that McKinley's extreme protectionist policies might once again invigorate the American free-trade movement.[59] A mutual fear of Jeffersonian silverite Bryan thus forced the Listians and Cobdenites into a final, albeit short-lived, rapprochement.

Conclusion

Despite mounting domestic opposition from globalization's discontents – its Populists, its silverites, its labor unions – Cleveland's second administration temporarily thwarted the Republican party's incipient imperialism of economic nationalism, its Listian expansionist path of coercion, retaliatory reciprocity, and high protective tariffs. Cleveland's Cobdenites

Papers. Walker had begun arguing against Carey's protectionism at the age of seventeen. See "Mr. Carey and Protection," *National Era* (Washington), January 21, 1858.

[58] Horner, *Ohio's Kingmaker*, 161; Beito and Beito, "Gold Democrats"; *Fiftieth Anniversary*, 55; *New York Times*, September 30, 1900, 1; Adams to Atkinson, September 24, 1896, carton 7, Atkinson Papers. Henry and Brooks Adams also came to sympathize with the silverites. Brands, *Reckless Decade*, 32–33, 37–38.

[59] Atkinson to Smith, June 10, 1896, carton 25, Atkinson Papers; Williamson, *Atkinson*, 211.

thereby haphazardly halted the Republican acquisition of a closed-door empire. In particular, the Cleveland administration overturned the McKinley Tariff's reciprocity provisions through the 1894 Wilson–Gorman Tariff, and undermined previous Republican annexationist designs upon Samoa, Hawaii, and Nicaragua. In contrast to both the antebellum Jeffersonian Democratic party and the postbellum Republican party, the Anglo-Saxonist Cleveland administration instead largely practiced and preached the anti-imperialism of free trade, seeking peaceful market expansion for surplus American goods while eschewing American formal and informal imperial expansion. The Listian–Cobdenite rapprochement and Cleveland's anti-imperialism of free trade, however, would prove fleeting after Listian nationalist William McKinley stepped triumphantly into the White House in 1897.

In May 1896, the *Washington Post* had erroneously reported how "the McKinley candidacy expects to use the Cobden Club as a punching bag." Rather, upon William Jennings Bryan's 1896 defeat to William McKinley, the Cobden Club grudgingly admitted that it "was gratified at the election of McKinley to the American Presidency, though he was merely the lesser evil." If Bryan the silverite had not been his Democratic opponent, however, the club's leadership "would have thought McKinley the worst possible man for the Presidency," the *New York Times* relayed. The London-based club suggested that free trade had not been an issue in the campaign; only the silver question had mattered. "If Bryan had been elected," a "commercial panic" would have ensued, as well as the club's "loss of faith in the democracy of the world."[60]

The subsequent election of William McKinley in turn signaled the demise of the Populist party, which folded itself into the Democratic party. More importantly at the time for transatlantic free traders, control of the Democratic party had been wrenched from the American Cobdenite grasp, to be held once again by its Jeffersonian wing.[61] As a result of such intraparty nearsightedness, the Cobdenites were unable to forestall the acquisition of an American closed-door empire under McKinley, let alone foresee its imperial maintenance by subsequent Listian nationalist administrations in the years to come.

---

[60] *Washington Post*, May 22, 1896, 6; *New York Times*, November 25, 1896, 5. See, also, "Prospects of a Bolt," *Nation* (May 21, 1896): 391; "The Gravity of the Crisis," *Nation* (October 15, 1896): 282; *Washington Post*, May 22, 1896, 6; *New York Times*, November 25, 1896, 5; Atkinson to Fowler, November 23, 1896, carton 25, Atkinson Papers.

[61] Worth Robert Miller, "The Lost World of Gilded Age Politics," *Journal of the Gilded Age and Progressive Era* 1 (January 2002): 65–66.

Conclusion

The nations of the world fully recognize the hostility of the free trade movement to their interest .... Even the British colonies ... have been forced to accept this system of protection ... a line of conduct which the free traders tell them prevents the brotherhood of man.

Charles Heber Clark (Pennsylvania), 1896.[1]

The great question put to us to-day is this: Is it possible for us to persevere in our solitary course of Free Trade and live; or shall we turn our backs on Adam Smith and Cobden, and put ourselves into line with other nations, and follow List and his School?

Russell Rea (Liverpool), 1905.[2]

Free trade in late-nineteenth-century America was *not* a conspiracy. But it was certainly perceived as such by Anglophobic protectionists, the ramifications of which can still be felt today. Richard Cobden's and Friedrich List's conflicting visions for the global economic order garnered adherents throughout the Victorian world, leading to a hard-fought battle over the course of economic globalization. By focusing upon the politico-ideological struggle within the United States and the British Empire, this global Cobdenite–Listian conflict comes clearly into view. On the one hand, Cobdenite cosmopolitans envisioned an ideal global economic order of free trade, non-interventionism, and anti-imperial market expansion. If the nations of the world would only open up their markets, Cobdenites believed, the resultant global interconnectivity, interdependence, and prosperity would ultimately make economic and military conflict obsolete. On the other hand, Listian nationalists viewed the world as being at perpetual war – whether economically or militarily – and espoused an economic nationalist doctrine that combined protectionism with coercive foreign market expansion to obtain regionalized economic integration. From the Listian perspective, the nations of the

---

[1] Charles Heber Clark, "The Policy of Commercial War," *A Tariff Symposium* (Boston, MA: Home Market Club, 1896), 12.
[2] Russell Rea, *Two Theories of Foreign Trade* (London: Henry Good & Son, 1905), 10.

world existed at different stages of industrial development, and economic nationalism was thus a necessary step before reaching the ideal stage of free trade. Listians also held a progressive protectionist worldview that found its complement in nationalistic imperial demands for foreign markets, in contrast to the more orthodox home-market protectionist tradition that decried foreign markets. In England, Cobdenism would prevail. In the United States and the British World of white settler colonies, Listian nationalism would reign triumphant for many years to come.

Cobden's and List's ideas reshaped the United States and the British Empire in myriad ways: from the intersection of British free trade and American abolitionism; the ideological formation and reorientation of the Republican party; the Civil War's transatlantic free-trade diplomacy; the struggle for North American commercial unity; the anti-imperial Cobdenite presidencies of Grover Cleveland; the Republican party's postbellum imperialism of economic nationalism; to the British Empire's imperial federation and tariff reform movements. The pervasive free-trade-protectionist debate thus provides a particularly illustrative example of how ideas have helped shape local and global history.

The Cobdenite–Listian battle allows for the exploration of the global dimensions of seemingly local ideological conflicts. First, it provides an alternative ideological interpretation of nineteenth-century US political history by overturning the common laissez-faire portrayal of late-nineteenth-century America. A study of the American turn to economic nationalism elucidates how the Republican party became riddled with infighting, and ultimately discarded what remained of its antislavery and free-trade roots to become the party of protectionism *in toto* after 1884. It likewise offers a new interpretation for why the Liberal Republican and Mugwump leadership ultimately threw their support behind Grover Cleveland and the Democratic party in 1884 and 1892, as well as the short-lived arrival of Listian–Cobdenite rapprochement during the 1896 presidential contest to defeat the Populist radicalism of William Jennings Bryan.

Tracing the Cobdenite–Listian politico-ideological conflict in the United States also illustrates the differences both between and within the free-trade and protectionist camps. American Cobdenism's first subscribers came primarily from the country's growing manufacturing centers in the Northeast and West rather than in the South, where the agrarian-based free-trade tradition of Jeffersonianism had held sway for so long. Cobdenism was a different strain of free-trade ideology, one that took root in the 1840s among northeastern abolitionist Anglophiles rather than within the slaveholding Anglophobic South. Throughout the last half of the nineteenth century, the search for foreign markets in turn would put the progressive Listian nationalists at loggerheads not only with American Cobdenites, but also with more orthodox protectionists who yet remained skeptical of the American economic need to access the global marketplace.

Much as the American influence of Victorian free-trade ideology was not a conspiracy, neither was its manifestation a shining example of British free-trade imperialism in the United States. But upon closer study, it is plain to see *how* American economic nationalists perceived a conspiracy surrounding Cobdenism in the United States, and *why* they sought to stymie what they saw as Britain's attempt both to precipitously pry open American markets and to control markets in Latin America and the Asia-Pacific. It also illustrates how the transatlantic crossing of a second generation of Listian nationalists in the 1870s, 1880s, and 1890s by way of the German Historical School further paved the way for the positivist and activist Republican imperial governance of the early twentieth century, encompassing the beginning of the "long Progressive Era."[3]

Second, tracing these politico-ideological underpinnings of American economic globalization provides for a reinterpretation of late-nineteenth-century foreign relations history. The predominant story of American late-nineteenth-century expansionism has long centered on a steady bipartisan market-driven course to empire. Yet this long-standing and influential free-trade or open-door imperial narrative has tended to ignore how economic nationalists, not free traders, drove the US imperial expansionist enterprise. It also glosses over how the American Empire arose amid substantial politico-ideological conflict. In doing so, revisionist open-door histories have brushed aside how American Cobdenites struggled against imperialism in both its formal and informal manifestations, most noticeably during the nonconsecutive Democratic Cleveland administrations.

The American spread of Cobdenism also calls for a reconsideration of the "special relationship" between the United States and Great Britain, culminating in the so-called Great Rapprochement that arose by the turn of the century. The Cobdenite adherence of the Liberal Republican leadership and Grover Cleveland's Democratic cabinets allowed for

---

[3] Rebecca Edwards, *New Spirits: Americans in the Gilded Age* (New York: Oxford University Press, 2006), 7. Similarly, see Sidney Fine, "Richard T. Ely, Forerunner of Progressivism, 1880–1901," *Mississippi Valley Historical Review* 37 (March 1951): 599–624; Fine, *Laissez Faire and the General-Welfare State: A Study of Conflict in American Thought, 1865–1901* (Ann Arbor: University of Michigan Press, 1956). On the relationship between Progressives and imperialism, see especially William E. Leuchtenburg, "Progressivism and Imperialism: The Progressive Movement and American Foreign Policy, 1898–1916," *Mississippi Valley Historical Review* 39 (December 1952): 483–504.

the peaceful settlement of various international crises with the British Empire – from the Oregon boundary dispute, to the *Alabama* claims, to the Venezuela border dispute. Cleveland's handling of the Nicaraguan canal issue, for instance, or the fisheries dispute with Canada, or the bimetallism issue, or the Venezuelan border crisis, quietly restored amicable relations with the British government while offsetting Anglophobic opponents where possible. Cleveland's Cobdenites eschewed imperialism and attempted various downward reductions of the tariff in order to develop freer trade in an era of imperial expansionism, Anglophobia, and high protectionism. Through their close transatlantic ties, a shared ideology of Cobdenism, and a mutual desire to maintain the gold standard amid powerful opposition from American protectionists and silverites, the Cleveland administrations thus strengthened the possibility of peaceful Anglo-American relations, and helped bring about the burgeoning "special relationship" at the turn of the century. In doing so, however, they also brought upon themselves charges of a vast transatlantic free-trade conspiracy. The resultant Anglophobic economic nationalist response of the United States sparked demands for protectionist retaliation throughout the British Empire. More progressive British protectionists correspondingly sought a regional vision of imperial trade preference and political union: the Listian idea of Greater Britain.

Anglophobic Listian designs for coercive market expansion thus formed a formidable stumbling block waylaying the late-nineteenth-century free-trade movement. Like American Cobdenism, Listian nationalism took root in the antebellum era. Unlike American Cobdenism, Listian nationalism manifested itself in a most revolutionary way during the Republican administration of Benjamin Harrison. The retaliatory reciprocity provisions of the 1890 McKinley Tariff, coupled with James G. Blaine's protectionist, western-hemispheric imperial vision, provided the regionalized blueprint for the subsequent turn-of-the-century American Empire. But it did not come about owing to the imperialism of free trade, as suggested by the prevailing open-door historiography. Rather, it was the imperialism of economic nationalism – a regionalized, protectionist, closed-door imperial approach to American global economic integration. The future of American economic globalization therefore rested upon this politico-ideological debate: a debate that Listian nationalists would win in the near term.

By the end of the century, it was clear that American Cobdenites had met their match. Listian nationalists had developed what turned out to be an effective response to the Cobdenite free-trade movement in the United States. American Listians were beginning to noticeably consolidate the country's protectionist forces behind their imperial vision, bringing on board many protectionists that had previously refused to consider foreign markets alongside the domestic.

Why did the late-nineteenth-century American free-trade movement fail to reach its goals? For one thing, despite marginal success during the Cleveland administrations, American Cobdenites often found themselves outmaneuvered politically by the entrenched power of protected industries, and intellectually by the disciples of Friedrich List. US Cobdenites did not have the financial backing of American "infant" industrialists, and were rather inept at national political organization, as demonstrated by the disastrous Liberal Republican campaign of 1872 and the ineffective Gold Democratic campaign of 1896. For another, American Cobdenites also proved unsuccessful at using the era's economic booms and busts as advantageously as the opposition. In addition to this, American free traders were independent to a fault, rarely able to agree on the degree of policy change to accomplish their shared goals, and prone to infighting and internal distrust. Furthermore, American Cobdenites sought large-scale political support for their liberal reforms, but at the same time they distrusted both the era's more radical social reform movements and an overly active federal government. Even with all their flaws, failures, and false starts, however, America's Cobdenites would maintain a semblance of cohesion and optimism as they took the free-trade fight well into the twentieth century. They would continue their struggle for what proponents and critics alike now commonly describe as an American-led neoliberal world order.

The neoliberal legacy of the free-trade "conspiracy"

The politico-ideological fight between Listian nationalists and Cobdenite cosmopolitans helped create two distinct phases of American economic globalization. The first phase, from the end of the Civil War until the Second World War, was that of a Listian, imperial, regionalized phase of globalization: a regionally integrative stage that owed much to the era's rapid development of modern technological tools of globalization, and reached its zenith following the First World War. This regional, imperial phase of economic globalization was thereafter replaced by the second more studied phase: a neoliberal and global approach to economic integration that began under the American auspices of FDR's Cobdenite Secretary of State Cordell Hull in the 1930s and 1940s.

In 1900, however, Cobdenism's universal principles had lost out to local economic nationalist realities. The US presidential election of 1896 not only led to a temporary Jeffersonian resurgence in the national

Democratic party, but, through the election of Republican William McKinley, also solidified the country's Listian nationalist approach toward economic and foreign policy for many years to come. A double dose of protectionism and imperialism thereafter became the preferred cure for American economic ills, at least until Hull's neoliberal trade reforms of the 1930s and 1940s. This progressive reform-minded Republican approach to economic expansion developed into a coherent policy of imperialism, the imperialism of economic nationalism, which would become closely tied to "dollar diplomacy" in the early twentieth century.[4]

Nor was the United States alone. Many nations throughout the globe turned to imperialism, protectionism, and the theories of Friedrich List. Imperial expansion and rivalry reached new heights. Empire-hungry European states established protectionist blocs of their own, even as List-inspired high tariff walls were erected around the emerging econo- mies of Japan, Canada, Latin America, South Africa, and Australasia. The imperialism of economic nationalism, owing to its global popularity, would soon receive its fair share of Cobdenite condemnation for the failures of the international system throughout the early decades of the twentieth century.

At the turn of the century, Cobdenism was in retreat: even, it appeared, in Free Trade England, where Cobdenite-turned-Listian Joseph Chamberlain famously led the Edwardian protectionist Tariff Reformers and imperial unionists in an attempted overthrow of the free-trade order. The Cobden Club truculently noted this perceptible ideological shift, as well as a fascinating new conspiracy theory: "Mr. Chamberlain was for fourteen years, until 1892, an eminent member of the Cobden Club .... He has lately asserted that the Club is supported by the money of these foreign members in the interest of their own countries, and against that of Great Britain."[5] F. C. Chappell, a propagandist for the Home Market Club of Boston, concurred with Chamberlain's new charge. It was "quite wrong to reckon" the Cobden Club of 1902 "a 'British' one. It is nothing of the kind .... It is a moribund institution kept alive by the activity of foreigners – aliens who are industrial foes to Britain."[6] At the annual dinner of the Cobden Club in 1914, Lord Bryce noted that a couple decades ago "there was no arrow in the Protectionist quiver more frequently used in the United States than this representation of the

---

[4] Marc-William Palen, "The Imperialism of Economic Nationalism, 1890–1913," *Diplomatic History* 39 (January 2015): 157–185.

[5] Cobden Club, *Fact versus Fiction* (London: Cassell & Company, 1904), iii.

[6] "The Cobden Club – A Melancholy Humbug," *The Protectionist* [Home Market Club, Boston] (December 1902): 479.

Cobden Club as a powerful secret conspiracy, whose aim was to destroy American industries in order that British goods might overflow the country." It had since disappeared, "owing to the fact that ten or eleven years ago" Joseph Chamberlain began his protectionist movement in England.[7] Since then, Chamberlain's Tariff Reform movement had begun transplanting the free-trade conspiracy from American to British shores.

In Canada, the Cobdenite front line was similarly falling back. Wilfred Laurier's Liberal party may have won on a free-trade plank in 1896, but it then turned to imperial trade preference in 1897. This abrupt about-face was attacked in the Canadian Senate. When Laurier "recently jubilated in England, he was welcomed there with unexampled effusion by the free traders as the true apostle of the gospel according to Cobden," one opposition senator suggested. "The Cobdenites presented him with a gold medal, as the outward and visible sign of his inward and spiritual free-trade grace." And Laurier stood there "the most solitary figure in the empire, outside of Great Britain, lifting his voice and testimony in favour of the only true fiscal faith." Yet he returned to Canada and passed a protective tariff, and "the pathetic figure of Free Trade Apostle Laurier fades and is lost alike to imagination and sight." Laurier's political enemies even speculated that his free-trade plank had been crafted solely to earn him a gold medal from the Cobden Club, before duplicitously turning to imperial preference. American-style free-trade conspiracies were finding new purchase within the British Empire.[8]

The Canadian Liberal party's 1897 turn toward protectionism not coincidentally occurred amid the passage of a new protective tariff in the United States under Listian President William McKinley. The 1897 Dingley Tariff was passed just two days after McKinley took office, and the bill accordingly contained both a retaliatory reciprocity clause and even higher average tariff rates than the 1890 McKinley Tariff. McKinley's Listians had once again laid the groundwork for the imperialism of economic nationalism.

Yet while Cobdenism may have been in retreat, it had not lost all of its potency at the turn of the century. In 1896, economic nationalist George Gunton observed the continued Cobdenite influence in the United States: "The idea that patriotism is a wholesome and necessary requisite to citizenship has so faded that to-day any considerable expression of it entitles one to be called a 'Jingo.' Cosmopolitanism has become the

---

[7] *Cobden Club Dinner, 1914* (London: The Cobden Club, 1914), 13.

[8] *Debates of the Senate of the Dominion of Canada, 1898*, 3rd Sess., 8th Parl., February 8, 1898, 17; John Davidson, *Commercial Federation and Colonial Trade Policy* (London: Swan Sonnenschein & Co., 1900), 75.

fashionable thing." This fashion suggested "there should be no lines of demarcation between countries, no artificial barriers between nations." Gunton, of course, disagreed with this idealistic worldview. After all, "the idea of development among nations" was but "part of the law of evolution" toward ultimate free trade. "No religious, social or political entity can exist unless it develops the means of self-protection," whereas precipitous "*laissez faire* ... would lead us on the road to anarchy."[9]

Cobdenite cosmopolitanism may have appeared *en vogue* to Gunton in 1896, but it turned out to have been more of a fad for turn-of-the-century America. Following the mysterious sinking of the *Maine* in 1898, the opposite sentiment held true as nationalism swept the nation. A US declaration of war against Spain was made all the more viable with Listian nationalist William McKinley in the White House. Although he himself was at first reluctant to go to war, his lifelong patriotic defense of the American System would soon find its complement in the nation's jingoistic response to the *Maine*. The formal and informal American empire acquired from the Spanish–American War was therefore obtained primarily owing to the efforts of the country's economic nationalists, and against the loud protestations of its Cobdenite cosmopolitans. Progressive and coercive economic nationalist policies would subsequently be implemented in Cuba, the Philippines, and Puerto Rico, as they became incorporated within an expansive, Republican, closed-door empire.[10]

US imperialism in Asia and Latin America at the turn of the century and beyond therefore should not be confounded with the imperialism of free trade. Rather, what revisionist historians have described as open-door or free-trade imperialism was in reality the imperialism of economic nationalism: an expansive, closed-door, Listian-led search for new markets. It is not surprising, for example, to find that McKinley's Secretary of State John Hay, author of the "Open Door Notes," was a former editor of the protectionist *New York Tribune*, as well as a protégé of Listian James G. Blaine; Cobdenite-turned-Listian Teddy Roosevelt played an instrumental imperial role as Assistant Secretary of the Navy and later as US vice president and president; *Tribune* editor, US minister to France, and the 1892 Republican vice presidential nominee Whitelaw Reid strongly advocated for retaining imperial control of the Philippines and Cuba; and Listian nationalist John Kasson helped craft the economic argument for Cuban intervention and took charge of arranging retaliatory

---

[9] George Gunton, "The Ethics of Patriotism," in *A Tariff Symposium* (Boston, MA: Home Market Club, 1896), 3–6.

[10] Palen, "The Imperialism of Economic Nationalism."

reciprocity treaties with British Guiana, Turks Island, Barbados, Jamaica, the Bermudas, Argentina, and France under the 1897 Dingley Tariff. Similar imperialistic undertones were soon to be found from among the Progressive Era's gunboat and dollar diplomats.[11]

Alternatively, if Cleveland and his anti-imperial Cobdenites had found themselves at the executive helm in 1898, the Spanish–American War would not have come about.[12] Their ardor for Anglo-Saxonism certainly provided them with an intellectual defense of the civilizing mission, and yet it was America's Cobdenites that spearheaded the country's burgeoning anti-imperialist movement. They came out in vocal opposition not only to the Spanish–American War itself, but also to the militant jingoist outpouring that helped bring the imperial project to fruition and the Republican party's subsequent coercive protectionist colonial administrations.

Following the American acquisition of a formal and informal empire, the Listian–Cobdenite battle continued. While Britain's Edwardian Cobdenite fortress fended off Joseph Chamberlain's Listian siege, American Cobdenites continued their free-trade assault upon the formidable citadel of American protectionism, gaining a brief glimpse of their goals – a glimmer that included a substantial lowering of the tariff in 1913 – during the Progressive Era administration of Woodrow Wilson, who considered himself "of the brand of the Manchester School."[13] Alongside tariff reductions, and against the formidable opposition of Listians like Henry Cabot Lodge, President Wilson also attempted further Cobdenite reforms in the international arena, desirous as he was for international free trade, freedom of the seas, and arbitration through the League of Nations. American protectionists stymied many of Wilson's internationalist goals, however, and soon regained the executive.

---

[11] Whitelaw Reid, *Problems of Expansion, as Considered in Papers and Addresses* (New York: The Century Company, 1900); Tom E. Terrill, "An Economic Aspect of the Spanish-American War," *Ohio History* 76 (Winter/Spring 1967): 73–75; Emily S. Rosenberg, *Financial Missionaries to the World: The Politics and Culture of Dollar Diplomacy, 1900–1930* (Durham and London: Duke University Press, 2003).

[12] The same could not be said of Jeffersonian William Jennings Bryan, the 1896 Democratic presidential contender, who initially proved quite susceptible to the jingo cry, donning his military uniform and enlisting in the imperial enterprise.

[13] Arthur S. Link, *Road to the White House* (Princeton, NJ: Princeton University Press, 1947), 7, 24, 127; David A. Lake, "The State and American Trade Strategy in the Pre-Hegemonic Era," *International Organization* 42 (Winter 1988): 48–56. For Wilson's Cobdenite sentiment, see *American Free Trader* (April 1883): 3; Clifford F. Thies and Gary M. Pecquet, "The Shaping of the Political-Economic Thought of a Future President: Professor Ely and Woodrow Wilson at 'The Hopkins,'" *Independent Review* 15 (Fall 2010): 257–277, 259; *Report of the proceedings of the International Free Trade Congress* (London: Cobden Club, 1908).

The Great Depression that struck in the late 1920s proved instrumental for the reorientation of the global Cobdenite–Listian conflict. Anglo-American free traders would continue their fight against protectionism in their respective countries, but with few immediately tangible results. American Listians in turn could claim a pyrrhic victory with the infamous passage of the extreme Hawley-Smoot Tariff of 1930.[14] Partly in retaliation to the new American tariff, Free Trade England itself – for so long the last bastion of Cobdenism – finally succumbed to the empire's protectionist demands. It abandoned the gold standard and joined the British system of imperial trade preference in 1932.

These various Anglo-American fiscal reformations had long-lasting effects upon the global economic order. Following the combination of Britain's turn to protectionism, the demise of the British-led gold standard, and the continued US adherence to Listian nationalism, American protectionists found themselves unable to place the lion's share of the blame for the twentieth century's Great Depression upon either the British Lion or classical liberal principles. Blame was laid instead at the pedestal of protectionism, paving the way for trade liberalization.

The argumentation on both sides of the free-trade-protectionist debate remained strikingly similar to that of the late nineteenth century. Under the auspices of FDR's Cobdenite secretary of state, Cordell Hull, the United States thereafter began instituting neoliberal reforms beginning with the Reciprocal Trade Agreements Act of 1934 – what Alfred Eckes calls Hull's "Tariff Revolution."[15] Against Republican opposition, the new act granted the president the power to lower rates by up to 50 percent and included the application of the unconditional most-favored-nation principle. Hull's reform efforts could claim even more success after 1947, when the first negotiation round of the General Agreement on Tariffs and

---

[14] Douglas A. Irwin and Randall S. Kroszner, "Interests, Institutions, and Ideology in Securing Policy Change: The Republican Conversion to Trade Liberalization after Smoot-Hawley," *Journal of Law and Economics* 42 (October 1999): 643–674. See, also, Douglas A. Irwin, *Peddling Protectionism: Smoot-Hawley and the Great Depression* (Princeton, NJ: Princeton University Press, 2011).

[15] Alfred E. Eckes, *Opening America's Market: U.S. Foreign Trade Policy since 1776* (Chapel Hill: University of North Carolina Press, 1995). For Hull as Cobdenite, see, also, Per A. Hammarlund, *Liberal Internationalism and the Decline of the State: The Thought of Richard Cobden, David Mitrany, and Kenichi Ohmae* (New York: Palgrave Macmillan, 2005), 13; F. W. Hirst, "Cobden and Cordell Hull," *Contemporary Review* 155 (1939): 10–17; Anthony Howe, *Free Trade and Liberal England, 1846–1946* (Oxford: Clarendon, 1997), 274, 299, 304; H. Donaldson Jordan, "The Case of Richard Cobden," *Proceedings of the Massachusetts Historical Society* 83 (1971): 45; J. Pennar, "Richard Cobden and Cordell Hull: A Comparative Study of the Commercial Policies of Nineteenth Century England and Contemporary United States" (PhD diss., Princeton University, 1953).

Trade (GATT) ended with the twenty-three participating countries slashing import tariff rates. The United States led the way, lowering its tariffs on average by 35 percent. The GATT would lead to the creation of the World Trade Organization in 1995.[16]

But the United States would remain reticent to play the lead neoliberal role in the international system. Cobdenites like Hull were still outnumbered, especially when the Republicans, reluctant to fully accept trade liberalization as official American policy, recaptured Congress in 1946.[17] Hull's hoped-for American free-trade vision remained incomplete.[18] Britain's Harold Wilson, at the time President of the Board of Trade, noticed how the world "had changed a great deal since Cordell Hull saturated the State Department at Washington with his almost religious convictions on the subject of Tariff Reductions."[19]

It would take many more decades for Cobden's free-trade ideology to supplant substantively the American protectionist impulse. And as a result, the influence of Cobdenism today can lay claim to various influential intellectual outlets. The so-called Austrian and Chicago School conceptualizations for reforming the global economic system were indebted to the Victorian cosmopolitan ideas of the Manchester School. From the 1920s onward, Adam Smith-inspired Cobdenite ideas would be revitalized by a new generation of classical liberal thinkers – Ludwig von Mises, Friedrich Hayek, Milton Friedman – who are more commonly associated with the

[16] Barry Eichengreen and Douglas A. Irwin, "Trade Blocs, Currency Blocs and the Reorientation of World Trade in the 1930s," *Journal of International Economics* 38 (1995): 1–24; Arthur W. Schatz, "The Anglo-American Trade Agreement and Cordell Hull's Search for Peace 1936–1938," *Journal of American History* 57 (June 1970): 85–103; Eckes, *Opening America's Market*, chap. 5; Stephen Meardon, "On the Evolution of U.S. Trade Agreements: Evidence from Taussig's Tariff Commission," *Journal of Economic Issues* 45 (June 2011): 482; Douglas A. Irwin, "The GATT in Historical Perspective," *American Economic Review* 85 (May 1995): 323–328.

[17] Douglas A. Irwin, "From Smoot-Hawley to Reciprocal Trade Agreements: Changing the Course of U.S. Trade Policy in the 1930s," in *The Defining Moment: The Great Depression and the American Economy in the Twentieth Century*, ed. by Michael D. Bordo, Claudia Goldin, and Eugene N. White (Chicago, IL: University of Chicago Press, 1998), 325–352; Irwin and Kroszner, "Republican Conversion to Trade Liberalization after Smoot-Hawley."

[18] Thomas Zeiler, "Managing Protectionism: American Trade Policy in the Early Cold War," *Diplomatic History* 22 (Summer 1998): 337–360; Douglas A. Irwin, "The GATT in Historical Perspective," *American Economic Review* 85 (May 1995): 323–328; Harold James, *The End of Globalization: Lessons from the Great Depression* (Cambridge, MA: Harvard University Press, 2001), chap. 3. Francis Gavin argues that the instability of the Bretton Woods system only added more obstacles to international free trade, in *Gold, Dollars, and Power: The Politics of International Monetary Relations, 1958–1971* (Chapel Hill: University of North Carolina Press, 2004).

[19] Howe, "From Pax Britannica to Pax Americana: Free Trade, Empire, and Globalisation, 1846–1948." *Bulletin of Asia-Pacific Studies* 13 (2003): 141.

modern neoliberal turn.[20] Cobdenism also holds a prominent place within a wide range of International Relations literature.[21] And it can be glimpsed in the writings of today's advocates of liberal economic globalization.[22] US Presidents Bill Clinton and George H. W. Bush have accordingly been branded with the Cobdenite label owing to their post-Cold War neoliberal leadership – a free-trade ethos that still holds sway among the American foreign policy elite.[23]

Neither has Listian nationalism fallen by the wayside. It was implemented to justify Pan-German nationalism during the Second World War, and was thereafter used to legitimize the European Union.[24] And as Leonard Gomes notes: "Whether they are conscious of the fact or not, development economists the world over owe a great debt to the memory of Friedrich List, for he was the champion of their cause against the ideology of free trade." So too has Ha-Joon Chang, in his 2002 book *Kicking Away the Ladder* (a paraphrasing from List's *National System*), provocatively called for a return to Listian infant industrial policies throughout the underdeveloped world to thwart the inequities of the global free market system.[25]

---

[20] See, for instance, Ludwig von Mises, *Liberalism in the Classical Tradition*, trans. by Ralph Raico (San Francisco, CA: Cobden Press, 1985 [3rd addition]), chap. 3; Friedrich A. Hayek, *The Constitution of Liberty* (Chicago, IL: University of Chicago Press), chap. 4 and Postcript; Milton Friedman, "Adam Smith's Relevance for 1976," in *Adam Smith and the Wealth of Nations*, ed. by Fred R. Glahe (Boulder, CO: Colorado Associated University Press, 1978), 7–20; Edwin van de Haar, *Classical Liberalism and International Relations Theory: Hume, Smith, Mises, and Hayek* (London: Palgrave Macmillan, 2009), 95–97.

[21] For such IR scholarship, see, for instance, Katherine Barbieri and Gerald Schneider, "Globalization and Peace: Assessing New Directions in the Study of Trade and Conflict," *Journal of Peace Research* 36 (1999): 387–404; Michael Doyle, *Ways of War and Peace: Realism, Liberalism, and Socialism* (New York: W. W. Norton, 1997); Patrick J. McDonald, *The Invisible Hand of Peace: Capitalism, the War Machine, and International Relations Theory* (New York: Cambridge University Press, 2009); John R. Oneal and Bruce M. Russett, "The Classical Liberals Were Right: Democracy, Interdependence and Conflict, 1950–1985," *International Studies Quarterly* 41 (1997): 267–294.

[22] See, for instance, Daniel T. Griswold, *Mad About Trade: Why Main Street America Should Embrace Globalization* (Washington, DC: Cato Institute, 2009); Daniel W. Drezner, *U.S. Trade Strategy: Free versus Fair* (New York: Council on Foreign Relations, 2006); Michael Lustztig, *The Limits of Protectionism: Building Coalitions for Free Trade* (Pittsburgh, PA: University of Pittsburgh Press, 2004); Thomas L. Friedman, *The World is Flat: A Brief History of the Twenty-first Century* (New York: Picador/Farrar, Straus and Giroux, 2007); Douglas A. Irwin, *Free Trade Under Fire* (Princeton, NJ: Princeton University Press, 2009, 3rd edition).

[23] Eckes, *Opening America's Market*, 280; Alfred Eckes, "Cobden's Pyrrhic Victory," *Chronicles* (October 1995): 14–16.

[24] E. N. Roussakis, *Friedrich List, the Zollverein, and the Uniting of Europe* (Bruges: College of Europe, 1968); David Levi-Faur, "Friedrich List and the Political Economy of the Nation-State," *Review of International Political Economy* 4 (Spring 1997): 154–178.

[25] Leonard Gomes, *The Economics and Ideology of Free Trade: A Historical Review* (Cheltenham: Edward Elgar, 2003), 66, 83–89; Ha-Joon Chang, *Kicking Away the Ladder: Development Strategy in Historical Perspective* (London: Anthem, 2002).

With today's neoliberal order reeling from global economic crises, free trade's critics are growing in number.

By tracing the nineteenth-century ideological influence of Cobdenite cosmopolitanism and Listian nationalism from their antebellum roots to their postbellum conflicts, a new interpretation thus arises to help explain the shifting patterns of Anglo-American relations, tariff policy, party politics, and the ideological history of American economic integration from the latter half of the nineteenth century to today. While many American political leaders continue to defend neoliberalism, critics worldwide decry it as American free-trade imperialism. Demands for economic nationalist legislation once again have arisen throughout the globe, a clear reminder that the story of economic nationalism is far from over.[26] Optimistic prophets of global free market capitalism – the ideological heirs of Richard Cobden – appear to have been precipitous in their predictions for the post-Cold War liberal order. Global free trade's promised panacea of prosperity and peace yet remains in question. The ideological conflict that arose in the mid-nineteenth century has returned with a vengeance, as both sides continue to struggle over the future course of economic globalization.

---

[26] Henryk Szlaijfer, *Economic Nationalism and Globalization*, trans. by Maria Chmielewska-Szlajfer (Leiden: Brill, 2012), 7.

Select bibliography

Manuscript collections

Adams, Jr., Charles Francis, Papers, Adams Family Papers, MHS
Atkinson, Edward, Papers, MHS
Bancroft, George, Papers, MHS
Bayard, Thomas, Papers, LOC
Bigelow, John, Papers, NYPL
Bigelow, Poultney, Papers, NYPL
Blaine, James Gillespie, Papers, LOC
Bowker, Richard Rogers, Papers, LOC
Bowker, Richard Rogers, Papers, NYPL
Bright, John, Papers, British Library, London, England
Bryant-Godwin Papers, NYPL
Carey, Henry C., Papers, Edward Carey Gardiner Collection, Historical Society
  of Pennsylvania, Philadelphia, PA
Cleveland, Grover, Papers, LOC
Cobden Club Manuscripts, Records Office, Chichester, West Sussex, England
Cobden, Richard, Papers, British Library
Cole, George Ward, Papers, State Library of Victoria, Melbourne, Australia
Field, Cyrus W., Papers, NYPL
Ford, Worthington Chauncey, Papers, NYPL
Galt Papers, Alexander Tilloch, LAC
Garfield, James A., Papers, LOC
George, Henry, Papers, NYPL
Greeley, Horace, Papers, LOC
Greeley, Horace, Papers, NYPL
Gresham, Walter Q., Papers, LOC
Haddon, Frederick William, Papers, State Library of Victoria, Melbourne,
  Australia
Harrison, Benjamin, Papers, LOC
Lodge, Henry Cabot, Papers, MHS
Macdonald, John, Papers, LAC
McCulloch, Hugh, Papers, LOC
McKinley, William, Papers, LOC
Morrill, Justin S., Papers, LOC
Olney, Richard, Papers, LOC

Post, Louis Freeland, Papers, LOC
Reid, Whitelaw, Papers, LOC
Schurz, Carl, Papers, LOC
Seward, William H., Papers, LOC
Smith, Goldwin, Papers, Cornell University Library, Cornell, New York
Sumner, Charles, Papers, Houghton Library, Harvard University, Cambridge, MA
Sumner, William Graham, Papers, Sterling Manuscripts and Archives, Yale University, New Haven, CT
Tilden, Samuel, Papers, NYPL
Walker, Amasa, Papers, MHS
Wells, David Ames, Papers, LOC
Wise, B. R., Papers, State Library of New South Wales, Sydney, Australia

Official government papers

Canada, Debates of the House of Commons
Canada, Debates of the Senate
Congressional Globe
Congressional Record
Foreign Relations of the United States (*FRUS*, US Department of State)
Parliamentary Debates (England)
Proceedings of the Royal Colonial Institute

Pamphlets and periodicals

The pamphlets, newspapers, magazines, and journals referenced throughout are primarily from the United States, Canada, England, Ireland, Scotland, and Australia. Most archives held numerous periodicals and pamphlets. Digital databases such as *Trove*, *Nineteenth Century British Library Newspapers*, and *Nineteenth Century US Newspapers* were invaluable.

The Appendix, along with the full bibliography for the book, can be found online at www.cambridge.org/9781107109124

Index

abolitionism, xxv, xxviii, 16, 21–22, 30,
119, 126, 268
  American, xx, xxi, 12–21
  and free trade, 13–21
  British, 15, 37
  legacy, xxix
  transatlantic, xxi, 3, 13–21, 35
Adams, Charles Francis, Jr., 68, 72, 76, 80,
262, 265
Adams, Charles Francis, Sr., 30, 44, 54, 78,
88, 94
Adams, Henry, 67–68, 76, 81, 94, 109
Africa, 118, 133–134, 148, 209
African Americans, xxvi, xxix, 3, 10, 14, 28,
38, 51, 70, 75, 85, 94, 114, 119, 126,
144–145, 177, 238
African Trade Society, 134
agrarians, xxvi, xxxvi, 18, 28, 90, 106,
110, 120, 128, 137–138, 163,
179–180, 188, 199, 226, 232, 238,
242–243
Alabama, 44, 59
Alabama claims, 57, 77–82, 160, 270
Alaska, 100
Aldrich, Nelson, 186
Allen, W. F., 177
American Commercial Reciprocity
League, 157
American Economic Association, 177
American Empire
  comparison to British Empire, xviii
American Free Trade League, 20, 57, 66,
67–76, 82, 87–92, 96, 105, 109, 110,
118–119, 124, 157, 220, 241
  and the Cobden Club, 69
  creation, 69
  influence in Australian colonies,
221–222
American free-trade movement. *See*
American Free Trade League;
Cobdenite cosmopolitans; Liberal
Republican movement

American Protective Tariff League, 61,
108, 143, 179, 237, 249, 263
American Revolution, 23, 160
American Social Science Association, 92
American System, xvii, xxi, 8, 9, 23, 29, 37,
61, 73, 75, 100, 110, 112, 116, 121,
129, 173, 188, 221, 245, 274
Americanization, xxi
Anglo-American Rapprochement, 23,
27, 250
Anglophilia, xxviii, xxxiii, 12, 23, 113, 260,
264, 268
Anglophobia, xvi, xviii–xx, xxviii, xxxiii, 7,
10, 12, 16, 22–28, 38, 44, 52–53, 55,
57, 59–60, 77, 79, 82, 87, 93, 97,
106, 110, 117, 128, 132–133,
150–157, 160, 172–173, 180, 182,
191, 193, 197, 199, 202, 241–242,
246, 248–249, 251, 255, 259, 261,
264, 267–268, 270
  definition, 23
Anglo-Saxonism, 20, 77, 97, 156, 166, 178,
250–253, 255, 260, 275, *See also*
Anglophilia
  and cosmopolitanism, 252
Annexation Manifesto, 160
annual message (1887), xv, 130, 139,
181, 188
anti-Cobden Club, 61, 180, 237
Anti-Cobden Hall, 61
anti-colonial nationalism
  South Asian, 7
Anti-Corn Law League, xxi, 1, 2, 13–22,
25, 27–28, 61, 65, 68–69, 72, 82, 87,
91, 117–120, 123–124, 126, 170,
201, 234, 245–246
  and American abolitionism, 13–21
  and Westward expansion, 22–30
  legacy, 61, 72, 90, 119, 123–124, 147,
200, 245–250
anti-globalization, xxxv
Antigua, 217

Printed in the United States
By Bookmasters